Global Ethnography

Global Ethnography

Forces, Connections, and Imaginations
in a Postmodern World

MICHAEL BURAWOY · JOSEPH A. BLUM · SHEBA GEORGE

ZSUZSA GILLE · TERESA GOWAN · LYNNE HANEY · MAREN KLAWITER

STEVEN H. LOPEZ · SEÁN Ó RIAIN · MILLIE THAYER

UNIVERSITY OF CALIFORNIA PRESS
Berkeley   Los Angeles   London

University of California Press
Berkeley and Los Angeles, California

University of California Press, Ltd.
London, England

© 2000 by
The Regents of the University of California

Library of Congress Cataloging-in-Publication Data

Global ethnography : forces, connections, and imaginations in a
postmodern world / Michael Burawoy . . . [et al.].
    p.   cm.
  Includes bibliographical references and index.
  ISBN 0-520-22215-6 (cloth : alk. paper).—ISBN 0-520-22216-4 (paper :
alk paper)
    1. Ethnology.   I. Burawoy, Michael.
GN320 .G56 2000
305.8—dc21   99-053114

Printed in Canada.

09 08 07 06 05 04 03 02 01
10 9 8 7 6 5 4 3 2

To Eudora, without whom this would not have been possible.

CONTENTS

At Home with the Global Ethnographer

The Global Ethnography project emerged in the fall of 1996 from a dissertation group working with Michael Burawoy in the Sociology Department at the University of California, Berkeley. This was not, at first sight, a writing group with a clear natural affinity. Our shared relationship with Michael reflected no unity of subject matter. The dissertation research we brought in for discussion ranged across countries, social groups, movements, and theoretical and political agendas. Our very research choices reflected to some extent our scattered origins. Only half of us are native born North Americans, the rest immigrants—Hungarian, Irish, Keralan, English.

What we did have in common in those early days was a broad commitment to "soft," hermeneutic sociology: participant observation, open-ended interviewing, ethnography. The one exception, Joe, was working on a historical study of labor relations in the ship-building industry. Michael persuaded him that his twenty-five odd years as a welder in San Francisco shipyards constituted invaluable sociological data that Joe could work into a side project. As with the rest of us, this supposed side project took on more and more weight.

Our initial dissertation discussion group taught us that most of our cases were in some way caught up by that great mishmash of migrations, capital flows, hostilities, and opportunities jostling within the hot signifier of globalization. Was the extended case method used by Michael Burawoy and the other authors of *Ethnography Unbound* flexible enough to link everyday life to transnational flows of population, discourse, commodities, and power? Michael proposed that this question could generate enough common threads to be the basis of a collective writing project. The rest of us were intrigued by the idea, but felt that our understandings of globalization were uneven, sometimes contradictory. We therefore needed to develop common conceptual tools by reading and discussing a variety of texts.

Casting around for readings on globalization from different fields and disciplines, we encountered a huge range of interpretations. We started with James Clifford's sketch of the cultural revolution wrought by the arrival of the "exotic on the doorstep" of the Western anthropologist, that is, the great migration of previously colonized people to the lands of their former oppressors. We then moved through concepts such as Giddens's disembedded time and space, Appadurai's fragmented global "scapes," and Grewal and Kaplan's "scattered hegemonies," on to the bewildering new capitalist totalities conjured by Castells, Harvey, and Jameson. "Globalization," it seemed, had become all things to all theorists, a black box of the nineties akin to "structure" in the seventies.

Whether derived from post-colonialism, political economy, cultural studies, or feminist theory, what our sources held in common was not so much their diverse definitions of globalization as their high degree of abstraction. Was it only possible to talk about "the global" in such broad terms, we wondered, or could our ethnographic microscopes enrich these theories from the ground up, perhaps modifying the gloomy globalized totality implied by the political economists? After all, we felt, the local cannot be merely read off as one segment of the global structure. Out of such murky considerations emerged this book, as a collective exploration of the different globalizations thrown up by our projects.

Our first task was to develop a constructive working relationship. Some parts were easier than others. Here was the usual bunch of cranky, individualist academics with varied personal and intellectual histories, trying to form a writing community strong enough to produce a book with a truly common vision. Politically, we have a fair amount in common, most of us having participated in anti-establishment social movements of one kind or another. Yet our investigations sprawled from Steve's critique of regional industrial policy to Maren's breast cancer support groups; from Sheba's politics of carol singing in a Syrian Orthodox church to Zsuzsa's contentions around a proposed waste incinerator in southern Hungary.

Each of us had started the group from different points in our research and writing process. Lynne was close to finishing, Teresa only beginning her dissertation research. As our common project grew into shape, most of our individual studies shifted. Some of the group took on participant observation where they had thought of doing only interviews; others incorporated new concepts into their theories, new questions into their conversations; some extended their dissertations to new countries and new time periods.

We got to know each other, our research, and our chosen problematics in weekly gatherings in Michael's Oakland apartment. Using the Internet, we sent extensive comments and counter-comments in advance, which greatly helped the level of discussion. Michael worked up extensive summaries of each meeting, so that even those not physically present could keep in touch. Several members of the group excelled in massive and speedy responses to other people's work, leading to many reflections on how easy it is to think and write fluently when it's not your own work at stake. Steve deserves special mention. Even though he moved to Pittsburgh, he remained an indispensable member of the group through his punchy, plain-talking essays.

Our weekly meetings provided constant intellectual stimulation and companionship, wonderful feedback on our individual chapters, plenty of short-term goals, and even good food and drink. The dinner served by a different person each week; the luscious gateaux unveiled by Michael after an intense first half; constant e-mail discussions of readings and chapter drafts; the odd brandy or Hungarian paint-stripper consumed late in the evening; the intense focus mixed with hilarity which characterized many of our discussions—all contributed to making this project a uniquely collective intellectual adventure. In short, *Global Ethnography* seduced us with everything the typical dissertation process lacks.

Once we moved from our initial exploration of the literature, we developed our papers through a grueling set of drafts. First five pages, then ten, then three or four full versions of each paper were produced, analyzed from many angles, and collectively reformulated over the next two years. We submitted the final manuscript to the press three years after we had begun the seminar.

The first line of fault turned out to be, predictably, gendered, or at least that is how it appeared at the time. Our earliest attempts to define globalization were framed in the language of political economy, and soon jokes were flying about "political economy boys" or "PEBs" (some of them female) taking over the group agenda. This prolonged banter helped us to work out very real divisions. While Michael's own work leans toward the PEB side, he is not averse to working with students who insist on "feeding the discourse machine," as he would put it. Correspondingly, unfamiliar terms and analytical habits marked a noticeable distance between those from a political economy background and those enamored of feminist or Foucauldian theory.

However, the rather limiting PEB/discourse divide that seemed overdetermined during the early months was decisively abandoned once we started to form an overall structure for the book. Without ever explicitly recognizing it, we searched the various projects for implications about globalization that would crosscut the obvious epistemological and subdisciplinary fault lines of the group. Our discussions started to turn around the various understandings of globalization that propelled the papers. After much talk and many schematic adventures on Michael's blackboard, we separated globalization into three "slices": transnational "forces"; flows, or "connections"; and discourse, or "imaginations."

Our papers became ethno-histories as well as ethno-graphies. Our readings in the globalization literature generated a stream of comments along the line of "What's so new about this?"; and we became determined to historicize our own project, both the overall theoretical structure and the individual cases. Once we took on this longitudinal perspective, most of us came to see our cases as evidence of unfinished, ambiguous transitions from one form of globalization to another.

As ethnographers carrying out research into globalization we found ourselves grappling with the huge stretch between the local sites and the global dynamics we were studying. Certainly those of us whose dissertation projects started out from a small-scale, ground-level, strongly hermeneutic approach have found it quite a strain reaching up to the big pictures suggested by theories of globalization. It was hard to relate our work directly to the large institutional and economic shifts delineated by the grand theories of Harvey, Castells, et al. This book represents our collective attempt to overcome this stretch and pursue manifestations of the planetary Zeitgeist within the mundane, the marginal, the everyday.

We wondered whether exploring the global dimensions of the local changes the very experience of doing ethnography. The narrow boundaries of the traditional ethnographic "site" as conceived by the Chicago school were, for us, permeated by broader power flows in the form of local racial and gender orders, free-flowing public discourses, economic structures, and so on. The idea of a contained site with its own autonomous logic seemed even more flimsy and artificial once we extended our gaze to the global. It occurred to us that perhaps our global lens entailed a shift from studying "sites" to studying "fields," that is, the relations *between* sites. The "connections" group decided to explore this idea with transnational, multi-site ethnographies. Yet they ran into great difficulties trying to study transnational connections "from both ends," as the strands linking different sites proved far more complex and cross-cutting than they had imagined. Despite their fieldwork in a range of locations they were each eventually pushed into taking one site as their primary perspective.

Globalization affected the other ethnographies differently. Those studying global forces came to trace the power of those forces precisely through their frustration at the absence of identifiable agents in their studies of marginalization and loss. The "imaginations" group, in contrast, discovered that local actors were themselves re-connecting to the global by re-imagining it or rejecting the concepts of the global that were being presented to them.

For each of us, pursuing globalization generated new understandings of our research. We also discussed the theoretical implications of our own global locations. Zsuzsa said that she would never have undertaken her project if she had stayed in Hungary and suggested that it is easier to grasp the global from locations of relative privilege, when one has the resources to travel and to study on a less practical, more abstract theoretical level. Others wondered if our concern with globalization was in part an artifact of the priorities and concerns of the situations in which we found ourselves. Indeed, as immigrants and traveling ethnographers most of us were connected to a number of milieux within and across different countries. Perhaps our migrations among friends, families, and fieldwork sites in different places had sharpened our focus on globalization as a way of making sense of what we saw.

Our choice of sites and research questions showed us to be a mostly white group steeped more in Marx, Foucault, and feminism than in postcolonial theory. We did not, therefore, have a sufficient basis for serious theorization of race and globalization, or of the effects of globalization on the most impoverished peoples of the world. On the other hand, we did draw on perspectives from various newly industrialized countries. We decided that globalization looked like a more positive force for the middle classes of Ireland, Brazil, and India than for the previously protected working classes of the United States and other "advanced individualized" countries. At the same time, upwardly mobile immigrants from the newly industrialized countries were subject to the backlash around race and immigration in the richest countries. Such real-world tensions were part of our own personal experiences, reflected in our ambiguous conclusions regarding global connections and their impact.

An alternative way of thinking of ourselves in global terms was posed by Seán when, seeing similarities with the software developers he worked with, he suggested that global ethnographers were essentially "symbolic analysts"—part of the elite of workers who manipulated knowledge and information and who interacted on a global scale with similar elites. This suggestion did not exactly please the rest of us, but we could not deny some of the similarities. Teresa wanted to believe we were not truly part of the monster, arguing that as ethnographers we make a conscious decision to hold on to the specificities of the local in the face of the global, and in doing so we uncover the specificities and power relationships obscured by the bland homogenization of global neoliberalism. Millie took our defense argument further—surely our commitment to analysis of the local was born of a commitment to politics, an activity which symbolic analysts rejected in favor of an untrammeled global market. In other words, the conditions of the global ethnographer are similar to those of the symbolic analyst but our commitments and practices are not.

Globalization described the analytical subject of our collective project, but it also characterized the concrete process of the group. While those of us studying locally continued to meet with Michael in Oakland, the other members of the group spent various periods in India, Ireland, the eastern United States, Brazil, and Hungary. Technology became crucial to our collective interaction, as the extension of the field in order to study globalization forced more global research and increased use of the Internet. Joe obtained his figures on Korean steel production over the Internet, showing that even for research conducted locally the global dimension of research is somewhat technology-dependent.

The global connections were not evenly distributed however. Seán was easily able to connect electronically to the group from his base in a software team in Ireland; in fact, his team leader helped him set up the Internet connection. Millie's access from Brazil was more patchy, while Sheba had no link to a computer and became an "absent other" for the six months she spent in Kerala. But even those such as Steve and Lynne, who remained within the United States and who were relatively well connected via e-mail and speaker-phone, lost something of the internal workings of the group. The group could send out summaries of its weekly meetings but the collective tensions, agreements, and underlying issues communicated through debate, banter, and the many one-on-one conversations during breaks were largely lost to those relying on the new communication technologies.

Computers, therefore, became essential to our work process. However, the fusing of body and machine into cyborg ethnographer met its physical limits in the increase in repetitive stress injuries (RSI) among members of the group. Autoworkers, cashiers, meatcutters, and others have suffered from such illnesses for years; now RSI is becoming an epidemic among symbolic analysts. The computer intensifies our physical efforts within a shrinking range of activities even as it opens up a wider view to our theory and research. The compressed keyboard of the laptop computer injured our hands, wrists, and elbows even as it allowed us to be globally mobile and connected.

When we began our discussions, one of the questions facing us was whether globalization had rendered ethnography, apparently fixed in the local, impossible or even irrelevant. Our experience working on this project has suggested quite the reverse: rather than becoming redundant, ethnography's concern with concrete, lived experience can sharpen the abstractions of globalization theories into more precise and meaningful conceptual tools.

ACKNOWLEDGMENTS

When our papers began to see the light of day, when we showed them to our friends, and presented them at conferences, then a whole new set of pressures and influences was brought to bear on the book's evolution. To name all those who helped us from one draft to the next would risk overlooking someone. However, we would like to thank Charlie Kurzman, Judy Stacey, and Ruth Horowitz for their extensive, critical, and generous comments; Leslie Salzinger and Jennifer Pierce for using the draft manuscript in their classes, reporting back on its reception and encouraging us individually and collectively; the Institute of Industrial Relations for funding research assistance; Naomi Schneider for her perpetual encouragement; Rob Browning for his meticulous copyediting; Rachel Sherman for zealous proofreading; Mark Reschke for seeing everything through to completion; and Judy Haier for always being there for us.

Teresa Gowan and Seán Ó Riain

ONE

Introduction

Reaching for the Global

Michael Burawoy

How can ethnography be global? How can ethnography be anything but micro and ahistorical? How can the study of everyday life grasp lofty processes that transcend national boundaries? After all, participant observation, as sociologists have crafted it, aims for the subjective interpretation of social situations or the foundations of human interaction. It was designed to elucidate social processes in bounded communities or negotiated orders in institutions. It was incontrovertibly intended for the small scale. It was certainly not meant for the global! Classical anthropology, likewise, made a fetish out of the confinement of fieldwork, the enclosure of the village, the isolation of the tribe. Studies of ritual and routine, custom and law, or lineage patterns were irredeemably local. By convention global ethnography can only be an oxymoron. This book, therefore, departs from convention.

A THEORETICAL IMPOSSIBILITY?

If the prospects for global ethnography are bleak from a methodological standpoint, they are no less dismal from a theoretical standpoint. Take Fredric Jameson's theory of the global postmodern.[1] It begins with early capitalism, where the global is directly accessible from the local, from the spinning jenny, the county manor, or even the stock exchange. Ethnography fits well here. This double transparency of the near and the far did not last long. As capitalism spread across the world the truth of the local moved outside itself, embedded in obscure and distant circuits of capital. It was impossible to appreciate the fate of Manchester textiles without knowing about America's slave South or the progress of colonization in India. With the help of science, however, it was still possible to discern the terrain of this new imperial order, the operation of cartels, the rise of finance capital, forcible incorporation of peripheries. With the help of theory, ethnography could, at least in principle, link up the local to the global. But today, under late capitalism, science is helpless to comprehend a fragmented, dispersed, volatile, lived experience, let alone connect it to what Jameson considers to be an impenetrable totality. The local dissolves into ephemeral imagery while the global becomes invisible. With no place to root itself, to develop a coherent point of view, there can be no ethnography, let alone global ethnography. The best we can do is to dwell on fleeting experiences, telltale anecdotes, or aesthetic works that offer glimpses into a fractured, fragmented, all-encompassing "globality."

If Jameson's enigmatic postmodern pronounces ethnography's death sentence, theories of the information society condemn it to life imprisonment. In Manuel Castells's three-volume treatise, information technology promotes a network society of global reach in which the space of flows—flows of information, technology, and finance—replaces the space of places, the rootedness of industrial work, the fixity of urban and rural life.[2] The information society divides powerless places from placeless power—the decaying shipyard from commodity markets, the welfare client from universal discourses of legitimate need. The instantaneous transmission of electronic media introduces timeless time and the dissolution of history. The world is polarized between those within the flows of critical resources and those excluded, between the network society and the marginalized populations. If ethnography has any place, it is irrevocably local, buried in black holes or locked in real virtuality. In either case there is no exit, no way of climbing out to the other world.

In David Harvey's theory of global capitalism, ethnography is allowed out of prison but only to wander around homeless and irrelevant.[3] In his account the postmodern condition is propelled by the dynamics and contradictions of capital accumulation. In the Fordist period, crises were solved by exporting them to other territories or postponing them into the future, what he calls "time-space displacement." Capitalists could extend markets to the noncapitalist world abroad or create new demands through warfare or the welfare state at home. They could increase profits by drawing on cheap labor or by infrastructural innovation. Having exhausted themselves, these solutions are now replaced by "flexible accumulation," accelerating the processes of production, exchange, and consumption. Capitalism seeks to overcome its crises by producing more things more rapidly and by turning consumers into digestive automatons. All realms of life become volatile and ephemeral, subject to "time-space compression." If ethnography manages to withstand the hurricanes that sweep through everyday life, it can do no better than record the devastation.

Working from the top down, John Meyer and his associates have argued that the modern world society causes the diffusion of common institutional models and patterns of legitimacy among nation states.[4] These are, of course, Western models—democracy, markets, educational systems, legal orders, and so on. Meyer and his colleagues have little to say about the power that lies behind this diffusion nor, what is more important for us, about the link between models or norms on the one side and concrete practices on the other. Instead of theorizing the link between models and practices, they talk of their "decoupling," making it difficult to understand concrete variation within the same formal structures. On the ground, liberal democracy, for example, is very different in South Africa, Russia, Sweden, and the United States. The neo-institutionalists do not deny this diversity, but they leave ethnographers, who work from the ground upward, without theoretical tools to delve into the connections between micro-practices and macro-structures. Once more ethnographers have no theoretical hoist out of the local.

Anthony Giddens creates a chink in the global armor by recognizing the new opportunities opened up by what he calls time-space "distanciation."[5] In Giddens's premodern world, time and space were inseparable, congealed in locale, that is in "place." Then time separates itself out. It becomes the abstract time of the calendar and the clock. Next, space separates itself from place. The compass, the map, and the planetary system point to a world beyond place, a world with its own logic. In this time-space distanciation, locales still exist but they are connected to each other through symbolic tokens (money), experts (doctors, lawyers, accountants), as well as by new technologies (language, radio, television, and the Internet). Through them everyday life is disembedded, lifted out of the local and attached directly to the global. For Giddens, however, these connections across space and time afford new possibilities as well as new anxieties.

But if the global is enabling as well as constraining, whom does it enable? In Robert Reich's new world economy, the beneficiaries are the labor aristocracy of "symbolic analysts" who spiral through the weblike structure of the elevated corporation, through workplaces connected across national boundaries, removed from local contexts.[6] These sky workers—"symbolic analysts" or Rosabeth Moss Kanter's "world class"—are detached from those stranded on the ground, production workers and the growing sector of in-person services.[7] Saskia Sassen drops a ladder down from the sky, tethering the "global city" of corporate executive, accountant, and banker to the armies of service workers, often immigrants, who scamper around like Lilliputians at the feet of Gulliver.[8] Ethnography can now be grounded but in a place from which the global is still largely invisible.

Is the prognosis for global ethnography, and indeed for the world, as hopeless as it looks? In this book we argue that it is not. Surprising though it may seem, even the bleakest of these theories extends a special invitation to the ethnographer. However they differ in substance, all these accounts share a common theme: globalization as the recomposition of time and space—displacement, compression, distanciation, and even dissolution. Here lies the connection to the ethnographer, whose occupation is, after all, to study others in "their space and time." In entering the lives of those they study, ethnographers attune themselves to the horizons and rhythms of their subjects' existence. The ethnographer has, therefore, a privileged insight into the lived experience of globalization. On that basis alone, if ethnography can establish a terra firma and deploy new cognitive maps, it can shed light on the fateful processes of our age—processes that leave no one, least of all ethnographers, untouched.

Indeed, global ethnographers cannot be outside the global processes they study. They do not descend tabula rasa into villages, workplaces, churches, streets, agencies, or movements. They are also embedded in the time-space rhythms, not only of intimate relations, academic routines, TV sitcoms, café life, household, and so forth, but also of distinctively global processes. This was especially true of us as we developed our collective project. Precisely because we were scattered all over the globe, embedded in sites in countries as far apart as Russia, Hungary, Brazil, Ireland, India, and the United States, we became the living embodiment of the processes we were studying. For three intense years, no matter where we were, there were only rare moments when any one of us was out of touch with the rest. Strung out over the earth, continually moving between places, we were virtually always connected by a global net, the Internet. We surveilled one another even as we surveilled others. The very structure of our labor process brought global and local together, hauled us out of sites and into a global connection.[9]

To be a global ethnographer is one thing; to do global ethnography is another. We had to rethink the meaning of fieldwork, releasing it from solitary confinement, from being bound to a single place and time. We had to endow fieldwork with the flexibility to adjust to the space-time coordinates of the subject population. We had to self-consciously combine dwelling with traveling.[10] We had to pursue Indian nurses working in the United States back to Kerala, follow the careers of Irish software engineers as they spiraled through transnational corporate webs, and hitch ourselves to the feminist discourses circulating between Brazil and the United States.

Even when our fields did not themselves stretch across the globe, and it was only the participants' imaginations that connected them to the global, our ethnography was no less multi-sited.[11] We sought to understand the incessant movement of our subjects, the mosaic of their proliferating imaginations, by ourselves continually switching places, moving among sites within the field. It was not possible to confine ourselves to a single breast cancer movement: we had to study them in relation to one another—their internal diversity, their interweaving, the dialogues through which they achieve their own trajectories. Union organizing campaigns that contest the global city cannot be understood in isolation but only in their multiple connectedness. The clash of global imaginations around toxic dumping in rural Hungary cannot be understood except through its connection to the source of waste—the Budapest Chemical Works. Within any field, whether it had global reach or was bounded by community or nation, our fieldwork had to assemble a picture of the whole by recognizing diverse perspectives from the parts, from singular but connected sites.

Even as we consciously elevated movement, we did not lose sight of dwelling. We were determined that our studies not dissolve into a welter of postmodern fracturing and fragmentation, that they did not become a pastiche of vignettes, and we did not become tourists tripping from resort to resort. We were determined to ground our ethnographies in local histories. It was never easy to recover pasts and we used any means available—oral histories, archives, official documents, newspapers, community memories. In this way our ethnographies also became ethnohistories. We used this grounding in the past to spiral outward and explore changes in globalization. The clamor of Hungarian welfare clients to be treated like "mothers" was traced to the penetration of new global discourses that demanded means-testing to replace universal policies of socialist welfare. The changing experiences of work in the San Francisco shipyards were traced to demilitarization and the restructuring of global shipbuilding and repair. In pushing their carts with energy and determination, homeless recyclers tried to reenact a world of blue collar jobs, of Pax Americana, a world that they had lost.

In short, welding ethnohistory to ethnography, combining dwelling with movement, all our studies accomplished three things: first, they delved into external forces; second, they explored connections between sites; and third, they uncovered and distilled imaginations from daily life. Forces, connections, and imaginations became the three essential components, the three axes of our studies. However, determining which of these three would become the focus in each case of specifically global analysis varied according to the particular experience of globalization—whether people experienced globalization as an external force to be resisted or accommodated, whether people participated in the creation and reproduction of connections that stretched across the world, or whether people mobilized and/or contested imaginations that were of global dimensions.

In order to explicate the methodology we practice, I have adopted two interconnected approaches. In the first approach I stake out the terrain of global ethnography by reference to what it is not. Much of what follows, in the first approach, discusses the limitations of sedentary and perspectival anthropology on the one side and of urban and institutional sociology on the other. The second approach to unpacking global ethnography is genealogical, tracing how we got to where we are. Here arrival, if not accidental, is also not inevitable. There were many twists in the road; we entered many blind alleys as we battled to uncover the global. Such paths, entered but not ultimately taken, will not appear here. Instead, my narrative dwells on my own critical engagement with two major traditions of ethnography—the sociology of the Chicago School and the anthropology of the Manchester School—leading to the extended case method and from there to global ethnography.

From today's vantage point it is easy to forget that earlier in this century, in the 1920s and 1930s, the science of sociology was almost coterminous with ethnography. In the period of Chicago School preeminence, social surveys were associated with muckraking reform and the crusading women around Jane Addams and Hull House, while participant observation was science—objective, hard, and male. Thus, I begin with Chicago's foundational classic, Thomas and Znaniecki's *The Polish Peasant in Europe and America*, which was published just after World War I. From the standpoint of global ethnography this was indeed a very promising beginning, but Thomas and Znaniecki's successors in the Chicago School narrowed the field's scope to local ethnography of the metropolis, and from there it disappeared into the interiors of organizations and institutions. Connection with history and the outside world was lost. As the object of ethnography became more limited, so its method became progressively more marginal within sociology.

The trajectory of ethnography within anthropology, however, was the reverse. In the early decades of this century, professional anthropologists sought to separate themselves from amateurs—missionaries, travelers, colonial administrators—by emphasizing the rigorous scientific practice of careful observation in situ. The mythical figure of the lone, secluded anthropologist surrounded by "curious natives" became paradigmatic. Malinowski, encamped in his tent on the Trobriand Islands, signified the new discipline. Not far from the anthropologist's tent a storm was brewing, however. The anthropologist's confinement was soon to be unsettled by the distant and sometimes not-too-distant drums of anticolonialism. Here I take up the history of the Manchester School of social anthropology as the vanguard of this anthropological awakening to a wider imperial order. Its perspective on ethnography, refracted through the class and race struggles of Southern Africa, was still limited by the imperial order upon which it depended. Standing, as we do, within a postcolonial world, it is easy to diagnose the limitations of the Manchester method—the extended case method—but we nonetheless take it, or at least its revision, as our point of departure for our global ethnography. Finally, we show how our sociological sensibilities differ from what is now a flourishing global anthropology,[12] or from that tendency within it that marginalizes history and overlooks the continuing importance of the nation state.[13] In the conclusion we juxtapose our own grounded globalizations to their perspectival global "scapes."

THE POLISH PEASANT IN EUROPE AND AMERICA

The scientific move in *anthropology* during the second decade of the century turned fieldwork into a professional rite of passage, and with it came the closing of "tribal" societies, stripping them of their history, severing them from their colonial and capitalist determinations.[14] By contrast, the scientific turn in *empirical sociology*, at least in the United States, began with a global vision, pioneered by W. I. Thomas and Florian Znaniecki's idiosyncratic, eclectic, and unwieldy classic, *The Polish Peasant in Europe and America*. Originally published in five volumes between 1918 and 1920, it became the foundation tome of the early Chicago School.

It begins with a vision of the Polish peasant (prior to 1850), living within an array of rural primary groups of which the extended family was the most important. It ends with the institutions and mores of Polish American society in Chicago. Extraordinary for its time, *The Polish Peasant* describes communities in flux, with histories at both terminals of the immigration stream. Its depiction of social change is reminiscent of Emile Durkheim's account of transition from mechanical to organic solidarity, but here the transition is more obviously precarious and is spatial (traversing the Atlantic) as well as temporal.[15] Thomas and Znaniecki saw the decay of the old order as taking two roads—either *disorganization,* in which group values no longer regulate individual behavior, or *reorganization,* in which new institutions emerge to foster the reintegration of the individual. The path to a modern, "rational," self-regulating order is racked by the contending forces of disorganization and reorganization. In Poland the balance favors reorganization and nation-building, while in Chicago disorganization assumes the upper hand as adaptive institutions are slower to develop.

While global in scope, *The Polish Peasant* is at the same time ethnographic in method, inasmuch as it relies on "human documents" to describe the experiences of seasonal migrants at home and immigrants abroad. Its more than two thousand pages intersperse sociological analysis and historical commentary with lengthy extracts from letters exchanged between family members, and with newspaper articles, court records, and autobiography. Interestingly, Thomas regarded documentary evidence as more reliable than the interview, which he thought distorted as much as it revealed life experiences. As authors, Thomas and Znaniecki are erased from the text, so that even the division of labor between them is a matter of dispute. We do know, however, that the project was Thomas's brainchild. He spent much time wandering around Chicago's neighborhoods, learned Polish, and between 1908 and 1913 spent eight months every year in Europe, where he collected materials, visited important towns, immersed himself in local history, and mingled with peasants. He had initially a more ambitious plan, eventually shelved, of comparing peasants from different parts of Europe. It was on his last trip to Warsaw that he met Florian Znaniecki, a social philosopher deeply acquainted with Polish peasant society. Forced into exile in 1914, Znaniecki landed on Thomas's doorstep and was thereupon invited to join the collaborative venture that was to become *The Polish Peasant*. It was Znaniecki who then collected the documentary materials on Chicago's Polish community.[16]

If this was ethnography, it was certainly very different from the form being pioneered by another Polish émigré, Bronislaw Malinowski, who was pitching his tent in New Guinea at the time that Thomas and Znaniecki were assembling *The Polish Peasant*. Where Thomas and Znaniecki sought to locate the subjective, lived experience of the Polish peasant in its widest historical and geographical context, Malinowski, reacting against evolutionary theory, was militantly opposed to history and consideration of the extralocal context. Thomas and Znaniecki's rich tapestry of traveling and dwelling is in sharp contrast to Malinowski's solitary confinement. Yet they do share one feature. Like Malinowski's isolation of the Trobriand community, Thomas and Znaniecki searched for an original, self-contained "peasant community." But the purpose of isolation was different: Malinowski wanted to diagnose the internal functioning and stability of the existing Trobriand community, whereas Thomas and Znaniecki sought a historical baseline from which to understand the changes wrought upon Poland since the middle of the nineteenth century. Their first volume, therefore, is devoted to the erosion of the peasant community brought about by the occupying powers, by the advance of industrialization and rural impoverishment, and by the changing class structure and social mobility.[17] Thomas and Znaniecki are very aware of how decay could lead in many directions—to disorganization, reaction, and even revolution. They describe all of these tendencies as well as the possibilities for a new type of cooperative society based on "rational" norms rather than unreflective custom.

Thomas and Znaniecki observe that the same forces that led to the weakening hold of the primary group and the rise of individualism could, under the right conditions, lead to the reorganization of rural society. The rise of what we would now call a national civil society depended upon new forms of intellectual leadership, education, secondary associations, and above all the press. Thomas and Znaniecki were especially interested in the formation of civil society under what was effectively colonial rule. Long before Benedict Anderson, they well understood the importance of print capitalism for constituting the nation as an imagined community.[18] Through newspapers as well as through letters exchanged across the Atlantic, the world of the peasant ascended to a global scale.

Such *global imaginations* extended to the actual creation of utopian communities in far-off lands, such as the proposed state of Paraná in Brazil, to which thousands of Poles flooded in the 1890s. Thomas and Znaniecki describe the "super-territorial organization of Polish American society," or what today we call the "deterritorialization" of the nation state.[19] Religious, cultural, and political associations linked communities in the United States to Poland. Indeed, Polish America became the "fourth province of Poland." More generally, global imaginations fed upon the *global connections* of immigrants and those left behind. Letters exchanged between Polish emigrants and their families back home are dominated by the latter's economic needs. Women stranded with their children in Poland describe a life of destitution as they beg for remittances, while emigrants are concerned about the fate of their relatives, the burial of their parents, the employment of a brother, the marriage of a sister. It is difficult to know what proportion of emigrants wrote letters, but the evidence of continuing contact is impressive. Besides an exchange of money, there was a continual movement of people, with emigrants sponsoring friends and relatives, who would bring the latest news and gossip from the village. Today, as we shall see in Part 2, the telephone, the video, and the computer make living in two worlds easier, but there is little evidence that the dilemmas of duality are much different now than they were a century ago.

What *global forces* propelled emigration? Here Thomas and Znaniecki lack any compelling theoretical framework. They were concerned with individual responses to social circumstances, rather than with explaining the circumstances themselves. In their methodological introduction, following Thomas's earlier work, they propose four underlying "wishes" that govern human adaptation—desire for new experience, desire for recognition, desire for mastery, and desire for security. They move from the social situation inward to the individual and psychological rather than outward to the macro and economic. Nonetheless, despite their general hostility to materialist explanations, in the chapter "Emigration from Poland," Thomas and Znaniecki do argue that the difference between seasonal migration to Germany and the more dramatic emigration to America was related to levels of rural impoverishment. Seasonal migrants were often small farmers seeking supplementary income, while emigrants were more likely to come from a poorer, landless rural proletariat. They do not, however, have a corresponding analysis of the labor demand—the steel mills, the meat packers, the new manufacturers, and the garment industry—that made Chicago a magnet of immigrant labor in the last decade of the nineteenth century and the first decade of the twentieth.

When they turn to the immigrants' experience in Chicago, they do describe the devastating effects of what they call "economic dependency," which are nothing other than the vagaries of wage labor under the unregulated capitalism of the early twentieth century. Thomas and Znaniecki focus not on wage labor, however, but on the shock to the immigrant accustomed to the stability of rural life; on the weakness of new institutions of social control (church, parish, mutual benefit society, shops, and press); and on the corrosive effects of the individualizing welfare agencies. Just as anthropology was silent about imperialism, so Thomas and Znaniecki were silent about capitalism. It was the unexamined backdrop to immigrant (mal)adaptation; by overlooking it they missed the very class forces that would later usher in the New Deal. As I shall have cause to repeat and as others have said before me, without an analysis either of capitalism or of the state, it is impossible to understand first the transformation of America and then of the world in the twentieth century.[20]

The Polish Peasant was, therefore, *global ethnography without a theory of globalization.* Such theories were, of course, available in the writings of Lenin, Luxemburg, Hilferding, and other socialists, but nothing could have been further from the liberal pragmatism of the early Chicago sociology. Without theory, global ethnography was bound to wither on the local vine. The possibility of taking *The Polish Peasant* in the direction of more global ethnography was firmly buried by Herbert Blumer's celebrated indictment of its methodology that appeared in 1939. Invited by the Social Science Research Council to pronounce judgment on *The Polish Peasant,* he chided the authors for not living up to their scientific pretensions.[21] Theory and data were, according to Blumer, at best loosely coupled. Thomas and Znaniecki's distinction between values and attitudes, their typification of personality, their concepts of disorganization and reorganization, were obtained independently of the human documents they were supposed to analyze. For Blumer this was a cardinal sin, rather than the defining feature of good theoretical work. The social-psychological program announced at the beginning of *The Polish Peasant,* where among other things Thomas and Znaniecki propose a situational analysis based on subjective interpretations and emergent microprocesses, became the basis of Blumer's subsequent work, but for now he was using it to pass a negative judgment on their empirical enterprise. Rather than using their rich historical data to develop a new macro theory, Blumer chose to bolster the scientific basis of Thomas and Znaniecki's social psychology. The time was not ripe, the interest was not there, and the training was absent for locating these so well documented transnational processes within their global context.

Blumer's critique of *The Polish Peasant* enunciated a conception of science as inductive, as rooted in and emergent from the data. It would become the foundation of "grounded theory," which took ethnography into ever more restricted waters.[22] Blumer became an early switchman who led Chicago sociology down the road to symbolic interactionism, to the study of negotiated orders within bounded spaces. As we shall see, there were many factors predisposing Chicagoans to forsake the bigger historical picture for *institutional ethnography,* but Herbert Blumer was a major architect and propagandist, and his critique of *The Polish Peasant* one of its founding documents.

But we are getting ahead of ourselves. Between Thomas and Znaniecki and the post–World War II Chicago institutional ethnographies of Howard Becker, Erving Goffman, Fred Davis, Anselm Strauss, Donald Roy, and other students of Everett Hughes is the classical period of the Chicago School under the leadership of Robert Park and, to a lesser extent, Ernest Burgess—the period of *local ethnography*, whose major studies appeared in the 1920s and 1930s.

THE INTROVERSION OF THE CHICAGO SCHOOL

After the University of Chicago dismissed William I. Thomas in 1918, Robert Park became the leading figure of the department and, with Ernest Burgess at his side, pioneered what came to be known as the Chicago School of urban sociology.[23] Where Thomas and Znaniecki had explored the national integration of the peasant community, both as a process within Poland and between rural Poland and urban America, Park and his followers confined their attention to the uncertain transition taking place on their doorsteps. Once again Durkheim, although largely unacknowledged, hovered in the background—not just his theory of anomie or disorganization but also his theory of social change.[24] According to Durkheim, urbanization brought increases in moral density, impelling competition and then differentiation on the basis of adaptation to the environment.[25] In adopting these ideas as their own, the Chicago School founded the field of human ecology—the study of the division of the city into natural areas, each performing distinctive functions for the whole.[26]

Archetypal in this regard was Burgess's famous depiction of the city as consisting of concentric zones—the central business district, surrounded by an area of transition invaded by business and light manufacture, leading into a zone inhabited by the working class.[27] Further out are the residential areas of higher classes, and at the city limits is the commuter zone of suburbia. Park and Burgess sent their students out to study these areas in detail—who lived there, where they came from, what they did, and the emerging forms of association and disorganization. The best came back with what became the classic local ethnographies of the hobo[28] and the slum of "Little Hell," at the back door of Chicago's greatest concentration of wealth along "The Gold Coast."[29] Louis Wirth studied the Jewish ghetto, tracing its two millennia of history from Eastern Europe, Spain, and Germany to America.[30] Most of Wirth's monograph details the settlement patterns in Chicago of two successive waves of immigration. Even more than in Thomas and Znaniecki, Wirth's gestures to a global ethnography were eclipsed by a concern with problems of adaptation and mobility within the city.

There were also studies of specific urban institutions. The most famous of these is Paul Cressey's study of the taxi-dance hall, where single men paid to dance with young women, hired by proprietors of the hall.[31] Cressey and his collaborators observed the "sex game" on the dance floor and interviewed both taxi dancers and patrons, showing how this novel institution was an adaptation to the anomic life of the metropolis, teeming with immigrants and displaced persons. In all these studies, beneath the chaos of urban life, its incessant movement and vibrancy, the Chicago ethnographers revealed an ordered segmentation. As Park was fond of repeating, Chicago was the ideal laboratory for the study of social processes, the discovery of universal laws of human interaction. In the end these laws were few and far between, often adding up to no more than loose generalities, such as Park's optimistic cycle of group interaction, from competition to conflict, to accommodation and finally assimilation.

Even as the early Chicago School confined itself to local ethnography, it studiously avoided the study of work and industry. Later, after the Second World War, such subjects would become a central focus of institutional ethnography. In the 1920s and 1930s the study of industrial relations was dominated by the Harvard-based team led by Elton Mayo. In their exhaustive investigations of Chicago's Hawthorne plant of the Western Electric Company, Mayo and his team, like the Chicagoans, tried to blot out what was happening on their doorsteps—the mounting class struggle of the depression. In the case of the Chicago School, the silence seems all the more deafening in view of Park's prodigious comparative experience: beginning as a journalist, he proceeded to postgraduate studies at Harvard and in Germany and then for seven years worked closely with Booker T. Washington at Tuskegee before coming to Chicago in 1913 at the age of 49. The Chicago School, even as it practiced a sociology of "the common man," was always hostile to anything that smacked of revolution or socialism. In focusing on urban settlement from the perspective of social control, they were oblivious to the very forces that were transforming the city.

The methodological lesson, however, is what concerns me here. The search for transhistorical laws obscured real history, namely, the seismic shifts in the political and social landscape of the 1920s and 1930s.[32] As Lizabeth Cohen has documented, under the shock of the depression, ethnic associations and paternalistic employers could no longer protect their communities.[33] Chicago's working classes, therefore, switched their allegiance from neighborhood, mutual benefit society, and church to trade union, political party, and state. The popular impetus behind class associations bridged ethnic and even racial divides, reconfiguring the very meaning of particularistic identities. Park's conceptual templates of invasion and succession, cycles of group interaction, the functions of "natural" areas, and so on, drained local ethnography of its local context and so missed dramatic transformations wrought by the rise of mass culture, political machines, trade unions, and a rudimentary welfare state.

The Chicago School had remarkably little to say about class relations, but there was one notable, usually overlooked, exception, which speaks volumes for the Parkian tradition. Ernest Hiller's *The Strike* is a conceptually rich and empirically concrete study of class consciousness, class mobilization, class struggle, and class compromise. It examines strikes from the "social situation" of workers, giving credence to their imagination and rationality as well as to the structural impediments to their success. It is ethnographic inasmuch as Hiller bases his analysis on all manner of human documents from all over Europe and the United States—socialist speeches, tactical pamphlets, newspapers, autobiographies, government documents, and conciliation reports. His range of reading was extraordinary for a sociologist of his time.

Yet, paradoxically, Hiller pays little attention to Chicago's own remarkable history of labor wars. As if to underline the irrelevance of place and time, he begins his book with a "typical" strike at a South Wales colliery! Strikes in diverse sectors—coal, steel, garment, railroads, docks, agriculture—are all lumped together irrespective of historical or national context with the single purpose of discovering (or illustrating?) *the* "natural history" of *the* strike—mobilizing for concerted action, maintaining morale, controlling strikebreakers, involving the public, and finally demobilizing and reorganizing. Natural history becomes history out of context.[34] As we shall see, the substitution of natural process for historical specificity is a consistent thread running through Chicago ethnography, from Park to Janowitz.

After World War Two the Chicago department found itself in disarray, as its various factions struggled for the Parkian mantle. The Chicago sociologists were only too aware that sociology was taking very different turns elsewhere and that they were losing their prewar preeminence. They faced competition from the East Coast, from Harvard where Talcott Parsons was pioneering the deductive theorizing of structural functionalism, and from Columbia where the Merton-Lazarsfeld team pursued quantitative research and middle-range theory. In searching for their own niche, Chicago sociologists—Everett Hughes, Louis Wirth, and Herbert Blumer—battled with one another to define a subjective and situational approach to behavior and an empirically grounded notion of theory.[35] Blumer became the propagandist against Parsonsian grand theory and abstracted empiricism, while Hughes and Anselm Strauss quietly trained cohorts of graduate students in fieldwork. Wirth died in 1952, and in the same year Blumer left to create the Berkeley department, leaving Hughes, now chair, to contend with an increasingly divided department. Before he left for Brandeis in 1961, however, he had nurtured an exceptional group of graduate students, the Second Chicago School, which included such luminaries as Erving Goffman,

Herbert Gans, Joseph Gusfield, Howard Becker, Fred Davis, Eliot Freidson, and Donald Roy.[36]

The classic ethnographies of this immediate postwar period shifted from the study of locality to the study of institutions, specifically to the enclosed spaces of prisons, asylums, hospitals, and factories. Their analyses focused on the creative impulse in human behavior that was already central to Thomas and Znaniecki.[37] The Chicagoans exposed the subterranean world of institutions (prisons, asylums, hospitals, concentration camps), how inmates of such institutions created an informal world of their own, and how they contended with formal organizational structures and managerial attempts to control behavior. Ironically, the Chicago studies revealed that institutions created the problems they were supposed to solve: inmates learned to behave like the insane, workers learned to restrict output. These institutional ethnographies presented a world as it appeared from below, from the standpoint of the worker, the inmate, the patient. There was little attempt, however, to study the external pressures that led managers to impose specific forms of control, how these may change over time, or how inmates might draw on outside resources to challenge institutional powers. They studied a closed and delimited world, a world taken out of history and out of its American context.

Closing ethnography off from its context had the advantage that its claims could be generalized across diverse settings. Decontextualization made Chicago theory preeminently portable and in that sense global. Thus, Goffman's remarkable insights—now commonplace—into how asylums produce rather than correct mental illness inspired and justified deinstitutionalization the world over.[38] In a parallel argument, Howard Becker pioneered new approaches to "deviance," or what Thomas and Znaniecki had called "disorganization." Taking the standpoint of the underdog, Becker argued that there was nothing intrinsically deviant about the marihuana smoker or the dance musician.[39] He showed that by labeling as outsiders those it regarded as disreputable, society exacerbated their "deviance." This was, of course, an old Durkheimian point, but it also demonstrated an oft-quoted maxim of Thomas's, that if a social situation is defined as real then it is real in its consequences. For Becker, as for institutional ethnography in general, it was sufficient to take the side of the underdogs and to show that they were being labeled deviants and punished accordingly. But he did not explore the broader context of labeling—who labels whom and why or how "deviants" contest their labeling.

In a famous clash of perspectives, Alvin Gouldner launched a holy war on what he perceived as Becker's moral complacency, his romantic fascination with the "exotic other," and subjected "labeling" theory to withering attack.[40] Becker might be critical of the immediate caretaker agencies for the way they treated delinquents, drug addicts, or alcoholics, but at the same time he was feeding the oppressive machinery of the welfare state. In documenting the lives of marginalized groups, he was providing material for their regulation. No wonder the welfare state was happy to fund such research. Becker, Gouldner averred, was therefore on his own side too, pursuing his own interests as a career sociologist, and unwilling to adopt a radical critique of the world that sponsored him. Rather than present deviants as social problems to be solved, Gouldner called for their representation as challenging the regime that regulated them. He focused on sociologists' implication in the world they analyze, on the symbiotic relation of participant and observer, deviant and sociologist, institution and ethnographer, locating them both in their wider historical and political context.[41] In so doing, Gouldner underlined the importance of power and reflexivity, so effectively obscured by the Chicago School's focus on social control. His critique of institutional ethnography laid the groundwork for more radical visions of ethnography that would be critical of the welfare state. Today his critique sounds anachronistic, since the welfare state has retreated and the global has encroached onto the national terrain. Writing in the 1960s, he did not imagine that the sociologist-ethnographer, studying urban occupations and institutions, was implicated in a world beyond the nation state. He could not imagine a global ethnography. For that we need to turn to the anthropologists.

THE EXTROVERSION OF THE MANCHESTER SCHOOL

As the postwar Chicago School turned in on itself, retreating from local ethnography to the even more confined institutional ethnography, so the workplace, the prison, the hospital ward, the classroom, became like the anthropologist's sequestered village. At the same time anthropology itself was awakening to the challenges of decolonization. Not surprisingly, therefore, it was from the periphery that new visions emerged, washing back against metropolitan shores. In Southern Africa, the rapid expansion of industry based on cheap African labor had brought whites and blacks together under the banner of communism. Here colonial anthropologists could not ignore the wider contexts of their fieldwork. Race and class conflagrations burst the mythology of the museum "native."

If *The Polish Peasant in Europe and America* was the founding classic for the Chicago School, then Godfrey Wilson's *The Economics of Detribalization in Northern Rhodesia,* also published in two parts in 1941 and 1942, is the forerunner of the Manchester School of Social Anthropology.[42] Both studies set out from small-scale peasant or tribal societies in a state of natural equilibrium that is disturbed from the outside. While Thomas and Znaniecki take off in the direction of *global connections and imaginations*—the transatlantic flow of people, letters, money, and ideas—Wilson explores *global forces* that

were wreaking havoc with tribal society. Wilson begins with the disequilib-
rium of the depression-era world economy in which capital accumulation
outpaces consumption, propelling the search for raw materials and new
markets. The global crisis has its local manifestation in Broken Hill, where
international capital had begun to excavate zinc in 1906. Broken Hill, like
the much larger center of Northern Rhodesian—today Zambian—industry
known as the Copperbelt, became a racially charged and class-divided community of Indian traders, skilled whites, and cheap African labor. The tribal
economy sank into distress as its young men were drawn off to the mines,
where they were paid less than was needed for family subsistence, housed in
single quarters, and expected to return "home" once they were no longer fit
for work. Where Thomas and Znaniecki focus on the contrary forces of
social disorganization and transnational civic associations in the Polish
American community of Chicago, Wilson hones in on the raw class relations
of Broken Hill, on the African adoption of Western consumption in clothes,
drink, and food, on the breakdown of the family ties, and on the proliferation of divorce and prostitution. Rapid incorporation into a world economy
multiplies tensions that reverberate into the furthest corners of this British
colony. This was a far cry from the conventional village anthropology.

At the time Wilson was writing his *Economics of Detribalization in Northern
Rhodesia,* Max Gluckman was penning his paradigmatic *Analysis of a Social
Situation in Modern Zululand.* If Wilson's panorama broke from anthropological confinement into a global context, Gluckman's contribution was
more methodological. His monograph begins with an account of a bridge-
opening ceremony in 1938 in Zululand, describing the relations among different personae of South African society—African chief, Zulu king, the
Chief Native Commissioner, the local magistrate, missionaries, Zulu police,
and the lone anthropologist. Gluckman saw in the "ceremony" interdependence but also conflict, equilibria but also instability—tensions endemic to
the everyday worlds of Zulu society, enmeshed in the rapidly industrializing
multiracial South Africa. There never was any isolated tribe here! The Zulus
were a proud nation that had fought valiantly and often successfully against
their Afrikaner and British conquerors. World capitalism and colonial history were the warp and weft of Zulu society.

Gluckman's archetypal "extended case method" laid the foundation of the
Manchester School of social anthropology. He himself moved to Northern
Rhodesia in 1939 to succeed Godfrey Wilson as director of the Rhodes-
Livingstone Institute, which had been established to study the impact of
"European civilization" on "native African society." Although no revolution-
ary by any stretch of the imagination, Gluckman's communist sympathies
made him the object of suspicion in the eyes of the trustees of the Institute,
and so his appointment was delayed.[43] Once in office, however, he laid out

plans that would shape his own endeavors and those of his collaborators for the next thirty years. Throughout the period, he retained strong ties to Northern Rhodesia even after leaving there in 1947 to take up first a two-year lectureship at Oxford and then to become professor of social anthropology at Manchester University. At Manchester he gathered around him a remarkable group of students and associates, many of whom did their fieldwork in Central Africa, elaborating, revising, and disseminating the Manchester gospel. They included such illustrious figures as Victor Turner, Clyde Mitchell, William Watson, A. L. Epstein, Bruce Kapferer, Moshe Shokeid, Elizabeth Colson, Ronald Frankenberg, Jaap van Velsen, and Freddie Bailey.

The Manchester anthropologists made four innovations. First, their accounts of village life highlighted *social process*. Unlike his Oxbridge teachers, Radcliffe-Brown and Evans-Pritchard, who saw fieldwork as unearthing symmetrical and static structures then to be typologized, Max Gluckman and his students focused on social process, the endemic conflicts and schisms of African societies. They showed how the ambiguity of kinship norms or succession rules led to continuous feuding, rebellion, and even civil wars that in turn paradoxically tended to reinforce rather than undermine political orders. Conflict was ubiquitous but it was also functional.[44]

Changes in theory dictated changes in *fieldwork technique*. This was the second innovation. The study of social process demanded careful attention to practices as well as to norms, to actual behaviors as well as to the rules they instantiated. Africans were not moral dupes who simply executed norms; like everyone else, they contended over the interpretation of norms, manipulating them in the pursuit of interests. The Mancunians, therefore, followed cases—kinship factions, succession struggles, property disputes—over extended periods of time, and from one setting to the next.[45] It was in social situations—"events," "dramas," and "crises"—that discrepant norms became visible, but equally in such public displays of contention that unity was paradoxically preserved.[46]

Discrepant practices and deviations from norms marked internal contradictions of African society, but they could also be traced back to *external forces*. This attention to the wider context was the third distinctive feature of the Manchester School. Thus, kinship strategies and factional struggles have greater fluidity when villagers can appeal to colonial officials (such as the magistrate) as well as to traditional ones (such as the chief). In the economic realm, agriculture is affected by the migration of men to the various mining centers of Southern and Central Africa. The Manchester anthropologists were not interested in recovering any pristine and fictional past of the self-contained tribe but instead studied the impact of the tribe's integration into the wider society, whether colonial administration supported or subverted the power of the village headman,[47] whether labor migration reinforced or undermined local economies.[48] There was no presumption that urbanization or industrialization would detribalize rural areas. It could just as easily lead to "retribalization."

This brings us to the fourth innovation of the Manchester School. Those external forces were not simply left unexamined, the province of sociologists, economists, or historians. Instead the Manchester anthropologists traveled to town with their notebooks and settled among the urban population of the Copperbelt. There they began to study the forces that were having such a dramatic impact on the rural areas. Ulf Hannerz writes, "Apart from the work of the early Chicago school, perhaps no other single localized complex of urban ethnography can match the studies which for a number of years came out of Central Africa."[49] The theoretical frameworks of the two schools, however, could not be more different. Where Park drew analogies from plant ecology, Gluckman was influenced by Marxism. Where the Chicago School focused on ethnic adaptation and the functionality of natural areas, the Manchester School began from the *class relations of colonial capitalism.*

The Manchester anthropologists did not study urbanism from the standpoint of the breakdown of social ties, the breakdown of tribal mores. Their point of comparison was not tribal life in the village but the industrial revolution in England.[50] Here again they differed from Thomas and Znaniecki, whose point of reference was the primary group of the pristine Polish village. How appropriate for the Manchester School to hark back to the English working classes in the study of Africa! The Manchester mantra was *A townsman is first a townsman and only secondarily a tribesman.* The tribal dance, argued Clyde Mitchell, as performed in the mine compounds, was tribal in form but urban in content.[51] The song, the clothes, the values were unmistakably part of an urban civilization, although Mitchell would be heavily criticized for claiming that Africans were drawing on Western lifestyles to evaluate one another. In A. L. Epstein's classic urban ethnography, the mines stamped their needs on the compound where the workers lived, its confinement, segmentations, and enclosures absorbing the ceaseless rhythm of the mine shift.[52] When the miners rose up against mine management in 1952, they cast aside their "tribal elders"—a system of management-sponsored representation—and vitalized their own fledgling trade union. Before Edward Thompson had wrought his revolution in the study of working classes,[53] Epstein was studying the self-formation of an African working class. To be sure there were limitations to this class analysis, which did not anticipate the disappearance of colonialism, but for its time it represented a radical break with anthropology.

Yet Manchester Marxism was only one side of the Manchester School, and not always the most prominent. It attained its most vivid expression when deployed against other anthropologists, as in the case of Gluckman's remorseless attacks on Malinowski for studying social change in South Africa as culture contact and for ignoring South Africa's peculiar history of colonial conquest and racial capitalism.[54] There was, however, another side of the Manchester School that was much closer to the Chicago School in its search for transhistorical generalities. The Mancunians wanted to demonstrate that African society was no less dynamic, no more "primitive," than Western industrial society. They had only disdain for those who would constitute the African society as fundamentally "different," "other," or "inferior." The internal contradictions, the gap between norm and practice, endemic strife, the peace in the feud, the functions of rebellion, were no less true of the British army, the university department, the shop floor, than of the Lozi and the Zulu. Indeed, when they returned to Manchester, Gluckman's students were expected to show the relevance of their African findings to the British context.

Victor Turner, for example, was interested in ritual, so he studied the Roman Catholic Church. In later work he showed how the interdependence of structure and antistructure (communitas), or the necessary phases of social dramas, were of universal applicability.[55] Concepts originating in his first study of the Ndembu[56] are applied to counterculture in the United States; to Muslim, Christian, and Hindu pilgrimages; and to the Hidalgo Revolt against Spanish rule. The drive for universality was akin to the Chicago School's pursuit of general laws. Turner's four phases of social drama (breach, crisis, redress, and reintegration) are strikingly parallel to Park's cycle of group interaction (competition, conflict, accommodation, and assimilation). Turner explicitly draws on Znaniecki for his idea of community as the source of human creativity.[57] In stretching their theoretical templates so widely they became very thin, in combating colonial ideologies of racial superiority with human universality, the Mancunians paradoxically overlooked the real consequences of colonial domination and also the way Africans might be organizing themselves to challenge that domination.

The liberal face of the Manchester School received no less relentless criticism than what Gluckman had meted out to Malinowski. It was the young South African social anthropologist Bernard Magubane who delivered lone, courageous criticisms of Manchester's universalism, accusing the white Mancunians of smuggling into their work assumptions of Western superiority, of denying Africans their cultural specificity, and of understating colonial domination and thus the potentiality of anticolonialism.[58] Too often, Magubane claimed, the Manchester School took the colonial order as given and eternal. Magubane was turning Manchester against Manchester, appropriating and extending Manchester Marxism and launching it against Manchester's other face, its liberal face. Many of Magubane's criticisms are now commonplace but at the time he delivered them, in the last years of colonialism, he was alone in piercing the radical self-image of Manchester anthropology.

At the same time that Alvin Gouldner was angrily denouncing the Chicago School for concealing the ethnographers' interest in the social problems they studied, revealing how both the problems and those who studied them were bound up with the welfare state, Ben Magubane in a similar vein and a similar tone was excoriating white anthropologists for failing to recognize their own role in upholding the colonial order. Gluckman could not understand these accusations. Had he not suffered at the hands of settlers and colonial administrators for his communist sympathies? Had they not held up his directorship? Was he not for the native? From the African's point of view, his protestations were beside the point. Magubane was correct to diagnose a liberal complacency in the Manchester School, the same complacency that Gouldner found so disturbing in the Chicago School—the complacency of academic "objectivity" that concealed the ethnographers' implication in the world they study. But the worlds in which the Chicago sociologists and the Manchester anthropologists were implicated were different. Gouldner referred sociologists to their entanglement with the regulatory agencies of the welfare state, while Magubane accused anthropologists of supporting imperial domination. As we shall see, this distinction proves important in the way sociologists and anthropologists conceive of the world order.

Taking his own fieldwork on the Copperbelt as point of departure, James Ferguson has recently added a respectful arrow to Magubane's quiver.[59] He digs up the theoretical premises of Manchester complacency, namely, their faith in progress and convergence. Even as it disdained traditional anthropology for casting the African as Other, Manchester anthropology subscribed to other modernization mythologies—the presumption that Africans would become urban dwellers like urban dwellers elsewhere, that the African industrial revolution would follow in the footsteps of its Western forerunners. They saw that Africans could switch back and forth between the roles of "tribesman" and "townsman," that there was no simple evolution of the *individual* from the former to the latter, yet they could not see the same indeterminacy in the historical process. They could not see that history too could switch directions, that it did not possess any more teleology than the circulation between town and country.

Ferguson's postmortem on the Manchester School comes twenty-five years after Northern Rhodesia became independent. In the 1950s Manchester anthropologists did not anticipate the end of colonialism, let alone the disillusionment of postcolonialism. They did not anticipate the precipitous decline of the Zambian economy, the ramifications of a falling copper price. They could not imagine massive unemployment, the devastating consequences of structural adjustment, the return to the village, or the trauma of AIDS. Looking back now, we can see that they needed to have extended the extended case method to the level of the world economy. They needed to have taken their Marxism more seriously. They needed to have returned to their forerunner, to Godfrey Wilson's pioneering work on global ethnography.

After Max Gluckman died in 1975, the Manchester School continued in name only. Its most able practitioners scattered and took up their own callings. The Manchester mantle had passed, at least in part, to a distant cousin, another social anthropologist, Pierre Bourdieu.[60] The parallels are remarkable if unrecognized—the focus on social process, the divergence of norms and practices, the manipulation of rules, the functionalism, and the concept of field. Even Bourdieu's concept of habitus can be found in Victor Turner's work. There are two telling differences, however. First, Bourdieu's analysis of reproduction focuses on domination rather than on the functions of conflict, the peace in the feud, and the ritual of rebellion. Second, his focus on reflexivity demands that we recognize that we are of the world we study, that we are accountable to the "natives," who now talk back. No longer can we pretend to any clear demarcation between us and them. The political and economic orders that upheld such divisions have fallen. In this respect Bourdieu is as resolutely "postcolonial" as the Manchester School was "colonial." What this might mean and might not mean for the development of the extended case method is the question that concerns me next.

IN BERKELEY WITH THE EXTENDED CASE METHOD

I arrived at the University of Chicago in September 1972 as a grandchild and disciple of the Manchester School. I had been in Zambia since 1968, a refugee from England. Since Zambian independence in 1964, social anthropology was no longer organized from Manchester but had decamped to the Institute of Social Research, the renamed Rhodes-Livingstone Institute, at the new University of Zambia. It was there in 1970 that I began my postgraduate studies in sociology and anthropology—in those days and in that place no one bothered to distinguish between the two—at the feet of two vigorous minds. They were Jack Simons, the South African communist cum social anthropologist, and Jaap van Velsen, a formidable second-generation figure of the Manchester School. Surviving these two redoubtable figures served me well when I had to cope with the cut and thrust of the Chicago sociology department.

When I arrived at Chicago's Hall of Social Sciences, I had already dabbled in the extended case method. For four years I had studied the "Zambianization" of the copper mines—how Zambian "successors" were denied the resources and authority of their expatriate predecessors and how these in turn were promoted into newly created positions to "oversee" Zambianization.[61] It turned into a study of the reproduction of the color bar, the principle that no black should have a white subordinate. Given that the first goal of the postcolonial Zambian government was to eliminate racial injustice, how was it, I asked, that the color bar persisted? I extended out from the racial dynamics of the workplace to the economic and political interests of Zambian workers, multinational capital, the new governing elites, and expatriate management. I showed how the configuration of *class* forces, inherited from colonialism, held the racial order in place. I continued my study of the Zambian "new class" of successors when I became an M.A. student at the then recently founded University of Zambia. There I spent two years participating and observing students on campus. Once again I adopted the Manchester method, examining a dramatic conflagration between university and government to trace the political lines of fault within the postcolonial order.[62] In each case study I deliberately, if mistakenly, resisted the neocolonial temptation to blame everything on forces beyond Zambia, on the continuing grip of Western imperial interests. In my view this was an ideology too easily deployed by the new Zambian elites to hide their own exploitation and domination of subaltern classes.

I left Zambia for Chicago expecting to find thriving discussions about development and a lively school of urban ethnography. I was in for a shock. Chicago's Committee on New Nations, a center of research on newly independent countries of Africa and Asia, was already defunct. I found Chicago sociology decidedly parochial and, even sadder, its ethnographic tradition moribund. What little there was seemed as closed off from the world as ever. William Kornblum's *Blue Collar Community* was about to be published. It paralleled Epstein's study of the Copperbelt in that it considered the relation between work and community on the South Side of Chicago, but it ignored history and context. Kornblum did not reach beyond the workplace to the imminent collapse of the steel industry nor beyond the neighborhood to the eclipse of machine politics. Kornblum worked inward to the primary group as the foundation of secondary associations rather than outward to economy and state. Similarly, Gerald Suttles's *The Social Order of the Slum*— the other minor classic of the period—cordoned off his community with geographical barriers, the tracks of the elevated railway, freeway construction, and the like. While the destiny of the Addams Area, one of the oldest slums of Chicago, was determined beyond its perimeters, Suttles focused on moral isolation and ordered segmentation within its artificial boundaries. Suttles and Kornblum brought Chicago ethnography to its final denouement, combining *institutional ethnography's* focus on the negotiated order with *local ethnography's* concern with urban community. Innovative though they were, these monographs were out of step with the times, ignoring the legacies of the Civil Rights Movement, the Antiwar Movement, and the Great Society Program.

For my own research, I was interested in becoming a Chicago factory worker. Using a kinship entrée, I managed to land myself a job as a machine operator in the South Chicago plant of a large multinational. By a stroke of fate, it was the same plant that the famous Chicago ethnographer Donald Roy had studied thirty years before.[63] My first instincts were to undertake a critique of institutional ethnography—Roy's failure to see beyond the walls of the factory, his failure to recognize the historical specificity of Geer Company and its place within American capitalism.[64] When I contemplated Roy's enormous dissertation, a rich compilation of description and analysis, my respect for him as worker and ethnographer grew. I realized that it would be more interesting to use his study as a historical base line with which to compare my own. I would thereby supplement ethnography with ethnohistory. In this endeavor I was influenced not only by burgeoning studies of the transformation of work, but by the strange sameness of Roy's and my experiences. Although work at the drills had not changed much, there had been changes in the regulation of work. Over the thirty years, managerial control had become more reliant on consent than coercion. There had been a shift from a more despotic to a more hegemonic regime of production.[65] In trying to explain this, I extended my attention out from the shop floor, first to the absorption of Geer Company into a large multinational and, second, to the broader changes in industrial relations of the postwar period.

This launched me on a twenty-year research program into the politics of production. I asked whether the hegemonic regime I observed in Chicago was peculiar to America, as distinct from other advanced capitalist countries, and from there how production regimes might differ in early capitalism, Third World countries, and state socialism, and with what consequences for class formation. For the most part I used available ethnographies and social histories to explore these variations.[66] My interest in working conditions under socialism was piqued by another fateful coincidence, the discovery of Miklós Haraszti's lurid description of his own trials and tribulations as a machine operator in Hungary in the early 1970s.[67] My desire to suffer in a socialist factory intensified when the Polish working class rose up against its rulers in 1981. With the help of Ivan Szelenyi, János Lukács, and many others, between 1983 and 1989 I made my way into various factories in Hungary—champagne, textile, another machine shop, and finally long stints as a furnace man in the Lenin Steel Mill.[68] As I searched on the shop floor for the seeds of democratic socialism, the edifice of state socialism was disintegrating from above. Since I was not interested in the transition to capitalism, I jumped ship for the Soviet Union as soon as I could. But disaster—

call it revolution if you will—followed me everywhere. Since 1991 I have been observing and participating in the reprimitivization, what I call the involution, of the Russian economy. Following fellow workers from the early nineties, I have turned my attention to women's survival strategies and the household economy. I have finally evacuated industry because industry is disappearing.

I trace my own biography here not only to indicate my relation to the Manchester and Chicago Schools, not only to offer examples of the extended case method, but also to underline the fact that while I was a traveling ethnographer, while I never shrank from drawing the broadest conclusions from the smallest details, while I moved from continent to continent, nonetheless my horizons were always limited by the nation state. When I explained the differences between my experiences in two machine shops, one in Chicago and the other in Hungary, I drew on the relation between state and economy or on the economic logics of shortage and surplus economies. When I contrasted the success of Chinese economic reforms and the abysmal failure of Russian market reforms, I focused on national factors, the embeddedness of the state. My sociological vision always stopped at national boundaries. I never became a global ethnographer. Globetrotter, yes—global ethnographer, no.

How to extend the extended case method to the globe? That is the task Teresa Gowan and Seán Ó Riain set for us in the preface. But first it is necessary to offer a little adumbration of my understanding of the extended case method itself. It was only when I arrived in Berkeley in 1976 and had to teach participant observation that I began to reflect on my own research and contemplate what a historically grounded, theoretically driven, macro ethnography might mean. Compared to Chicago, Berkeley sociology was much more hospitable to the sort of ethnography I did. On the one hand, there was a long history of comparative and historical inquiry, stretching back to Frederick Teggart through Reinhard Bendix, Philip Selznick, Seymour Martin Lipset, Neil Smelser, Franz Schurmann, and Robert Bellah—a tradition that continues to thrive to this day. On the other hand, there was a deep commitment to ethnography begun by Herbert Blumer's mini-transplant of the Chicago School to Berkeley, bringing on board David Matza, Erving Goffman, Bob Blauner, Arlie Hochschild, and Troy Duster. Today the ethnographic tradition is stronger than ever with Barrie Thorne, Loïc Wacquant, Martin Sanchez Jankowski, Raka Ray, and Laura Enriquez. My aim was to marry these two traditions: the comparative historical and the ethnographic. Outside the department there was the inspirational work of anthropologists such as Aihwa Ong, Nancy Scheper-Hughes, and Paul Rabinow, and of the geographers, Dick Walker, Michael Watts, Allan Pred, and Gillian Hart. For them the extended case method was the very air they breathed.[69] Geography and anthropology could don the latest ethnographic fashions unencumbered but also undisciplined by the heavy weight of the sociological canon. At Berkeley, then, I got all the encouragement I needed to situate ethnography within its historical and geographical context!

When it came to teaching participant observation, I quickly learned that the best way was to cast students out into the sea and let them swim for themselves. You learn ethnography through practice, and perhaps a little bit of apprenticeship. There are guidelines but few rules. More or less anything goes. It was in those seminars, meeting twice a week, that we collectively engaged each other's projects. That is where we learned the lore of participant observation and the strategies of "extending out." At the end of one especially collaborative seminar during the fall of 1988, I proposed turning the studies into a book. The students, mainly in their second and third years, seemed up for the challenge. With varying degrees of enthusiasm they conducted further research and endlessly revised their papers. The process proved much more arduous and lengthy than any of us expected, but eventually our labor bore fruit and *Ethnography Unbound* appeared. Here were studies of social movements around AIDS activism and the peace movement, of workplaces in welfare agencies and a bread cooperative, of immigrants from Cambodia and Central America, of schooling in the classroom and in an after-school tutorial college, of ethnographers working in an AIDS-prevention project, and, finally, one brave individual studied us. The ethnographies aimed to confound conventional stereotypes of participant observation as atheoretical, ahistorical, and micro. Each study sought to reconstruct, revise, or simply elaborate preexisting theories to accommodate its empirical findings to wider contexts of determination. The studies showed how labor markets shaped work organization, how the state defined spaces for collective mobilization, how welfare agencies limited the effectiveness of reform, how the local network economy could foster cooperative enterprises, and so on.

The authors of *Ethnography Unbound* had immersed themselves in the local metropolis to come up with a composite picture. In this they were similar to their Chicago predecessors, but the portrait they painted had a very different tone, style, and perspective. Instead of "social control"—the leitmotif of the Chicago School—they focused on the dynamics of domination and resistance; instead of a group's capacity for "self-regulation," they studied the "hegemony" of one group over another. To use Habermas's language, the Berkeleyites emphasized the way the external "system" colonized the subject lifeworld and how that lifeworld, in turn, negotiated the terms of domination, created alternatives, or took to collective protest. The Chicagoans, on the other hand, had focused on lifeworld autonomy as if there were no world beyond—the natural urban communities of Hoboland and Gold Coast, patients in the hospital or workers on the shop floor. The sociological habitus of the Berkeleyites, with a little nudging from myself, led them beyond their sites to their constraining structures, whereas the Chicagoans celebrated self-regulation and bracketed the outside world.

The practitioners of the Chicago School occupied a non-Marxist and pre-feminist space in which the accumulation of knowledge was viewed as emancipatory. The post-Marxist and feminist Berkeley students of the late eighties, on the other hand, regarded knowledge with suspicion. Foucault had seeped into their imagination so that from their point of view knowledge was all too easily implicated in domination. But that didn't stop their practicing sociology. Rather, it made them averse not only to grand narratives and grand theory but also to the Chicagoan proclivity toward empiricism, in which abstraction followed closely on the heels of observations. Berkeley students took the middle road, searching for theories that might make their observations interesting, theories that would make their findings unexpected or anomalous, and then elaborating those theories. Apart from a general interest in domination and resistance, in how people participated in recreating or contesting the conditions of their oppression, there was little theoretical unity to *Ethnography Unbound.* What bound us together was method, in particular the extended case method.

We are not the only ones to use the extended case method. Many ethnographers approach their work with sensitivity to process, systematically incorporating historical and geographical context with a view to reconstructing existing theory. Thus, community ethnographies have not always stopped at the tracks, so to speak, but have incorporated the wider contexts of racism and labor markets[70] as well as urban political regimes.[71] Workplace ethnographies, traditionally confined to "plant sociology," have also taken external factors into account, such as race and ethnicity, citizenship, markets, and local politics.[72] Participant observation studies of social movements have located those movements in their political and economic context.[73] Ethnographies of the school have always sought to explain how education is shaped by and at the same time influences wider patterns of social inequality.[74] Family ethnographies have found it impossible to ignore influences beyond the household.[75] It is worth noting that many of these ethnographies are feminist in character, which is not an accident since, following Dorothy Smith, they have been concerned to dislodge essentialist explanations for gender domination by identifying external forces that have confined women in subordinate positions.[76]

My purpose here is to pull together a concept of what all these studies do in common, an elaboration of the dimensions of the extended case method with a sensitivity to questions of power and reflexivity.[77] The first dimension is the one common to all participant observation, *the extension of the observer into the world of the participant.* Rather than bringing the "subject" into the laboratory or into the world of the interviewer, the observer leaves the security of the university for the uncertain life of the participant. This is something shared by all three approaches—Chicago, Manchester, and Berkeley. There is a huge literature on covert and overt participant observation, different levels of immersion, insider and outsider status, and the role of informants, but what makes this relationship most problematic is the relation of *domination*, which distorts the mutuality of exchange.

The second dimension refers to *extensions of observations over time and space*. Ethnographers don't stick their toe in the water only to pull it out a second later. They spend extended periods of time following their subjects around, living their lives, learning their ways and wants. Believing that situations are important in determining both actions and beliefs, the ethnographer's problem becomes one of understanding the succession of situations as a social process. The early Chicagoans paid lip service to process, while the later ones took it more seriously, but it was the Mancunians who pioneered new forms of data gathering that were event- or case-centered. Such a reduction of situational observations to social process involves underscoring the contribution of some agents at the expense of others. It necessarily involves the second face of power—*silencing*.

The third dimension refers to *extending out from micro processes to macro forces*, from the space-time rhythms of the site to the geographical and historical context of the field. This was, as I have said above, a distinctive innovation of the Manchester School, and notably absent in the Chicago Schools. One way to think of the macro-micro link, but not the way we think of it, is to view the micro as an expression of the macro, discovering reification within the factory, commodification within the family, bureaucratization within a school. Some putative principle that governs society is found in its every part. For us the macro-micro link refers not to such an "expressive" totality, but to a "structured" one in which the part is shaped by its relation to the whole, the whole being represented by "external forces." That determination is often made accessible by explaining the divergence of two similar "cases." For example, in my work I explained the difference in work organization between my plant and Donald Roy's by reference to the different corporate context and the changing industrial relations context. I explained the difference between my experiences in Chicago and Haraszti's in Budapest by reference to the different political and economic orders of advanced capitalism and state socialism. The danger here is from the third face of power—*objectification*. That is to say, constituting the extralocal as forces gives them a false sense of durability. After all, forces are only the historically contingent outcome of processes that are hidden from the ethnographer. Objectification can be a powerful source of mystification, since we often believe we are in the grip of forces beyond our control which turn out to be quite fluid and susceptible to influence. Whatever the risks of objectification, the discovery of extralocal determination is an essential moment of the extended case method. Such discovery is impossible, however, without prior theory that would identify those external factors likely to be important.

The fourth dimension, therefore, is the *extension of theory*. Rather than being "induced" from the data, discovered "de novo" from the ground, existing theory is extended to accommodate observed lacunae or anomalies. We try to constitute the field as a challenge to some theory we want to improve. What makes the field "interesting" is its violation of some expectation, and an expectation is nothing other than some theory waiting to be explicated. We have seen how resistant the Chicago School was to adopting prior theoretical frameworks (even their own!) in order to refine, elaborate, revise, or reconstruct them. The Mancunians were also suspicious of starting with theory, although implicitly they almost always did. As social scientists we are conventionally taught to rid ourselves of our biases, suspend our judgments so that we can see the field for what it is. We cannot see the field, however, without a lens, and we can only improve the lens by experimenting with it in the world. There is an element of power here too, the fourth face of power—*normalization*. We are in danger of straitjacketing the world we study, disciplining it so that it conforms to the framework through which we observe it. We must expose our theories to continual critique from those they presume to understand, we must search for anomalies that challenge our theories, if we are to avoid the sorts of power effects that Edward Said, for example, discerns in "Orientalism."[78] Indeed, much of this book aims to expose the limitations of fatalistic and naturalistic interpretations of "globalization."

These in a nutshell are the four moments of the extended case method: extending from observer to participant, extending observations over time and place, extending from process to external forces, and extending theory. The fact that each dimension is limited by a corresponding face of power is not an indictment of the method but of the world. The shortcomings of our method only underline the ubiquity of domination, silencing, objectification, and normalization. The extended case method seeks to highlight those limitations not by ignoring them but by centering them— by entering into a dialogue with those we study, by encouraging different voices to challenge our emergent accounts of process, by recognizing there can be no one-way determination between processes and forces, and by developing theory through a process of dialogue with other theorists as well as with the world we encounter as ethnographers. We are engaged in a reflexive science in which the limitations of method become the critique of society.

FORCES, CONNECTIONS, AND IMAGINATIONS

We can engage and problematize each of the four dimensions of the extended case method but any given study will inevitably focus on one or two at the expense of the others. *Ethnography Unbound* focused on the fourth, the elaboration and reconstruction of theory. The authors used their studies to improve existing theories in one of five substantive areas—social movements, work, immigration, schooling, and the practice of sociology. However, they made no attempt to understand the specificity of the Bay Area as a modern metropolis—as postindustrial economy, center of innovative politics, or multicultural agglomeration. The Bay Area was simply the container for our ethnographies. The extralocal was never problematized or defined as something we shared. It was specific to each case study—regional economy, labor markets, state, education system, and so on.

In this book, from the beginning, we were concerned to define a common context that we all shared, whether our sites were in the Bay Area, Pittsburgh, Middle America, Ireland, Hungary, India, or Brazil. That common context was the "globe." It was not simply a container for our researches, nor a variegated, taken-for-granted background. It became instead an object of theorization in its own right. Where *Ethnography Unbound* deliberately opened up context, here we reenclose our studies not within a village or a nation but within the globe. We do this to contribute, individually and collectively, to an understanding of globalization. This is where we depart from those contemporary anthropologists who open up their studies to the world without the world's becoming an object of investigation.

In effect we are problematizing the third dimension of the extended case method, the extension from micro to macro, from local to extralocal, from processes to forces. It is not simply that we take external "forces" to a global level but we problematize the very concept of forces. The danger here, as I have already suggested, is *objectification*—that global forces will appear inevitable and natural. We have adopted three strategies to counter objectification. The first is to consider global forces as constituted at a distance. The focus of the ethnography then is on the way global domination is resisted, avoided, and negotiated. The second strategy is to see global forces as themselves the product of contingent social processes. Here forces become the topic of investigation; they are examined as the product of flows of people, things, and ideas, that is, the global connections between sites. The third strategy, the most radical, sees global forces and global connections as constituted imaginatively, inspiring social movements to seize control over their immediate but also their more distant worlds, challenging the mythology of an inexorable, runaway world.

We begin with *global forces*. We draw on all sorts of secondary constructions to create a picture of the "global" economy, polity, and culture as composed of forces constituted beyond our sites. The global force makes itself felt through mediators that transmit it as their interest or as the subjective internalization of values or beliefs. The locality in turn can fight back, adapt, or simply be destroyed. Lynne Haney works through the entire chain starting from men in suits, messengers of welfare efficiency and discipline, sent out by international agencies. They appeal to Hungarian sociologists and welfare administrators, who latch onto the rewards for adopting neoliberal discourses, and in turn direct welfare agencies to put those principles into practice. The ethnographic chain ends with protesting welfare clients, outraged by the materialization of their needs. They appeal to welfare regimes of the past to defend their interests in the present.

Like Hungary's "welfare mothers" held in disrepute, San Francisco's homeless recyclers mobilize their nostalgia for an era when they were included in American society. Teresa Gowan portrays them as reenacting that past, doggedly clinging to their work and their independence as recyclers, even as they are rejected as no better than the refuse they collect. They live near San Francisco's decaying shipyards, reminding workers there that tomorrow it could be them.

Twenty-five-year veteran boilermaker Joe Blum knows only too well how the yards have changed. He has experienced the long process of degradation not so much of the work itself but of the craftworker and the way he is treated. As sociologist, Joe Blum looks beyond changes in the immediate production regime to the transformation of the global shipbuilding and ship repair industry and to demilitarization. He and his fellow craftworkers show great ingenuity in finding new ways to labor in the shadows of globalization, in an effort to avoid the final degradation of homelessness. In each of our three cases, global forces descend on participants from without. These forces are not presented as abstract and inert, but as concrete and dynamic, evoking fluid patterns of resistance and accommodation.

The second approach takes us into the belly of the whale to see how global forces are constituted by global connections. While all of us are engaged in multi-sited ethnography, while none of us is riveted to a single place and time, it is only in the study of *global connections* that multi-sitedness becomes the object of theorization. Studying connections between sites, however, proved to be much more problematic than we had anticipated, mainly because from any one site connections fan out in multiple directions, so that the relations between any two sites are usually thin. Sheba George, for example, studies Christian nurses who migrate from the state of Kerala in India to Central City, U.S.A. They come from all over Kerala and not just a single community, so her ethnography tends to be more extensive and thinner in Kerala as compared with her more focused fieldwork in the parish of St. George's in Central City. She focuses her attention on the nurses' upward mobility as they migrate, and discovers that this is by no means an unalloyed American success story. Even in the United States, the nurses are pulled back into Indian patterns of gender and class stigma. She describes the finely balanced compromise between the downwardly mobile husband and the breadwinning wife and how this leads "nurse-husbands" to reclaim status in the religious congregation. The immigrant community is no victim of global forces but actively reenacts its global connections to Kerala through the flow of marriage partners, babysitting kin, children, priests, videos, and monetary remittances, and through short visits for funerals, marriages, and births.

Seán Ó Riain has to concentrate on the Irish end of his study—software engineers who have the world in their heads, spiraling across the Atlantic through corporate webs. The global workplace, however, is firmly embedded in local as well as global networks, customs, and prejudices. Space and time, rather than being disembedded, are intensified by the global workplace, as the workteam is subordinated to the almighty deadline, emanating from American headquarters. As they plot their careers, they participate in and reproduce global connections. Like Sheba George and Seán Ó Riain, Millie Thayer burns the candle from both ends, but like them she too has to concentrate on one end, in her case Recife. She offers us the most optimistic picture of global connections—Brazilian feminists appropriating academic theories to engender popular social movements. The downside here is that the discourses and lessons learned in Brazil don't flow back to engender poor people's movements in the United States.

Unemployed shipyard workers, homeless recyclers, and means-tested welfare clients experience *global forces* as degradation and individualization, powers that dominate them and to which they must submit. Resistance there may be, but it is effective only in carving out small arenas of autonomy at the margins, enough autonomy to stymie rather than ignite rebellion. When we enter these anonymous forces and explore the processes of which they are composed—chains, flows, networks, in short *global connections*—we discover a more open and less determinate picture. From this second perspective the new world order offers new opportunities, new horizons, the expansion of geographical boundaries, an escape from the oppressive enclaves that had confined migrant nurses in Kerala, software engineers from Dublin, and feminists from Recife.

The third perspective demystifies globalization as something given, natural, and eternal—an ideology behind which corporations, governments, parties, unions, and so forth all justify their self-interested action as driven by global pressures. We study how different images of globalization are produced and disseminated, and how they can galvanize social movements.[79] Zsuzsa Gille shows how struggles over the distribution of resources and dangers in a small county in postsocialist southern Hungary suck global actors—multinational capital and the Greens—into a whirlpool of local politics disconnected from the central state. An ideological war is waged around the benefits of incineration and the hazards of waste. Steve Lopez documents the way unions in Pittsburgh refuse the logic of globalization and reverse attempts to privatize nursing homes by appealing to homegrown counter-ideologies. The global imaginary deployed by Pittsburgh's new elites comes up against an equally powerful local imaginary. Maren Klawiter's study of breast cancer activism goes one step further. She shows how the medical-industrial complex, through changing medical practices, lays the foundations for local social movements, whose imaginations are then projected onto a global plane. Zsuzsa Gille explores the warring ideologies of globalization; Steve Lopez analyzes a local battle against the neoliberal ideology of globalization; and Maren Klawiter shows how ideologies springing from novel social movements can rise to the global level where they clash with other global imaginations.

Here then are the three strategies of global ethnography, strategies that correspond to real experiences of globalization. Transnational connections are the most directly global experience. Of course, as such, these are not new. Elites have always been connected across national boundaries, and international labor migration is certainly as old as capitalism. New means of transportation and communication, however, have made transnational links more universal, extending them in particular to such professional classes as software engineers, feminist organizers, and nurses. Still, not everyone is connected across the globe. Many experience globalization as a remote force that seems beyond human control. Especially, those expelled from a previous era of globalization who cannot find a niche in the new order—welfare mothers, redundant shipyard workers, and the homeless—can be overpowered by the effects of globalization. They experience globalization as loss. These "rejects" from the old order can resist or negotiate, but they do not have the wherewithal to contest globalization. That is the prerogative of those who have managed to accumulate resources with which to launch their challenges. Service workers can exploit their indispensability to the new global city. Hungarian villagers have turned their disused land with its toxic dumps into bargaining weapons against transnational capital. Women have appropriated control over their breasts, the most colonized part of the their body, putting the cancer industry, at least temporarily, on the defensive. These groups have challenged globalization by welding their resources to global or consciously counterglobal imaginations. Global imaginations reconfigure what is possible, turning globalization from an inexorable force into a resource that opens up new vistas.

BEYOND THE NATION

Recent reconstructions of the history of sociology and anthropology have drawn attention to their "preclassical" concerns with cultural diffusion and social difference on a global scale. At the beginning of this century anthropology narrowed its global focus to accommodate a professionalization that was marked by devoted and extended fieldwork, by dwelling rather than traveling, by enclosing community in both space and time. When anticolonial struggles burst around their tents, when ethnography's imperial pillars collapsed, anthropologists rediscovered the global context of their studies. Such openings were pioneered in the 1950s by, among others, the Mancunians whose broader visions reflected the peculiar conditions of southern Africa—advanced industrialism, white settler colonialism, and burgeoning struggles of racialized classes.

Anthropology is now returning to its forebears of the nineteenth century, when European novelists, missionaries, colonial administrators, and sundry travelers painted the lives of "distant, exotic peoples." To be sure, today there is every attempt to hear multiple voices and perspectives, to deny difference's claim to superiority, and to recognize the location of the anthropologists relative to their subjects. For all the difference, however, the old and the new global explorations have something profound in common— the bypassing of the nation state. If the early anthropologists reflected a period before the rise of the modern nation state,[80] their contemporaries today have sprung straight from village to the world as though the nation had already deceased. Arjun Appadurai articulates this tendency when he writes of the way electronic media and transnational migration have liberated modernity from the nation state.[81] Modernity, as he says, is now at large, settling and unsettling localities everywhere, creating diasporic public spheres, dissolving the past in the present, prompting a nostalgia without memory, stimulating and releasing imagination in everyday life. The cultural landscapes—ethnoscapes, technoscapes, financescapes, mediascapes, ideoscapes—are the fabricated lens of a fragmented, imaginary world in which the nation state is pulled apart, enfeebled and dissolved.

Appadurai has influenced our own study of global connections and imaginations, but being sociologists we have a different legacy to contend with. As Robert Connell has insisted, sociology also set out in the last century with unabashedly imperial ambitions, concerned with mapping out hierarchies of difference—gender, racial and ethnic—on a global scale.[82] But its first major ethnography, *The Polish Peasant,* was remarkable in leaving behind those early discourses on "progress" and superiority. Thomas and Znaniecki took the standpoint of the colonized in prosecuting Polish nationalist renewal against the occupying powers. As we have seen, the Chicago School shrank this global ethnography into local ethnography, and from there it disappeared into the interiors of organizations. With the diminution of scale, with the turn to micro-sociology, ethnography became increasingly marginal—where before it had been central—to sociology, whose object had become civil society and its connection to the state.

Classical sociology, what is now retrospectively called the canon, was born between 1890 and 1920 as part of a nation-building enterprise. Its hidden premise was not only the justification of imperialism, global difference, and domination of "primitive other," but the flip side of this—the metropole's domination, but with the consent of, its subordinate classes. Sociology participated in Gramsci's project of "national hegemony"—the expansion of the state's ideological apparatuses, and its penetration into the newly constituted civil society. Classical sociology was born together with the railroads, the police, universal schooling, the welfare state, the popular newspaper, the trade union, and the mass political party. Its message was solidarity, legitimacy, and bureaucracy. To this day its major subdisciplines—family, organizations, political sociology, crime and deviance, health and medicine, stratification, and so on—focus on the stabilizing and destabilizing tendencies of civil society. World system analysis is not a challenge to sociology but the apotheosis of sociology as we know it, because it presumes national hegemony to be unproblematic, a world order constituted of relations among nation states. Indeed, rather than challenge sociology, world system analysis, at least in its early incarnation, is itself challenged by globalization, by processes that are supranational, transnational, and postnational.[83]

Anthropologists can simply evacuate their villages and communities and move straight into the global arena, blissfully unperturbed by the tenacity of the nation state. Their discipline has never taken the modern nation state seriously and they are not about to do so now. Sociologists, on the other hand, are still haunted by the nation state as their discipline's raison d'etre. That is why when we talk of global forces we mean *supranational* forces, forces that operate above the nation state. The logic of the world market, and of its constituent institutions such as the United Nations, European Union, and International Monetary Fund, takes the existence of nation states as its premise. What is novel is the fact that states are now pulled not only from below but also from above. But the effects reverberate downward. As civil society loses its influence over the state, it turns outward, developing what we have called *transnational* connections—flows of people, information, and ideas, and the stretching of organizations, identities, and families. The dense ties that once connected civil society to the state are being detached and redirected across national boundaries to form a thickening global public sphere. Yet these connections and flows are not autonomous, are not arbitrary patterns crossing in the sky, but are shaped by the strong magnetic field of nation states. Taxation, welfare, labor markets, regional centers of economic agglomeration, natural resources, education, political regimes, and ideologies—all mark out national grids for the transnational. Just as global connections are transnational, global imaginations are *postnational* in that they react against the nation, reinvigorate the local, demand regional autonomy, or clamor for universal identities. As our studies show, abstract ideas such as environmental justice, human rights, and feminist discourses have their effects only when they are embodied in movements on national soils. Even if it is true, *pace* Appadurai, that global imaginations have emancipated themselves from the nation state and that the cultural is rapidly disconnecting from the nation state, that should not blind us to the latter's continuing influence in the realm of forces and connections.

If we are more cautious about the disappearance of the nation state than anthropologists, we are not saying nothing has changed. Indeed, it is the project of this book to specify what is new about the global, what distinguishes the global postmodern from the more familiar global imperialism out of which it is emerging. As sociologists we take Stuart Hall very seriously when he asks what it might mean to constitute hegemony not at a national level, which is the old sociological project, but at a global level: that is the new sociological project.[84] We return to these issues in the conclusion, after ethnography has put flesh on the bones of our schemata.

NOTES

I would like to thank Kathleen Schwartzman, Charlie Kurzman, Margaret Cerullo, Erik Wright, Ruth Horowitz, Ruth Milkman, Jennifer Pierce, and Leslie Salzinger for their comments on earlier versions of this chapter.

1. Fredric Jameson, "Cognitive Mapping." See also his *Postmodernism or, The Cultural Logic of Late Capitalism,* and *The Cultural Turn.*

2. Manuel Castells, *The Information Age,* vol. 1, *The Rise of the Network Society;* vol. 2, *The Power of Identity;* and vol. 3, *End of the Millennium.*

3. David Harvey, *The Condition of Postmodernity.*

4. John Meyer, John Boli, George Thomas, and Francisco O. Ramirez, "World Society and the Nation-State"; and John Meyer and Brian Rowan, "Institutionalized Organizations: Formal Structure as Myth and Ceremony."

5. Anthony Giddens, *The Consequences of Modernity,* and *Modernity and Self-Identity.*

6. Robert B. Reich, *The Work of Nations.*

7. Rosabeth Moss Kanter, *World Class.*

8. Saskia Sassen, *The Global City.*

9. Indeed, Seán Ó Riain's account of the global labor process in this volume (chapter 6) provides a good model for our own work relations. In the beginning we went through an intense introverted phase, focused on establishing the parameters of our collective endeavor, followed by an extroverted phase in which centrifugal forces drove us apart. After the first year it was difficult to recapture our early solidarity. From then on we were held together by occasional meetings, informal support groups, and a continuous stream of deadlines that took us through successive rewrites and revisions, new field work, and reorientation of the overall mission. At times I felt much like Ramesh in Seán's description, trying to hold course from a distance and imagining the circulation of subversive e-mail exchanges beyond my vision. For their part, my collaborators saw me as their Bela Karoly, the tyrannical Olympic coach remembered for his incessant urgings, endless demands, and emotional blackmail of his young female gymnasts.

10. James Clifford explains the early anthropologists' devotion to extended fieldwork in a single place, their concern with dwelling rather than traveling, as an

attempt to demarcate themselves from missionaries, travelers, and colonial administrators, who also indulged in descriptions of the tribes and peoples they came in touch with. Systematic observation, sustained over time in one place, was to make them scientists as distinct from dilettantes. See Clifford, "Traveling Cultures," and "Spatial Practices." Paul Rabinow's *Reflections on Fieldwork in Morocco* was one of the first ethnographies to break with professional codes by back-staging "dwelling" and front-staging "traveling," traveling to, through, and out of the field. Finished with the preliminary rituals of graduate school in Chicago, Rabinow takes off for the "field," arriving in Sefrou, one of Morocco's regional cities. His motion narrative takes the reader from the city's colonial outposts to its Ville Nouvelle (where he finds his first Arabic teacher) and from there to the Medina where he meets his capricious contact to the village. He negotiates entry with the village elders and, once in, he is passed from one informant to another. Finally, he meets a Moroccan soul brother who leads him to deeper self-realization. The reflections end with Rabinow returning to Chicago a changed person, even more alienated from graduate school than when he set out. The book is saturated with the language of movement. In displacing the ethnographer as dweller and centering movement, he violates all conventional norms.

11. George Marcus elaborates the idea of "multi-sited" ethnography in his *Ethnography through Thick and Thin*, especially chapters 1 and 3.

12. For recent reviews of the literature, see Michael Kearney, "The Local and the Global," and George Marcus, *Ethnography through Thick and Thin*, chapter 3.

13. There are many important anthropological figures who have resisted the temptation to marginalize history. Eric Wolf, *Europe and the People without History*, was a central figure in pioneering the location of ethnography in its global and historical context. Other anthropologists have become sensitive social historians. See, for example, John and Jean Comaroff, *Ethnography and the Historical Imagination*, and Jean and John Comaroff, *Of Revelation and Revolution*.

14. See Joan Vincent, *Anthropology and Politics*, for a fascinating historical reconstruction of the field of anthropology, which shows how this closing of the tribe came about, and Eric Wolf, *op.cit.*, for an anthropological reconstruction of history through a world system lens.

15. Durkheim, *The Division of Labor in Society*.

16. This narrative is drawn from Morris Janowitz's "Introduction" to his collection *W. I. Thomas on Social Organization and Social Personality* and from Martin Bulmer, *The Chicago School of Sociology*.

17. I am here referring to the 1927 two-volume edition of *The Polish Peasant in Europe and America* and not to the original five-volume edition. The contents are identical, just slightly rearranged. Thomas and Znaniecki mainly focus on parts of Poland occupied by Russia and to a lesser extent on those regions occupied by Germany, hardly mentioning Austro-Hungarian Poland.

18. Benedict Anderson, *Imagined Communities*.

19. See, for example, Basch, Schiller, and Blanc, *Nations Unbound*, or Rachel Sherman, "From State Extroversion to State Extension in Mexico: Modes of Emigrant Incorporation, 1900–1997."

20. See, for example, Eli Zaretsky's "Editor's Introduction" in his abridged edition of Thomas and Znaniecki, *The Polish Peasant in Europe and America*.

21. Blumer, *An Appraisal of Thomas and Znaniecki's* The Polish Peasant in Europe and America.

22. The locus classicus here is Barney Glaser and Anselm Strauss, *The Discovery of Grounded Theory.*

23. Thomas was arrested in a Chicago hotel room with a young woman on charges of disorderly conduct, false registration, and violation of the Mann Act. The event attracted a lot of negative publicity, especially as the woman's husband had just sailed for France to fight in the war. Thomas himself had always been a controversial figure, not least for his adamant support of women's rights. The staid University of Chicago wanted nothing more to do with him, despite protestation from some of his colleagues.

24. In their textbook, *Introduction to the Science of Sociology,* Park and Burgess do draw on Durkheim in their introductory chapter, using his notion of "collective representation" to establish the grounds for their key concept of social control. The only significant reference to Marx in the more than a thousand pages is to his "ponderous tomes" to which orthodox socialism appeals. Simmel, by contrast, is a dominant influence throughout.

25. Durkheim, *The Division of Labor in Society,* Book 2.

26. The locus classicus of the early Chicago School, known as the green bible, was the textbook by Robert Park and Ernest Burgess, *Introduction to the Science of Sociology.* Park became famous more as an essayist than as the author of original monographs. See, for example, the collections in Park and Burgess, *The City,* and Ralph Turner, editor, *Robert E. Park on Social Control and Collective Behavior.* The best biography of Robert Park is Fred Matthews, *Quest for an American Sociology.*

27. Ernest Burgess, "The Growth of the City."

28. Nels Anderson, *The Hobo.* While this ethnography is by no means global in scope, it does locate migratory labor and homelessness in the context of capitalism. Anderson had been a hobo himself and his account, like Teresa Gowan's study (chapter 3 below), is unusual in giving centrality to work. But there is a difference. Whereas Gowan's independent recyclers try to reenact a world they have lost, the hoboes described by Anderson are more forward-looking, less oppressed by stigmatization, more community-oriented, and more politically engaged (often with the IWW). Indeed, in a new introduction, written in 1961, thirty-eight years after the book's publication, reflecting on the hoboes' disappearance, Anderson referred to them as "heroic figures of the frontier" (xxi)—a far cry from contemporary pathologization of the homeless, to be sure, but notably lacking in critique of the material and discursive world that had produced the degradation he had so effectively described. From the point of view of Park and the Chicago School, *The Hobo* offered a case study of a self-regulating community.

29. Harvey Zorbaugh, *The Gold Coast and the Slum.*

30. Louis Wirth, *The Ghetto.*

31. Paul Cressey, *The Taxi-Dance Hall.*

32. This is how Park and Burgess distinguish sociology from history: "As soon as historians seek to take events out of their historical setting, that is to say out of their time and space relations, in order to compare them and classify them; as soon as the historians begin to emphasize the typical and representative rather than the unique

character of events, history ceases to be history and becomes sociology" (*Introduction to the Science of Sociology*, 8).

33. Lizabeth Cohen, *Making a New Deal.*

34. Hiller's book anticipates much social-movement literature of today—the pursuit of universality comes at the expense of history. The studies in the third part of this volume by Gille, Lopez, and Klawiter adopt a different, contextualized approach to social movements.

35. This narrative is taken from Abbott and Gaziano's "Transition and Tradition," a detailed account of factional fighting and feuding within the department, which reports that the department was in effective receivership from 1950 to 1957.

36. See Gary Fine, *A Second Chicago School?*

37. In his various writings Hans Joas has made the Chicago School's focus on the creative dimension of social action its defining trait, tracing this back to John Dewey and G. H. Mead. See Joas, *G. H. Mead, Pragmatism and Social Theory*, and *The Creativity of Action* (chapter 3).

38. Erving Goffman, *Asylums.*

39. Howard Becker, *Outsiders.*

40. Alvin Gouldner, "Sociologist as Partisan."

41. Alvin Gouldner, *The Coming Crisis of Western Sociology.*

42. The Manchester School was composed of white social anthropologists who came to study with or under the redoubtable Max Gluckman, chair of Manchester University's Department of Anthropology from 1949 to 1975. Gluckman had been director of the Rhodes-Livingstone Institute in Northern Rhodesia, which was to become Zambia in 1964. Even after Gluckman moved to Manchester, much of the fieldwork of his students continued to be conducted in Southern or Central Africa, although his international reputation attracted scholars to Manchester from all over the world.

43. See Richard Brown, "Passages in the Life of a White Anthropologist."

44. See Max Gluckman, *Rituals of Rebellion in South-East Africa, Custom and Conflict in Africa*, and *Order and Rebellion in Tribal Africa.*

45. See, for example, Jaap van Velsen, *The Politics of Kinship*, which in many ways anticipated Pierre Bourdieu's analysis of kinship-based society in Algeria and his book *Outline of a Theory of Practice.*

46. See, for example, Victor Turner, *Schism and Continuity in an African Society.* Max Gluckman distinguishes the use of cases as "apt illustration" from their being the object of study in themselves, when they become the embodiment of social process. See Gluckman, "Ethnographic Data in British Social Anthropology."

47. Max Gluckman, *Order and Rebellion in Tribal Africa*, chapter 5.

48. William Watson, *Tribal Cohesion in a Money Economy*, and Jaap van Velsen, "Labor Migration as a Positive Factor in the Continuity of Tonga Tribal Society."

49. Ulf Hannerz, *Exploring the City*, 119.

50. Max Gluckman, "Anthropological Problems Arising from the African Industrial Revolution."

51. Clyde Mitchell, *The Kalela Dance.*

52. A. L. Epstein, *The Politics of an Urban African Community.*

53. Edward P. Thompson, *The Making of the English Working Class.*

54. Gluckman, *Order and Rebellion in Tribal Africa*, chapters 8 and 9.

55. Victor Turner, *The Ritual Process,* and *Dramas, Fields, and Methods.*

56. *Schism and Continuity.*

57. *Dramas, Fields, and Methods,* 32–33.

58. Bernard Magubane, "Crisis in African Sociology," and "A Critical Look at Indices Used in the Study of Social Change in Colonial Africa."

59. James Ferguson, *Expectations of Modernity.*

60. The parallels are most clear in Bourdieu's *Outline of a Theory of Practice* (see pp. 22–30 for references to Gluckman and van Velsen) and its updated version, *The Logic of Practice.*

61. Burawoy, *The Colour of Class on the Copper Mines: From African Advancement to Zambianization.*

62. Burawoy, "Consciousness and Contradiction: A Study of Student Protest in Zambia."

63. Donald Roy, "Restriction of Output in a Piecework Machine Shop," "Quota Restriction and Goldbricking in a Machine Shop," "Work Satisfaction and Social Reward in Quota Achievement," "Efficiency and the Fix: Informal Intergroup Relations in a Piecework Machine Shop."

64. I was influenced in this regard by Tom Lupton's parallel Manchester study *On the Shop Floor.* Lupton, also an experienced worker, developed a view similar to Roy's, that the amount of effort delivered by workers was quite rational and that if this did not come up to managerial expectations it was because management had got the incentive system wrong or because the necessary material conditions were absent or because the work was poorly organized. Lupton, however, compared two different firms where he worked—a transformer factory and a garment factory—with a view to explaining differences in productive behavior on the part of workers. The differences between the shops allowed him to "extend out" his study to include such explanatory factors as labor markets, product markets, competition between firms, and labor costs as a proportion of total costs. It was this extension beyond the workplace that was never even contemplated by the Chicago School.

65. Burawoy, *Manufacturing Consent.*

66. Burawoy, *The Politics of Production: Factory Regimes under Capitalism and Socialism.*

67. Miklos Haraszti, *A Worker in a Worker's State.*

68. Michael Burawoy and János Lukács, *The Radiant Past.*

69. One should not forget that Berkeley's anthropology department had its own close and distinguished connection to the Manchester School, one of Manchester's rare women, Elizabeth Colson.

70. See, for example, Elliot Liebow, *Tally's Corner,* and Philippe Bourgois, *In Search of Respect.*

71. See, for example, William Foot Whyte, *Street Corner Society;* Ida Susser, *Norman Street;* and Lynne Haney, "Homeboys, Babies, Men in Suits: The State and the Reproduction of Male Domination."

72. See, for example, Louise Lamphere et al., *Sunbelt Working Mothers;* Robert Thomas, *Citizenship, Gender and Work;* Vicki Smith, *Managing in the Corporate Interest;* Linda Blum, *Between Feminism and Labor;* and Ching Kwan Lee, *Gender and the South China Miracle.*

73. See, for example, Rick Fantasia, *Cultures of Solidarity;* Paul Johnston, *Success While Others Fail;* and Raka Ray, *Fields of Protest.*

74. See, for example, Paul Willis, *Learning to Labor;* Jay MacLeod, *Ain't No Making It;* and Brian Powers, *Making Marginality.*

75. See, for example, Judith Stacey, *Brave New Families;* Marjorie Devault, *Feeding the Family;* and Pierrette Hondagneu-Sotelo, *Gendered Transitions.*

76. Dorothy Smith's "sociology for women" begins by debunking abstract, decontextualized, and universalistic sociology as the ideology of ruling men and turns to the concrete lived experience of women as point of departure. The microstructures of everyday life, which women direct, become the foundation and invisible premise for macro-structures controlled by men. When one includes the injunction to participatory research, this looks like the extended case method except that it claims to have no theoretical premises. Looking at Smith's empirical studies, on the other hand, I find them saturated with Marxism. See Smith, *The Everyday World as Problematic.*

77. Compare Jaap van Velsen's "The Extended Case Method and Situational Analysis," published in 1967 as one of the most advanced formulations of the Manchester method, with a more recent version, published by his student thirty years later, Burawoy's "The Extended Case Method."

78. Said, *Orientalism.*

79. We follow the lead of Allan Pred and Michael Watts, who study the cultural forms of protest, or what they call "symbolic discontent," that accompany capital accumulation in geographically and historically specific situations—from Islamic millenarianism sparked by Nigeria's integration into a world oil economy, to the renegotiation of gender identities among Gambian peasants instigated by the spread of contract farming, to linguistic resistance of California construction trades, to anti-union strategies of Korean capital. They show how movements are not only generated on the terrain of competing ideologies but such movements in turn often compose further alternative, compelling visions of their own (Pred and Watts, *Reworking Modernity*).

80. I am borrowing Eric Hobsbawm's periodization in *Nations and Nationalism since 1780.*

81. Appadurai, *Modernity at Large.*

82. Connell, "Why Is Classical Theory Classical?"

83. More sophisticated world systems analysis seeks to understand the way location in the world economy sets limits on the possibilities of national hegemony. For an exemplary study in this genre, see Kathleen Schwartzman's *The Social Origins of Democratic Collapse.*

84. Hall, "The Local and the Global: Globalization and Ethnicity," "Old and New Identities, Old and New Ethnicities," and "When Was the 'Post-Colonial'? Thinking at the Limit."

PART ONE

Global Forces

Introduction to Part One

All three of our projects take globalization as a constellation of forces that impinge upon people's lives. We do not want to argue that globalization is "new" in and of itself. But significant economic, political, and technological changes in the world in the last quarter century have led to a shrinking world, an ever more integrated global economy, and an information and technological upheaval, whose ongoing logic continues to reshape lives and institutions. New forms of globalization are taking shape in the contemporary world—new constellations that both coordinate and disrupt the lives of specific populations in historically unique ways.

A global, completely interdependent world economy has emerged, working as a single unit in real time. All economic processes affect each other, as distant regions of the planet are brought together by flows of labor, capital, information, and commodities. The increasing mobility of capital leads to contradictory effects for domestic labor. Capital flight leaves many previously semisecure workers in the position of having a home and established relations in a community in which they are no longer economically viable and in which occupational opportunities no longer exist for them to maintain their lifestyles. They must either chase capital to new locations and myriad uncertainties, or face certain downward mobility. For others, ranging from some traditional immigrants to the symbolic analysts of the new digital realm, the reconfiguration of capital provides new and sometimes lucrative opportunities.

These shifts in relations between capital and labor have contradictory implications for the nature and workings of contemporary nation states. Governments' ability to control transnational capital has diminished. States and other subdivisions within national entities have become competitors, attempting to attract, maintain, and retain increasingly global networks of markets, industries, and factories.

The efforts of governments to discipline and restrict both labor and the ordinary citizen, on the other hand, have greatly increased. Across the richer countries, economic transformation has coincided with a shrinking of citizenship rights. The European Community has turned itself into Fortress Europe and the United States denies many social services to immigrants. Along with restrictions on citizenship, states have begun to scale back welfare benefits and social provisions. Once designed to provide social rights and entitlements to recipients, welfare states have become more discretionary, introducing both means-testing and time limitations. In the United States, the so-called Personal Responsibility and Work Opportunity Act of 1996 abolished AFDC (Aid to Families with Dependent Children), the primary safety net for poor families, and affirmative action on behalf of minorities was outlawed in many states. At the same time, the repressive nature of the state has increased, as those discarded by market forces feed a burgeoning prison population.

Our accounts of globalization examine how these forces have reconfigured both sides of the once impenetrable divide between the Soviet and Western spheres of influence. Our essays begin from a period of difference—a historical moment when the industralized world was split into two opposing "camps" vying for hegemony. On one side of the divide, Joseph Blum shows how the economic and political configurations of the Cold War United States were largely dependent on this global order. Joseph's subjects are Fordist workers—men whose stable jobs, military positions, and political citizenship were intimately connected to the success of United States hegemony. While they were by no means the architects of this order, their interests were both coordinated and served by it. Lynne Haney examines how the state socialist world of Hungarian full employment and societal welfare was also contingent on this global arrangement. Her subjects were formerly socialist mothers—women positioned as the reproducers of the national labor force and therefore entitled to support from the state.

While our essays begin with the divergent worlds of West and East, they end with a story of convergence. The collapse of the Cold War world system was accompanied by the "end of history," the triumph of neoliberal economic, political, and societal models. As it traveled, neoliberalism gobbled up all alternatives and assigned all challenges to the historical dustbin. Governments have become more tightly focused on the facilitation of capital accumulation, and are adopting authoritarian methods for dealing with those members of the society unable to prosper within the corporate machine. Structural approaches to the problems of the poor and excluded are discredited as economically infeasible and historically obsolete, just as within the economy alternative modes of industrial work and union organizing are deemed inefficient and outdated. Thus, our studies reveal the discursive homogenization that has surfaced with the collapse of the Cold War divide.

With this gobbling up of historical alternatives, we also find the subjects of our studies experiencing quite similar forms of domination. The convergences are striking. Once situated in different locations, United States blue collar men and female Hungarian welfare clients confront common processes of marginalization. They all experience economic disenfranchisement, in both real and relative terms. They all face heightened insecurity and instability in their work and everyday lives. And they are all surveyed and stigmatized in new, potentially deeper, ways. In short, they all bear the brunt of forceful global processes of homogenization and domination.

The marginalization and disenfranchisement that our subjects encounter is not simply related to their being from the two key sides of the Cold War order. Not all populations in the United States and Hungary experience this global reshuffling as a time of destruction or loss. Here we must remain attentive to these groups' subject positions within their particular national contexts. While the groups in our studies were located on the two key ends of the previous global divide, they also were included in the "core" of their respective sides.

In both Hungary and the United States, the Cold War period was also the time when the bulk of the working classes were for the first time integrated into secure, decently paid work, protected by their governments from the fear of poverty through aging, unemployment, or sickness. Following the considerable union successes of the thirties, American workers became constructed into a national workforce, with unions joining large corporations and government to regulate the boom and bust tendencies of competitive capitalism.

Hungarian mothers were similarly central to the socialist model of the Hungarian nation, intrinsically valued and financially rewarded for their labor in reproducing the next generation of Hungarian workers. In theory at least, the government took responsibility for the well-being of mothers in a broadly inclusive framework, including protection from male violence, and help with employment and with housing provision and conditions.

In both Hungary and the United States, therefore, the hegemonic concept of nationhood was intimately tied to the fate of the "ordinary" man and woman. This core citizen was in both cases implicitly white, as opposed to the Romani in Hungary or various peoples of color in the United States. However, even subordinate minorities gained during this period. In the United States, a much-expanded professional military provided employment for millions of poor young men and women, especially African Americans and Latinos, who might otherwise have remained excluded from the corporatist bargain. The victories of the civil rights movement further broadened the base of working-class integration, as various levels of the government were required by affirmative action to employ large numbers of African Americans. In Hungary, Romani women might be given a lower standard of service by the social welfare offices and caseworkers, yet the rights guaranteed to all mothers within state socialism gave them automatic access to substantial resources.

Lynne Haney describes how the state's broad conception of women's needs under socialism has contracted under neoliberalism into a narrow, stigmatized place, framed in purely economic terms. The increasing stigma, bureaucratic barriers, and means requirements have successfully dissuaded most mothers from demanding help from the state. The remaining claimants are therefore women with no other means of support, largely women from poor and already stigmatized communities.

Like the poverty of American mothers on AFDC, that of Hungarian claimants is increasingly understood by social scientists and social workers as a product of their pathologies. Correspondingly, their meager welfare benefits become loaded with morality tests and exhortations to self-improvement. Detached from their former community with Hungarian mothers as a whole, such women can no longer legitimately claim the role of producers of the national workforce.

The blue-collar men described by Joe Blum and Teresa Gowan are similarly displaced from former positions of integration and security. Joe and his coworkers have gradually lost union power, income security, and respect from management for their skills. Yet, unlike many former industrial workers in the Bay Area, they still have some work. The homeless recyclers studied by Teresa Gowan have been less fortunate. Many who were previously longtime employees of unionized local corporations and the military now struggle for basic subsistence by reclaiming garbage for the international recycling industry. Like the Hungarian welfare mothers, their poverty is taken as a symptom of inner weakness and disease.

What these three chapters have in common, therefore, is their examination of how globalization has destroyed formerly "core" collectives. The more broadly inclusive constructions of working-class employment, entitlement, and citizenship characteristics of the Cold War period have been fragmented in different directions. While some have prospered under the so-called free market, those unable to adapt to the hucksterism of the new order have fallen through the cracks. The recent Asian crisis shows that even the winners in globalized societies are not safe from the fluctuations of the economy without borders.

Without former social entitlements, both the opportunity to better one's position and the possibility of rescue from disaster have been pushed back into the private sphere. As in previous periods of low market regulation, family wealth and cultural capital become a person's primary protection against the insecurity of the risk society. Those without such resources live in constant danger of social fall, and, once fallen, recovery is unlikely. Degraded, marginalized, and often stigmatized by the broader society, such casualties attempt with difficulty to reclaim the rights and respect they have lost.

Joseph A. Blum, Teresa Gowan, and Lynne Haney

TWO

Global Discourses of Need

Mythologizing and Pathologizing Welfare in Hungary

Lynne Haney

When I began this research on the Hungarian welfare system, I thought of myself as a "hardened" ethnographer. Having just completed grueling ethnographic research in the California juvenile justice system, I was confident that I could handle anything I encountered in Hungary. As it turned out, my previous experience did not prepare me for a crumbling welfare state that was replete with pain and dislocation. On the one side were the clients who struggled to keep themselves afloat materially, socially, and emotionally. On the other side were welfare workers—women who were frustrated by work they found unfulfilling. It was difficult to watch these workers become increasingly powerless and lash out defensively at clients. I knew they were not malicious or mean-spirited women. Yet, when confronted with abysmal working conditions, they reacted in understandable (although not commendable) ways. At the everyday level, there was no one to blame. There were no clear-cut bad guys; there was just a lot of pain and suffering.

My struggle to cope with these experiences of loss pushed me beyond the world of welfare agencies in two directions. First, I became unwilling (and unable) to limit my study to welfare offices alone. Instead of conducting a "traditional" ethnography of a single site, I insisted on multilocality—that is, on taking the whole terrain of Hungarian welfare as a "field" of sites. This meant that I spent a considerable amount of time conducting the research; I worked in my field of sites for over eighteen months. It also meant that, as I did

the research, I continually maneuvered from agency to agency, from
research institutes to welfare offices, and from welfare "experts" to
welfare workers. Through this maneuvering, I first became aware of
a disjunction between ideology and practice. I attended welfare conferences and heard celebratory speeches about Hungary's new autonomy, but then I watched as local government officials scrambled
to adhere to International Monetary Fund (IMF) and World Bank
demands. I met Hungarian academics who celebrated the opening
up of the "civil society," but then I read their research reports that
propagated the welfare models of the international organizations
funding them. And I attended training sessions where welfare workers were told that means-testing would rationalize their workloads,
but then I returned to the pandemonium of welfare institutions.
Thus, by remaining multiply situated, I connected different welfare
sites to uncover the gap between ideology and practice.

Another disjunction between ideology and practice surfaced
through my second movement beyond the current world of welfare
agencies. Faced with the suffering of the present, like many clients,
I turned to the past. Initially, I thought I could simply interview
caseworkers about the work of their predecessors. Yet the accounts
relayed in these interviews were rarely satisfying; they were more like
ideological commentaries on state totalitarianism than concrete reflections on state practices. This prompted me to conduct my own
historical excavation, which took me beyond "traditional" ethnography into ethnohistory. After gaining access to welfare agencies'
archives, which consisted of millions of records stretching back to
the inception of state socialism, I randomly sampled 1,203 case files.
In interpreting these historical records, I ran into a methodological
problem: how could I justify a comparison of the past, based on caseworkers' records, and the present, based on my own observations? I
confronted the problem by supplementing my observations with an
analysis of case files from the past and the present, which gave my
data some consistency over time. I also approached these data in
similar ways—eliciting caseworker and client accounts as expressed
in their words and/or actions and as acted out in front of me and/
or in written statements. It was through this mediation that I encountered yet another disjunction between ideology and practice:
in actual practice, the state socialist welfare apparatus had given
clients more room to maneuver than either the ideology of the past

or the present would lead us to believe. Once again, multilocality in time *and* space enabled me to unearth ruptures in past/present ideologies and practices.

Hence, my analysis of global discourses of need grew out of an ethnohistory of the field of Hungarian welfare. From this wider lens, I reveal how Hungarian social scientists were lured into an ideological flirtation with global policemen from the IMF and World Bank— a flirtation that eventually evolved into material appropriation and discursive co-optation. From this field perspective, I also expose how these discursive exchanges translated into institutional changes that altered the terms, the organization, and the connotations of welfare. Finally, I argue that the practical and discursive space surrounding clients has contracted, leaving them increasingly stigmatized and pathologized. In short, this paper debunks the euphoria associated with the political transition in Eastern Europe, and shows how rapid democratization limited clients' ability to articulate and defend their interests.

On March 12, 1995, after days of negotiations with the Hungarian government, four men in expensive suits boarded a plane from Budapest to Brussels. As they departed, Prime Minister Gyula Horn appeared on Hungarian television to announce the "Bokros csomag," a proposal to restructure the Hungarian welfare system by means-testing all cash benefits. The repercussions of the announcement were felt throughout Hungary; in stores, workplaces, and pubs all talk revolved around the plan. Yet nowhere were the effects felt as acutely as in local welfare offices, where female clients converged *en masse*. In one office, clients gathered around caseworkers' desks, demanding an explanation for the proposal. Caseworkers nervously tried to justify the plan, arguing that means tests were not so bad and were used all over the world. Unconvinced, clients protested that the plan would leave them more vulnerable and powerless. One woman even staged a sit-in at a caseworker's desk, ordering her to call Prime Minister Horn to revoke the proposal. In effect, these clients viewed the reform proposal as a curtailment of their social rights; they contested reform which they believed would undercut their social protection and well-being.

In sharp contrast to the angry protests launched by female clients, social scientific analyses of democratization in Eastern Europe tend to be infused with euphoria. Unlike the scholarship on the economic transition, which acknowledges the conflicted nature of privatization and debates the desired outcome in property forms, the scholarship on democratization is less cautious and more optimistic. There is little debate over the desired goal—the transmutation of "the party/state into a liberal state" and of "the people into civil society."[1] Similarly, the virtues of democratization go uncontested by these scholars; they presume that the blossoming of political parties and movements will offer East Europeans more space for the articulation of interests and the formation of social identities.[2] To the extent that scholars of democratization exhibit caution, they worry that the political freedom unleashed in the region will meet an institutional vacuum, and thus become channeled into right-wing politics or nationalism.[3] Should this scenario be avoided, and liberal political institutions implanted, then the virtues of democracy will prevail.

The optimism in the democratization literature is even more pronounced in the scholarship on the welfare state transition. Here one finds a consensus that the collapse of state socialism marks an end to "bureaucratic state collectivism."[4] While welfare scholars recognize that economic liberalization underlies welfare restructuring and cuts in welfare funding in the post-1989 period, these shifts are obscured by their celebration of the "democratization" of the state. At the political level, these scholars see new space for political contests over whose social needs will be met by the state.[5] At the policy level, they foresee new opportunities for citizens to become involved in the conceptualization and implementation of provisions to satisfy their needs.[6] And at the institutional level, they project a flourishing of new social initiatives of self-help and philanthropy as well as the pluralization of welfare agencies.[7] Scholars working on Hungary exhibit even more optimism—with one theorizing that the "bourgeois activity by citizens in the interstices of Kadarism" equipped Hungarians to become active subjects in the post-1989 welfare regime change.[8] In short, these scholars assume that the expansion of political citizenship will breed new forms of social citizenship, and that the extension of political rights will lead to the enlargement of social rights in the region.

The opening up of "civil society" did have profound effects on Hungarian welfare, but they were not of the sort imagined by these optimistic East Europeanists. Once pried open, this social realm was quickly filled by a global discourse of need—a poverty discourse that embodied new assumptions about what the population needed and how to meet those needs.[9] Ascendant worldwide, this poverty discourse surfaced in contexts as diverse as North America, Latin America, Scandinavia, and Western Europe. Yet this discourse of need was not a disembodied phenomenon; it did not float around the world, mysteriously rearranging welfare states as it journeyed. Rather, it was produced and transmitted by a collection of transnational policing agencies and actors. Armed with neoliberal economic theory, these men in expensive suits from the IMF and World Bank spanned the globe, counseling governments about "appropriate" levels of social spending. They arrived in Hungary with prepared modes of argumentation:

they claimed market economies could not work with "encompassing" entitlement criteria that subject the state to soft budget constraints; they deployed Hungary's large foreign debt to instill fear of an economic collapse; and they proposed "welfare with a human face" through poverty programs and means tests. These men had power. They bolstered their poverty discourse with loans and debt-restructuring plans. And they justified their blueprints by referring to "success" stories of countries they had visited in the East, West, North, and South. Their discourse of need was global in its appeals and effects; the homogenization of welfare systems was an openly stated goal.

While this discourse of need was a global force, it had to be indigenized and planted in local soil as it traveled. In Hungary, this implantation process involved both global and local actors. This paper analyzes the dynamics of this discursive transfer and its effects on Hungarian welfare clients. Although the poverty discourse that seeped into postsocialist Hungary was certainly part of the economic liberalization project to trim the welfare state, its implications were decisively political as well. This discourse was first translated into Hungarian through an interactive process that locked into local expert systems—Hungarian social scientists latched onto this discourse to serve their own ideological and material interests. Once localized, the poverty discourse had concrete institutional effects: It altered the conditions of welfare work and transformed caseworkers into eligibility workers; it narrowed the practical and discursive space available for female clients to protect their well-being—what I term "client maneuverability"; and it heightened clients' subjective sense of stigmatization. Hence, my analysis challenges the optimistic claims so often advanced by scholars of Eastern Europe, the self-described "transitologists"—revealing how welfare restructuring undermined the democratic project of increased social participation and led to a contraction, rather than an expansion, of the space in which Hungarian clients could defend their interests.[10]

THE POLITICS OF DISCURSIVE INDIGENIZATION

In order to grasp the full extent of this contraction in space, some historical context is needed. We must go back to the "state" of Hungarian welfare under late socialism—an era often overlooked in euphoric accounts of the transitologists. During the last two decades of state socialism, the Hungarian welfare regime developed into a strong system of social entitlements and guarantees. At the core of this system was a series of full employment and work-related provisions that linked Hungarians' access to socialized goods and services to participation in the labor force.[11] Until the mid-1980s, the Hungarian state guaranteed all Hungarians employment. In fact, it required Hungarians to participate in wage labor—those who did not avail themselves of the right to work were deemed "publicly dangerous work avoiders" (*közveszélyes munkakerülés*) and subjected to fines and even imprisonment. On the more positive side, the national state subsidized most basic necessities and provided the population with numerous socialized goods and services. These included subsidized childcare, housing, education, and transportation. At the enterprise level, workers had access to additional benefits. While the availability and the quality of these goods and services varied by workplace, many workers were given subsidized eating facilities, childcare, housing, clothing, household goods, and vacation packages through their workplaces. The principle underlying all of these benefits was that Hungarians' social contributions as workers entitled them to material supports and a basic standard of living.

Moreover, beginning in the late 1960s, a subsystem of welfare arose on top of this work-based system to tie eligibility to motherhood. This maternalist welfare apparatus consisted of four key provisions. First, after 1968, Hungarian mothers were entitled to three years of paid maternity leave (*Gyermekgondozási Segély/Díj* or GYES/GYED).[12] Available to all women regardless of their class or occupation, the grant guaranteed mothers reemployment in their previous positions upon completion of leave.[13] Second, Hungarian parents with at least two children received family allowances (*csaladi potlék*) attached to their wages. While the amount of the allowance varied by family size, it constituted 10 to 15 percent of the average monthly wage. Third, Hungarian mothers had their own system of short-term leave provisions: once a month they could take a "housework holiday" from work, and six to eight times a year they could take paid child-care leave.[14] Finally, beginning in 1974, mothers could apply for special childrearing assistance (*Rendszeres Nevelési Segély*). These were income-maintenance funds given to women as rewards for "good" mothering.[15] None of these provisions were allocated according to material need.[16] Rather, this welfare regime was based on encompassing entitlement criteria linked to recipients' social contributions as workers and/or mothers.

In effect, the state socialist welfare regime was just the kind of expansive welfare system that provokes anxiety in representatives of the IMF and World Bank. Yet the first attack on this system did not come from global policemen; it was launched locally. And this early attack did not fault the welfare regime for its bloated size; it criticized the regime for not going far enough to meet the population's needs. In the mid-1980s, years before the official "collapse" of state socialism, Hungarian social scientists began to critique the existing welfare system for failing to address material problems adequately. Many of them based their critique on studies that revealed a dual system of stratification emerging: at the top were new entrepreneurial classes with access to the second economy, while at the bottom were Hungarians without the skills or resources to secure second-economy incomes.[17] The latter group, constituting over 30 percent of the population, began to experience real pauperization. Other social scientists discovered inequalities among Hungarian families, as female-headed households and urban families slipped into poverty in the early 1980s.[18] Still others unearthed poverty in their studies of Romani communities and in their work with poor-relief groups like SZETA.[19] In summary, Hungarian sociologists revealed that different social groups were falling through cracks in the welfare system, with their social problems going unresolved. As a result, they called for the creation of targeted policies and institutions to meet the material needs of the impoverished.[20]

Initially, this poverty work was an oppositional move, an attempt to use social democratic politics to critique actually existing state socialism. Hence, sociologists' reform proposals of the mid-1980s rarely called for the destruction of the entitlement system *per se*. Rather, they drew on West European and Scandinavian social democratic welfare models to argue for a system that coupled social entitlements with poor relief.[21] Yet as these sociologists formulated their proposals, another discourse of need began to surround them, seeping into Hungary through its increasingly porous borders. This was the discourse of need articulated by the IMF and World Bank, both of which had stepped up their policing of the Hungarian economy to guide it toward liberal capitalism. These agencies entered Hungary much earlier than they did other countries in the region; they surfaced in Hungary in 1982, but did not reach Poland until 1986 and Czechoslovakia until 1990. Beginning in the late 1980s, these agencies issued a series of policy reports designed to convince Hungarians to develop more restrictive eligibility criteria. Using Western mythologies of how welfare states "should" operate, they pushed to introduce means tests and a discretionary welfare state. It was here that these global and local forces converged. This poverty discourse soon found its way into local sociologists' reform programs. Sociologists used this discourse as ideological ammunition—appropriating it to bolster their critique of socialist welfare and to argue for the creation of more discretionary social policies.[22]

Just as Hungarian sociologists mobilized internationally recognized poverty discourses in their local struggles, the reverse was also true: international policing agencies used sociologists' poverty work to market their welfare agenda. In their research reports published in the late 1980s and early 1990s, these agencies based many of their reform proposals on the empirical work of Hungarian sociologists. On the one hand, they drew on sociological analyses of the bureaucratic privileges embedded in the socialist entitlement system to call for the creation of a more targeted system. Without clear means tests and income tests, they argued that the Hungarian welfare system would continue to operate according to informal bargaining that put the poor at a disadvantage.[23] On the other hand, they pointed to studies suggesting that universal entitlement criteria were unduly advantageous to the wealthy, who could afford to pay "market price" for subsidized goods and services.[24] Here these agencies proposed "welfare with a human face"—arguing that replacing expansive entitlement criteria with more restrictive ones would protect the poor and vulnerable.[25] Hence, these agencies selectively appropriated local social scientific work. They ignored sociologists' commitment to social entitlements, but endorsed their ideas about poor relief. While their political goals may have been different, there was a (partial) ideological affinity between international agencies and Hungarian professionals.

What began as ideological flirtation between these global and local forces evolved into a full appropriation by the early 1990s. By this time, the global discourse of need had become fully absorbed by local expert systems. The nature of their relationship changed—it became less ideological and more material. Many of Hungary's most prominent welfare experts joined the payrolls of the IMF and World Bank. They received money to produce studies in line with these agencies' policy recommendations. For instance, the Hungarian Institute of Sociology conducted regular social policy studies for these agencies. Sociologists did micro-level investigations of the new patterns of social inequality in the transition period.[26] These studies showed that large sectors of the population were slipping into poverty and that universal welfare policies were ineffective in halting this slide. Thus, they made a case for means tests to alleviate new forms of poverty. Sociologists also conducted studies that made similar arguments at the macro-level.[27] Using comparative data on welfare expenditures, they argued that Hungarian expenditures were inconsistent with the country's level of economic development.[28] They attributed this to Hungary's inability to apply a consistent "principle of need" to welfare allocation.[29] They claimed that these rates were economically disastrous and "morally offensive" since they lacked "solidarity" with the poor, the weak, and the needy.[30] Needless to say, these were just the kind of arguments that the agencies funding this research yearned to hear.

In addition to funding local research, international agencies also subsidized the emergence of new journals and educational institutions to further ground this global discourse of need. Here a series of other international agencies and foundations entered the picture. What has become the most influential Hungarian social-policy journal, *Esély*, was established with the financial support of groups as diverse as the World Bank, USIA, UNICEF, the European Union, and the Soros Foundation.[31] This journal publishes the work of Hungarian and Western welfare scholars and operates out of Hungary's first degree-granting Department of Social Policy and Social

Work at the University of Budapest (ELTE). Founded in the late 1980s, this department relies so heavily on international support that the department chair holds the title of "European Union Chair of Social Policy."

Since the formation of this department, over a dozen smaller schools of social work have sprouted up in Hungary. They also receive funding from abroad. The curricula of these schools include required courses on means-testing and poverty regulation. Many students learn about these subjects from their visiting professors from Western Europe and the United States—faculty brought to Hungary by international agencies and foundations. Others learn about these topics from their U.S., French, and British text-books—books translated into Hungarian with the funds of international agencies and foundations. A social worker once showed me the core text-book used in her school. Written by a UCLA professor, it devoted three chapters to the detection of welfare fraud, instructing social workers to search for expensive items such as Nike sneakers and CD collections while on home visits. "This is a problem I face every day in Hungary," the social worker ironically remarked. "Real helpful."

Perhaps the clearest example of the indigenization of this global dis-course of need occurred in the conferences organized and funded by inter-national agencies. In these conferences, Western experts were deployed to teach Hungarians the tools of the welfare state trade. Held every few months, these gatherings were organized in similar ways: opening speeches by Western experts on the theory and practice of the targeted welfare state, followed by workshops in which Hungarians learned to administer such pro-grams. The information transmitted in these meetings always flowed in one direction, from Westerners to Hungarians. Sessions included workshops on the "newest" techniques of means-testing in the West and on the "new assis-tance philosophy" in Western Europe, as well as roundtables on the rela-tionship between poverty and child abuse. Some sessions bordered on the absurd. In one a Dutch expert spent an hour discussing how a new video sys-tem installed in her office detected clients' deep-seated "ambivalence" about work. The Hungarian audience sat in awe, staring at this woman as if she were from Mars.

Such absurdity aside, it was through these kinds of appropriation that the global poverty discourse was localized in Hungary. By subsidizing Hungarian research, policy journals, schools of social work, and confer-ences, local welfare experts were saturated by this discourse of need. Yet they did not reject it. Far from it—most Hungarian social scientists and wel-fare experts swallowed the discourse. They had an interest in swallowing. It gave them access to resources that were rapidly evaporating in the Hungarian state and academy. It also enabled them to carve out places for themselves in the welfare apparatus, as welfare analysts and policymakers. They became the "experts," the ones with the knowledge to formulate, adjust, and administer the new discretionary programs of the targeted welfare state. Hence, in the newly "democratized" state sphere, global experts met up with "needy" local experts—with the former using the latter to ground their poverty discourse, and the latter using the former to secure and promote their own professional ascendancy.

REGULATING POVERTY, LIMITING CLIENT OPTIONS

This poverty discourse did not remain confined to policy journals, schools of social work, research institutes, or conferences. Once appropriated, this discourse was translated back into Hungarian to reshape the welfare apparatus itself. Out of the policy studies came new recommendations for the introduction of discretionary welfare programs. So, by the late 1980s, local welfare agencies were distributing benefits according to means tests; by the mid-1990s, national-level welfare benefits had been income-tested. Out of the schools of social work came new cadres of welfare workers trained to target and treat poverty. Hence, by the late 1980s, the institutional welfare apparatus had expanded to include networks of poor-relief agencies and social workers. Out of the international conferences came new institutional models and casework approaches. Thus, postsocialist welfare institutions began to employ new surveillance techniques to monitor clients' lives and livelihoods.

It was, of course, through this reworking of the Hungarian welfare apparatus that this poverty discourse was transmitted to clients. Within welfare institutions, female clients discovered that their needs would be assessed in strictly material terms. Clients learned this through the reorganization of casework and social work. They experienced it through the new means tests administered by welfare offices. They encountered it through the new techniques designed to survey their material lives—home visitors with assistance forms that included questions about the size of their flats, the value of their furniture, and their access to electronics, automobiles, and telephones. Together, these welfare practices grounded the poverty discourse in female clients' everyday lives. Their effects on clients' lives were far from the optimistic projections of East European welfare scholars. While providing new possibilities for "identity formation" and "interest articulation," these practices reduced the resources available to clients.

To understand the extent of this reduction in resources, we must once again return to the state socialist welfare system—this time from the perspective of its female clients. This welfare regime was distinctive not only because of the size of its policy apparatus, but also because it acknowledged women's multiple needs. By linking eligibility to clients' social contributions, this regime established a fairly broad terrain upon which clients could seek state assistance. This had implications for the discursive and institutional resources at their disposal. Discursively, this welfare regime offered an array of rhetorical possibilities for claims-making. It allowed clients to couch appeals for state support in several idioms; they could speak of their needs as workers, mothers, and/or family members. As workers, women could claim a series of benefits through their workplaces, such as subsidized housing, health care, vacation packages, and eating facilities. As mothers, women could obtain state support for their childrearing. They could demand more time, in the form of maternity and child-care leave, and they could claim special financial support, in the form of childrearing assistance. As family members, women could appeal for state support to fulfill their familial responsibilities—family allowances to offset the costs of childrearing; marital allowances to enable married couples to set up house; and elderly assistance to permit them to care for sick and aging parents. In the state socialist welfare system, female clients could frame assistance claims around a variety of social positions and needs.

Moreover, in this past regime, clients could make discursive connections among their different needs. At work, women often emphasized their responsibilities as mothers and family members. In my archival research, I discovered that women regularly drew on their family demands to improve their work lives. Of those who cited their living conditions at work, 39 percent did so to secure more flexible work schedules, 31 percent to upgrade their working conditions, and 30 percent to increase their access to socialized goods and services. "I have a husband and two sons, and more mouths to feed and more dirt to clean," a female factory worker wrote to a union official in 1966 in order to obtain a new oven and vacuum cleaner from her workplace.[32] Similarly, when appealing to the main welfare office of the period, the Gyámhatóság, female clients frequently drew on their positions as workers. They used their positions as workers to coax caseworkers to intervene in their family lives. "I am a diligent seamstress who suffers pain at the hands of my husband," one woman wrote to the Gyámhatóság in 1965. "I ask for nothing more than an end to this pain."[33] Thus, by maneuvering among their different social roles, clients manipulated the prevailing "needs talk" to stake claims to a multiplicity of state resources and supports.

Accompanying these discursive resources was a plethora of practical tools clients could utilize in their everyday lives. These institutional resources were not simply financial in nature. Although this past regime did accord female clients material support, it also gave them the tools to become socially integrated. On the one hand, clients regularly mobilized Gyámhatóság caseworkers to resolve work problems—approximately 58 percent of my sample of state socialist case files involved clients who sought assistance to enter the labor force. Many of them mobilized caseworkers to locate and gain employment. They also used caseworkers to improve their work relations with colleagues and supervisors. On the other hand, clients appropriated caseworkers to help them integrate their nuclear and extended families—roughly 72 percent of my sample of case files involved such familial work. Clients who felt that their families were falling apart often turned to caseworkers. Women who had been abandoned by their spouses or lovers had caseworkers track down these men—convincing caseworkers to use their control over paternity investigations, child custody, and child support to undermine men's ability to shirk their domestic responsibilities. They also drew on welfare workers to help repair severed ties with extended kin—using caseworkers to help them make contact with larger kinship networks or to work out issues they had with adult siblings and parents. As one woman wrote in a thank-you note to a state counselor in 1977: "I know that my ambivalence toward my daughter comes from my mother's anger toward me. I thank you for your help uncovering this and resolving and improving this relation."[34]

In addition to receiving this integrative assistance, female clients used state socialist welfare offices to help alter the nature of their familial relations. They mobilized caseworkers to help make men better spouses and parents. Gyámhatóság caseworkers were willing to scold unruly husbands or irresponsible fathers. "He calls me a whore in front of the little ones," a woman confided to her caseworker in 1975. "They have no respect for me as a result."[35] On subsequent visits, the caseworker reprimanded the man for his "inappropriate" language. In another 1978 case, a woman informed her caseworker that she had to apply for assistance because her husband "refused to work hard."[36] On later visits, the caseworker lectured him about his "laziness" and pressured him to work more. Caseworkers were also used as bargaining chips in clients' domestic battles. They often gave clients copies of their home visit reports to mobilize as weapons. "Look what the tanács said about us," one woman exclaimed to her husband in 1980 in order to convince him to stop drinking.[37] And caseworkers regularly threatened to withdraw clients' support or to institutionalize their children as a way of forcing men to improve their behavior. For example, in 1969 a female client made a deal with her caseworker—the caseworker temporarily institutionalized her son to prove to her husband that his abusive behavior had "consequences."[38] In a 1975 case, a woman had a state psychologist require that she tutor her sons daily in order to equalize the domestic division of labor. As the counselor recounted after a home visit: "I arrived at the home at 6:30. The mother was in the back working with the boys while the father was heating up the food. When I asked about it, she smiled and said he did this since our therapy started."[39]

Thus, by recognizing women's social contributions and responding to a variety of needs claims, the socialist welfare regime gave female clients a considerable amount of room to maneuver; it allowed them to articulate and defend their different interests. It was precisely this practical and discursive space that narrowed with the entrance of a global discourse of poverty regulation. First, at the practical level, this discourse limited the number of institutional resources at clients' disposal. In contemporary Hungary, all clients' problems are interpreted as material issues. With the introduction of means tests in the 1980s, caseworkers began to see their clients strictly through the lens of the material. Caseworkers used these tests to identify their clientele; only those women who could demonstrate material need became clients. The reversal has been striking. In the two districts covered by my research, 92 percent of female clients in the state socialist period were thought to have problems related to their work and/or family lives. In contemporary Hungary, 78 percent of these offices' clients are defined as strictly "materially" needy.

This dramatic shift in welfare workers' conception of need has shaped the kind of assistance provided to clients. Caseworkers now deal with clients in one of two ways. In most cases, they just distribute financial assistance. They allocate poor relief to clients and assume it will solve their problems. Since the mid-1980s, the overall number of Hungarians receiving occasional poor relief has increased by 2,000 percent; the number of recipients of ongoing poor relief has risen by 1,000 percent.[40] Similar increases occurred in the two Budapest districts of my research: the proportion of clients receiving childrearing assistance soared from 8 percent in 1985 to 77 percent in 1992. These increases are deceiving if interpreted without an appreciation for the broader changes in state redistribution. Poor-relief programs provided recipients minimal amounts of money: in 1995, they provided clients between 1,500 and 3,500 forints ($20–40) from three to six times a year. Moreover, such boosts to clients' incomes paled in comparison to the material losses they suffered in the last decade—with the end of price subsidies for basic necessities and housing, state-financed childcare, employment guarantees, and work-based benefits, the socialist safety net has largely evaporated. Even those Hungarians who were able to pool all of the available state supports remained unable to bring their families above the subsistence level.[41] This may explain why, in 1995, 30 to 35 percent of the population lived below the minimum subsistence level, and an additional 20 percent hovered around it.[42] Hence, while caseworkers did distribute more poor relief, these funds were nowhere near sufficient to counter the financial losses confronting clients.

In addition to distributing poor relief, caseworkers placed large numbers of their clients' children in state care. Institutionalization was the primary way that caseworkers dealt with clients they believed to have severe material problems. Among the 517 cases I reviewed from the period, I found poverty to be the main justification used to remove children from their homes. In these cases, welfare workers offered elaborate accounts of these clients' material conditions and their inability to provide basic necessities for their children. They used detailed data on the size and value of clients' flats to justify institutionalization—41 percent of the institutionalization cases in my sample cited "inappropriate housing" as the sole reason for removing children from their homes. "Did you see how they lived?" a caseworker once exclaimed to me after a home visit. "Six people in one room. Of course I will pull the kids. How could they imagine otherwise?" Caseworkers used income data in similar ways. Approximately 39 percent of the institutionalization cases I reviewed cited "low wages" as a justification for placing children in state care. As a caseworker put it in a 1990 case: "With their low wages, it is impossible to raise three children. They lie about their income or they live in extreme poverty. Either way, the children must go."[43] Data collected by welfare offices confirm these findings: in 1984, 29 percent of the children placed in state care were said to be materially (*anyagilag*) endangered; by 1992 the number had increased to 87 percent.

This focus on targeting and treating poverty meant that a whole range of issues fell outside the state's domain. Many kinds of state assistance ceased to be available to clients—they were no longer able to use caseworkers to foster their social integration or to reshape their domestic relations. Rather, caseworkers were skilled at reducing all of their clients' problems to material issues. For instance, they never addressed the domestic abuse that so many clients were subjected to.[44] In my archival and ethnographic research, I determined that roughly 32 percent of current welfare cases involved some sort of domestic violence—abuse that was consistently ignored by welfare workers. Instead, caseworkers turned this violence into a material problem. "Don't talk about the fights with your husband," a social worker once advised a public assistance applicant. "Just tell them that your husband lost his job and you have no heat. That's the real problem." A good example of this was the case of Mrs. Lakatos, a Romani woman who came to a Family Support Center in 1994 ostensibly for help paying an overdue utility bill. As her meeting with the social worker progressed, she began to remove her clothing to show us the scars and burns covering her body. By the end of the meeting, she had broken down in tears—admitting that her husband beat her and begging for help. What kind of help did she receive? A few hundred forints for medicine to treat her wounds and a referral to a local soup kitchen.

Caseworkers also collapsed their clients' childrearing problems into material issues. Whereas in the state socialist period "child protection" encompassed a wide range of domestic arrangements, by the late 1980s it had been defined in strictly material terms. A caseworker who began work in the early 1980s defined it in this way in an interview: "Child welfare is saving children from poverty and the dangers of it. What else could it mean? It is simple. Children are healthy and secure when they have food, a home, and clothing."[45] In practice, this meant that caseworkers simply refused to deal with clients whose childrearing problems were not accompanied by poverty. "I am sorry, I cannot help you," a caseworker once told a woman seeking help on behalf of her delinquent son. "You have the resources to deal with the problem, but try a probation officer." Those clients with both childrearing concerns and material problems had the former reduced to the latter. Caseworkers attributed all sorts of childrearing difficulties to material deprivation, thus ignoring the other issues that impinged on mothers' lives. As a caseworker analyzed in 1986: "The mother is angry and abusive with her son because since his birth, the family slid into poverty."[46] Caseworkers frequently linked juvenile delinquency, rebellion, and poor school performance to low family income. In one 1991 case, a welfare worker even attributed a teenage girl's sexual promiscuity to her family's poor material circumstances. As she wrote in her case notes: "Five people live in one room. There is no bathroom in the flat so they use the collective one in the building. . . . The girl escapes this with her irresponsible and disorderly behavior with older boys."[47]

Clients with severe alcohol problems received similar treatment. It was not uncommon for such clients to come staggering into these offices. Most of them were looking for someone to talk to. Yet they rarely found sympathetic listeners. As a caseworker told me when I asked her how she dealt with such clients: "Well, we never give them money. You know where it will go. We have special food packages for them, so they get the nutrients they need." Other clients received lectures on the connection between alcoholism and poverty. "How many forints do you spend on pálinka?" a social worker quizzed one such client.[48] "Imagine, if you had that money, you would not be here." Similar kinds of "assistance" awaited clients with psychological problems or emotional troubles. All of these clients were collapsed into one category, the materially needy. And all of them were thought to be in need of one kind of assistance, poor-relief.

As a result, in this welfare system it was almost impossible for clients to acquire state resources to resolve nonmaterial issues. I observed numerous clients become dismayed as they told stories of domestic turmoil to the blank, uninterested faces of caseworkers. All caseworkers had a few clients whom they called "chronically long-winded" due to their continual attempts to draw caseworkers into their domestic lives. They avoided these clients like the plague. In one office, two caseworkers developed a "rescue system" to avoid dealing with such clients. Whenever one of them got stuck with a long-winder, she would kick the adjacent wall—prompting the other caseworker to come over with an "emergency" to end the meeting. As one of them remarked after a successful rescue mission, "You'd think she [the client] would learn. I don't want to hear about every fight with her husband. What does she think I can do?" Other caseworkers were less subtle in their refusal to engage in clients' domestic lives. One home visit comes to mind. When we arrived at Mrs. Janos's flat, she was cleaning and her husband was sleeping. As the caseworker made her usual calculations, the client whispered stories of the man's heavy drinking and violence. When the caseworker interrupted her to ask if she had a car, the woman began yelling about how no one cared and the Gyámhatóság was no good. The caseworker responded that she was assessing her eligibility for childrearing support, not the "quality" of her marriage. As we left, the woman returned to her sweeping with a defeated look on her face. For Hungarian women like these, the materialization of need was a constraint that limited their room to maneuver.

In addition to reducing clients' practical maneuverability, the materialization of need has also narrowed the discursive space within which clients can advance their own definitions of need. By collapsing clients' identities into one identity, all "needs talk" has been confined to the material. Acceptable modes of argumentation have been limited to poverty claims. This welfare regime hears only the appeals of certain classes of women. And it responds only to appeals couched in terms of poverty. Appeals not framed in material terms fall on deaf ears. "Did you hear me," one Romani woman exclaimed as her caseworker measured the size of her flat. "I said that he goes to those prostitutes on Rákóczi square. This is dangerous for the little one, with all the diseases. Are you writing this down?"[49] The caseworker rolled her eyes and pretended to write something down. Other caseworkers were even less polite. For instance, many clients brought their children to welfare offices and staked claims to state assistance on their behalf. Caseworkers regularly mocked these clients. One woman who had her son sing and dance for caseworkers to bolster her request to exchange her flat was accused of using her child as a "circus animal." Her request was rejected and she became known as the "circus woman."

As I have noted, the new discursive terrain also became less malleable. Just as clients found it impossible to squeeze practical resources out of these agencies, they were unable to expand the discursive space to speak of a wider range of needs. Female clients who couched appeals in maternal terms were silenced. Caseworkers simply did not hear their confessions of maternal isolation or exhaustion. Domestic violence loomed large in these offices, but was never addressed. Clients' complaints about unruly husbands resounded throughout this welfare apparatus, but were never discussed. And clients who voiced needs they had as women were treated as if they spoke a foreign language. A 1995 home visit to a woman referred to the Gyámhatóság by her son's teacher is illustrative of this silencing. When we reached her flat, located in an elite area of Budapest, the client had us sit down for coffee. She then recounted story after story: how her husband left her for a secretary; how she lost her job at the Ministry of Culture due to her communist background; and how her family banished her because they could not deal with her "nervousness." Her words literally floated by the caseworker, who sat drinking her coffee and calculating the value of the client's expensive furnishings. After discovering how large her disability pension was, the caseworker abruptly got up, walked out of the flat, and dropped the case. On the way back to the office, she turned to me and asked, "What was that woman about? Please, I have clients who can't even feed their kids. What did she want from me?"

As this incident reveals, an impenetrable discursive barrier was erected between clients and caseworkers. On one side of this barrier were female clients, socialized in the state socialist welfare regime, who expected caseworkers to assist them both materially and socially. As their appeals for broad social protection remained unrecognized, their room to maneuver contracted; as their nonmaterial pleas went unacknowledged, they became disgruntled. On the other side were caseworkers, trained in new schools of social work and armed with means tests and surveillance techniques. As their material handouts were met with requests for further aid, they became frustrated; as their poor-relief and soup-kitchen referrals led to demands for additional social intervention, they became annoyed. In effect, the materialization of need enlarged the social distance separating caseworkers and clients. Out of this yawning chasm emerged mythologies about the stigmas and pathologies of the "new" Hungarian welfare client.

MATERIALIZED NEEDS, STIGMATIZED WELFARE CLIENTS

This pattern of interaction between caseworkers and female clients repeated itself over and over again, surfacing in all of the welfare offices I studied. The situation was frustrating for everyone—clients left the office unsatisfied with their forint handouts, while caseworkers remained on to face the next predictably ungrateful client. These interactions took on an assembly-line quality and left caseworkers feeling like alienated, piece-rate workers. As caseworkers sat in their collective offices, processing case after case, they expressed an extreme dislike for their work. They had good reasons to be disgruntled: Their working conditions had changed in ways that transformed them into eligibility workers; the new office division of labor undermined their control over cases and clients; and the limited resources at their disposal made them feel powerless, given the enormity of the problems they confronted.[50] Caseworkers' struggles to make sense of their lot were made more difficult by their newness to the job. The overall censoring of the past left them without a comparative perspective on their welfare practices and working conditions.

For many welfare workers, these feelings of frustration were exacerbated by the fact that the welfare reforms being enacted around them had negative effects on their lives outside of work. Most welfare workers were lower-middle-class women who lived just above the subsistence level. Thus, while they experienced a decline in their standard of living, they remained ineligible for the new poverty programs they oversaw. In effect, the poverty tests they administered disadvantaged women just like themselves. Welfare workers frequently referred to this. As they distributed childrearing assistance and household maintenance funds, caseworkers often noted that they could use some extra money to raise their kids or to renovate their flats. Such comparisons became even more prevalent in the mid-1990s after the "Bokros reforms" income-tested the family-allowance and maternity-leave programs—thus cutting many welfare workers from these benefits and heightening their sense of economic insecurity. Once implicitly connected through universal provisions, there were no longer any policies joining caseworkers and clients; there were no programs that both groups of women shared. One caseworker put this best when she explained the Bokros reforms to me in an interview: "I don't know what the clients complain about; with their income they will get support. Mothers like me will be harmed. If I do not have my baby in the next year, *I* will be without support, not *them*."[51]

In response, most caseworkers displaced their sense of powerlessness onto their clientele. Their frustration evolved into full-scale hostility and anger toward clients. This surfaced in numerous ways. Most common were caseworkers who read new meanings into their clients' appeals for assistance. They began to interpret such appeals for evidence of individual pathology and defect. These interpretations soon gave rise to the icon of the "welfare cheat" and a new language to describe her: she is a lazy, uncultured, simple, and disorderly woman. She is a woman who cannot be trusted. She is a woman capable of forging income documents or hiding electronics in closets. All of these welfare agencies had institutional archives of stories to support this image: home visitors who found costly household goods hidden under beds or in neighboring flats; caseworkers who discovered fake work records or unreported income; and clients who came to the office covered with expensive jewelry. Caseworkers then used these stories to explain client poverty. "Clients are different today," one older caseworker revealed in an interview. "They lie, cheat, and steal. Even the Hungarians do this now. Terrible."[52] Once reserved for Romani clients, the myth of the "welfare cheat" now applied to all clients. Whatever their ethnicity, all clients were thought to be potentially pathological and capable of extreme acts of deception.

Quite often, this image of the "welfare cheat" was coupled with mythologies about clients' aggressive and "out of control" behavior. Most caseworkers believed their clients were capable of outrageous acts of violence and thus needed to be contained physically. All of the welfare institutions I studied employed "security guards." In some agencies these guards were male social workers trained to "keep order"; in other offices they were actual policemen who wielded weapons. When I asked about the need for these guards, welfare workers half-jokingly told me that these men "herded" and "tamed" their clientele. Actually, this was exactly what these men did. They stood outside the agency doors, blocking the entrance and deciding whom to let in. They escorted clients into the office and routinely watched over their meetings with welfare workers. To intimidate potentially aggressive clients, these men walked through the office and asked, "Is everyone okay here?" or "Does everyone feel safe?" When clients got visibly angry, these men forcibly removed them from the office. In general, clients were perceived to have become "out of control," to be in need of continual surveillance. As a female client once screamed as she was physically removed from the Gyámhatóság: "She has taken my children away, why do I need to be taken away too? You would also be upset, am I not allowed to be angry?"

Caseworkers' defensive attacks on their clients frequently descended beyond their presumed personality traits to their physical characteristics. The sight, the smell, and the feel of clients' bodies were common topics of conversation among caseworkers. Many caseworkers used animal metaphors to describe their clients, referring to them as cattle and pigs. Caseworkers called those days when assistance applications were due "slaughterhouse days" because of the large number of clients who gathered outside Gyámhatóság offices to submit applications. Even more demeaning were the jokes that caseworkers told about their clients' appearances. They regularly made fun of deformities in their clients' bodies. "Was that person human? Man, woman, or beast?" a caseworker once joked about a client. They came up with degrading names for clients. There was the "toothless one," a woman whose front teeth had been knocked out by her husband and who could not afford replacements.[53] There was the "legless one," a woman who had lost part of her left leg in a "domestic accident" and who could not pay the medical costs to repair it.[54] There was even the "voiceless one," an elderly man who had throat cancer and spoke through a device attached to his mouth.[55] In a 1989 case, a particularly poetic caseworker used the metaphor of a "battlefield" to describe a client's body: "She works on Rákóczi Square. [This is] appropriate. Bruises all over, like a war. . . . Tattoos on the skin, like mines . . . and the mouth of a soldier."[56]

Moreover, caseworkers spoke incessantly about the "smell" of their clients. They often berated clients for not washing regularly. "I used to wash before work," a caseworker once remarked to me. "Then I realized that there is no use, so now I clean myself as soon as I return from work." Another caseworker told the office a "funny" story about how her two sons once remarked that she "smelt like a zoo" when she arrived home from work. While her story provoked hysterical laughter among her colleagues, it prompted the clients in the room to drop their heads in embarrassment. Then there was the caseworker with whom I rode the metro to work each day. Whenever we exited the metro station, located over three blocks from the office, she began talking about how she could already smell her workplace. To deal with this, she brought air freshener to the office. She kept it by the door and continually sprayed it around to rid the office of the "sickening smell" of poverty.

Given their disgust with the sight and smell of their clients, welfare workers avoided all contact with clients' bodies. In effect, clients had become "untouchables"—contaminated bodies not to be felt. This may have been another reason for the security guards: These men handled the contaminated. When situations arose that necessitated physical contact with clients, caseworkers called in the guards to do the dirty work. On one occasion an elderly client lost her balance and fell to the floor of one Gyámhatóság office. Unable to get up, she was forced to lie on the floor until a caseworker called a guard to help her up. While the caseworker never discussed the incident, it was clear that she feared physical contact with the client. Another caseworker articulated this fear explicitly when she once saw me touch a client. The client's son had been institutionalized, and she came to beg for his return. After a caseworker rejected her appeal, the woman wandered the office, eventually ending up at my desk. As she sat crying, I touched her hand in an attempt to comfort her. The caseworker looked on, mortified. I was immediately reprimanded: "Never touch a client. Wash your hands immediately because you never know what you can get from them."

As horrific as these mythologies about clients' deficiencies and pathologies sound, it is important to recognize the source of caseworkers' defensive attacks. Caseworkers were themselves cogs in the system. To a large extent, their attitudes reflected changes in their working conditions—changes that, in effect, sliced clients into small pieces and turned caseworkers into piece-rate, eligibility workers. Caseworkers played no role in the importation process through which this larger poverty discourse seeped into Hungary. Others spearheaded this process: global policemen and local social scientists who appropriated and co-opted each other to serve their own interests. Thus, caseworkers were simply the messengers of a reductionist welfare model; they were the bearers of a stigmatizing message they had little input in formulating.

While caseworkers may have been merely the conduits of a prepared message, clients viewed them as the source of the new mythologies looming over them. They perceived caseworkers as heightening their sense of stigmatization; they saw caseworkers' new welfare practices as threatening and pathologizing. Thus, they reacted to the message through the messenger. In doing so, clients sent their own powerful messages about the discursive and practical losses they are currently suffering. Their reactions took a variety of forms. Most often they exhibited embarrassment when interacting with caseworkers. Clients frequently came into welfare offices with their heads down, whispering as they listed the different kinds of poor relief they received. Many clients told me that they dreaded coming to these offices and felt "ashamed" when they begged for state assistance. They complained about the degradation associated with caseworkers' investigations into their material lives, frequently calling caseworkers uncaring, brutal, and cold. As a female client once said to a friend as they left the Gyámhatóság, "I always feel dirty here. They are so despising."

For others, this embarrassment evolved into anger and rage. These clients engaged in shouting matches with their caseworkers, refusing to accept their new rules. "Why do you need evidence of my mother's pension?" one young woman snapped at a caseworker. "Isn't it enough that I am a single mother with two kids?" These clients challenged the narrow focus on the material and forced caseworkers to explain why their other needs no longer mattered. In these angry exchanges, clients asked penetrating questions. Why was it important if they had televisions or VCRs? And why was it not important if they felt disconnected and isolated? Why was it relevant if they knew how to economize or budget? And why was it not relevant if their husbands beat them or abandoned them for their secretaries? Few clients ever got answers to such questions. The materially "needy" ones got a little money and were shuffled out of the office, while the others were just shuffled out.

Finally, for some clients this degradation was too much to handle. As a result, they broke off contact with these agencies, despite serious personal and material problems. Vilma was one such client. I met Vilma in 1993 when she came to her local Family Support Center because her husband had lost his job. Initially, Vilma made no mention of the bruises and scars that covered her face. She simply came in every Friday to pick up food coupons and packages. With time, Vilma became more talkative, describing the beatings inflicted on her by her husband. Just as she began to open up, the Center ran out of welfare benefits. Her social worker referred Vilma to the Gyámhatóság and instructed her to apply for poor relief. While on a home visit to assess her eligibility for such funds, the caseworker discovered a problem: Vilma's husband owned some expensive musical instruments that put their disposable income over the assistance cut-off level. If she did not sell the instruments, her family would be denied aid. This prompted a series of fights between Vilma and her husband—fights that he apparently won, since she was given only temporary aid for which she had to reapply every two months.

On subsequent visits, Vilma's bruises became more visible, as did the signs of severe alcohol abuse. No one ever mentioned these symptoms. When Vilma lost her job in 1994, rumors began to circulate that she had turned to prostitution. Her caseworker then confronted her, threatening to withdraw her assistance if she did not stop her "illegal activities." Bombarded by accusations, Vilma sat with her head down and adamantly denied the charges. Clearly deflated, she was being "hit" from all sides. I saw Vilma last in early 1995. Her body was emaciated, bruised, and battered. She had come to the office to place her kids in an institution for neglected children. As she filled out the necessary paperwork, she turned to me and nervously remarked, "I had no choice. At least I won't have to come here and see them [the caseworkers] anymore."

GLOBAL WELFARE SHIFTS AND THE MATERIALIZATION OF NEED

The IMF and the World Bank promised Hungarians "welfare with a human face." Hungarian sociologists promised them a welfare system that was more sensitive to the needs of the vulnerable and deprived. Democratization scholars promised them new possibilities for "identity formation" and "interest articulation." What clients like Vilma got instead was a poverty discourse that narrowed their room to maneuver. They faced a discourse of welfare that constituted them solely as needy, materially deprived individuals. They confronted a newly reformed welfare apparatus that accorded them few practical or discursive resources. And they felt stigmatized and pathologized in new ways. Rather than having more opportunities to secure their own well-being, these Hungarian clients experienced a contraction in the space they had to protect themselves in their everyday lives.

The poverty discourse underlying these welfare shifts is not unique to Hungary. This same discourse has been at work across the globe, restructuring welfare systems in contexts as diverse as North America, Western Europe, and the South Pacific. With these shifts, the diversity in welfare models characteristic of the postwar era has given way to a convergence. Once organized to meet the collective needs of workers, mothers, and/or families, these welfare states have become more class-based. Gone are the days when many welfare states operated with expansive conceptions of need that guaranteed their citizens everything from employment to universal childrearing supports to comprehensive family benefits. As entitlement systems are scaled back and means-tested, definitions of need have been narrowed and individualized. And as need-definitions have been individualized, welfare states have become focused on the bureaucratic regulation of poverty and the "needy." Moreover, the vehicles for these structural and discursive shifts were often international agencies. The IMF and World Bank did not restrict their policing activity to the Second and Third Worlds. They were also active participants in negotiations over European integration, especially in the debates over social expenditures. And they always brought their welfare blueprints home with them as they restructured debts and transformed welfare systems throughout the West.

While this poverty discourse has become globally hegemonic, it must still be indigenized in specific locales. In this regard, Hungary and other post-communist societies were in a somewhat unique position. With the ascendancy of the new poverty discourse, countries like Hungary were characterized by special historical conditions that made their soil particularly ripe for planting. Unprotected by the historic shield of the party/state, they were wide open for this discourse of need to flood in through the newly-opened sphere of civil society. Itself in transition, the Hungarian state was unable to serve as a filter or a buffer for these global forces. These conditions also made local experts particularly "needy" and more inclined to participate in this discursive indigenization. With resources drying up in the local state and academy, Hungarian sociologists were readily co-opted by these global forces. They were lured into an ideological flirtation, unable to resist the political and material resources offered by the international policemen. Before long, they had embraced this discourse and translated it into Hungarian. Instead of freeing Hungarians to articulate new identities and interests, rapid democratization allowed global forces and local actors to institute new surveillance techniques and disciplinary welfare practices.

In this way, the welfare shifts experienced in postcommunist Hungary may be a sign of what is to come on a more global scale. Hungary's vulnerability to global inundation, combined with its censoring of the past and rejection of universalism as a standard for welfare, simply hastened processes underway elsewhere. As a potential vanguard of the new liberal welfare regime, Hungary may provide an example of what this global discourse of need breeds as it runs its course. In addition to pointing to the economic losses that accompany neoliberal welfare restructuring, the Hungarian case warns of the political repercussions of such reform: It reveals the practical and discursive limitations of this liberal welfare model and the pathologization and stigmatization unleashed by overly materialized conceptions of need.

NOTES

This research was supported by grants from the International Research and Exchanges Board (IREX) and the Joint Committee on Eastern Europe of the American Council of Learned Societies and the Social Science Research Council. I thank the many friends and colleagues who commented on this paper, including Lisa Brush, Liena Gurevich, Barbara Heyns, Ruth Horowitz, Robert Jackson, Jayati Lal, Suava Salameh, Andras Tapolcai, and members of the Workshop on Gender and Inequality at New York University. Finally, I am most grateful to the Hungarian sociologists, social workers, and clients who generously shared their ideas, their time, their space, and their lives with me.

1. Christopher Bryant and Edmund Mokrzycki, "Introduction: Theorizing the Changes in East-Central Europe."

2. See Zygmunt Bauman, "After the Patronage State: A Model in Search of Class-Interests"; and Gail Kligman, "Reclaiming the Public: Reflections on Creating Civil Society in Romania."

3. See Andrew Arato, "Revolution and Restoration: On the Origins of Right-Wing Radical Ideology in Hungary"; and Arista Maria Cirtautas, "In Pursuit of the

Democratic Interest: The Institutionalization of Parties and Interests in Eastern Europe."

4. Robert Deacon, "Social Policy, Social Justice and Citizenship in Eastern Europe," p. 7; János Kornai, "Paying the Bill for Goulash Communism: Hungarian Development and Macro Stabilization in a Political-Economy Perspective."

5. Zsuzsa Ferge, "Recent Trends in Social Policy in Hungary"; Jan Adam, "Social Contract"; Claus Offe, "The Politics of Social Policy in East European Transitions: Antecedents, Agents, and Agenda of Reform."

6. Deacon, "Social Policy, Social Justice and Citizenship in Eastern Europe"; Péter Gedeon, "Hungary: Social Policy in Transition."

7. See Iván Szelényi and Robert Manchin, "Social Policy under State Socialism: Market Redistribution and Social Inequalities in East European Socialist Societies"; Deacon, "Social Policy, Social Justice and Citizenship in Eastern Europe"; and Gábor Hegyesi, "A Szociális Munka."

8. Júlia Szalai, "Social Participation in Hungary in the Context of Restructuring and Liberalization."

9. Nancy Fraser, *Unruly Practices.*

10. The label "transitologists" is frequently used by scholars of Eastern Europe to denote their expertise in the study of political, economic, and social transition in the region.

11. Zsuzsa Ferge, *A Society in the Making: Hungarian Social and Societal Policy, 1945–1975.*

12. See Központi Statisztikai Hivatal (KSH), *A Gyermekgondozási Segély Igénybevétele és Hatásai; A Gyermekgondozási Díj Igenybevétele és Hatásai.*

13. See Júlia Szalai, "Some Aspects of the Changing Situation of Women in Hungary."

14. See István Kollar, *The Development of Social Insurance in Hungary over Three Decades.*

15. See Ágota Horváth, "Egy Segély Anatómiája"; and Lynne Haney, "But We Are Still Mothers: Gender and the Construction of Need in Postsocialist Hungary."

16. Until the mid-1980s, they were not even tied to the mother's income—all mothers received the same flat-rate grant. And all households received the same amount in family allowances.

17. Szelényi and Manchin, "Social Policy under State Socialism."

18. See Zsuzsa Ferge, *Szociálpolitika Ma és Holnap;* and Szalai, "Some Aspects of the Changing Situation of Women in Hungary."

19. SZETA was a nongovernmental charity organization established and run by oppositional social scientists and activists in the 1980s. In addition to distributing poor-relief to the impoverished, SZETA exerted political pressure on local-level government officials and offered legal aid to the poor.

20. See Zsuzsa Ferge, *Javaslat a Szociálpolitikai Rendszer Módosítására;* and Géza Gosztonyi, "Hatóság + Szolgálat."

21. Zsuzsa Ferge, *Szociálpolitika Ma és Holnap.*

22. Zsuzsa Ferge and Júlia Szalai, *Fordulat és Reform.*

23. See World Bank, *Hungarian Health Services: Issues and Options for Reform; Housing Policy Reform in Hungary.*

24. See World Bank, *Hungary: The Transition to a Market Economy: Critical Human Resources Issues;* and IMF, *Social Security in Hungary.*

25. See World Bank, *Hungary: The Transition to a Market Economy; Hungary: Reform of Social Policy and Expenditures.*

26. See Júlia Szalai, "Poverty in Hungary During the Period of Economic Crisis"; "Urban Poverty and Social Policy in the Context of Adjustment: The Case of Hungary"; and Júlia Szalai and Mária Neményi, *Hungary in the 1980s: A Historic Review of Social Policy and Urban Level Interventions.*

27. See István Tóth, "A Jóléti Rendszer az Átmeneti Időszakban"; Rudolf Andorka and István Tóth, "A Jóléti Rendszer Jellemzöi és Reformjának Lehetöségei."

28. Tóth, "A Jóléti Rendszer az Átmeneti Időszakban."

29. János Kornai, "Lasting Growth as the Top Priority," p. 20.

30. Tóth, "A Jóléti Rendszer az Átmeneti Időszakban"; Gedeon, "Hungary: Social Policy in Transition."

31. The name of this journal, "Chance" or "Prospect," is itself quite indicative.

32. Enterprise archive, Csepel Vas és Fémmüvek 21–3310: 21. All translations of records and case files are the author's.

33. Gyámhatóság case file #01311–102–2.

34. Nevelési Tanácsado case file #0137788908–189: 125.

35. Gyámhatóság case file #081129: 120.

36. Gyámhatóság case file #013221: 152.

37. The "tanács" was the Hungarian local-level state apparatus, which included welfare agencies as well as district government offices and the police. Gyámhatóság case file #013002: 183.

38. Gyámhatóság case file #087750: 139.

39. Nevelési Tanácsado case file #082211212–123/89.

40. Zsuzsa Ferge, "A Magyar Segélyezési Rendszer Reformja II."

41. Zsuzsa Ferge, "A Célzott Szociálpolitika Lehetösegei"; and Rudolf Andorka and Zsolt Speder, "A Szegénység Magyarországon 1992–1995."

42. Ferge, "A Magyar Segélyezési Rendszer Reformja II," p. 29.

43. Gyámhatóság case file #08009: 1002.

44. See Krisztina Morvai, *Terror a Családban.*

45. Author's interview #013112: 24.

46. This case is indicative of the interpretive shift. The woman had been abused as a child, had mental-health problems, and had an abusive husband. In the previous system, all of this information would have been used to analyze her anger toward her son. Gyámhatóság case file #0137794: 712.

47. Gyámhatóság case file #0811776: 909.

48. Pálinka is a Hungarian brandy known for its strong, inebriating effect.

49. Rákóczi square is a notorious Budapest gathering place for prostitutes.

50. See Alice Burton, "Dividing Up the Struggle: The Consequences of 'Split' Welfare Work for Union Activism," for a similar connection between the organization of welfare work and caseworkers' attitudes toward clients in the United States. Her analysis reveals how the shift to eligibility work bred hostility between welfare workers and recipients in another, very different context.

51. In fact, after the Bokros plan, there was a rush among caseworkers to have children before the reforms went into effect. When I returned to the field after a year, 70 percent of the caseworkers I knew were on maternity leave.

52. Author's interview #013112: 31.
53. Gyámhatóság case file #0811776: 1102.
54. Gyámhatóság case file #013221: 1034.
55. Gyámhatóság case file #086689: 1198.
56. Gyámhatóság case file #081998: 992. Her account made a metaphorical connection between Rákóczi square, the gathering place for prostitutes, and the Rákóczi war of independence which occurred in the eighteenth century.

THREE

Excavating "Globalization" from Street Level

Homeless Men Recycle Their Pasts

Teresa Gowan

A San Francisco paramedic is eating with his firefighter colleagues in the fire station kitchen. He complains of yet another call to haul a collapsed wino covered in vomit out of the gutter. "I should have slipped him something." Eyes shift uneasily. Some of the firefighters chuckle, others pretend not to hear.

I tell this anecdote to one of the homeless recyclers, Anthony. He laughs. "Put us out of our misery, I guess. Didn't I tell you we rank down somewhere with the stray cats? . . . That kind of attitude, that's the whole point with recycling. When I'm working hard right before their eyes no one can say I'm just a smelly drain on the public purse."

Studies of homelessness do not dwell particularly on smelliness, yet sickness and inadequacy take center stage, resulting in a literature that neglects to analyze independent income-generation. Anthony and many of his colleagues take their work very seriously, and I decided that work, rather than disability, should be my starting point.

The material in this chapter is the product of several episodes of ethnographic research with some twenty-five homeless recyclers living and working in various San Francisco neighborhoods. Following my decision to prioritize work, I approached the recyclers in the street, or in the recycling company yards, rather than through the service agencies catering to the homeless. Using a combination of participant observation and informal interviewing, I got to know the men by working with them and spending leisure time together, as well as through recorded interviews.

Over time we climbed into dumpsters together, shared beer under the freeways, and met up for occasional fry-ups in my kitchen. They brought me pans, sweaters, and jewelry from dumpsters and acted as my protectors in dodgy situations. I helped with welfare and disability claims, giving them breakfast or a place to shower or visiting them in jail.

In this fieldwork I focused primarily on those who were the most serious about their work, the most productive. And the interest was often mutual. Approaching men as recyclers, and explicitly starting with a curiosity about recycling as work, I find that my work appeals most to those men whose life-worlds support my thesis. Men who are investing recycling with a great deal of meaning, using scavenging to practice a specifically worker identity, respond instantly and enthusiastically to my inquiries about the recycling life. Certainly some of the sample group, including Sam and Clarence, are champion recyclers, carrying some of the biggest loads in the city.

I initially framed the homeless recyclers as survivors, making a place for themselves in a growing third-world-style informal economy. Yet the work of homeless recyclers makes little sense outside the context of their general isolation and rejection by the broader society. As Anthony's comment suggests, the recyclers tend to interpret their work as an escape from stigma. But they do not escape, really. They are still homeless, mostly addicts and alcoholics, and few observers appreciate their efforts.

The "they are workers too" angle, while providing legitimate positive images, came to feel blinkered. One limitation of doing ethnography with the marginalized is that it is hard to see the mechanisms of exclusion. You can study the agencies trying to mop up the problem, but you, like your subjects, are cut off from the larger social turns—institutional, economic, political—that provide the context (although not necessarily the proximal cause) of their miseries. In Castells's terms, people like the recyclers are stuck in a stripped, decaying "space of places," unable to hook into the "space of flows" of the information age.

In this paper, the instrument I use to hook into the big picture is nostalgia, the nostalgia of the dispossessed for the lives they have lost. In each case, individual regrets and losses connect to the large-scale social shifts set off by what we call "globalization." Unlike many homeless Americans, Sam, Clarence, and Desmond have not always been marginalized and destitute, and their attempts to maintain self-respect through "honest labor" reflect value systems learned in more prosperous times. They are the subjects of this chapter because their nostalgia for the past helps us to explore globalization as loss, not because they are more moral, or more "deserving" than other poor Americans.

"Are you a twenty-first-century man?" asks a *Details* magazine quiz, inviting its hipster targets to "see if you're headed for the dustbin of history or the fast track to the future." High scorers are praised for their adaptability:

> Congratulations. You're wary of any and all organizations, you rely on no group, government, or organized religion. . . . you let expedience guide your lifestyle choices, you are able to think on your feet and sanguinely shift jobs, friends, lovers, and residences at the drop of a virtual hat. In other words, you're ready for the twenty-first century.[1]

Details puts a positive spin on the nineties economy, encouraging its young male readers to embrace flexibility over predictable career paths, opportunity over job security. The tone may be ironic, but only with that Generation X kind of superficial ironic gloss, which lacks a critical referent under its raised eyebrows and knowledgeable smirk. The message prevails. Safety is for sadsack losers, but you, dear reader, are smart, independent, healthy, suave, entrepreneurial enough to play to win. You're *money*, baby.

The *Details* reader knows he has to stay lean and hungry, always with an eye to better opportunities, new niches. Jobs-for-life are gone, but the new economy offers quick bucks and stellar careers for the best and the brightest. Like the man with no name, the entrepreneurial individualist can come into his own, proving his courage and self-reliance in the Wild West of flexible capitalism.

Much of this is boyish escapism. The kinds of entrepreneurs profiled in the magazine are hardly the unattached warriors celebrated in the quiz, what with their telltale signs of vital contacts made at top-tier colleges, of helpful investments from family members. It is a different kind of risk if you can return to managing Mom's apartment buildings when things are not working out.

Can twenty-first-century man be found among more marginalized Americans? The writers at *Details* are unlikely to conceive of their supremely adaptive flexible being as a sex worker, migrant farm laborer, or prep cook, let alone a homeless crack addict, panhandler, or thief, yet the insecurity,

mobility, flux, and fragmentation of *Details'* "twenty-first century" is far truer
for the poor than for college-educated professionals. Broadly speaking, the
lower you go down the economic scale, the less stability you find, and there
is nowhere in America where the basic conditions of everyday life are more
volatile than on skid row. In the public soap opera played out endlessly in
skid row streets across the country, only continued poverty and disappointment can be relied on. Devastating stabs of ill-luck become mundane, and
for those without shelter the knocks seem to follow faster and harder. Any
time, almost any place, such naked lives lie open to predators biological,
criminal, voyeuristic, bureaucratic. Pneumonia, arrest, AIDS, robbery, or
the official confiscation of those personal effects carefully nursed through
the wilderness, maybe even murder: any or all become possible, even likely,
for a person reduced to the status of homeless derelict.

Indeed some homeless men respond to the unstable conditions of life on
the street with a remarkable flexibility. The bastard brothers of the entrepreneurial techno-yuppies targeted by *Details,* such twenty-first-century
(nineteenth-century? third-world?) have-nots adopt a "hustler" mode of
homeless life.[2] They improvise their daily needs through combinations of
panhandling, plasma sales, selling the *Street Sheet* newspaper, dumpster-div-
ing for things to sell on the sidewalk, prostitution, using soup kitchens and
other charity organizations, petty theft, recycling, selling personal posses-
sions, and small-time drug dealing.

The "Hustler as twenty-first-century man" fits the perspective on homeless
workers developed by David Snow and his collaborators.[3] They describe the
money-making strategies of the homeless as a set of improvisations for survival, a constant ad-libbing for daily needs. And much of what they have to
say about the unpredictability and constant crisis of homeless life rings true
in the lives of the men featured in this chapter.

Yet man rarely lives on junk and booze alone. The stigma, assaults, and
casual insults of street life knock away most external referents for self-
respect, making the project to *be someone* more crucial than ever. But what
kind of *someone* feels like the real you? That depends in the main on who you
already are, on who you have been before.

The homeless recyclers featured here—the "pros"—are most reluctant
to see themselves as playing the system. Instead, they stride across the city,
working hard and fast. Usually following established routes and stopping
places, they sort their findings into great bags of bottles and cans tied on to
their shopping carts, heaving up to two hundred pounds to the recycling
companies each run. The most strenuous toilers treat themselves as beasts
of burden, harnessing themselves to pull two large carts at once. For others
it is more important to use their work to reconnect socially with the non-
homeless, or to assert their claims to public space as legitimate trash work-

ers. But what the pros hold in common is the resolve to turn their backs on the painful boredom of skid row life, as they try with all their strength to create lives that are still "decent" in their own eyes.

For these men have not always been poor. In comparison with homeless street vendors or drug dealers, who tend to share much more uniformly marginal and impoverished life histories, many of the pro recyclers have suffered massive drops in income and status. In earlier lives they were long-distance truckdrivers, dockers, mechanics, career soldiers, industry electricians, welders, and delivery drivers. Many of them had union jobs, and most of those who did not were still entitled to health benefits and some degree of job security.

Those earlier lives are gone, dissolved in a compound of poisons equal parts unique and commonplace. Within the current social context of exclusion and intolerance, misfortunes or wrong turnings surmountable in kinder times now serve as life sentences. The inexorable decline of the recyclers' "prospects" since the 1970s has reacted and multiplied with joblessness, family tragedies and unravelings, despair, hallucinations, myopias born of substance love, self-disgust, or incarceration. Connections to institutions that could save them from this dramatic social fall have corroded and crumbled, leaving them to scramble for day-to-day survival.

Yet while the lives of the pros are inescapably overshadowed by their immediate needs, they do their best to minimize their time spent in hustler mode. Instead they play down their desperation in favor of the peculiar comforts of routinized hard labor. Recycling, as their major means of subsistence, becomes not only an essential economic floor, the bare bones of survival, but a broad project to recover and celebrate the routines, productivity, skill, and solidarity of blue-collar work.

The efforts of the recyclers to carve out normality from stigma and to create routine from the anomie of unemployment is by no means reflected in the main body of the academic literature on homelessness. The vast social welfare machine dominates the field, converging on the failures, sickness, or cultural incompetence of the homeless individual. This perspective therefore "brackets" the broader social context of the vast increase in homelessness since the mid-seventies. Large-scale authoritative research projects on poverty are usually seduced into such methodological individualism by the government agencies that can provide their bread and butter.

One advantage of cheap, small-scale qualitative research is that one does not need to work within these limitations. Therefore, instead of using my spotlight on these homeless men to test the dominant theories on homelessness on their own grounds, I use it to illuminate their relationships with the bigger picture, the picture of changing America, the world outside the brackets. The idea is to dig up local traces of the huge shakeup we call "globalization," experienced in the United States as a systemic turn away from the

Keynesian social contract among government, corporations, and unions the postwar years toward the contemporary period of deregulation, welfare state dismantling, and union busting.

If we take globalization to mean the transformations of locales by processes instigated or maintained from outside national borders, the United States has been at the center of various forms of globalization for hundreds of years, as both a site and an agent of raw collisions among Europe, America, and Africa. Today, in the richest and most powerful nation on earth, this new "globalization" does not represent a new shattering of the integrity of the local; our "locals" were already globally connected, expansive, reflexive. What Americans *are* experiencing is instead a gradual replacement of the previous military, Keynesian form of globalization with a fresh neoliberal coalition, one representing changed forms of capital, different sensibilities, new winners, and new losers, as well as a resurgence of traditional "conservative" discourse.

Conservative theory defines men like the recyclers, able-bodied single men, as high-functioning deviants in rebellion against the market. The solution, say the rhetoricians of market freedom, is to force the dependent poor to adapt to the current economic structure by removing the safety nets that guarantee their subsistence. Severe penalties for crime will ensure that these newly stimulated energies toward subsistence will be channeled to legitimate activities. Only then will such men be forced by their need for subsistence to learn new skills, or to take jobs at wage and status levels they might previously have found demeaning.

Conservative policies have been put into practice at all levels of government over the last ten years. Financial entitlements have been transformed and safety nets removed, culminating with the 1996 abolition of the sixty-two-year old AFDC program, and the devolution of responsibility for the unemployed to the local level. States are sanctioned with the withdrawal of federal support if they do not institute lifetime welfare limits.

Local governments increasingly require work in exchange for the bare subsistence allowed to prisoners and welfare recipients. The number of welfare recipients in compulsory work programs is expected to reach one million within the next few months.[4] As of June 1997 there were nearly 3,000 "workfare" workers cleaning San Francisco's streets, buses, parks, and housing projects for roughly one tenth of the pay of regular city employees. The new welfare laws could add up to 25,000 more workfare workers within the next two years.[5]

Entitlements to freedom of movement have also been withdrawn. While a million and a half men and women swell the penal colonies, the space outside is more subtly restricted. All over the United States public space is being redefined both formally and informally as private space with selective access for people who do not look poor. New downtown developments use anti-homeless architecture that closes off "public" space to pedestrian access.[6] In the same commercial strips where consumers are encouraged to browse and linger, homeless people are moved on, cited, and arrested for "encampment" or "obstructing freedom of movement." "Quality of life" offenses not enforced since the depression have been reactivated all over America, making many basic human functions (sleeping, urinating, and so on) illegal to those outside.[7]

The San Francisco version of "quality of life" enforcement was initiated by the "Matrix" program under Mayor Frank Jordan's administration, starting in August of 1993. Under Matrix, homeless people received ten to fifteen thousand citations a year for offenses such as "encampment," "drinking in public," "aggressive panhandling," "urinating in public," or "obstructing freedom of movement." While Matrix's status as an official high-profile political campaign was officially terminated in 1996, the ticketing policy has persisted. The fine for the average citation is $76, rising to about $180 and an arrest warrant if left unpaid. Most homeless people are unable to pay these fines, leaving thousands of them with outstanding warrants.[8]

THE NOSTALGIA OF THE DISPOSSESSED

There are so many mediating institutions, biographical particularities, and quirks of fate lying between the forces of "globalization" or "neoliberalism" and any one individual. It is hard to justify a simple causal line from structural sea-change to individual disaster. Yet across the industrialized world there are striking correlations among increased corporate mobility across national borders, conservative political ascendancy, and the return of mass indigence, both on and off the streets. The conceptual and political difficulties involved in actually *proving* some causal relationship between the huge and the personal should not foreclose its exploration. Otherwise we have nothing to work with but the decontextualized, sometimes degrading, personal details revealed by the disease model of the social welfare institutions.

The tool of exploration I use here is the concept of nostalgia. Kathleen Stewart defines nostalgia as the attempt to place oneself in time and place, creating "an interpretive space" in reaction to the alienation of postmodern life.[9] She draws a distinction between two different forms of nostalgia within "late capitalism."

> . . . it depends on where you stand: from one place in the cultural landscape nostalgia is a schizophrenic exhilaration of a pure present that reads images for their own sake; from an other place it is a pained, watchful desire to frame the cultural present in relation to an "other" world—to make of the present a cultural object that can be seen, appropriated, refused, disrupted or "made something of."

Stewart defines the first kind of nostalgia as the act of taking possession: "Here, individual life narratives dramatize acts of separation (freedom, choice, creativity, imagination, the power to model and plan and act *on* life)."[10] In such a way the disappearing blue-collar lifestyle mourned by many homeless recyclers is appropriated as kitsch in front of their eyes by pseudo-Bohemian multimedia programmers wearing vintage work shirts with "Johnny" or "Ray" sewn on the chest.

In contrast to this first nostalgia with its power to choose, to freely appropriate, Stewart presents her "other" nostalgia, which might be called the nostalgia of the dispossessed. The "others," who live away from the highways of power and self-determination, experience nostalgia as a "painful home-sickness," which aims at "the redemption of expressive images and speech." Those deprived of former certainties and thrown into chaos and loss use nostalgia as a way of placing themselves *inside* a surrounding world which makes sense.[11]

As a collective attempt to reclaim a past world, nostalgia can sharply point up the places where a person's life-turns most clearly knit into a bigger fabric of experiences common to others in similar social locations. For each of the recyclers, the past is a primary referent. Although their pictures of the past are both similar and different, they all see the present in relation to how things "used to be." Each of them makes a life on the street where he can make use of skills, habits, and ways of thinking learned under quite different conditions. In this they are no different from most of us. What is less commonplace about the recyclers is the massive changes in their social standing between then and now. Stigma and extreme downward mobility make them favor the past with the intensity of dying men.

Stewart's "nostalgia of the dispossessed" describes how I understand the attempts of the homeless recyclers to recreate familiar worlds out of the disorientation and degradation of life on the street. They assert values and life-ways drawn from the past as both critique and shield against the alien landscape of the new, that landscape we attempt to contain and describe with the encompassing hot signifier, "globalization."

For the pros, the current version of globalization feels different from the Pax Americana of their past. This version has no place for them, and consequently appears as a collection of alien forces. Experiences of globalization are all about subject position. For the purposes of this chapter, I focus on three of the pros, Sam, Clarence, and Desmond, taken from a broader fieldwork sample of twenty-five. They are not composites, but discrete individuals who happen to share certain histories, sensibilities, and strategies with others of the group.

As they mourn and try to keep alive the worlds of their earlier lives, the particular nostalgias of each man point up particular elements of the shift from Keynesianism to the neoliberal new world order. The homeless ex–manual worker Sam has been marked for life by deindustrialization and the decline in secure employment. The homeless veteran Clarence has witnessed the doors closing on the giant work-creation program provided by the postwar military. And the homeless ex-convict Desmond laments the civil war on the African American working class represented by the War on Drugs.

WORK WILL SET YOU FREE: SAM

Sam is a muscular, taciturn Polish American in his early fifties. He spent his youth working on his own hot-rods and playing a lot of football, and he married straight out of high school. He never saw the need for schooling, he says, being confident in his mechanical abilities. Sam became a highly skilled mechanic, holding down a couple of long-term union jobs repairing trucks and industrial machines before he became unemployed, and then homeless.

Sam's knees ache from old sports injuries, but he works continually, putting in two heavy shifts every day and rarely stopping to rest. Keeping his cart on the road he steams along, head down and leaning hard into the weight of the recycling. As he picks up bottles and cans he keeps his eyes on his work, fast sorting each piece into the proper category. One of the less vigorous recyclers who shares Sam's turf calls him "Robocan."

For Sam, it is very important to have his recycling already sorted, because he does not really like to spend much time at the recycling plants. Being around homeless people who are less obsessively workaholic than he is really bothers him. He assumes laziness in other recyclers on the basis of any public rest-taking or excessive talking. Black recyclers are particularly suspect. "I just don't want any of that bullshit," he told me after a black recycler I know had tried to initiate conversation with the two of us. "I'm not interested in shooting the shit. I don't come here for fun. This is work." Sam himself never takes a break anywhere in clear public view.

When Sam hit forty he was still living with his second wife in his own house in Pittsburg, a working-class town in the East Bay. He has hinted on occasion that his second marriage ended "badly," saying that he does not blame his wife for kicking him out. "She couldn't believe what she married. Nor could I." He has four children and two grandchildren, but he does not see any of them except when there is a marriage or death in the family.

Sam explains the deterioration of his second marriage as a result of unemployment and subsequent heavy drinking. (This is not unusual. The divorce rate is around 50 percent higher than the national average in families where the father has lost a job and cannot quickly find an equivalent one.[12]) First Sam was laid off from well-paid union work repairing engines for a utility company in 1985. He had been working on the same vehicles for years, and knew them inside out. But engines changed, and he could not get motivated to learn the new technology. "Hit me hard, being on the scrap heap, I'll admit that. . . . You don't much consider about unemployment, you know, till it happens to you. Then it's too late to get your bearings." Electronic tinkering with new models "controlled by a stupid piece of plastic" offended his deep love of "real" cars, to which he had dedicated both work and leisure hours since he was a teenager.

Sam found it very hard to deal with his declining position in the labor market. His last job was with a nonunion corporation specializing in brake repair, where he never actually got to work on cars, but instead had to follow a monotonous and rigidly enforced routine. Even though the pay was lower than ten years before, Sam started spending half his income on cocaine. "My heart wasn't with my job anymore, and the manager was always pushing me. He gave us no respect. . . . So I got to putting half my paycheck up my nose. No woman to check up on me." [Sam winks.] "I was generally demoralized, you know. Everything had gone to shit."

When homeless recyclers like Sam express disbelief at their decreasing abilities to command either decent wages or respectful treatment in the years before they became homeless, they are pointing to a phenomenon bigger than their own personal shifts in social location. Call it what you will—a "space of flows," disorganized capitalism, the condition of postmodernity, or late capitalism[13]—there are several ways in which the Bay Area economy of the nineties manifests qualitative breaks with the situation twenty years ago.

On the national level, large-scale, collective, wage-bargaining structures have disappeared. Monopolies have broken out of state regulation almost entirely, and manufacturing jobs have either gone elsewhere or been transformed into minimum-wage, temporary work—work designed for women, immigrants, and young men who do not have the memories of better conditions that might make them mutinous.

California suffered the effects of this restructuring later than the older manufacturing regions of the United States. The state was insulated from the manufacturing collapse of the early 1980s by its disproportionate share of defense contracts, its large share of computer and bio-tech companies, and a real-estate frenzy financed by the Los Angeles-based junk-bond boom.[14]

The early nineties revealed the inability of these industries to sustain general prosperity. Working-class Californians suffered from a prolonged and severe recession, losing 1.5 million jobs in 1990–92, including a quarter of all manufacturing jobs. Construction, always the best bet for unskilled male labor, practically stopped—the rate of housing starts in the early nineties was the lowest since the Second World War.[15] Several white recyclers have

mentioned that journeyman work used to earn them twelve to fourteen dollars an hour. By 1994 it was down to six or seven. In the Bay Area the disjunction between the decimation of heavy-industry work and the booming
computer industry added to the problems of blue collar workers by bringing in large numbers of younger people with high disposable incomes who
are able to pay increasingly fantastic rents and house prices.

The unemployment crisis for manual workers has contributed to the
blossoming of the local informal economy. Unlicensed and tax-avoiding
entrepreneurs and their employees flourish, working as under-the-table taxi
drivers, carpenters, house cleaners, hair dressers, recyclers, mechanics, dog
walkers, electricians, junk vendors, garment-makers, psychics, roofers, manufacturers, nannies, and gardeners.

Rather than providing competition for the more formal enterprises,
much informal work actually interlocks with it, increasing the profits to
large companies.[16] In the case of San Francisco recycling, the garbage giant
Norcal dominates both the legal and the informal economies in trash.
Norcal holds the city contract for both garbage collection and curbside recycling. The company also owns the two largest recycling companies in the
city, both of which buy the overwhelming majority of their materials from
the scavengers of the informal economy.

Sam and other ex–manual workers picking up bottles and cans on the
streets of San Francisco are participants in a great slide from secure wage
labor in the formal economy to insecure "survival strategies" outside of any
protective regulation. But the pros will not accept the idea that recycling
represents a reactive, hand-to-mouth existence, a desperate scrabbling at
the bottom of the heap. Rather, they all appreciate and take pleasure in
their work as a challenging, socially useful activity, which gives structure to
their days. In Sam's case, recycling is a vehicle for him to bring his old
mechanic persona alive again, competent and industrious. But in order to
convince himself with this act of will he needs to continuously distance himself from the apparition of the lazy scam artist.

Sam and most of the other white pros are quite explicit about differenti-
ating themselves from less hard-working homeless people. They often discuss the hopeless dependence, laziness, and irredeemable "snakishness" of
other poor men, men who are not "workers" in their eyes. Sometimes they
have good reasons for suspicion. Sniping across the timeworn frontier
between the deserving and the undeserving poor, they effortlessly slip into
a repertoire of contempt instilled in more prosperous former lives.

Their contempt is racialized: poor African Americans are the most common targets. However, most of the white recyclers make a point of expressing respect and collegiality toward the black recyclers, as long as they are
fiercely gung-ho about their work. Derick, a thirty-something African
American veteran, credits Sam with getting him going as a successful recy-

cler. "You wouldn't know it, but he's tight, Sam. There was a time I was really losing it, but he persuaded me recycling could make me some decent money. [He] . . . gave me a bunch of good tips."

Sam marches the streets to escape the ghost of himself as an undeserving pauper. Other pro recyclers conjure up more positive, even evangelical, understandings of their vigorous work ethic. David, another white recycler with a much more countercultural history than Sam, talks passionately of how the moment-to-moment sense of purpose, the rhythmic physical effort of it all, keeps him human.

> I don't know about other people but if I wasn't able to recycle, I'd lose hope. I'd lose hope for being able to put one foot in front of the other. A lot of times it's a challenge. Takes determination. . . . I'm not doing so well, I push harder. It's like it accelerates you. . . . Some days I get to feel like the old Dave. . . . I mean, I just get on with my work, no fuss, just like other guys.

While the physical work itself is usually solitary, the cultural work of the pro recyclers can become a collective project. Many of the men naturally talk about their work lives in terms of "we," especially when appealing to the social usefulness of recycling vis-à-vis other occupations of the homeless. Taking time out under the freeway one day, Anthony, Bill, and Javier discussed the superior morality of the recycling life:

> *Anthony:* We're just trying to be decent, you know. I mean I could be a drug dealer, because I do happen to have a connection. [Laughter.] But recyclers, we want to choose the other road, not preyin' onto people's kids or stealing or something. Just cleaning up the neighborhood.

> *Javier:* But people disses us anyway. No respect. You're a bum, you're scum.

> *Bill:* Not everyone disses us. OK, those ignorant mother-fuckers don't see it, but at least we know, and people with eyes know how we're doing a good job out here, the recyclers. The best we *can* seeing as things are this fucking rough. Well, most of us anyway.

> *Anthony:* Except Javier. [He shoves Javier affectionately.]

> *Bill:* You tore into those bags like a pack of coyotes, man. Definitely letting down the profession. . . .

> *Javier:* Never knew I was a professional. Well whaddaya know. I finally made it! [General amusement.]

SERGEANT TO SCAVENGER: CLARENCE

As he tells it, Clarence was a mama's boy. Raised "strict" in a Baptist family in a tract home in South Central Los Angeles, he was rarely in trouble and spent most of his free time playing sports. But he was not altogether a happy child.

His fear of his father, a man who combined substantial drinking with hellfire sermonizing and righteous whippings, led him to escape the neighborhood as soon as he could. Leaving his family for good, he joined the army right out of high school and did pretty well. Not seeing himself as the macho type, he gravitated toward "wheelin' and dealin'" from his post as a supplies clerk. In his eight years stationed in Germany he built up several links to the local underground economy. "I bent the rules some, but didn't do no harm— everyone does it," he says. This made him plenty of friends, both on base and off. Clarence really liked Germany and misses his German friends intensely. From where he is now, his years in Germany appear both impossibly far and close to his heart. The details of his life over there, his daily routines, the names of acquaintances, of local bars, shops, and parks, all are extraordinarily fresh in his mind. Like many African Americans, he experienced living in western Europe as a release from the type of racism he had grown up with in Los Angeles. "You never know what's your good time till it's all over. That was my good time, I guess." He sometimes dreams of getting together the airfare, but he knows it would be real different without the army.

Clarence is now 42 and a homeless recycler. He was discharged from the Presidio army base in the late eighties, after failing a second random drug test. In shock, he unsuccessfully floundered for subsistence and housing. All he knew was the army and its ways and means, and he had long lost touch with his family. He considered trying to find his mother. Maybe his father was dead, or perhaps they had separated. In the end, Clarence was so ashamed of his cocaine habit he could not face his mother anyhow. "I mean, I was the *good* son, you know, not the crackhead. Funny thing is, I still am, after all." Not knowing other poor people, it took him six months to find the soup kitchens and to get on General Assistance. During this time he lived only a few minutes walk from his former base, camping on Baker beach and eating out of garbage cans. "I was too depressed to get my shit together, too ashamed to ask for help. But one good thing, I got clean of cocaine, seeing as I had no cash. Didn't last though. . . . Drugs mess you up, but once you're down, it's all you've got."

Most of the day Clarence pushes two large carts around the city, following a recycling routine that he calls his "patrol." Several restaurants save him bottles and boxes. Apart from the obvious benefits of stabilizing income, such connections are important points of pride, ways to convince himself and others that people who are not homeless rely on his services and trust him to keep to a routine. His manner is polite but preoccupied, avoiding casual eye contact. He often has a puzzled, distracted look, as if he cannot remember where he put something.

Clarence has made quite a success out of recycling, winning the respect of both suppliers and peers for the size and quality of his loads. He considers his work socially useful and insists that others realize this:

The company, Norcal, doesn't mind us talking to the public and asking permission to pick up their recycling. They're working toward an environmental consciousness. I believe they want to make sure the trash goes to the right place. We're sorting it out so it doesn't break down an' . . . [make] poisoned contaminous toxic waste in the soil.

To put Clarence's interpretation in context, many other recyclers have extremely antagonistic relationships with the same company, whose workers are sometimes physically violent to homeless recyclers. One manager tried to persuade the Immigration and Naturalization Service to prosecute another of the pros. Yet Clarence himself *has* achieved a cordial relationship with some Norcal staff, even working for them as a security guard on a few occasions. Few "street" homeless people can make themselves acceptable enough for wage labor, but Clarence manages to keep himself supernaturally clean and well laundered, even though he sleeps in the same clothes out on the bare sidewalk every night of the year.

Clarence has a similar approach to his relationship with the welfare bureaucracy. Welfare officials often act as though clients not only have no jobs, but no legitimate lives outside their claimant status. It is therefore easy for them to treat such third-class citizens as though they have nothing better to do than wait in line for seven hours or spend weeks collecting the right forms for entitlement to maintain their bare subsistence. Men and women on GA are publicly shamed by street-sweeping duties, which display their dependent status to the general public. Yet Clarence rejects the more common role of resentful, passive client, thinking of himself more as dutiful taxpayer than stigmatized pauper.

Uniquely among the pros Clarence declares his earnings to the city:

> You know, with General Assistance we're allowed to make money, and we mail in our receipts once a month. I'm on this program now. We don't have to sweep the streets and we can do recycling. Actually, we still go to workfare but we're allowed to work part-time. We're allowed to earn up to four hundred bucks—well even more actually. Every one hundred dollars we earn we are minus twenty dollars from our General Assistance . . . but we're in the plus zone for, well, eighty bucks.

I mentioned to another recycler, Walter, that at least one recycler I knew sent in his recycling receipts to GA. He was amazed. "That's not conscientious," he said, "that's just insane." Walter thinks that it is pointless to pursue any legitimate relationship with the city, given that homeless people are not treated like other citizens. "Why kid yourself?" was his take. But Clarence will not participate in his own marginalization any more than he has to. One afternoon Derick was complaining of his treatment in the GA office. Clarence said, "OK, maybe. But you can't give attitude, brother. Act respectful and that's what you get." Derick shook his head, incredulous.

"Respect! Right! You crazy man?" After his characteristic pause for thought, Clarence answered, "Not really. Not yet."

Clarence's story is not unusual. The streets are full of homeless veterans. As the biggest public works program of the postwar years, the military provided millions of jobs for working-class men and women, with job security and decent benefits for veterans. For many African American and Latino men, it opened a much-needed door into middle-class America. But warfare is being transformed into a high-tech, highly mechanized affair, and the mass-employment model is being gradually shed, removing the most reliable employment and training option for the young men of low-income communities.

The changes mirror the shift in the rest of the American economy toward a dual economy composed of well-paid symbolic analysts on the one hand and a mass of low-paid and insecure service and assembly workers on the other. A core of elite military officers and technicians land well-paid and stable employment, while millions of enlisted men and women clean floors and stand guard at minimum-wage level. Basic military pay is $199 per week before taxes, and unit commanders frequently use "Article 15" punishments to further dock the soldiers' pay for minor infractions. One in three recruits drops out before completing his or her first term of enlistment.[17]

The restructuring of the military is a substantial area of deindustrialization. Like the Fortune 500 companies, the post–Cold War military has used drug testing to push through large-scale redundancies. Started by the Navy in 1981, a heavy regime of compulsory random testing spread to other branches of the military, under the title of "surprise and deterrence." By the end of the eighties the Pentagon was claiming to have reduced illegal drug use by two-thirds, leaving Clarence and many like him dishonorably discharged.[18]

Making the best of his bleak chances as an unskilled forty-something African American, Clarence turns a brave face to the world, usually acting as if sleeping on the sidewalk and pushing around four hundred pounds of bottles is just fine with him. He tries to have faith that others will see him as the upright, hard-working man he is. Yet sometimes he gives signs of what might lie underneath this upbeat facade. Once I asked him why he slept out on the sidewalk beside a garment factory rather than finding a hiding place like most of the others. "I've got nothing to hide," he answered. "There's no need." As Clarence tends to keep some cash on him, I asked him, "But couldn't you get jumped for your cash?" He shook his head and paused. He screwed up his eyes, sighing. "Look, you can't be givin' them a reason, any reason." He changed the subject quickly. What he meant, I later understood, was that he didn't want to give other "decent" folk, let alone the police, any reason to classify him as a furtive criminal. He is no smalltime dealer with a stash of rocks, no petty thief concealing his spoils, only an honest worker of the underworld, with nothing to hide but his pain.

Clarence is not the deluded fool that Walter thinks he is. He knows that his status as a homeless black crack-user is the archetype of the violent criminal in mainstream popular culture. His response to this dilemma is to create a transparent, strenuously legitimate life, which leaves no room for suspicion.

In his struggle for respectability Clarence does his best to have the same kinds of relationships with his suppliers, with the church, even with government that he would choose to have if he were not homeless. This is an incredibly difficult task. For example, Clarence tried at one point to join a church congregation, attending services for several weeks running. This attempt to join a community of housed people on equal terms went into a spin when two companions from the street insisted on joining him. They slept through most of the service, then ran off with the collection money. "That was just so depressing," he said. "I knew they were up to something, but I couldn't be sure, you know." Not only does Clarence act as if he is not automatically stigmatized as a homeless man, but he also gives his companions the same benefit of the doubt he requests for himself. In his own words, "You know, when you lose trust that's it. You're gone."

Clarence's attempts to be "normal" mark his refusal to participate in the stigmatizing process by pretending he does not see it. Trying hard not to "default" on his "schedule," he converts what most people consider a highly informal hand-to-mouth subsistence practice into a legal, transparent routine. From informalizing the military, he has moved to formalizing the informal economy.

Clarence's project of transparency and connection is quite different from Sam's compulsion to throw himself passionately into his physical labor. Without reducing either man to racial stereotypes, it seems clear that for Clarence dignity is not to be achieved by back-breaking labor, "slaving." Such donkey work is all-too-connected with the legacy of slavery to be a source of self-esteem. James, another African American pro, is equally disparaging of "pure" labor, commenting: "My old man slaved himself to an early death laying tarmac. He wanted something better for me." Most of the African American recyclers underplay the physical effort involved, although many of them work very hard indeed. For them, the pure effort and bodily strength they put into recycling is not the primary honor in the work, not the part that they say makes them feel more human. They are more concerned to see themselves as skilled and knowledgeable, able to make and maintain relationships with their suppliers. Sam, in striking antithesis, draws on the longtime notion of the white Republican worker, for whom vigorous, taciturn work habits form the cornerstone of individual freedom and opportunity. Slavery and racial identity are touchstones of work identity for whites as much as for African Americans. Sam's embrace of (self-imposed) physical extremes that Clarence and James call slaving is partly about distinguishing himself from the "lazy" African Americans he will not speak to. In similar, self-deceiving ways the white artisans of the pre-Civil War free states attributed their freedom to their ability to independently discipline themselves, while they scorned the supposedly dependent and present-time-oriented slave.[19]

LIFE SENTENCE: DESMOND

Desmond is a tall, slender black man in his early fifties. He has a charming, quiet confidence—unlike most of the pros he gives the impression of complete social competence—but his marginal status is marked by his cart and his missing front teeth. He collects his cans in the North Beach area of the city, which is the part most visited by San Francisco's tourist hordes.

After a traumatic early childhood with a violent father, Desmond spent a peaceful protected youth with his older sisters and grandparents. They lived in Newark, New Jersey, where his grandparents both worked in the local hospital, Grandma in the laundry, Grandpa delivering supplies to the wards.

> They were from the South, real traditional country people. They tried to raise us respectful, but everything was so different outside the house. Newark was jumpin' back then, and I just lost my soul to music. And I don't mean gospel music! . . . By fourteen years old, I'd say, I knew that was what I was gonna do, not waste my life in servitude like the old folks. That's what I was thinking.

Desmond started to work as an informal roadie at clubs a couple of evenings a week, checking out soul bands. He traded his mother's fur-trimmed coat for his first electric guitar and amplifier. His grandma was not pleased, but let him have his way as long as he stayed in school.

> Then I met Jimmy, my best buddy. He played bass for Sam McGee. . . . Sam was *big* on the East Coast back then. Jimmy got me a job as roadie with that outfit. See, he told Sam I was eighteen, but really I'd only just turned sixteen. I wasn't even shaving yet, but yes Ma'am, I just left Mama Betty and the girls and took off with those dudes. . . . Grandpa was already passed from his stroke, you see.

Over the next fifteen years Desmond gradually worked himself up from roadie to bass to rhythm guitar with McGee. On tour in Washington, D.C., he fell in love with a Trinidadian singer, who went on the road with the band. They married and started a family. This was when things started to get difficult financially. Shirley, his wife, made some money doing nails, but the take-home pay from the aging band was not getting any better. Touring with a kid was crazy, they decided. Desmond tried in vain to find a slot in a local cover band, which was making decent money. After their second child was born in 1983, Desmond quit the band and tried to get some "regular" work. A few weeks surveying the wreckage of the Newark economy moved them to drive out to Los Angeles, where Desmond's sister had settled. The situation there looked more promising, but months of pounding the pavement failed to turn up a job with "prospects" of any kind.

> See, I never knew it would be so hard. All that time I was with the band, I used to think how everything would be easier with the family if I just gave up playing out for a while, put in my time doing some honest labor. . . . [Laughs.] Guess I wasn't reading the papers. I would have been more responsible if I had only got to build up seniority somewhere, but I wanted to follow my dream. I should say our dream in fact.

Later, Desmond qualified his regrets, saying, "See, I coulda been responsible and still got screwed. Seniority is a long shot too, these days. I don't see too many of us out there." He meant black men working in the trades. Desmond insists that the dismal labor market pushed him into drug dealing.

> I couldn't find *anything*, only jobs for kids. So after a few months starving my babies and losing my self-respect at Taco Hell I quit. . . . Then I started dealing bud [marijuana] instead. In fact, not instead exactly—I kept a part-time day gig at another fast-food joint, dealt out the back door, just like everyone else.

Marijuana got more and more expensive during the eighties, due to a heavy crackdown on the growers upstate. Crack cocaine, on the other hand, became far cheaper and more easily available. Like a couple of other men in the sample, Desmond slipped from marijuana into dealing crack cocaine without really thinking about the difference between the drugs.

> It was around 1987. I was still into reefer myself, but crack was where to make the easy money. That's what the people want now. Back in the seventies we wanted to be mellow, now it's "Beam me up, Scotty," "Make me crazy." Now maybe if I'd had a decent-sized place I would have grown it [the reefer] myself, but that wasn't an option with four people in a one-bedroom.

In 1989 Desmond was caught sitting in his car with over six grams of crack in his inside pocket. Unfortunately for him and thousands of other black Californians, the federal mandatory sentencing laws which had come into effect the previous year required that he serve at least five years in prison. This was a first drug offense and Desmond was a minor street dealer, yet ironically this relative "innocence" left him vulnerable, with no bargaining chips. Dealers with more connections, more information, can usually reduce their sentences in exchange for naming some names.[20]

Desmond had rarely been in trouble, his worst previous encounter with the law being a drunk-driving offense several years before. Now he was ripped from his family, leaving them destitute. Once inside, he suffered the panic, humiliation, and despair common to first-time prisoners. He did not know how to fight:

> See, I grew up with womenfolk, and then, well, the music world, there's a bunch of mellow dudes. . . . You don't want to know the shit I went through in there. Losing my teeth, *that* wasn't the worst of it. . . . I got myself through by reading and watching too much TV. . . . Staying out of certain people's way, trying not to rattle this or that psycho's chain, that's a full-time occupation.

It is easy to be a felon if you are a working-class black man. While the military has cut back on its role as mass employer for unskilled working-class men and women, the rising prison industry has taken up many of them. In California the number of prisoners has tripled since 1980, while nationally 7.9 percent of the black population was either locked up or under supervision by 1990, compared with 1.7 percent of the white population.[21]

Taken together with the downsizing of the military, the vast expansion of the incarceration industry since the end of the Cold War is emblematic of certain changes in the priorities of American government. The gradual erosion of the mass military and growth of a mass system of penal colonies has been particularly significant for working-class black men. African Americans have been disproportionately represented in the lower ranks of the armed forces since the Second World War, and have at the same time been disproportionately hit by deindustrialization in the civilian economy. They now account for over 90 percent of prisoners convicted of crack cocaine dealing, and the majority of homeless men in most large American cities.[22]

Drug possession and trafficking convictions are the engine of the incarceration boom. In the years 1986 to 1991 the African Americans doing time for drug offenses in state prisons increased by 465.5 percent.[23] This law enforcement emphasis on the predominantly black and Latino crack cocaine trade is a relatively recent development. Until 1982 heroin was the primary target of Drug Enforcement Agency (DEA) and local police antidrug activity. Around that time the mass consumption of powder cocaine mushroomed, primarily among the middle and upper-middle classes. The economic structure of these sectors was quite hierarchical, and therefore relatively stable. The popularity of crack cocaine, taking off in the mid-eighties, "flattened" the structure of the drug trade. Anyone with cooking equipment and baking powder could convert powder cocaine into rocks and join the competition. The ensuing turf-wars became more and more violent, justifying increasing police focus on this new, more horizontal industry. It seems that as the crack trade has consolidated, the crack-related homicide rate has declined. The decline may, however, be too late to change public opinion. Media perceptions of the problem were manipulated by the Reagan administration and the DEA, until most journalists, and therefore most Americans, accepted as common sense the idea that street crack dealers were the primary agents of the decline of the quality of life in the inner cities.[24]

Desmond's experience would suggest a more complex relationship between devastated inner city neighborhoods and the crack trade. For him dealing was a last resort rather than a longtime project. He says that he certainly had no ambition to rise in the business, only hoping to find something else and get out. That is why he was halfheartedly working a street corner at the age of forty. "It's ironical how, well, I wasn't really suited to dealing. Not at all. For a start, I'm too softhearted. Some poor fiend come beg me for credit I found it hard to resist. Especially women. I'm a family man."

The mandatory sentencing required by the 1986 Anti-Drug Abuse Act slammed down on Desmond and his companions in the vast pool of "clockers" (street dealers), most of them African American and Latino men. Drug arrests and convictions soared. Squeezed into dealing for subsistence by tight labor markets, long-term poverty, racial segregation, and incremental welfare destruction, thousands of nonviolent poor men and women were pulled into the jaws of the expanding penal-industrial complex.

When she realized how long Desmond's sentence was, Shirley took the girls back to Trinidad, promising to come back when he was released. According to Desmond, his wife's mother, an evangelical Christian, was horrified by his offense, and put pressure on Shirley to divorce him during his fourth year in prison. He has never seen any of them since. On release, Desmond was paroled to San Francisco, where he hoped to make a fresh start in a place where no one knew him as a dealer. He did not contact his sister, hoping to surprise her with good news later on. "Donna was good to Shirley, but shamed of my fooling. I never could get her to visit me in the joint," he said.

Good news never reached Donna. Desmond's spirits were not high leaving prison, and he easily sank in the Tenderloin district's sea of indigent ex-cons. Work seemed harder than ever to find, as he had no friends among the working population. It was at this point, staying in a welfare hotel with a prison acquaintance, that Desmond developed a crack habit for the first time. "I *knew* what I was getting into. I was thinking, OK, things can't get any worse. May as well get *high* before I die." With no one to turn to, crack quickly exhausted his minimal income and he could no longer afford his share of the room.

Recycling, he says, is the best street life offers. "Less of the bullshit, maybe a fraction more of the respect." Keeping his cart in the mouth of one of three alleyways, Desmond can sit out on one of the main drags, retrieving containers as soon as people discard them. Every fifteen minutes or so, he makes a small collection with a plastic bucket from the nearby public trash-cans and sorts it into his cart. The rest of the time he sits on doorsteps, reading the paper or talking. A few workers from the Italian restaurants will bring him bottles, all stopping to discuss the weather or the news. He has great "people skills," a low-key charm and an ability to connect with a great variety of people. "Yeah, I've always been sociable," he explained. "I used to work the audience real good. It was a pity I wasn't a great singer." Most days Desmond sets off with his heavy load in the early evening, toward a recycling company three miles across town. This is one of the few places where he can sell his wine bottles. With the money he can usually afford two hamburgers, a five dollar hit of crack, and some bourbon to get him through the night. Compared to many homeless men, Desmond's crack habit is quite well controlled. He gets the crack and bourbon in the Tenderloin on his way back to North Beach.

Desmond's friend Julio, a Salvadoran bus boy at one of the upscale Italian restaurants, arrives every couple of days with a load of empty wine bottles and a spliff of marijuana to share in the alley. Sometimes he brings leftovers. When they first became friends, Julio was convinced he could eventually get Desmond a job as a dishwasher. "Have to keep trying, amigo. You'll do good, I know." Desmond would play along, "Maybe, we'll see," but told me privately that Julio was a great guy but he did not understand America yet.

> Not black America anyway. I'm not saying it's impossible for blacks to get ahead, because I see plenty of them every day up here. Even those traveling college kids with the sucker bags [back packs], some of those are black kids now. But for us it's always been one strike you're out. Me, I'm out, literally. [Desmond laughs.]

A couple of months after this conversation, Julio got Desmond an interview with his manager. Desmond was ambivalent about going, but eventually came to my place to spruce up, saying he did not want to hurt Julio's feelings. By the time he had to leave, he seemed optimistic, cracking jokes about those free meals he would serve us when he was promoted to waiter.

Apparently the manager spent only about one minute talking to Desmond and said he thought he already had someone for the job. Julio and Desmond came away with different stories. Julio seemed frustrated that Desmond acted too unenthusiastic, telling him, "You got to look like you *want that* job." Desmond was softly unyielding:

> Look, hombre, I knew he wasn't interested. He took one look at my face and knew I was on hard times. I doubt they ever hire blacks in those joints any more, even if I wasn't a bum and a felon. . . . But my mouth doesn't help. If I was really serious about employment, I need to get me Medicaid and see about some dentures.

Like all the recyclers, Desmond feels that the nature of "society" has changed, not just his own circumstances:

> I'm sure of it, people in general, across the board, now they more out for themselves. Proud to be selfish. You hear it all over, like "I'm getting me mine" and all that bullshit. . . . I'm all for self-help you know, but, hell, we need some unity, people.

Another ex-con recycler, a white man called George, feels much the same way:

> I went to prison in '81. When I got out in '88, I found the change. Nothing changes in prison, but when you come out, you know, into society, things are always changing. When I came out, I found so many "snakish" people, people who didn't give a care about nothing.

I asked George if the change was not more that now he was associating with poorer people, unemployed or homeless. After all, he was in a very different position in those days, as a delivery driver with an apartment and a girl friend.

> It's true, no one gives a homeless guy the benefit of the doubt. But back then you wouldn't let a guy go homeless. Not unless he was truly fried [drug damaged]. It didn't seem so much of a problem. There was work, you know, so you wouldn't get stuck. . . .

Desmond also complains of the difficulty of creating community on the street, given the mutual fear and hostility among too many street people. He talks of street life as a young man's world, requiring the energy and apparent invincibility of brutal youth:

> Oh, I dunno. Sometimes I think I'm just too old now. I never was real hard, and now, now I *sure* can't deal with the kind of bullshit going down out here. I mean, I sound like an old-timer: "things ain't how they used to be." Can't crest the wave so I got sand in the mouth. Shit.

Later that night Desmond ran over a variety of jobs he thought he could do successfully. "I don't ask for much right now," he said, leaning his forehead against an alley wall. "Just give me a minimum-wage job and the appearance of basic respect and I'll *be* that old-timer."

INTO THE DUSTBIN OF HISTORY?

Despite their differences, Sam, Clarence, and Desmond share a common past in which they earned decent money and were generally treated respectfully. As a musician, Desmond was never in the solid financial position of Sam and Clarence in their good days, but he moved in similar circles and never doubted that a solid job would be his for the asking. Desmond remarked that "In the old days, you know, it felt like something to be American, even for us" [black Americans]. "I used to know a couple of dudes from India. . . . We'd talk about how you'd never get that kind of extreme shit over here. Not since slavery. But now. . . ." Desmond pointed to a wheelchair-bound homeless man trying unsuccessfully to relieve himself discreetly. "Now we've got *that*."

Clarence, Sam, and Desmond may not have considered themselves fortunate at the time, but in retrospect their old days are bathed in a golden glow. They experience the new order as a set of forces against them, which they cannot harness to their advantage. However, the reason the recyclers see deindustrialization, military downsizing, and the War on Drugs as antagonistic forces is not because they are inherently external, but because these forces are part of a social order in which they have no part. Flexible nineties America doesn't harness *their* interests, or articulate their experience. The era of Keynesianism and the Pax Americana was equally "big," but there they felt part of the bigness. Indeed, as soldiers, unionized workers, and consumers of goods subsidized by American market control, they *were* part of it. Even Desmond made his living catering to a prosperous black working-class audience, now either scattered outside the historical black communities or suffering in their decay. The swinging club strips fed by the postwar black prosperity have diminished or disappeared.

This new order introduced by the Reagan administration, like its Keynesian predecessor, is not only global but profoundly local. It presents itself to individuals in the form of both overwhelming constraints and novel opportunities. Here in San Francisco the winners and losers are painfully thrust together. The disproportionately black and Latino working class, the elderly, and the poor of the city are progressively displaced into Oakland and smaller depressed suburbs by all the young people from suburban backgrounds pouring in to take advantage of the flexibility, good pay, interesting work, and pseudo-Bohemian lifestyles offered by the computer industry in the Silicon Valley and San Francisco's Multimedia Gulch. San Francisco has lost over half of its African American population since 1970. As for the homeless, the software takeoff has nothing to offer them beyond a glut of mineral-water empties. Emaciated panhandlers with hunted eyes creep into the less well lit restaurants and bars, trying to hustle a buck before expulsion.

The pros feel left behind—Sam explicitly calls himself a "relic." But in their homeless state, the pros are in their own way integral manifestations of resurgent conservatism in the United States. Mass homelessness is the most visible and, to many, the most disturbing result of the end of the Keynesian tax-and-spend model. The recyclers are therefore not exactly *typical* but are *emblematic* in their fall from working-class respectability into indigent marginality.

The recyclers are also emblematic in that the poor—most specifically "welfare mothers," ghetto dwellers, the homeless, or destitute addicts—are the most common targets of the compulsion to *adapt* that is the Zeitgeist of the last fifteen years.

Newt Gingrich, coordinator of the Republican 1996 "Contract with America," said that "we simply must abandon the welfare state and move to an opportunity society."[25] Most Democrats concur, intoning that removing government support from the disadvantaged is the truly compassionate choice, the only way to save them from isolation and degradation. In the second presidential debate of the 1996 campaign, Bill Clinton claimed:

> I started working on welfare reform . . . because I was sick of seeing people trapped in a system that was increasingly physically isolating them and making their kids more vulnerable to getting in trouble.[26]

Both parties would have us believe that the solution to endemic poverty is good honest work, yet the conditions of available jobs for unskilled workers are unlikely to pull a person, let alone a family, out of poverty. Workfare workers are not covered by federal wage legislation. Indeed, under the terms of the Personal Responsibility Act they do not have to be paid anything over their basic welfare benefit level. The entry of both high numbers of workfare workers and workers previously on welfare is likely to depress wages considerably in low-wage labor markets, where workers already struggle to pay for housing, medical treatment, and childcare.[27]

Protecting the wages and working conditions of citizens is no longer a realistic approach in a globalized world, explains Robert Reich, the center-left secretary of labor during Clinton's first term. Contemporary government should resign itself to the reality that multinational corporations can set the basic terms of the work environment. Government should concentrate on leading the population into the most favorable niches in the international economy. In their turn, the American public should concentrate on skill acquisition so that as many of them as possible can become symbolic analysts, the only workers who can expect decent pay and working conditions.[28]

Even before they became homeless, there was little chance of middle-aged, relatively uneducated men like the pros moving into the areas of job growth. Too young for retirement, too old for radically new directions, most of the recyclers have neither the education for high tech jobs nor the capacity for "emotion work" necessary for most service jobs.[29] These kinds of life histories tend to produce men who are both uncomfortable and inexperienced at using their "personality" for direct economic gain. Besides, even minimum-wage employers are likely to dismiss such job applicants as potentially overly assertive and unlikely to learn new work practices. And they might well be right. After all, what the recyclers took for granted about their old work, and what they recreate in recycling, is the minimum level of "emotion work," hustle, and "sucking up." Such jobs are now hard to find.

HOMELESSNESS: SYMPTOM OR DISEASE?

So what about the experts, the researchers in academia, social welfare institutions, and policy think tanks? Rather than exploring the relationship between homelessness and neoliberal America, most have adopted a disease model which focuses on the grubby, addicted, and depressed poor themselves. Where hardline conservatives see intentional homelessness and criminality, the disease model places the homeless under a fine microscope, separating them into various categories of disability. Mental illness, addiction, and family dysfunction are each measured in order to build a composite model of the problem.

The disease model did not always dominate the debate on homelessness. A structural model that focused on war and economy had its currency in the early 1980s when the Reagan revolution took an ax to the remaining Great Society programs and a century of labor rights. Many New Left activists eagerly responded by taking up the cause of homelessness, as a case in which the poverty and desperation of the victims were indisputable. Here, perhaps, corporate downsizing, union busting, and Reaganomics could be shown to be inhumane, just as the homeless "Hoovervilles" had served the reform discourse of the depression era.[30] No doubt the popular perception of homeless people as relatively racially diverse, compared to the ghetto poor, helped this construction of deservingness. Similarly, the prior military service of many homeless men continues to be an important source of sympathy and funds.

And so for a time during the eighties the activists were considerably successful with their structural analysis. Liberal mass media often presented the homeless as ordinary people down on their luck, especially emphasizing homeless two-parent families, which are in fact relatively rare.[31] The homeless Vietnam veteran, alternately wounded everyman and modern-day gunslinger, became a stock figure, played in Hollywood by Sylvester Stallone, Liam Neeson, and Jean-Claude Van Damme.[32]

Both conservatives and health professionals eventually developed critiques of this "ideological" hyperbole, agreeing that the activists grossly overestimated the numbers of homeless, and that their conception of a large working-class pool "at risk" of homelessness relied on ridiculous claims of similarity between the homeless and the general public. The National Coalition for the Homeless and various city-level advocacy groups and organizations of the homeless continue to articulate a structural interpretation, but the disease model counter-interpretation now dominates the press, the Democratic party establishment, and the more liberal state and local governments.

From the point of view of most health professionals in the field, homelessness is a symptom of the severe mental illness and substance abuse of the few, and has little to do with working and housing conditions for the many.[33] This individualization of the causes of homelessness restricts legitimate research to examinations of the individual characteristics that prevent homeless people from fitting in and to studies of the best ways to help them move back into society. The nature of the society they are expected to fit in to is rarely subject to debate. While the "homelessness industry" provides essential practical services to the homeless, its resistance to structural interpretations and solutions echoes the "sobriety plus hard work" prescription of the urban missions of the early twentieth century. Like those of the free market conservatives, such interpretations naturalize the relatively recent social and economic structure of the United States in the nineties into a given—"jobs and housing"—forgetting the administered, sometimes negotiated terrain that was the norm for fifty years after the New Deal.

The better shelters, drug rehabilitation centers, and even prisons do reach out to help those who have hit rock-bottom, provided they are willing to acknowledge their sickness and take the approved steps out of it.[34] Those diagnosed with depression and other mental disorders must promise to stay *on* their drugs, while those diagnosed as addicts must strive to stay *off* theirs. Yet at the same time, low wages, harsh sentencing policies, and cuts in welfare and disability entitlements keep pressing down on the poorer members of the working class, steadily increasing the number of the near-homeless and despairing. The homelessness industry can do little about the constant supply of clients, only try its best to turn a few of them around with little more than "self-esteem," Prozac, or the fellowship of Narcotics Anonymous to help them.

The proponents of the disease model are right in noting that the structural perspective of homeless activists and advocates tends to underplay addictions and mental instability among the homeless. Most clearly, there is no doubt that the isolation and extreme poverty of a sizable minority of the homeless that suffer from organic mental illness has much more to do with misguided policy and changes in family structure than with changes in the labor market. However, the disease model sets up a false antagonism between "proximal" causes, such as depression or substance abuse, and structural conditions beyond the individual's control—the shrinking market for manual laborers, for example. This line of thought tends to obscure the complex relationship between the personal and the structural. For men like Sam, there is rarely a simple one-way relationship between drinking, getting laid off, marital breakdown, and homelessness. Or, again, between a long prison sentence, drugs, and depression, in the case of Desmond. Similarly, the same self-destructive or unstable behavior carries very different outcomes, depending on a person's degree of family support and his or

her position in society. If Clarence had had a close, loving family to return
to, technical or educational qualifications, or even just friends with civilian
employment know-how, it is unlikely that his discharge from the military
would have left him so fundamentally alone.

Drug and alcohol use and abuse, after all, are endemic to society, both in
urban and rural areas. Yet most people with addictions continue to function
in their work lives. Cocaine, in particular, is favored by workers in high-stress
jobs—high-end restaurant workers and lawyers, as well as the overtime
hounds of the working class. One of the other recyclers developed his habit
while working as a house painter. "The money was no good, so they paid us
a bonus in cocaine. I'd never done it before. It used to be expensive. But on
that painting crew there was a fair amount of peer pressure. You know, if
you're not one of the boys, you won't get called next time. Some jobs it's
beer, some jobs it's coke, or crack. You work better on coke, of course."

The connection among drug use, hard labor, and impoverished men
goes way back. Like the Bolivian miners chewing their coca leaves, the
tramps and hoboes who built America used alcohol heavily to numb their
regrets and and reward their back-breaking labor. Nels Anderson tells how
the "hoboes" served an intermediate role in developing the West in the late
nineteenth and early twentieth centuries. They arrived too late for the
great land grabs, but served a vital "in-between" role as cheap, flexible labor
power for the extractive industries that fueled the American juggernaut.
The hobo labor market centered on the railway hub of Chicago; half a million transients passed through that city every year. Too poor to marry, too
proud to do service jobs, the hard-drinking, rebellious hoboes became a
class of their own, often ending up dependent on the urban missions when
economic slumps, old age, or industrial injury cut them down.[35]

It was not their hard drinking that destroyed the hobo class. Just as the
steel mills, auto plants, and other heavy industries of the postwar period
closed their doors on the industrial worker of the 1970s and 80s, the industrial frontier gradually lost its use for the hobo. Mechanization, corporate
consolidation, and family settlement of the West lowered the demand for
large numbers of migrant workers to build railroads, work temporary mining camps, harvest ice, and move crops. In this later phase, in the 1920s and
30s, the underemployed hobo became a burden on the cities, as more and
more former transients turned into "home guards"—low-paid petty workers, panhandlers, and con artists.

Like the homeless in the 1980s, the "transients" of the 1920s became a
much-discussed social problem. Charitable municipal communities were
instituted, and the hobo became an early subject of the new discipline of
psychopathology. Specialists generally presented the problem in individual
terms. Even though it was the demand of the frontier for a tough, flexible,
bachelor workforce that had created skid row, its culture, and characteristic

institutions, the psychopathologists and social workers assessed the "hobo problem" purely in terms of the personality defects of the homeless man, his immature "wanderlust," "egocentricity," "emotional instability," and, above all, his drinking.

Anderson, who was a former hobo and the child of a transient worker, tended to a more holistic analysis:

> All the problems of the homeless man go back in one way or another to the conditions of his work. The irregularity of his employment is reflected in the irregularity of all phases of his existence. To deal with him even as an individual, society must deal also with the economic forces which have formed his behavior, with the seasonal and cyclical fluctuations in industry. This means that the problem of the homeless man is not local but national.[36]

For Anderson, the primary solution to the hobo problem would be the "decasualization of labor," to be achieved by instituting a well-funded national employment system with the job of regulating employment agencies, providing public works for periods of business depression, and regulating unemployment insurance in vulnerable industries.[37]

And indeed this is what came to be in the New Deal era. First, the great depression pulled so many of the population into skid row that the structural interpretation of vagrancy gained unprecedented strength. The Roosevelt administration set up the Works Progress Administration and the Civilian Conservation Corps work programs, and the new Social Security entitlements rescued the elderly from skid row. In the wartime and postwar boom, the skid rows of America shrank to a fraction of their old glory, the radical tramps of the IWW died out, and the majority of the white working class found the means for marriage and stability in the new tax-and-spend commonwealth.

Now the shape of the society has changed again, and the 1990s are not so very different from the 1920s. It is an age of hype and glitter, and there are new fortunes to be made, but at the same time large numbers of workers have been displaced, and are roaming the country for work. This time, the labor surplus is less about the closing of the second frontier and the mechanization of farming, and more about globalization and the collapse of heavy industry and union labor. As then, free-market politics are in ascendancy and imprisonment rates are high. And, once again, hundreds of thousands of single indigent men and women crowd the skid row areas of the major cities, panhandling, working by the day, selling papers, selling sex, and operating various minor scams. This time they are younger, and more of them are black or brown-skinned. The poorest of them are homeless.

Like Anderson's hoboes, today's homeless men are a hard-drinking, hard-drugging crew, with a disproportionate number of free-thinkers, ex-convicts, orphans, and other misfits.[38] If they have enough money they may stay in one of the few remaining single-occupancy hotels. The cage hotels and flophouses that enabled their forerunners to sleep inside for a minimal fee have disappeared. Now they can either sleep in shelters similar to the old missions or lie outside in the streets or under bridges, in doorways, or over steam vents. Like the mission stiffs of the twenties, a disproportionate number of the homeless and near-homeless are sick or disabled. Around 30 percent are said to show signs of serious mental illness.[39] A significant modern development is that illness has become much more lucrative than it was in the past. Now, a crippling hit-and-run injury or the diagnosis of a life-threatening illness is surprisingly often assessed as "worth it" by a man exhausted from years on the street. Now he will qualify for disability payments and can finally move inside, into his own place. Disability becomes a solution as well as a cause of homelessness for some individuals.

Today, however, the problem of homelessness is even more international than it was in the Great Depression. In all the richest countries of the world, large numbers of men of working age are sleeping rough. In Japan, for example, homelessness has become a major issue since the recent economic crisis. In urban underpasses armies of men sleep in cardboard boxes, their shoes neatly positioned beside them. France, Russia, Britain, Italy—all the European countries have their own manifestations of the problem.

Like the psychopathologists of the twenties, most policy experts on the subject of homelessness and indeed poverty in general, agree that the growth of homelessness in the eighties and nineties has little to do with labor or housing markets but is generated by diseases of the mind, dysfunctional families, and demon drugs. Like the reformers of the past, some favor outreach and treatment, others prohibition and imprisonment.

The radical homelessness advocates see the homeless as canaries in the mine, the vulnerable or unlucky few who are the first to succumb to the dangerous gases around all of us. And many poor and working-class people agree that they are "one paycheck away from homelessness." Lillian Rubin says that "Nothing [better] exemplifies the change in the twenty years since I last studied working-class families than the fear of being "on the street.""[40]

Yet at the same time, policy experts, politicians, and other opinion leaders continue to medicalize homelessness, telling us that the canaries are suffering from a specific disease of their own. All we can do is help the best of them back into the mine, where work shall set them free. With such lordly discourses we render natural and inevitable the grand social upheavals of our times: the sweeping destruction of blue-collar living standards, the mass incarceration of black men, and the wholesale abandonment of the poor.

NOTES

In the academic field I received wonderful encouragement and guidance from Leslie Salzinger and Amy Schalet. Back home, my band—Andrew, Josh, Gina, and

James—and my chosen family—Tricia, John-boy, Kev, and Mark—all did their best to keep my feet on the ground and my heart full of music during a difficult period of my life. My biggest thank-you goes to all the recyclers who helped me with this research, especially Sam, Clarence, and Desmond, all fictitious names. I dedicate the chapter to those who didn't make it. Rest in peace, brothers.

1. *Details,* January 1997, p. 53.

2. Both *Details'* flexible man and the street hustler model are primarily masculine visions, *Details'* because such levels of disaffiliation are neither appealing nor realistic for most women, the hustler model because poor women with children have been differently positioned vis-à-vis law, benefit entitlement, and the state. They have greater access to money and shelter because of their roles as mothers and victims of domestic violence, while poor unemployed men receive little to no financial support and are overwhelmingly caught up in the criminal justice system. One work which explores the differentiation and separation of the poor by gender is Joanne Passaro's *The Unequal Homeless: Men on the Streets, Women in Their Place.* The new time limits on AFDC are likely to transform the gender differentials. Already sharply rising rates of women's imprisonment suggests that the decline of welfare benefits to poor women will be reflected in increasing criminal activity.

3. David A. Snow et al., "The Homeless as Bricoleurs: Material Survival Strategies on the Streets," p. 6.

4. Sabra Chartrand, "Unions Try to Secure a Place in the Changing Work World."

5. *Street Sheet,* June 1997, p. 6.

6. See Mike Davis, *City of Quartz,* chapter 4 ("Fortress LA"), pp. 221–64.

7. Talmadge Wright, *Out of Place: Homeless Mobilizations, Subcities and Contested Landscapes;* and Erich Brosch, "No Place Like Home," *Harper's,* April 1998, pp. 58–59.

8. In April 1996 a judge marked the official termination of the Matrix program under the new administration of Mayor Willie Brown by dismissing nearly 40,000 citations and warrants, most of them issued for drinking in public. However, since Brown was elected the Matrix citations have actually increased in some categories, especially for sleeping in parks. According to the figures kept by the Coalition on Homelessness, the 4,692 citations given in the first four months of the Brown administration exceeded the 4,360 citations issued to homeless people in the first four months of 1995, at the height of the official Matrix program (*San Francisco Bay Guardian,* April 17, 1996). The primary difference between the administrations is that the populist Brown does not promote the public image of himself as scourge of the homeless.

9. Kathleen Stewart, "Nostalgia as Polemic," p. 252.

10. Stewart's elitist nostalgia of power, exhilaration, and flux perhaps underplays the discomfort, even desperation, that can tinge elite romanticizing about the primitive, the authentic, the working-class, the black, and so on. I prefer Renato Rosaldo's "imperialist nostalgia," which describes white frontiersmen and imperialists concealing feelings of doubt and guilt by mourning the passing of what they themselves have transformed as if such passing were inevitable. Rosaldo, *Culture and Truth: The Remaking of Social Analysis,* chapter 3.

11. Stewart, p. 253.

12. "The Downsizing of America," *The New York Times,* March 3, 1996.

13. These are terms used, respectively, by Castells (1989), Lash and Urry (1987), Harvey (1989), and Jameson (1991).

14. Dick Walker, "California Rages Against the Dying of the Light." California received up to 23 percent of all United States defense contracts in the Reagan years.

15. Ibid., p. 45.

16. By subcontracting into the informal economy, enterprises can avoid the "indirect wage" of benefits and at the same time increase labor control by restoring arbitrary dismissal. Work becomes a joint attempt by worker and manager to avoid legal detection, making it almost impossible for workers to use any outside leverage in their relationships with management. In the context of rising competition from the global economy, American informalization is increasingly ignored by state regulatory agencies, as it provides much-needed jobs. For politicians committed to curbing the political power of labor, informalization helps to suppress the mobilization of workers through formal democratic channels or unions.

17. Kevin Heldman, "On the Town with the U.S. Military," p. 24.

18. *Los Angeles Times,* March 20, 1988.

19. Roediger's study of the evolution of white working-class identity shows how white republican independence was historically counterposed to the unfree slaves. In an early version of blaming the victim, African Americans were held to be inherently incapable of these same republican virtues and therefore the enemy of righteous free labor. David R. Roediger, *The Wages of Whiteness: Race and the Making of the American Working Class,* chapter 3.

20. Troy Duster, "Pattern, Purpose, and Race in the Drug War: The Crisis of Credibility in Criminal Justice," p. 266.

21. United States Bureau of Justice Statistics, excerpted by *Prison Legal News* on the World Wide Web at http://www.ai.mit.edu/people/ellens/PLN/4.3/ FEDERAL_PRISON.html.

The prison system has taken up some of the slack from job losses in industry and the military by multiplying prison-related jobs by four since 1980. Most prisoners are also workers, though hardly employees, given that they are usually paid under fifty cents an hour. Prison production from the federal Unicorp program alone is worth $1.35 billion per year, creating ultra-low-wage workers on the inside out of those who might refuse such work on the outside (*San Francisco Bay Guardian,* July 17, 1996). It is unlikely, however, that the high costs of maintaining a prison population—now approaching $30 billion a year, at least five times greater than in most industrialized nations—can be rendered cost-effective by such measures.

22. William Julius Wilson, *The Truly Disadvantaged: The Inner City, the Underclass, and Public Policy,* pp. 40–41. Drug offenders accounted for more than a third (36 percent) of the national increase in the state prison population from 1985 to 1994 and more than two-thirds (71 percent) of the increase in the federal prison population for this period (Marc Mauer, *Intended and Unintended Consequences: State Racial Disparities in Imprisonment*).

23. Mauer.

24. Katherine Beckett, *Making Crime Pay: Law and Order in Contemporary American Politics,* pp. 44–48.

25. Newt Gingrich, *To Renew America,* p. 9.

26. The increased discussion of minority "isolation" in newspaper columns and

political speeches of the nineties reflects the broad influence of William Julius Wilson's *The Truly Disadvantaged* in policy circles.

27. Adolph Reed, Jr., "A Slave to Finance," p. 27.

28. Robert B. Reich, *The Work of Nations*. Reich implies that union mobilization in the low-wage, routine production and service sectors is no longer a viable strategy, as capital will only move elsewhere. In keeping with his argument that corporations are increasingly supranational, Reich does not approve of preferential government support for United States–owned businesses, as they are no more likely to provide decent jobs than any foreign corporation.

29. For discussion of "emotion work," see Arlie Hochschild, *The Managed Heart: The Commercialization of Human Feeling*.

30. An academic structural analysis of contemporary homelessness is provided by Joel Blau in *The Visible Poor*. Blau retains a consistent focus on the pathologies of the wider society rather than on those of the homeless themselves, moving from large-scale phenomena such as unemployment, underemployment, and welfare contraction to more specific structural changes such as rent inflation and the destruction of America's skid row hotels.

31. Two-parent families do not figure highly in statistics of the homeless. Apart from the huge stresses that poverty and insecurity put on relationships, institutions such as AFDC, safe houses, and family shelters have made it economically possible, and often desirable, for poor women to leave their partners.

32. The prototype for the homeless Vietnam veteran as the contemporary rendition of the Western movie's man-without-a-name is the first "Rambo" movie, *First Blood* (1982), directed by Ted Kotcheff and starring Sylvester Stallone (Ronald Reagan's favorite movie). Rambo first comes into conflict with the hick cop badguys of the movie when they arrest him for vagrancy. Neeson starred in *Suspect* (1987), directed by Peter Yates, Van Damme in *Hard Target* (1993), directed by John Woo.

33. See, for example, Alice S. Baum and Donald W. Burnes, *A Nation in Denial: The Truth about Homelessness*, p. 125; Stephen F. Redburn and Terry F. Buss, *Responding to America's Homeless: Public Policy Alternatives;* and Dennis P. Culhane, June M. Avery, and Trevor R. Hadley, "Prevalence of Treated Behavioral Disorders among Adult Shelter Users: A Longitudinal Study."

34. Most drug rehabilitation programs piggyback onto the nonprofessional twelve-step movement, which offers strong peer support and frequent activities for the recovering addict.

35. Nels Anderson, *The Hobo: The Sociology of the Homeless Man*.

36. Ibid., p. 121.

37. Ibid., p. 268.

38. Both Nels Anderson, in 1923, and Snow, Anderson, and Koegel, in 1994, remark on the high numbers of orphans and foster children in their samples.

39. Interview with Peter Rossi, a longtime student of the vast homelessness literature. See Benedict Giamo and Jeffrey Grunberg, *Beyond Homelessness: Frames of Reference*, chapter 1.

40. Lillian B. Rubin, *Families on the Fault Line*, p. 114.

FOUR

Degradation without Deskilling

Twenty-five Years in the San Francisco Shipyards

Joseph A. Blum

I am of this world and this essay is an attempt to step back and make coherent sense of social processes that most of the people living through them find almost impossible to comprehend. I worked as a boilermaker, welder, and shipfitter in the shops, shipyards, and construction sites of the Bay Area from the early 1970s until I retired from the actual physical labor of the trade in late 1997, soon after I finished the research for this paper. Since then I have been the Recording Secretary and Dispatcher for Boilermakers Local Lodge #6. Thus, as both a skilled worker and as a union official, I have experienced the systematic assault on my craft and the erosion of the power of my union. In this paper I attempt to analyze the effects and the causes of the sharp decline of the Bay Area ship repair and heavy steel fabrication industries over the past couple of decades from the workers' perspective. Global competition, the end of the Cold War, and the transition of both the national and local economies from the industrial to the information age have decimated the industries in which we try to earn our livelihood. Steady work for thousands, so plentiful in the mid-1970s, is a thing of the past. Those thousands have been reduced to the several hundred workers who retain seniority at the few union shops and shipyards still in business. Hourly wages, the envy of metal trades workers around the world during the four decades following the start of World War II, are now less than the average earned in the advanced industrialized countries, and some "unskilled" positions are being paid wages, especially in nonunion yards, comparable to those of shipyard workers in South Korea. Even at these wage rates, things would not be so bad if the work were steady, but most of the members of my Local work no more than half of the year at their trade. With the decline of the industry has come a parallel dimi-nution in the power and the quality of representation that the unions provide for the workers. Rank and file participation has declined steadily, and contact and solidarity among the crafts has lessened. Labor-management relations, which in the past were the product of compromise between relatively powerful unions and bosses who at least recognized the need to elicit the cooperation of our skilled labor, had deteriorated by the mid-1990s to virtual management dictates. Shipyards, heavy steel fabrication, and con-struction are inherently dangerous industries to work in, but speed-up, the lack of real union representation at the job site, the breaking down of respect for the practice of traditional crafts, and the failure of management to provide for the training of a new generation of workers over the last two decades have made the shipyards far more hazardous. The most important reason for my leaving the trade at a relatively young age (fifty-six) was my belief that the local shipyards are an accident waiting to happen, and I did not want to become one of their victims.

Detaching oneself from the field of study is a problem that proba-bly plagues all ethnographers. This is especially true for me. Working as a metals trades craftsman has not been the quaint, the exotic, or the unknown for me. Unlike most academic ethnographers, I did not go to the shipyards to do fieldwork; I went there to earn a living. My participation preceded by almost a quarter of a century the kind of systematic and conscious observation that I have undertaken in the last several years. I made scattered diary entries over previous years, but did not begin to make systematic field notes until I began to conceptualize this paper. Thus, much of my firsthand knowledge of earlier years is drawn from memory and present-day discussions with other workers remembering their past. While memories can be faulty and distorted because they are reflections through the lens of our present-day understandings, my account can claim the authenticity that comes from long acquaintance with the subject.

My experiences over the years are very similar to those of other workers. I know what it is like to do the work every day, to be laid off at inopportune moments, to vote on contracts with my livelihood at stake, and to decide to what degree to risk my personal safety in order to keep my job. My presence did not "contaminate" the research site. The social processes that I am attempting to analyze were not altered by my presence, at least not as a researcher. As a Jew who entered the trade *after* receiving my B.A., who got my master's degree twenty years later, and who became a Ph.D. candidate in sociology at UC Berkeley while still working in the yards, I have always appeared to be very different from almost all the other workers; and in some respects I certainly am. I have been nicknamed "Rabbi" and "Professor" and been called a lot worse, but first and foremost over the years I became one of the guys. That is how I defined myself at work, and that is how I am seen both by my fellow workers and by management. Dozens of rank-and-file workers are either friends or acquaintances. I had a respectful, although at times contentious, relationship with the previous Business Manager of my local. I have a close and cooperative relationship with the present Business Manager, for whom I have worked. I am on good terms with the officers of many of the locals of other crafts. I have had ongoing dialogue with members of management, including those at the highest level. My research questions were formulated after I already had intimate knowledge of the social processes at work and were refined as my research continued. This essay is informed by these firsthand experiences: I know the work, I know the people, I know what is real and what is not.

I am of this world and I cannot leave. I am personally, emotionally, and intellectually welded to these workers and these industries. Yet I partially detach from them when seeking the perspectives needed in my various projects to document our lives. I have written about the history of our predecessors in the trades, and I am in the process today of memorializing aspects of our labor process through black and white photography. But I am reluctant to assign finality to social processes that are still unfolding. For all the inexorability of those "global forces," individuals have their own ways of challenging them, negotiating them, eluding them. Even as I write, I know that tomorrow I might return to the dregs of those dreaded shipyards to earn a needed dollar and exchange an insult with my bosses. This is my world. It is the world of the academy that remains exotic and difficult for me.

Almost every day, but especially on Thursday, which is payday, shipyard workers hurrying to and from work at San Francisco Drydock walk past Kevin Harris (not his real name) and are reminded just how precarious is their hold upon their jobs. Until the early 1990s, Kevin was employed in the shipyard as a journeyman welder, driving a late-model four-wheel drive vehicle and, if not prosperous, was certainly getting by with a reasonably high-paying, but no longer steady, unionized craft job. An accident on the job, or a dispute with management (accounts from workers who knew him while he was still working differ), has made him unemployed, forced him into homelessness, dependent upon SSI and donations from workers who knew him when, and who still have their jobs. Seemingly unable to sever his connections with the workplace that has discarded him, Kevin apparently sleeps among the debris around the shipyard's industrial area. Although he is an extreme case, Kevin is hardly unique. His plight illustrates how, over the last twenty-five years, conditions have deteriorated for men, like myself, who seek to earn their livelihood in the San Francisco Bay Area metal trades, mostly in steel fabrication and shipyard repair work.

Though Kevin and his predicament are rarely discussed, he cannot be far from the minds of local shipyard workers. The possibility of falling from skilled craftsman to "homeless bum" has become perhaps our greatest nightmare. We see the world we know, the one in which we play such a vital role and from which we draw our sustenance, identity, and security, disintegrating before our eyes. Few of us will actually plunge into homelessness, but all are confronting the demise of our trades, the virtual elimination of our occupations, as a result of the reconfiguration of global economic and political forces far beyond our control. The process is not new, but the endgame is at hand. It has been going on for at least two decades in a steady and relentless fashion. In the last five years it has become clear to everyone that the decline is permanent. The condition of the last major unionized shipyard in the area is a metaphor for a dying industry.

The physical plant itself is obsolete and worn out, located in a decaying industrial area. Weeds push their way up around portions of the grounds, which are strewn with discarded metal and assorted industrial debris. The walls of both of the drydocks are patched with hundreds of large and small "doubler plates" to maintain water tightness. All kinds of minor repairs and constant vigilance are required just to keep them functioning. From high atop the wingwalls of the drydock one can see the rotting timbers of the piers of an adjacent shipyard that closed down fifteen years ago; half a mile beyond lie the now idle concrete piers of still another yard that went bankrupt in 1996. Four years earlier one of the biggest yards on the Bay closed down, sold its state-of-the-art floating drydock to a Singapore firm, and permanently laid off almost five hundred workers. Many of the cranes and some of the heavy equipment, in this, the last of the large yards, no longer work. On big jobs, the tool room is often forced to issue grinders, drills, and other hand tools that are thirty years old. The small administration building out on the pier, a beautiful turn-of-the- century brick structure, is closed and roped off, its useful life terminated by the Loma Prieta earthquake in 1989. The much larger buildings on the perimeter of the yard, closest to downtown, which used to house corporate personnel, sales representatives, estimating departments, and engineering and drafting offices, have been closed for more than a decade. Administrative and clerical work today is done in temporary trailers, the kind found at many construction sites, which are located just inside the main gate and line the pier leading to the wharfs and drydocks.

The dilapidated condition of the yard is matched by the precarious employment opportunities accorded the workers. Although hourly wages (at least for journeymen) are still high compared to much blue collar and service work, steady employment is virtually impossible to attain. A cycle of "feast and famine" prevails. Short-term jobs, lasting at most several months and requiring hundreds of workers, are run at breakneck speed, often seven days a week, in twelve-and-a-half-hour shifts, day and night, only to be followed by periods of enforced idleness, also lasting months at a time. Although, according to the contract, overtime is not mandatory, rare is the worker who feels he can turn down any extra hours offered at premium pay; all are driven by the understanding that they had better get it while they can. Although this sprawling shipyard has been here for over 115 years, every job could be its last one, and its appearance conveys that; its future is precarious. Sitting on the edge of the Bay in the best micro-climate in the city, the land seems ripe for sale to a developer to put in an upscale marina along with some condos, restaurants, and retail shops, as has been occurring for years further to the north all along the waterfront. Most of the workers in the yard believe it is only a matter of time before the city's oldest industrial establishment will be closed for good, making their chances for earning a livelihood in the metal trades in the Bay Area almost nil.

How are we to explain what can only be seen as the degradation of work, the loss of our status, security, and indeed of our very place in the modern American economic landscape? In his seminal work, *Labor and Monopoly Capital*, published in 1974, Harry Braverman put forward the bold proposition that "With the development of the capitalist mode of production, the very concept of skill becomes degraded along with the *degradation of labor*."[1] Yet, all the evidence I have been able to gather, as both a participant and an observer for the last twenty-five years, indicates that the labor process in San Francisco shipyards has been relatively impervious to change. The technological requirements of shipyard repair work have varied very little, and the core of workers plying their trades have been journeymen for at least a decade, many of them for three and four times that long. We remain very much the equal of our counterparts of the past few generations in terms of technical competence, and we have even learned to work with some new materials and processes. But our basic skills, tools, and relative autonomy with regard to the labor process have remained virtually the same.[2]

Given our retention of skill, perhaps Michael Piore and Charles Sabel are the more relevant theorists. They assert that the *flexible specialization* required in craft production inevitably leads to a "community of equals" who participate in a production environment of "industrial democracy."[3] But I saw little "yeoman democracy" in my years in the shipyards. True, when the unions were strong we did have considerable rights and protections, but now that the industry is in decline we have lost most of those powers and we face a more authoritarian regime. Like Braverman, Piore and Sabel have no way of understanding the independent variation of the labor process and the politics of production. They conflate the labor process with the regulation of that process. As Michael Burawoy points out, these two aspects can be separated analytically, and as I will document, they can and do vary independently in the real world. The labor process involves the actual operations carried out by the workers, in Burawoy's words, the "coordinated set of activities involved in the transformation of raw materials into useful products."[4] The control of that process is achieved through what Burawoy calls the "production regime," the "*political apparatuses of production,* understood as the institutions that regulate and shape struggles in the workplace."[5] These include management-union relations, the distribution of workers into places, and indeed the very constitution of individuals as workers.

The production regime of two decades ago was a class compromise based upon the employer's ability and willingness to grant us substantial yet limited material concessions, both because of the employer's dominant position in world markets and because of our crucial and irreplaceable role in the production process, combined with our organizational strength in exclusive craft unions and our consequent ability to impose the closed shop. The result was a regime I call "flexible hegemony." The flexible craft labor process, with its wide latitude of worker autonomy, was necessary to perform the actual production tasks in the uncertain world of ship repair, steel fabrication, and construction work. The hegemonic regime was the result of compromise between two powerful and organized class forces. The unions were taken in as junior partners with some influence over the evaluation and placement of workers, and both management and labor agreed to an elaborate system of mutual rights and obligations. Today, under the impact of macro, global economic and political forces, which compel our bosses (those who have not taken their capital elsewhere) to compete internationally for every job, and which have resulted in the virtual decimation of our unions, management has chosen to abrogate the class compromise and impose a much more oppressive regime of increasing control, one that I call "flexible discipline." The flexible craft labor system necessarily remains unchanged, but the regime is now characterized by the reassertion of managerial prerogatives, unilateral imposition of contracts, redistribution of skills, control over the evaluation and placement of workers, and the regulation of individual workers through disciplinary practices aimed at the body.

Neither Braverman nor Piore and Sabel are very helpful in understanding these changes in the production regime. Braverman assumes that workers are more or less immune from degradation as long as they retain their skills. His analysis and focus on the labor process at the point of production largely disregard wider economic, social, and political forces, or assume that the monopoly corporations he was studying had reached the point where they could control and dominate these outside forces. Piore and Sabel err in the same direction. They fail to specify the kind of "macro-regulatory requirements" that would be necessary, in conjunction with craft production, to promote a more democratic workplace.[6] Neither seems to recognize the profound effect that competition in the product and labor markets has not only upon employment opportunities, but also upon the industrial relations that workers and employers agree upon in formal contracts, relations which they negotiate and renegotiate informally on the shop floor every minute of the working day.[7]

This chapter will first present evidence for the continuity in skill levels in shipyard repair work in San Francisco over the last quarter of a century. The second section will describe and analyze the production regime under conditions of flexible hegemony. The third section will analyze and document the change to the new production regime, flexible discipline. The fourth section seeks to explain these changes in terms of global forces. The concluding section turns to the responses of the workers affected by these changes.

A MOST RESILIENT LABOR PROCESS

Before writing *Labor and Monopoly Capitalism*, Harry Braverman was for many years a shipyard worker in a four-year apprenticed craft. He viewed the naval shipyard as "probably the most complete product of two centuries of industrial revolution," a place where the "interlocking processes" of both ancient and modern crafts were carried on cooperatively in close proximity. Although his trade, coppersmithing, suffered a "rapid decline with the substitution of new processes and materials, . . . the trade of working copper provided a foundation in the elements of a number of other crafts."[8] He was able to utilize those related skills and find craft employment in railroad repair, sheet metal work, and heavy steel fabrications shops. Thus, as late as the 1940s and 1950s, Braverman presents evidence for the persistence in United States industry of skilled craft workers, who, although not as autonomous as their pre-industrial revolution ancestors, nevertheless more closely resembled them than the degraded homogeneous labor power the scientific managers sought to produce. These workers played an indispensable role in the production process and therefore were able to extract rewards from their employers to ensure their cooperation and continuing loyalty.

The inherent power, control, and autonomy embedded in the skilled craftsperson is, according to Braverman, incompatible with the laws of the accumulation of capital. Therefore, via the vehicle of scientific management, epitomized by Taylorism, capital consciously and systematically collects, concentrates, and appropriates for its exclusive use all of the knowledge embedded in the craft skill and then uses "*this monopoly over knowledge to control each step of the labor process and its mode of execution.*"[9]

For Braverman, the history of capitalism, especially in its monopoly phase, is the successful unfolding of this "law," the wresting away of these craft skills from the workers by the capitalist class. In that process, skill, work, and human labor are all degraded, the latter being cheapened and reduced to "the level of general and undifferentiated labor power,"[10] capable only of carrying out the mindless, simple, detailed tasks dictated by capital.

Braverman failed to recognize the limited ability of even the capitalist labor process to deskill many jobs. For some work the limits are virtually technologically determined—the very work process itself is not amenable to rationalization under the present state of technical knowledge at a cost that would allow the firm to increase its accumulation of capital. A great deal of ship repair work falls into this category. Unlike new shipbuilding, which, with the development of modular construction techniques, was greatly simplified and rationalized during World War II, ship repair continues to require flexible work organization and skilled people of various trades. Systematic surveillance, a prerequisite to deskilling, is almost impossible for management to achieve on work scattered about in the honeycombed bowels of a ship. Even if feasible, the policing costs would be prohibitive, and policing would surely trigger resistance from the workers. Not only must the workers be skilled in their particular crafts—pipefitter, electrician, boilermaker, machinist, shipfitter, and so on—but they must be able to carry out their work in confined spaces with a minimum of disruption or damage to existing structures. Although routine tasks requiring minimal skill are frequently performed, each job presents unique problems. All require new measurements, different kinds of materials, and different methods of access. Plans change constantly as the work itself often inadvertently disrupts previously agreed-upon designs. Indeed, fights over "change orders," which alter the original contract between the ship owner (or his agent) and the shipyard doing the work, occur constantly, as the very process of repair often reveals new damage previously hidden from view. The work contains too much uncertainty to allow management even to consider attempting to dictate completely the details of the work process. Obviously this kind of work is not amenable to the essential principles of Taylorism, the vital element of which is, according to Braverman, "the systematic pre-planning and pre-calculation of all elements of the labor process, which now no longer exists as a process in the imagination of the worker but only as a process in the imagination of a special management staff."[11]

The technological imperatives of ship repair work change very slowly over time. The work is virtually impervious to the kind of deskilling that Braverman found in other industrial branches of the same trades, because it is highly resistant to the introduction of machinery. As in the past, shipyard repair work is carried out almost exclusively with hand tools under the control of the individual worker. Each time I hire in for a new job, I am issued a journeyman shipfitter's toolbox. It contains a twenty-five-foot tape measure, a combination square, a chalk line, a center punch, a small (two-pound) ball pein hammer, an angle divider, a chisel, and assorted screwdrivers, pliers, and adjustable wrenches. I also check out a welding hood, burning goggles, a stinger (the tool that holds the electrode in electric arc welding), and a burning torch (in case I need to work without the assistance of a combination welder). At least rudimentary welding and cutting skills are a requirement of my craft, and many experienced fitters are excellent welders. Like most other shipfitters, I bring my own "beater," or heavy hammer, a five-pounder with a fourteen-inch hickory handle, suitable for most fit-up work. These are the basic "tools of the trade." No power tools are issued, although almost daily I will be called upon to use one or more small hand-held grinders, impact wrenches, or hydraulic jacks, the latter to move structural steel pieces too stubborn to submit to my "beater." As in the past, the use of wedges, "dogs" (steel pieces cut with a notch and used in conjunction with wedges to raise or lower adjacent steel plates), saddles (similar to dogs, but usually larger), and other devices usually creatively fashioned on the spot to conform to the unique situation encountered, forms the basic techniques applied by the shipfitter.

As persistent as the tools are the skills shipyard workers are required to possess. Journeymen shipfitters, pipefitters, boilermakers, and machinists are expected to read blueprints, and when they do not exist, which is often, make their own sketches of the work to be done. They are expected to do layout—that is the process of transferring the information contained in the prints and sketches onto the actual steel. They are required to make templates out of wood or cardboard, so that pieces of steel or pipe cut to exact specifications can be fabricated by others in the shop. Most important, they must know the art, science, and techniques of cutting, fitting, and fusing metal. Shipfitters must know how to fit up the heavy primary structural components of a ship's hull and shell plate, as well as the lighter, secondary structural pieces comprising decks, bulkheads, and foundations; and all craftsmen must be able to accomplish their tasks to critical tolerances, often to variations of no more than one-sixteenth of an inch.

In addition to the necessary skills of the craft, the shipyard repair worker of today, just as in the past, is often required to work in exceedingly cramped, remote, almost inaccessible, dark, damp, hazardous, and extremely smoky spaces. It is not unusual to have to string hundreds of feet of electrical line just to provide temporary lights and power for hand-held tools. All workers must (or should) wear and use a variety of safety clothing and devices. Hard-hats and steel-toed shoes, as well as burn-resistant clothing (often supplemented with heavy leather welding jackets), are necessary for elementary bodily protection. Safety glasses, earplugs, and respirators are also mandatory. The cutting, fitting, and welding of steel, especially in the marine environment, and in confined spaces, can be exceedingly noisy and produces toxic fumes. Workers are forced to rely upon individual protective devices to preserve their health because management rarely installs engineering solutions sufficient to eliminate the hazards. Although absolutely necessary, many of these devices make communication among workers much more difficult (hearing and speaking are both restricted) and require an increase of energy and effort; for example, breathing through a respirator is more difficult than without.[12]

It is evident that the requisite skills persist largely unaltered and undiminished. A changing labor process is not the place to look for an explanation of the degradation of conditions for Bay Area metal trades workers. Rather, we must turn to the transformation of the way the labor process is regulated, what I call the production regime.

FLEXIBLE HEGEMONY

The production regime which I have labeled "flexible hegemony" was in effect for more than forty years, from the beginning of World War II through the early 1980s. It was predicated upon United States economic superiority in the world market and the continuation of the Cold War, which together provided steady employment for thousands of Bay Area men and a handful of women in steel fabrication, construction, and ship repair. Even in the late 1970s, being a mechanic, working out of Boilermakers Local #6 in San Francisco, was something to be proud of. Fathers still brought willing sons into the trades. I had joined the ranks of skilled craftsmen who were building the gigantic machinery necessary to strip-mine the West, develop the Alaska oil and gas fields, construct and maintain the infrastructure of the region, and repair and recondition the Navy's Pacific fleet. It only seemed reasonable that our working hard and playing by the rules should bring their just material rewards; and for a while they did.

Achieving journeyman status in the union and receiving one's "book" virtually assured one a secure job (or a continuous series of temporary jobs), with relatively high wages and benefits, including contributions to a pension plan and full medical, dental, and eye care coverage for the worker's entire family. Work in a closed union shop, shipyard, or construction site conferred the accrual of certain rights and protections (seniority and grievance procedures), considered virtual birthrights, for the industrial craftsman, who was playing a vital and indispensable role in keeping the United States the dominant industrial and military power in the post–World War II era.

The class compromise embodied in flexible hegemony had three major characteristics: 1) a relatively nonconfrontational partnership between management and ten strong craft unions organized into a Metal Trades Council, which had influence upon job descriptions and distribution, and which, after receiving input from their rank-and-file memberships, negotiated coastwide contracts, whose terms were mostly honored in practice; 2) a union-sanctioned traditional craft labor system, with a modified apprenticeship program, which conferred honor, dignity, and respect upon the craftsman; and 3) an elaborate series of mutual rights and obligations in which management agreed not to interfere with the worker's private life and to provide a relatively safe working environment and appropriate sanitary and eating facilities at the worksite, in return for hard work and high productivity from skilled craftsmen.

Strong Unions—Negotiated Contracts

The unions' strength was based upon their large numbers and upon government intervention during the war, which granted them the closed shop and allowed them to monopolize access to the necessary skills of the metal trades. As late as the mid-1970s, five Boilermakers locals had master agreements with three different branches of the industry: field construction, steel fabrication shops, and shipyards. These locals had approximately ten thousand members and, although they were by far the largest of the metal trades unions, accounted for only about 65 percent of the workers employed in the industry. They worked in at least nine Bay Area shipyards and twenty-five fabricating shops, some of substantial size and importance to the regional economy. The largest of the employers were long-established, well-known names in American industry: American Bridge (United States Steel), Kaiser Steel, Todd Shipyards, Bethlehem Steel, FMC Corporation, Paceco (Freuehauf Corporation), while others were substantial regional and local businesses.[13]

The evolution of the union's exclusive bargaining rights can be traced to the beginning of World War II and the federal government's interest in the production of war materials without labor disputes. In 1941, just prior to the extraordinary expansion of the West Coast shipbuilding industry, the Metal Trades Council, led by the Boilermakers Union, signed a Master

Agreement, sanctioned by the Navy, the Maritime Commission, and the War Production Board, establishing the closed shop in all shipyards from just north of Los Angeles to the Canadian border. The contracts they negotiated made West Coast metal trades workers the highest paid in the world.[14] After the war, union-controlled hiring halls, which monopolized access to the necessary skills and regulated the external labor markets, helped ensure relatively high wages and increased benefits, internal labor markets strongly influenced by seniority, and the existence of an "internal state," applying rules of "formal industrial jurisprudence," which guaranteed us industrial conditions, including citizen rights on the job, equal to any enjoyed in the world under capitalist production relations.[15]

The ability to continue to gain such favorable contracts, and for the most part to enforce them, was due in no small part to the active participation in union affairs by substantial groups of rank-and-file workers. We regularly attended meetings, pushed for democratic reforms such as the election of shop stewards, demanded that the union take a more active role on the shop floor, held the officers publicly accountable on fiscal affairs, and generally attempted to keep the leadership responsive to the needs of the ordinary worker. Although none of the traditional craft unions making up the Metal Trades Council was known for its democratic procedures, the membership has always had the right to ratify all contracts and elect local leadership. For months before any contract was negotiated, hundreds of ordinary workers would attend boilermaker meetings insisting that our demands be presented in contract negotiations.

Despite the unions' ability to negotiate decent contracts, management and control of all "business matters" resided with ownership (or their managers in the larger concerns), including the most crucial of all business decisions, whether to keep their capital invested in the metal trades industry at all. Neither the union nor the workers were ever consulted concerning questions of capital investment, market or product selection, the acceptable rate of return on the money invested, and, finally, and most crucially, alternative investment opportunities.

Union-Sanctioned Craft Labor System

During the post–World War II boom years, and well into the early 1980s, the Bay Area metal trades industry closely resembled Piore and Sabel's ideal-typical model of craft production, the shop-floor organizational foundation for their notion of flexible specialization. Our wages were tied to our skill, and not to the job we performed. Only two levels of skill were recognized, journeymen or mechanics, and apprentices or trainees, and the classification of individual workers was *negotiated* between management and the unions, both of whom were required to follow contractual rules. Journeymen were presumed to possess comparable skills and were paid a single rate, while learners received a sliding scale, eventually reaching mechanic's level as their skills accumulated over time. Shop floor supervisors, at least up to the foreman level, were invariably drawn from the ranks of craftsmen. They retained their membership in the union and often floated back and forth between lower management and mechanic. The fact that lower-level supervisors tended to be our union brothers, who might be back working with the tools on the next job, tended to keep relations with many immediate supervisors fairly friendly and easy-going, although both the shops and the yards had their full share of authoritarian foremen.

Ten separate metal trades craft unions controlled access to all jobs within their clearly defined areas of jurisdiction. A member in good standing was virtually assured of full-time work year-round. Out-of-work members would register with their respective halls and would be called upon in order as new jobs became available. Showing up at a job site with a dispatch slip from your union practically guaranteed you the job. In the not-so-distant past, a time many of the current workers can remember, a phone call to the union hall following a layoff at one job could often land you a new job the following day. Many workers, wanting a break of a week or two, a breather during which they could do some fishing, catch up on home repairs, or just kick back and recover from the hard physical labor, while collecting a week or two of unemployment insurance, would avoid reporting immediately to the union's out-of-work list because they would be technically and legally ineligible for unemployment benefits if they were dispatched to another job and turned it down.

Most important, craft production implies at least the semblance of a community. Because "construction is always based upon a unique design (or the unique adaptation to local circumstances of a standard design), the organization of the work has to be defined each time *de novo;* with their technical knowledge, the workers are integral to the drawing up of the plan, just as they are essential for solving the inevitable problems that arise in its execution."[16] Piore and Sabel assert that this makes collaboration among management, workers, and the union a necessity, and in the flush days, under the discipline of a relatively tight labor market, this was true to a limited extent. Because of our vital role in the production process, workers in the Bay Area metal trades industry achieved a significant influence over the detailed daily decisions concerning the labor process. Cooperation and collaboration were limited to labor process decisions and always took place within a clearly defined hierarchical order. Management generally retained its prerogatives pertaining to shop floor production decisions, not always with favorable results for the company.

Rights and Obligations

While control over production was ceded to management, they in turn were contractually obligated to maintain certain standards in their workplaces and to accord their workers a certain degree of respect and care. Until the early 1990s management made no attempts to monitor or regulate the bodies or the private lives of their employees. Indeed, the contract even specifically outlawed any "Doctor's physical examination [or] age limit, except as required by law," as a condition of employment.[17] Article 16 of the contract required the employer to "exert every reasonable effort to provide and maintain safe working conditions," while complying with all government laws and regulations. Specifically spelled out were obligations on maintaining safe "staging, walks, ladders, gangplanks and safety appliances," as well as guards for eye protection around welding operations and the provision of "prompt ambulance service and first aid" for injured employees on all shifts. Several subsections of Article 16 were devoted to requirements regarding the proper procedures for ensuring the ventilation of "noxious or poisonous gases" from properly lit confined spaces, for frequent checks on people working in confined spaces, and for blood and urine tests, if required by the Occupational Safety and Health Administration (OSHA), to monitor for potentially dangerous substances. Finally the provision of "special protective devices and equipment," supplied at the employer's expense, where needed, was mandated.[18]

Respect for our creature comforts was also contractually required. Management was charged to provide clean, "properly heated and ventilated" toilets and washrooms, lunch areas "separate from toilet facilities," drinking water, and secure personal lockers.[19] Employers were required to pay double time for "dirty work," which was broadly defined, and to provide adequate time and facilities to clean and change oil- or water-soaked clothes.[20] When compliance was not forthcoming, grievances were often filed, and occasionally we took direct action. When we failed to receive "dirty pay" while cutting ten thousand feet of pipe out of the bilges of the aircraft carrier *Coral Sea*, several workers brought in and distributed copies of the relevant part of the contract, and after lunch hundreds of us refused to return to the job.[21]

While not all contractual obligations were honored in practice, most of them were. This was especially true all through the mid-1970s and early 1980s, when hundreds of Bay Area rank-and-file workers took an active role in their union affairs, insisting that their shop stewards demand that the bosses comply with their responsibilities and meet their contractual obligations.

FLEXIBLE DISCIPLINE

Rather than becoming the foundation for the development of an industrial yeoman democracy for the production regime of the twenty-first century, the craft production regime of flexible hegemony, even with the active participation of hundreds of rank-and-file workers, has been transformed under the pressure of macro global economic and political forces into a new and far more oppressive production regime of "flexible discipline." The class compromise which conferred upon both workers and managers mutual rights and obligations, which granted to unions influence over job definition and distribution, and which honored and respected the "knowledgeable" craft work embedded in the body and mind of the journeyman has been abrogated.[22] Management, in the face of competitive pressures, especially from several new small local nonunion yards, which bid competitively on all available work, and unable to rationalize and modernize the labor process, has opted for an authoritarian strategy.

While the production regime of flexible hegemony endured for many decades, the present regime of flexible discipline represents an unstable transitional stage. It is characterized by conflict between an aggressive employer strategy seeking to impose its will against a relatively enfeebled, mostly ineffective, and disorganized worker resistance—but a resistance nevertheless. In many shops and shipyards the workers still retain their unions, the ability to negotiate contracts, and a measure of citizen rights on the job, gained from previous struggles. If the unions can reorganize their strength, they may be able to achieve a more favorable form of class compromise than is the case today. Should the employers prevail, they may well be able to break the unions completely and establish a truly despotic production regime.

The present transitional regime of flexible discipline has three major characteristics: 1) a confrontational relationship between an aggressive management and ten separate and weak craft unions, with virtually no rank-and-file participation, resulting in either the elimination of the unions entirely or an imposed contract requiring increasingly oppressive conditions; 2) the replacement of the traditional craft labor system with a multilevel stratification system, which not only introduces craft-less "utility workers," but stratifies the category of journeyman via management-dominated evaluation schemes measuring both skill and *attitude;* and 3) the imposition of a regime of discipline that subjects workers to mandatory drug tests, thus regulating workers' bodies and activities both on and off the job, and, through speed-up, cost-cutting, and the elimination of many reciprocal rights and obligations, results in deteriorating safety and sanitary conditions for workers who cannot be deskilled.

Aggressive Management, Weak Unions

Capital flight and its attendant job losses have decimated the workers' organizations, the once powerful metal trades unions. By the spring of 1997, the last remaining shop/shipyard local of the Boilermakers Union, my local, #6, had fewer than nine hundred workers on its rolls, a drop of more than 90 percent since the late 1970s. Even with this reduced number, during many months of the year 30 to 40 percent of the members will be out of work.[23] As the union's power and membership have diminished, so too has any semblance of rank-and-file participation in the local's affairs. In the mid-1980s all significant local, rank-and-file initiatives were rebuffed as unconstitutional by the union's international leadership headquartered in Kansas City, which, because of the constant turmoil, placed the local in receivership. Although local leadership was eventually restored, the mild insurgency had been quelled. In recent years Boilermakers Local #6 has been unable to get a quorum for its regular monthly meetings, even when elections of officers or contract negotiations are the business of the day.[24]

Taking advantage of the weakened state of the unions, which are no longer able to provide steady work, and the increasing gulf between the average worker and even the lowest officers of the union (the shop stewards, who are increasingly reluctant to fight for workers' rights on the shop floor) the management of San Francisco Drydock was able to force through a contract in 1996 which the rank-and-file clearly recognized as against our interests. Despite the endorsement of the Metal Trades Council and the leadership of all participating unions, the workers originally rejected the proposed contract by 85 percent. On the same day that the election results were announced, the Boilermakers shop steward, along with management, called a meeting to begin implementing the provisions of the very contract that we had just rejected. About a month later, with at least the tacit consent of the various local union officers, management rammed through the identical contract by the slimmest of margins, while more than 90 percent of us were on lay-off.[25]

The terms of this new four-year contract, "ratified" in July 1996 between the management of the last large Bay Area unionized shipyard and the unions of the Metal Trades Council, formalize the transformation of power relations in the yard.[26] Although presented as an "industry recovery labor agreement" designed to ensure the survival of "profitable union shipyards," paying "family wages and benefits," and couched in the language of cooperation and mutuality, the contract is a manifestation of management's strategic decision to respond to the global challenge by substituting discipline for class compromise.[27] In traditional terms the agreement is not even a binding contract. Article 2.3 states, "The Parties Agree to amend the content of the contract by mutual agreement when bidding against non-union shipyards."[28] Since there are virtually no other union shipyards in the area, the contract is subject to renegotiation at any time.

The Destruction of the Craft Labor System

The traditional craft labor system with its two levels of skill, journeyman and apprentice, has been obliterated and replaced with a scheme that stratifies and divides workers along several lines. Most egregious, and breaking with more than one hundred years of tradition, the contract provides for an entirely new tier of nonapprenticed labor, the non-craft-specific "utility worker," whose starting wages closely approach those now being paid ship-yard workers in South Korea.[29] Management is now entitled to employ up to 30 percent of the workforce at below journeyman scale. Although "utility worker" is a new classification, the contract provides no specifics on, or lim-itations to, their role in production. These workers, remunerated at slightly more than one-half the journeyman rate, are being used as the spearhead of a more generalized trend toward "cross-crafting," which journeymen are expected to comply with as well. As the contract puts it, "Jurisdiction and past practices shall be relaxed to allow for all skills and abilities of all employees to be utilized to perform the available work safely in the most efficient manner."[30] In addition, management is allowed to designate up to 10 percent of the workforce as "key employees," who "may be retained and recalled out of seniority."[31]

While the traditional partition between journeymen and apprentices is formally preserved, the mechanic's classification has been divided into four separate levels with different rates of pay and status for each. Although the majority of the men will be retained as mechanics, others will be demoted and a minority will be rewarded with higher wages and more secure employ-ment. The methods used to reconfigure the traditionally unitary journey-man classification have left no doubt in the minds of the majority of work-ers that their employers regard them with contempt. Mechanics' status, despite union certification, years of experience in the trade, and even seniority rights, is no longer taken for granted, but is subject to continuous reexamination. Journeymen with up to forty years of experience are now subject to annual reviews by management-dominated craft-evaluation boards. Invoking the discourse of both scientific management and "human relations," the company asserts that the evaluation program's purpose is a cooperative labor-management "system," which benefits both "the organi-zation" and "the employee" by acknowledging accomplishments, improving communication, raising productivity, and improving morale.[32]

The evaluation process itself is framed in scientific terms, and purports to normalize the workers not only according to our craft skills, but also to the quality and quantity of our work, our attendance and dependability, our compliance with safety regulations, and our cooperation and teamwork. Each worker is rated on a standard ten-point system (from unsatisfactory to exceptional) for our ability in each component of our craft, as well as our attitude. Bonus points are given to those workers whose "versatility" allows them to qualify as a journeyman in more than one craft. A worker must obtain an overall rating of at least 5.0 in order to retain his journeyman's status and rate of pay. Those workers, previously classified as mechanics, who fail to achieve that minimum score, are "grandfathered" in as journey-men and have their wages frozen at the level of the last contract. In some crafts, up to 30 percent of the workers may be designated above journey-man level, as "craftsman," and 5 percent as "master craftsman," the highest rating. Over the course of the four-year contract, the wage gap between the ordinary mechanic and the new higher classifications grows each year, while those "grandfathered" in will fall even further behind.[33]

Most rank-and-file workers see the evaluation process as just one more way to devalue them. They see the evaluation boards as rigged in manage-ment's favor, consisting, as they do, of two supervisors (the general foreman and a leadman in their craft) and one "peer" (considered by most to be a toady). The evaluation process began immediately after the ratification of the contract, but to my knowledge members of the boards never went out to the ships and actually observed the men at work. A worker's evaluation was a reflection of his foreman's opinion of his skill, ability, and attitude. The boards served merely as rubber stamps, a means of conferring a degree of legitimacy on a management decision. They invariably ratified the supervi-sor's judgment and assigned it a "scientific" designation: a series of numbers on an elaborate, official looking computer-generated form, calculated to intimidate and bamboozle shipyard workers unaccustomed to having their skills and attitudes translated into numerical values.

Many of the evaluations had little to do with the worker's actual skill and ability. I use myself as an example. Although I have been a journeyman welder for more than twenty-five years, for the last four years I have hired in as a journeyman shipfitter, and was evaluated in that craft. Five percent of the shipfitter's skill assessment is based upon his ability to burn and tack (make small welds), essentially the tasks of a combination welder. My score in that category was 5.0, the minimum needed to be accorded journeyman status. But I also received 5.0 for all sixteen categories, for my skill, ability, and attitude. Clearly no real assessment was made of my work. Each worker was given his evaluation in a private meeting with the supervising foreman of his department. Part of management's plan was to break down what small amount of solidarity remained among journeymen and to fragment and individualize each worker's industrial relations. When a large number of workers refused to allow the union shop steward to be present at those meetings, it appeared the strategy was working.

But the process has also produced countertendencies. Even before the evaluations were completed, the men resented this extraordinary break with tradition and began slowing down on the job. After being evaluated, men who felt they deserved higher ratings, openly began to say, "If I'm only a 5.6, then I will work like a 5.6." And they did. Although it has existed under the surface for a very long time, social pressures to "bear a manly attitude" both toward the boss and toward each other reemerged with the imposition of the new contract.[34] I myself was brought to heel under this discipline. After lunch one day, when I had not had a very productive morning and was concerned that I would not finish my task for the day, I began walking, not quickly, but certainly faster than the regular and socially sanctioned "shipyard shuffle," back to the job. Before I got a few feet ahead of my mates, a chorus of boos and criticisms rang out: "Hey Professor, trying to get on steady?" "Hey 'Kissy-Kissy,' what's the rush?" To maintain my status, I immediately dropped back into step with the others and, upon reaching the drydock, went out of my way to strike up two or three brief conversations with fellow workers. I also made an unnecessary stop at the tool room for a pair of earplugs even though I had several pairs in my pocket. I was thus the last man to get back on the ship that afternoon and I was able to make a show of returning later than several of my friends who were already on the job.

Workers even mounted a degree of organized resistance, exercising their still-existing industrial citizen rights (which do not exist in the nonunion yards) and forcing the union and management to abide by the contract. At least 10 percent of the workers appealed their evaluations. Power on the appeals board was more evenly distributed, as management got only one seat, with a local union representative and a peer from another craft holding the other two. Even when appeals were won, however, and several were, retroactive pay was not granted.

Despite token resistance, management's transparent goals in developing the new labor scheme have mostly been achieved. They have emulated the strategy of the nonunion yards by securing a core group of highly skilled and reliable workers in all crafts, including many with cross-craft skills, are compensating them above journeyman scale, and are allowing them to supervise craft-less, low wage utility workers, thus reducing the required number of mechanics, and thereby bringing down overall labor costs. Previously employed, highly skilled journeymen, along with additional utility workers, now form a peripheral reserve army of labor to be employed intermittently on large jobs.

Regulating Bodies and Activities

But whether in the core or on the periphery of the workforce, all workers when they hire in are required to submit to a demeaning mandatory drug test. The stop at the medical office for the test is an ironic twist because, given the erratic nature of employment, at least three-quarters of the workers lack medical coverage, having failed to get the necessary hours in the appropriate quarter to qualify under an ever more restrictive health plan. The company does however have the resources for piss tests, at least for nonmanagement personnel. Three years ago management insisted on a contract requiring yearly drug tests for all unionized workers. The new contract goes much further, requiring "pre-hire, for cause and unannounced/random" tests. It is not unusual for new hires, especially the low-wage utility workers, to disappear after about a week on the job, never to be seen again. Workers with seniority who test positive are allowed to sign a "last chance agreement" and are enrolled in a drug rehabilitation program; new hires are terminated on the spot the minute their "dirty" test comes back from the lab.[35]

The surveillance of our bodies is conducted with great scientific rigor, resulting in enhanced control at the workplace through the effective monitoring of our private, off-site activities. The justifying discourse is safety. The company asserts that its commitment to a "safe, healthy and productive work place" makes drug-testing imperative. Substance abuse by any worker endangers everyone, including the public and the company.[36] Even the unions ignore much greater threats to our safety, the unsafe conditions that management fosters by its business practices. Virtually every job is a rush job, and the company declines to spend the necessary money or time to prevent hazards or engineer solutions to ones that exist. Thus, despite a strict drug policy for the last three years (recently strengthened again), the accident rate on some of the most recent jobs has been alarming. In the winter of 1996, a ship in the yard spilled a large quantity of oil into the bay. Rumors began to circulate among the workers that the costs would put the yard out of business. The General Manager told all the yard workers that not only was the company insured in case they were found liable, but that he would prove "us" innocent of any blame. Either way he said, the spill posed no economic threat to the company. The real threat, he said, was the unacceptably high accident rate, which could drive the company out of business. The onus was immediately put back on the men. Either we must learn how to work more safely or our jobs would be in jeopardy. Conditions were so bad that somebody blew the whistle, and the emasculated safety-regulation agency, OSHA, wrote the company a letter alleging "inadequate ventilation and lighting" in "enclosed and confined spaces," as well as "fire protection systems on the piers and drydock" with "frozen valves and broken gauges."[37] Dozens of equally serious hazards, including inadequate staging, man-lifts with broken controls, obsolete air-powered and electric hand tools—often lacking safety guards—and broken ladders, were never mentioned. Although the company denied the existence of any hazards or violations, every worker in the yard knows that the place is loaded with accidents waiting to happen, and the most conscientious exercise extreme caution to make sure, not always successfully, that they do not happen to them.[38]

Management's response is to run weekly safety meetings which constantly emphasize individual responsibility in a "naturally" hazardous industry. The men sit around these mandatory meetings paying little attention, socializing with friends, drinking coffee, or just spacing out, glad for a break before the start of the day's work. Virtually all see the meetings as useless, still another way for the company to cover its ass, while insisting that we do the impossible: finish speeded-up jobs with quality workmanship under hazardous conditions without getting hurt.

Elementary standards of sanitary decency previously provided are now denied. The locker rooms are filthy, their roofs leak, and their heaters do not work. Half of the large industrial communal sinks in the washrooms are broken, and there are no more than two or three functioning showers in the whole plant. Many of the toilets do not even have doors, making privacy, to say nothing of dignity, difficult to maintain. Many workers, myself included, train themselves to avoid, if at all possible, the need to use these facilities. On graveyard shift, especially on weekends, there is a good chance that toilet paper, soap, and paper towels will all run out, as management tries to save the money it costs to bring in a maintenance worker on over-time. There is no cafeteria or food service, only a "roach coach," which arrives in the morning and at lunch (at least on day shift), a few soda and snack machines, and a smattering of tables, the most concentrated group in front of the main tool room, outdoors and exposed to the elements.

The mutual rights and obligations of an earlier era are all but gone, mostly replaced by greater demands and more restrictions on the workers. The latest contract makes almost no demands upon management concerning safety, stating only that "Employees and Management share responsibility for the prevention of injuries and illnesses," although the latter are called upon to "eliminate hazardous conditions and practices." Compensation for "dirty work" has all but been eliminated, as it is restricted to work considered "exceptionally dirty" by the company. The theme of this contract is greater control over our bodies—through disciplinary practices and self-discipline. Several paragraphs oblige us to correct the productivity problems arising from the "historical employee abuse of time" at shift changes and lunch breaks, insisting that we remain on the job from whistle to whistle. Despite our retention of skill and ability, management increasingly treats us as degraded labor.

The extraordinary differences between the authoritarian production regime of today and the regime of flexible hegemony that existed only a decade or so ago can only be fully explained if we look far beyond the local worksite.

INTERNATIONAL COMPETITION—THE END OF THE COLD WAR

Global forces, that is macro-economic and political developments of national and international significance, have always had a profound influence upon the fortunes of the Bay Area metal trades industry and its workers.

The local iron industry got its start, in the middle of the nineteenth century, supplying tools and machinery, first for the California Gold Rush and subsequently for the fabulously rich, deep underground mining of silver in

Nevada's Comstock Lode. The Union Iron Works (now called San Francisco Drydock) was transformed from a foundry and machine shop into one of the world's most modern shipyards in 1883, expressly to construct warships for the Navy as United States Imperialism expanded into the Pacific. By the beginning of the 1890s, San Francisco shipyards were doing $3.5 million worth of work a year as they built the heavy cruisers and battleships that comprised Commodore Dewey's fleet, the naval force that destroyed the Spanish Armada in Manila Bay on May 1, 1898.[39] During both world wars, but especially the second, San Francisco became the hub of one of the premier shipbuilding areas of the world. At its peak, during the Second World War, shipyards from Marin County to Richmond in Contra Costa County employed upward of 250,000 workers. Although there was an extraordinary drop-off after the war, with shipbuilding—except for an occasional barge—phased out, the ship repair and heavy steel fabrication industries continued to flourish. During all of these boom periods, relatively high wages and decent working conditions prevailed, although they were achieved only through struggle by workers organized in strong trade unions.

In the last two decades, however, a once-vibrant Bay Area metal trades industry has virtually been destroyed by international competition and the end of the Cold War. In the late 1970s, the development of productive capacity in other parts of the world began to generate competition in many of the market areas traditionally dominated by Bay Area fabricated steel products. Since the end of World War II Bay Area shops had been major suppliers of steel pipe and structural weldments for the Middle East, Asia, and even Europe. However, the development of a lower-wage, modern, and more productive Japanese steel industry, and the emergence of newly industrializing countries, led by South Korea, as well as revitalization in Europe, convinced the owners of West Coast fabricating plants that, rather than competing, their capital could be invested more profitably in other enterprises. American Bridge, the fabricating division of United States Steel, located in South San Francisco, was the first big plant to close. Although hundreds of workers agreed to significant concessions—both a pay freeze and a change in working conditions designed to boost production—the company shut its doors for good in 1983, permanently laying off about five hundred workers.[40] In the next decade virtually every fabricating shop in the area shut down or scaled back appreciably. Today fewer than four hundred workers are covered by the union's shop contracts.

With the official end of the Cold War, the Navy, after more than one hundred years of economically and politically nurturing and sustaining the ship construction capabilities of the Bay Area, has withdrawn the fleet and with it the maintenance and repair contracts that sustained so many businesses and provided the major source of income for thousands of metal trades craftsmen and their families. Well into the mid-1980s, the ship repair business thrived on virtually guaranteed profits from more than $150 million a year in "cost-plus" maintenance contracts from the United States Navy on scores of ships, including two nuclear aircraft carriers home-ported in the Bay Area.[41]

While the Navy was by far the largest customer for the shipyards, significant additional commercial business came from local shipping lines, cruise ships, container ships, and tankers calling at local ports. By the late 1980s much of the Navy work had been transferred to other areas, and the biggest multinational corporations, first Bethlehem Steel and then Todd shipyards, closed down their local operations, resulting in huge job losses. Virtually all of the commercial ship repair business went to lower-wage areas of the Pacific Rim (Japan, South Korea, Taiwan, and Singapore).[42] Even Navy repair work, which requires workers to be citizens when performed in United States yards, was partially transferred during the Reagan years to Japanese yards.[43] Mare Island Naval Shipyard, the oldest Navy facility on the West Coast, was closed in 1995. The Alameda Naval Air Station, homeport to several aircraft carriers and numerous support vessels, was closed in 1997, as the Navy scaled back its surface fleet from more than 600 ships during the Reagan years to 340, and in the process closed selected bases.[44] By the end of 1997, the last of the Bay Area Navy contracts had been completed.

Powerless to control either the increased international competition or the withdrawal of lucrative Navy contracts, and unable to reorganize the labor process, management's principal strategy is to redistribute skills by resurrecting the nineteenth-century craftsman-helper labor system. The loss of jobs has left a large and highly skilled industrial reserve army of labor and severely weakened the influence of the unions over how workers are classified. Presented with a plentiful supply of skilled craftsmen stripped of most union protections, management has abandoned compromise and pursues short-term, cost-cutting strategies of union busting, wage freezes, benefit reductions, and, especially, labor force reconfigurations that reward a select few but cheapen and debase the majority of the workers they still employ. The workforce has been stratified into a highly skilled core group, which continues to work with the tools, performing the difficult and precise tasks inherent in the ship repair labor process, assisted by "craft-less" utility workers, "helpers," who work alongside them under their immediate supervision. Management believes that up to 30 percent of the work previously done exclusively by mechanics can be performed by utility workers at one-half the wages. Almost all the new nonunion shipyards, as well as the biggest of the union yards, are organized around this principle—paying key craftsmen over scale (even over union scale) in return for their acting simultaneously as both workers and low-level supervisors. More often than not, the "helpers" are former journeymen whom management is now able to employ at bargain rates. Many men recently employed as mechanics, but not selected for the core group, and facing permanent unemployment, accept positions as utility workers in a desperate effort to secure steady work.

This new labor force configuration and its supervisory scheme tends to produce resentment and division among workers previously united in the single classification of journeymen. Management further enhances its ability to maintain discipline by heightening the uncertainty and insecurity that all workers experience. Determining who will be allowed into the core and how long they will remain there is the work of a capricious and elaborate company-controlled system that regulates individual workers through evaluations of skill and *attitude* and through disciplinary practices. Individualized evaluations, drug tests, company-determined paths of advancement, and favoritism ("key employee" designation, for example), combined with the constant threat of possible demotion and layoff, breed considerable competition and conflict among workers seeking the coveted jobs, while spurring at least a core of workers to greater effort and loyalty to the company, especially when their unions fail to offer protection or promote solidarity. This strategy also breeds fear, contempt, and sometimes resistance, especially among peripheral workers, who remain essential for completion of the big jobs. These workers find collective action difficult to achieve, however, because they are dispersed and isolated, get little support from their unions, and when they finally do get hired are mostly concerned with getting as much work as possible before their inevitable next layoff.

In a recent book, David Gordon analyzes United States corporate managerial strategy and its effects on workers, in the face of increasing global competition. He discusses both the "high road" attempts to "build economic growth and prosperity through cooperation and strong worker rewards" and the dominant model, the "low road," which applies the "stick strategy," characterized by falling or stagnant real wages, increased "conflict and insecurity," and a system of discipline and control relying upon "harsh worker punishment."[45] Clearly, San Francisco Drydock has chosen the low road. Whether it will make the company competitive and profitable is dubious.

GLOBAL IMPASSE, LABOR IN FRAGMENTS

Bay Area metal trades workers have always been affected by forces beyond our control, buoyed and buffeted by precious metal bonanzas, wars, depressions, and the economic cycles of industrial capitalism. But this time is different! For the last two decades we have been suffering the local effects of a profound reconfiguration of global economic and political forces, resulting in the transformation of the United States from an industrial to a postindustrial society. This transition has already expelled the vast majority of us from our crafts and forces those of us who remain in the trades to labor under deteriorating and degraded circumstances. In response to either an absence of work or intermittent employment under increasingly disciplinary conditions, almost all of us are seeking alternative ways to earn a living, before we are crushed. Most hold in contempt the low-wage service sector jobs that we fear we might be forced to accept, but the emerging postindustrial world offers us few other opportunities.

The end of each big job always results in a kind of diaspora as each worker is left to fend for himself. By early January 1997, the last of hundreds of boilermakers, machinists, pipefitters, and others who came together, for a period of up to three months to repair the S.S. *Chesapeake*, the S.S. *Cape Mohican*, the S.S. *Green Valley*, and several other ships, were laid off. A series of small jobs provided periodic work for most, but not all, workers with seniority in many trades during the rest of the year. In the following six months, carpenters, painters, and pipefitters obtained some work, as ships requiring painting below the water line came in for drydock work. But no significant steel job was undertaken in the following year.

Some of those who have been dispersed are living on unemployment benefits, on the wages of their spouses, or by working on some union job in outside construction, known as the "field" (a very small minority). Others find employment in nonunion shops, in shipyards or construction jobs, or operate in the underground economy, somehow managing to get by by hook or by crook. How many will be called back when, and if, new work arrives is unknown. Some of those recalled will never return. The end of virtually every job produces some attrition, even among the most skilled in their prime wage-earning years, workers who finally give up their trade and seek other work to feed their families.

Kevin, whom I described at the beginning of this chapter, has already lost everything: his job, his home, his family, his dignity, his self-respect, and his status in the community. He has become a beggar. Those who pass him every day—a few stop to chat, some to give the brother coffee, food, and/or a smoke—are seeking ways to cope as their employment world disintegrates too. Many have plans, realistic and not, for getting out before they are inevitably thrown out permanently. Steve, a foreman in the steel department, who got hired on as low-level management at the Drydock when the yard he was working in closed down a year or so ago, is in the process of opening a limousine business. He has bought the car and applied for all the licenses, and although he has aspirations to own several cars, and employ men to drive them, he knows that in the beginning *he* will be the driver. Because he is so well integrated into the lower management old-boy network, he has more room to maneuver than most. As long as the yard remains open, his knowledge, connections, and skills virtually assure him employment (he could certainly hire in as a journeyman shipfitter). In his early forties, with young children, he sees the risks, work, and uncertainty of this small business venture as far more promising than reliance on the yard alone to provide his family with a livelihood.

The vast majority of the men, those without seniority who work only when a big job comes in, are in an even more precarious situation. Harry, an experienced and capable shipfitter, and the organizer of the most successful and efficiently run sports pools, has grown weary, like so many, of the feast and famine nature of the work in the yards. He was quite sick with a bad cold or the flu as we worked the graveyard shift out on the open decks in the heavy winds and rain last winter, fabricating and installing lifeboat foundations. He spoke bitterly and passionately about not having medical coverage, although he works every job the union, of which he is a trustee, dispatches him to. Harry has left the trade, taken his early retirement pension, and is driving a cab for a living. George, a journeyman welder for more than twenty years, and a foreman at another yard during a time not so long ago when work was much more plentiful, now makes ends meet by managing the apartment building he lives in, taking every shipyard job the union dispatches him to, doing nonunion jobs if necessary, and collecting unemployment benefits. Last year, for the first time, his unemployment insurance ran out before a new ship came in. After the last job, he too spoke repeatedly of quitting, and is actively pursuing a job at a new casino being opened on the Peninsula. Bob and Pete, two brothers, both excellent welders, recently gave up their shipyard seniority and took jobs with a nonunion construction firm. Despite a long commute and an uncertain future, they felt the jobs would be safer and would provide steady work for at least a year or two. More importantly, during the first month on the job they felt that their skills were recognized and honored and their persons respected. They eventually quit after repeatedly being pressured to work mandatory overtime and are now once again seeking work in the shipyards.

Even these accomplished and enterprising workers realize they do not have the skills, either technical or social, to function in the computerized occupational world that has recently emerged, the world where the good jobs of the future will be located. At best, they float between degraded metal trades craft work and the world of "in-person services." I am virtually unique among them because I have the ability to escape that dilemma. Unlike them, I can *choose* either to fit steel or to write about it. Unlike them, I can move into the world of "symbolic analysts," where my skills at utilizing concepts, computers, words, and ideas can potentially earn me greater material rewards and certainly more recognition, honor, and higher status than the most proficient craftsmen will ever get in the fabrication shops or the shipyards. Unlike the overwhelming majority of them, I can face the future with some security. The tragedy of this situation is especially poignant because these very workers and their predecessors have built the infrastructure that makes the technological marvels of the twenty-first century possible. They have laid the groundwork for a new world in which they no longer have a place.

NOTES

I could not have written this essay without the unstinting aid of two very special people, Lincoln Bergman and Elisabeth Garst. My best friend Linc, a superb editor and sensitive scholar, read and constructively criticized every version of the paper, as well as every e-mail comment and critique I received. He steadfastly encouraged me to tell this story as I lived it and as I was coming to understand it. Lizzie's copy-editing somehow managed to bring my writing into some proximity to the "King's English," and she was the source of numerous incisive comments and beneficial critiques. A generous two-semester research grant from the Institute of Industrial Relations, University of California, Berkeley, was indispensable and greatly appreciated. An earlier version of this paper won the 1997 Braverman Award from the Labor Studies Division of the Society for the Study of Social Problems.

1. Harry Braverman, *Labor and Monopoly Capital: The Degradation of Work in the Twentieth Century,* p. 444. My emphasis.

2. The description given by Keith McClelland and Alastair Reid, regarding the fundamental consistency in skill requirements during the transition from wood to iron shipbuilding more than one hundred years ago, accords almost perfectly with my observations of conditions during the last twenty-five years in the ship repair and steel fabrication trades in the Bay Area. According to these authors, "What is striking is the extent to which the industry *remained* based upon hard physical labour and the skills, judgement and experience of workers and, concomitantly, *tools rather than machines—i.e., equipment that was the instrument of labour rather than vice versa.*" See Keith McClelland and Alastair Reid, "Wood, Iron and Steel: Technology, Labour and Trade Union Organisation in the Shipbuilding Industry, 1840–1914," p. 163. My emphasis.

3. Michael J. Piore and Charles F. Sabel, *The Second Industrial Divide: Possibilities for Prosperity,* pp. 115–20, 303–7, and 321.

4. Michael Burawoy, *The Politics of Production: Factory Regimes under Capitalism and Socialism,* p. 87.

5. Ibid. Emphasis in original.

6. "If the macro-regulatory requirements of mass production are relatively well-defined, those of flexible specialization remain the *least developed aspect* of the model." Paul Hirst and Jonathan Zeitlin, "Flexible Specialization versus Post-Fordism: Theory, Evidence and Policy Implications," pp. 4–5.

7. Of all the writers concerned with the relationship between skill and craft, D. J. Lee makes the strongest case for the importance of the labor market as "a source of deskilling in its own right." He treats the labor market as a "*series* of social filters intervening between productive skill and class structure." He concentrates on three "shifts" or "effects": industry shifts, cyclical shifts, and occupational shifts. His treatment of cyclical shifts, or those caused by recessions, are most relevant to the Bay Area metal trades workers. Lee argues that cyclical unemployment is a form of deskilling for three reasons. First, it is likely to be permanent, especially if workers

are in the latter stages in their life cycles. Second, even with recovery "many *individual* workers" will experience "substantial dislocations" because of "organizational, financial and geographical shifts in the locus of employment." Finally, "recession (and not labour process deskilling) provides the most direct and tangible form in which the initially relatively privileged groups, such as skilled workers, experience proletarianization. In short, cyclical deskilling is likely to be highly relevant for understanding how key groups of workers *experience* the unfolding of class relationships in a society." If we substitute Lee's concept of "absolute industry shifts," for "cyclical shifts," we have a very accurate description and analysis of what has happened to Bay Area metal trades workers over the last quarter of a century. D. J. Lee, "Skill, Craft and Class: A Theoretical Critique and a Critical Case," pp. 60–61, 66.

8. Braverman, p. 5.

9. Ibid., p. 119. Emphasis in original.

10. Ibid., p. 121.

11. Ibid., p. 119.

12. In some limited-safety areas, workers today are better off than they were twenty-five years ago. Then it was hard to find a boilermaker who had been in the trade for any time at all who could still hear. I was several years in the trade before a "progressive" monopoly corporation, United States Steel, began insisting on the use of ear protection in its fabrication shops. First, of course, we were given hearing tests, so that we could not sue for previous damage. The greatest safety improvements have been in the availability and quality of personal respiratory devices, although engineered methods of ventilation may have deteriorated during the same period.

13. My information comes from personal discussions with Boilermakers Union Business Agents and with Arthur E. Johnson, Director, Labor Relations, California Metal Trades Association, winter 1996 through spring 1997, and from "Master Agreement between The Plate and Tank Division, California Metal Trades Association and International Brotherhood of Boilermakers, Iron Shipbuilders, Blacksmiths, Forgers and Helpers of America, AFL-CIO. July 1, 1974–June 30, 1977."

14. Joseph A. Blum, "The African-American Struggle for Equality In the World War II West Coast Shipyards."

15. The concept of the internal state at the workplace is most fully developed by Burawoy. "The term 'internal state' refers to the set of institutions that organize, transform, or repress struggles over relations in production at the level of the enterprise." Its form changes as capitalism grows and matures from despotism under competitive capitalism to hegemony under monopoly conditions. "With the rise of the large corporation and trade unionism, the institutions of the internal state have become disentangled from the managerial direction of the labor process and embodied in grievance procedures and collective bargaining. The emerging internal state protects the managerial prerogative to fashion and direct the labor process by imposing constraints on managerial discretion and by endowing workers with rights as well as obligations." *Manufacturing Consent*, p. 110, and see especially chapter 7.

16. Piore and Sabel, p. 117.

17. "1983–1984–1985 Pacific Coast MASTER AGREEMENT: The Pacific Coast Shipbuilding and Ship Repair Firms and the Metal Trades Department of the A.F.L.-

C.I.O., the Pacific Coast Metal Trades District Council, the Local Metal Trades Council, the International Unions Signatory Thereto," ratified October 13, 1983, Article 16.10 ("Physical Examination"), p. 7. This contract is hereafter referred to as "1983 Contract."

18. Ibid., Article 16, Subsections 1–7, 11–12, pp. 6–7.

19. Ibid., Article 16, Subsection 8, pp. 6–7.

20. Ibid., Article 12, p. 5.; Article 16, Subsection 6 (b), p. 6. The "Dirty Work" provision called for double-time pay not only when working in "tanks, bilges, sumps, or under floor plates where oil or water has accumulated, or in boiler, uptakes or stacks," or "when cleaning or working in septic or holding tanks containing human waster [sic] where entry is required," but also "in areas in the machinery spaces where an unusually dirty conditions [sic] exists."

21. While double-time pay was not given by management, a small raise was granted to everyone working in the bilges.

22. Shoshana Zuboff's description of "knowledgeable" work, as work based upon "knowledge that accrues to the sentient body in the course of its activity, knowledge inscribed in the laboring body . . . ," "knowledge filled with intimate detail of materials and ambience," knowledge derived from "action and displayed itself in action, knowledge that meant knowing how to do, to make, to *act-on*," most accurately captures the nature of skilled ship-repair work. *In The Age of the Smart Machine: The Future of Work and Power,* pp. 40–41. Emphasis in original.

23. As of July 15, 1997, Boilermakers Local #6 had 884 members, with about 200 on the out-of-work list. By July 1, 1999, membership had fallen below 750. Figures from earlier times and other union information was obtained in ongoing conversations with the Business Agent and Assistant Business Agent of Local #6. The most recent figures are based upon my personal knowledge as Dispatcher and Recording Secretary of Local #6.

24. A meeting in July 1997, to nominate officers for the local, failed to produce a quorum. According to the then Local Business Agent, the local has failed to obtain quorums since 1994. In mid-1998 this trend was at least partially reversed. A more democratically oriented Business Manager has held regular meetings with about 3 percent of the members attending. He has revived rank-and-file meetings with various shops and shipyards when contract negotiations begin, and he has appointed shop stewards more responsive to the average worker.

25. The first vote, in which the contract was overwhelmingly defeated, was a mail ballot. The second vote took place at the shipyard under the watchful eyes of foremen and other members of the management team. It was ratified by a vote of 111 to 106, with one blank ballot (Official Notification by Pacific Coast Metal Trades District Council, Richard E. Harden, Executive Secretary-Treasurer, July 31, 1996).

26. If the unions are able to get any contracts these days, they are almost invariably with a single firm. Long gone are the coastwide agreements that guaranteed identical wages and conditions all along the Pacific Coast north of Los Angeles, thus making it impossible for employers to play one area against another in order to get limited work.

27. "General Presidents' Pacific Coast Master Shipyard Industry Recovery Labor Agreement" (Negotiated Between San Francisco Drydock, Inc., and The Metal Trades Department of the AFL-CIO, The Pacific Coast Metal Trades District Council. The Bay Cities Metal Trades Council and The International Unions Signatory

Thereto, Effective July 30, 1996 through June 30, 2000), p. 2. Hereinafter known as "Contract."

28. Ibid., Article 2.3, p. 3.

29. Starting wages for utility workers for all four years (1997–2000) of the contract are $9.00 per hour. They can rise as high as $13.00 per hour the first year, $13.25 in the second and third years, and $13.50 in the final year, but no criteria or protocol are specified as to when or if a worker is entitled to a raise. In 1993, the latest year for which statistics are available, the average hourly labor cost for shipyard labor in Korea was $8.32 per hour. The Korean figures include fringes; the local figures do not. The fringe benefit package at the shipyard is believed to be worth about $3.83 per hour. "Contract," Schedule A, p. 26. The source of the Korean statistics is the United States Bureau of Labor Statistics as supplied on the World Wide Web by Colton and Company at http://www.coltoncompany.com/index/shipbldg/wages.htm.

30. "Contract," p. 9. Many of the newly hired utility workers are former journeymen in various crafts. Lacking seniority, they were failing to get steady work in their craft. Because management knew many of them to be reliable workers, they were offered the new lower-paying classification with the promise of more hours of work. Each is assigned to one or another of the crafts, but they no longer have journeyman status. Nor, given the lack of work in the yard, have their hours gone up appreciably. Other utility workers are new hires from off the street. In at least one case, the same worker was laid off one day as a journeyman shipfitter and hired back the next as a utility worker. He was promised journeyman status on the next job but said he preferred work as a utility man at lower wages to no work at all. Seniority is granted to utility workers on a yard-wide basis regardless of trade after they have worked a cumulative 120 days in a one-year period. "Contract," p. 18.

31. Ibid., p. 20.

32. Company handout touting the advantages of the evaluation process to both management and workers, labeled "*EP.*"

33. Grandfathered journeymen will remain indefinitely at $15.85 an hour. Journeymen get $16.25 the first year and increases of $0.25 per year, reaching $17.00 in the year 2000. Craftsmen start at $17.00 in the first year and increase $0.50 per year, reaching $18.50 in the last year. Master Craftsmen begin at $18.00 and reach $20.00 in 2000. "Contract," Schedule A, p. 26.

34. This "craftsman's ethical code," with its stress upon autonomy, dignity, and equality, was first identified and analyzed by David Montgomery, *Workers' Control In America: Studies in the History of Work, Technology and Labor Struggles*, pp. 11–15.

35. "Contract," pp. 25, 27–31. Of thirty pages of text in the contract, six are devoted to substance abuse.

36. Ibid., p. 27.

37. Letter from Leonard Limtiaco, Director of Enforcement & Investigations, Occupational Safety and Health Administration, U.S. Department of Labor, to Carl Hanson, General Manager, San Francisco Drydock Inc., Case Number 72601040, December 26, 1996.

38. Letter from Alex Williams, Safety Coordinator, San Francisco Drydock, Inc., to Pauline M. Caraher, Occupational Safety and Health Administration, Phoenix, Arizona, January 2, 1997. The letter denied all charges of violations and supplied photographs "proving" adequate lighting and ventilation in all confined spaces.

39. The most complete account of the early San Francisco iron and shipbuilding

industry is found in Joseph A. Blum, "San Francisco Iron: The Industry and Its Workers—From the Gold Rush to the Turn of the Century."

40. The closing of this plant by United States Steel took place during the same period of massive closings of their steel mills in Pennsylvania and Ohio. In 1982 the corporation invested $6 billion in its purchase of Marathon Oil. For details concerning capital flight, see Barry Bluestone and Bennett Harrison, *The Deindustrialization of America.*

41. According to James Ruma, a contracts administrator in the office of the Supervisor of Shipbuilding Conversion and Repair, United States Navy, San Francisco Division, repair contracts on United States naval vessels remained at well over $100 million per year and peaked in the late 1970s and early 1980s at over $150 million. Today that figure has reached zero (numerous conversations, fall 1996–spring 1997).

42. The emergence of Korea as a shipbuilding power is perhaps the most dramatic. Korea constructed its first shipyard in 1974, delivered its first ship in 1981, and today is the second largest shipbuilding nation in the world. In 1994 Korea delivered 115 vessels totaling 5.17 million gross tons, representing 27.3 percent of the world total. Only Japan, which also had no shipbuilding industry after World War II, had a larger share of the shipbuilding world market. See "The Shipbuilding Industry in Korea" on the World Wide Web at www.iworld.net/Korea/industry/f206.html.

43. Discussions with Boilermakers Business Agents.

44. "Background," from the Center for Advanced Ship Repair and Maintenance, Norfolk, Virginia, on the World Wide Web at www.odu.edu.gnusers/miatc_v/casrm1.htm.

45. David M. Gordon, *Fat and Mean: The Corporate Squeeze of Working Americans and the Myth Of Managerial "Downsizing."*

Global Connections

Introduction to Part Two

The book's first part emphasized global forces—a vision of the global as an overarching structure experienced as an external force by individuals, groups, and localities. However, we see the global as an increasing interconnectedness among diverse places and groups and especially across national boundaries. In the past, the nation state was more likely to be able to "contain" social relations and discourses. Today, new communities are increasingly being formed of people with a foot, either physically or "virtually," in many places around the world. Discourses cross borders with these "travelers" and on electronic pathways. The studies in this part uncover the importance of particular institutions, movements, and organizations as brokers and mediators of this process. While the picture they present is quite different from that presented in the first part, it is a complementary view taken from the perspective of different social actors.

What is the nature of the emerging global connections in which these actors participate? The transnational economic is perhaps the clearest system of global linkages. However, while economic connections play a critical part in our stories, our theoretical focus is the "transnational social"—transnational public spheres that emerge in the spaces between institutionalized power structures.

Nancy Fraser has argued, in relation to the capitalist welfare state, that, as needs spill over from the "private" spheres of the family and the economy, they enter the realm of "the social," where they are politicized and become an object of struggle.[1] The welfare state responds by attempting to enclave these needs into a safe administrative framework where they can be managed, and partially satisfied, without any threat to the existing public and private power structures. Maneuvering in this nebulous arena between the privatization of needs and their public administration, the social is the arena in which social movements mobilize and genuine communicative action and democratization are possible.

Fraser's concept of the social is similar to the concepts of the public sphere or civil society. However, she sees the social as a much less structured phenomenon than these more institutionalized public spaces. Beyond that, the social is more fragmented and consists of overlapping public spheres with inequalities within and between them, rather than one coherent, structured discursive space. As such, it offers more opportunities for expression by those "subaltern publics" excluded from white, male-dominated civil society.[2]

In our studies, we borrow and extend Fraser's concept of the social by analyzing the way it overflows the borders of the nation state to become the "transnational social." The weakened ability of states to enclave particular expressions of needs facilitates the increasingly transnational nature of the strategies for meeting those needs. This in turn further weakens the ability of the state to contain such needs. While a coherent global civil society clearly does not exist, the concept of the "social" captures the emergent nature of the transnational connections we discuss and the shifting social and discursive relations around them.

We recognize the power of economic forces and connections, but the social relations we study cannot be reduced to the direct effects of such forces. Social links can generate economic activity, but in some cases they will not. Economic ties will produce social relations, but these in turn cannot be totally enclaved and administered within the economic sphere. Neither do any of us see the social as a purely discursive arena. Rather, we analyze the way emerging global connections create new regimes or sets of social relations in which the "material" and "discursive" moments are inextricably linked. In this way, the transnational social occupies a social space that escapes the efforts of the national state to administer social needs and the efforts of transnational economic interests to privatize those needs.

This transnational social is in many ways a precarious place within the world-system, but it is also a place of privilege, albeit limited. During the postwar era, the groups described here were enclaved inside national borders, within a restricted range of relatively rigidly defined identities. But in the contemporary period, crossborder human, economic, technological, and cultural flows have brought together and juxtaposed distinctive material and discursive regimes, destabilizing old identities and offering opportunities to a new, more heterogeneous set of actors for cultural challenges, economic advancement, or social transformation. Whether or not these possibilities are realized, for certain groups in newly industrializing countries and other semiperipheral states the connections forged in contemporary globalization are connections of inclusion into the world-system. This is true even as globalization is experienced as loss and exclusion by many social groups in core and peripheral countries, including those described in the studies in Part 1 of this book. Indeed, it is the emergence of semiperipheral groups onto the world stage that in many ways defines our view of the contemporary era of globalization.

The studies in this part are from the perspective of those in the middle class from the semiperiphery who have the skills, contacts, and other resources to allow them to incorporate into global economic and discursive flows. Sheba George shows how migration to the United States of Indian nurses has opened up new economic opportunities to these women but has initiated a struggle over the class and gender ideologies of the immigrant community. Seán Ó Riain describes how Irish software developers take advantage of increasing opportunities in an emerging industry and use their social networks and job-hopping strategies to negotiate their place in local and global labor markets. Millie Thayer analyzes how feminist activists in Brazil draw on feminist discourses from the core, translating and adapting them for local realities, as they engage with a constellation of global and local institutions.

Clearly not everyone in Brazil, India, and Ireland has benefited from globalization and many have suffered from its effects. However, the three studies that follow do identify at least potential benefits for Brazilian feminists, Indian nurses, and Irish software developers. These groups are also attached to emerging sectors in the world economy—to nongovernmental organizations and to health and information technology. Indeed, the dominant way in which these semiperipheral groups have advanced themselves has been through attaching themselves to emerging sectors where global power structures have not yet been fully institutionalized.

But the social is not just an area of inclusion. The very fact of incorporation of the new social groups also produces a transformation in social relations as the relations within and among core and semiperipheral countries and social groups are renegotiated. Power differentials persist and are often exacerbated, and the potential of the social for emerging groups depends a great deal on the conditions of their inclusion in the world system.

Racial and ethnic-national hierarchies must be renegotiated as connections are forged between the mainly white core and the mainly nonwhite semi-periphery. In particular, the assumed superiority of core practices is challenged and undermined by the emergence of the new connections to the semiperiphery. Inclusion does not necessarily mean homogenization, as assimilation to the dominant culture is often actively resisted. Brazilian feminists in nongovernmental organizations reject certain imported conceptions of "gender," and reinterpret and incorporate others into their practices in novel ways. At the same time, the efforts at "translation" of these same feminists, considered "white" in their national context, are resisted by black Brazilian women with their own visions of social transformation. Irish software engineers socialize happily with their United States managers into the small hours of the Dublin night but complain long and hard about them the following Monday. While Indian nurses and their families are marginally incorporated into the United States economy, they maintain their own public spaces in which they struggle over social relations, with India as a main point of reference.

This, then, is the common view of the transnational social that underlies our studies. We each focus on the experience of a group from a semiperipheral country in negotiating its way between a variety of institutionalized power structures to create new patterns of inclusion and relative privilege. The relation of each to the world system and to the social groups in its own locality or country is transformed by the conditions of its inclusion.

Nonetheless, the transnational social is a heterogeneous space, and internal differences emerge from each study. The source of the global connections, the space available to the social sphere, and the implications of the transnational social for the semiperipheral populations as a whole vary considerably among the three cases. In contrast to Fraser, we do not find that the emergence of the transnational social necessarily leads to the politicization of needs, but rather to a continuum of responses, from suppression and containment, to individual autonomy, to collective critical practice.

In Sheba George's study of Indian nurses in Chicago, a transnational community is formed by the international demand for nurses. The new economic resources available to the nurses and their newly acquired social position threaten community norms around gender and family practices. However, the transnational Indian community "reprivatizes" the nurses' needs quite decisively in its own religious space, and the liberating potential of the transnational social is effectively contained.

The software developers studied by Seán Ó Riain are better able to maintain their autonomy within the transnational social sphere than the Indian nurses. However, this is largely because of their increasing disconnection from the Irish transnational community as a whole. Individual software workers form an uneasy alliance with the transnational corporations that dominate the industry.

The Brazilian feminist social movements that Millie Thayer studies clearly express the greatest opportunity for the ongoing politicization of social needs on a global scale. The transnational social provides crucial material and discursive resources to feminist groups in Brazil. However, their own discursive reach and influence on feminists in the North is limited and their reliance on international funding poses some danger of enclaving their movements' expressed needs within the agenda of the funding agencies. Different conditions are pushing the groups toward a flourishing feminist transnational social, on the one hand, or an incorporation and administration of womens' needs by the funding institutions and their agencies, on the other.

The studies in this part therefore suggest a variety of ways in which needs can be expressed, mobilized, enclaved, and administered through a vast range of transnational connections. The implications for local and transnational politics, for the ties that bind transnational groups to their "home" locales, and for a democratic form of globalization depend greatly on the circumstances surrounding each different set of global connections—circumstances and connections described in the following studies.

Sheba George, Seán Ó Riain, and Millie Thayer

NOTES

1. Nancy Fraser, "Struggle over Needs: Outline of a Socialist-Feminist Critical Theory of Late Capitalist Political Culture," in *Unruly Practices*, pp.161–87.
2. Nancy Fraser, "Rethinking the Public Sphere."

FIVE

"Dirty Nurses" and "Men Who Play"

Gender and Class in Transnational Migration

Sheba George

This paper is the product of over two years' fieldwork in two places: Central City, U.S.A., and the state of Kerala, India. In 1994 and 1995 I spent eighteen months in Central City at St. George's, an immigrant congregation with Kerala origins.[1] I visited the homes of thirty couples from the congregation, interviewing husbands and wives separately and jointly.[2]

In those homes I watched and listened to how couples accommodated to an unusual immigration pattern in which women, recruited as nurses, preceded their husbands. When the husbands arrived, even when they had professional experience or advanced degrees, they had to take up menial jobs. What concessions, if any, did they then make to their breadwinning wives? I studied the variety of new household partnerships in cooking, in childcare, in financial decision-making. To explore how on-the-job experiences might be affecting nurses, I regularly visited a nursing home where many Kerala women were employed. But what of the men? If they suffered downward mobility in the labor market and an erosion of their authority at home, was there another arena where they could recover their lost status? As an active participant in the religious life of the community, I watched men carve out their own preserve in the church. There they assumed positions of leadership and built a sense of community and belonging.

In quite subtle ways, however, their reactive compensation was only partially successful. They could not escape the class and gender stigma that clung to them as the husbands of nurses who were their

families' primary breadwinners. It was as if they had created for
themselves their own "little Kerala" in the midst of Central City.
How was such a specifically Indian stigma transmitted to and embedded in such a far-away place as Central City? To explore this
transnational re-creation of norms I studied the dense flows of
meaning, people, and commodities between the two locales. I
rejoined the flow myself, traveling to Kerala for six months to seek
out the kin of the Central City couples and to see what immigration
looked like from the perspective of the sending community. I submerged myself in a Kerala church community to compare it with St.
George's. Finally, from individual and group interviews with nurses,
I learned how their labor was stigmatized, indeed more stigmatized
as their wages became more prized. By recreating this global field for
myself, I saw how norms were reproduced in Kerala and from there
transmitted and appropriated in the community around St. George's.

All these fieldsites were familiar to me. All my life I had been part
of the very process I was studying. Having immigrated to the United
States from India as a young girl, I had spent a good part of my
childhood years involved in a church community similar to St.
George's. Entree into the research site was, therefore, relatively
easy but that also created tensions. I often found myself straddling
or caught between competing identities. At St.George's I was both
researcher and churchgoer, although they regarded me as neither
adult nor child (I was in my late twenties, too old to be a child, and
unmarried, in a community where adulthood is attained by entering
marriage). Having immigrated at the age of twelve, I was neither a
first- nor a second-generation immigrant but a "one-point-fiver," as
we are called. In Kerala I was no less a hybrid. I spoke Malayalam
fluently, I looked like a Malayalee, and I dressed like other young
women, but I could never hide my difference. My cousin said it was
the way I carried myself and made eye contact. Still, it was my "in-
betweenness" and my "liminality," which I usually considered an
autobiographical headache, that gave me the room to maneuver
among different identities and see the field from different points
of view. I could associate with both the adults and the teenagers,
with both men and women, nurses and non-nurses without being
bound to any one group.

But it was not all easy going. The fluidity of identity made it a
constant challenge to position myself. I would be asked to follow

scripts that no one else could follow. The priest asked me to organize the young people for a Christmas-caroling venture, which, at St. George's, was an exclusively adult male activity. While I was close to the teenagers and wanted to help the priest, I did not want to be in the limelight of controversy. In retrospect, despite difficulties, it turned out to be a uniquely revealing experience that helped me understand the importance of church participation for the immigrant men. As a young, unmarried woman, my presence among the company of men generated varying expressions of resistance that threw cultural and religious assumptions into relief. If I had taken the safe way out by remaining solely an observer, I would not have seen the significance of caroling—it had been redefined as an adult male domain forged in "reactive compensation" for their loss of status at home and at work. Breaking the rules allowed me to see what the rules were.

Similar transgressions in Kerala brought their own insights into the unstated presumptions at both ends of the migration stream. While traveling in an auto-rickshaw with my aunt, I asked the driver to stop at a particular place. He did not seem to hear me, so I tapped him on the shoulder to get his attention. My aunt was aghast: "He could get the wrong idea about you," she exclaimed. I had broken one of the cardinal rules of male-female interaction—I had touched a male stranger. From this and other such incidents I began to understand better why immigrant nurses in Central City harbored the view that they were regarded as "dirty" women. I reflected on those young aspiring nurses who, twenty to thirty years ago, left behind a Kerala that probably had even stricter prohibitions against the interaction of the sexes. These same women who were not allowed to enter the living room when male visitors came to their homes had to touch, clean, and nurture hundreds of male strangers as part of their professional duty. My aunt's reaction in 1997 to my touching the driver gave me a momentary insight into the almost tangible gender boundaries among the Kerala immigrants of Central City. Although my study relies heavily on interviews, it is only through the transgressive ethnography of breaking rules and through getting my own hands "dirty" in the fields of Central City and Kerala that I have been able to understand the views expressed by people at both ends of this transnational migration.

At an informal tea party Mrs. Thomas brought up an incident from her last visit to India. After being in the United States for over fifteen years, she was back in India, traveling by train with her children and her sister-in-law. When they got on the train, there were two empty seats, each next to a man. Mrs. Thomas sat down in one of them but her sister-in-law did not do the same. Eventually, her sister-in-law took one of the children and sat down in the other empty seat. But she made sure that she separated herself from the man next to her by squeezing the child in between. Observing this uncomfortable maneuver, Mrs. Thomas realized that her highly educated sister-in-law must have thought of her as only a "dirty nurse" because she had sat next to a man. When I asked Mrs. Thomas why she thought that, the four other immigrant nurses listening all proceeded to tell me how nurses back home were seen as "loose," "spoilt," and having low moral values.

Six months later I am interviewing Mr. Mathen about politics at St. George's, an Indian immigrant congregation in the United States. Surprisingly, to explain the contentious nature of church politics, he refers to the dynamics of the immigrant family:

> Most of our people came here as a spouse—rather most of the men—as a spouse of a nurse. . . . In the house, the husband does not have his proper status. In the society, you are an Indian—what status do you have? For men—where are they going to show their "macho" nature? That's why they play in the church. This is what is going on in our churches and I am not just talking about St. George's.

These vignettes capture the gender and class paradoxes facing Indian Christians who immigrate from Kerala, the southernmost state of India, to the United States. The immigration pattern is unusual in that women arrive first as nurses, and only once they are settled do they sponsor their husbands and families. The paradox confronting Mrs. Thomas and all Indian nurses is that despite their professional standing in the United States, despite their influential position as breadwinner, and despite their extended family's dependence on them as sponsor, they are still stigmatized as "dirty nurses." Mr. Mathen's comments, on the other hand, emphasize a second paradox, that of the "nurse-husband." Despite their prominent roles as church committee members and their serious devotion to the religious community, men like Mr. Thomas are seen as "playing" in the church. Try as they may, they cannot escape the stigma that attaches to their wives. Given the professional success of the nurses and their families, these negative evaluations of nurses and their husbands do not make sense from the point of view of the wider American society. Rather, they reflect the way the tightly knit immigrant community in the United States absorbs and appropriates meanings from India, meanings that become the undercurrents for the negotiations of class and gender relations.

Sociological literature has difficulty understanding either of these paradoxes. Overall, attempts to theorize the impact of immigration on gender relations do not give enough attention to the important ways in which the ongoing connections to the native country shape the discourses and practices of immigrants in the United States. The meanings of nursing operating in the opening vignettes illustrate how the point of reference for this immigrant community is Kerala rather than the wider United States society. To be sure, there is an emerging field of "transnational" studies, which looks at the processes by which post-World War II immigrants maintain linkages and identities that cut across national boundaries and that bring two societies into a single social field.[3] This literature, however, fails to examine whether transnational connections reaffirm or erode gender and class hierarchies. As the anthropologist Sarah Mahler notes: "Much of the literature to date on transnationalism from below paints it as empowering, democratic, and liberating, particularly in light of other global trends toward the concentration of wealth and power. This subaltern image needs to be tested consistently."[4]

An exception is Pierrette Hondagneu-Sotelo's ethnography of gender relations in a Mexican settlement community in California.[5] Unlike other migration scholars, Hondagneu-Sotelo examines both ends of the migration stream to see how the originating family promoted or undermined gender hierarchy in the receiving community. Her study in fact upholds the conventional wisdom that immigration promotes a more egalitarian household division of labor, more equal participation in decision-making, and greater spatial mobility for women. She criticizes Patricia Pessar and others who explain the diminution of male dominance in immigrant families as the result of women entering the labor market and men losing economic resources.[6] Arguing that employment alone is too narrow an explanation, Hondagneu-Sotelo focuses on the social context of the community of incorporation and on resettlement experiences shaped by migration patterns. She argues that when the community of incorporation was mainly one of men, the "bachelor" living style forced them into "domestic work," and so without any sense of emasculation they were amenable to helping their spouses when the latter joined them in California.

While Hondagneu-Sotelo's work captures the connections between native and host societies, and does recognize different realms within the immigrant community, she nevertheless oversimplifies the interrelations between these realms. In particular, she fails to acknowledge the possibility that men may balance the emergent egalitarianism in the household with the reconstitution of patriarchy in other social arenas. She assumes that men lose out both in private and in public spheres, that what happens in one sphere reinforces, rather than counterbalances, what happens in other spheres. Yet it is quite possible that the same Mexican immigrant men who agree to do housework may not be as willing to own up to this in front of their friends, with whom they may instead reassert their masculine prerogatives.

Hence, without detracting from the major contributions she makes, I believe that Hondagneu-Sotelo nonetheless falls into what Yen Espiritu argues is an all-too-common problem with scholarship on immigration.[7] Focusing particularly on Asian-American studies, Espiritu writes: "Reflecting sociologists' concerns with economic issues and the structures of immigrant opportunity in the United States, most studies of post-1965 Asian Americans have focused on Asian-American relations with and adaptation to the larger society rather than on relations among group members."[8] By not examining those exclusively immigrant public spaces, Hondagneu-Sotelo misses a crucial arena where gender and class hierarchies may be contested as well as affirmed. Among Kerala Christian immigrants, the religious congregation plays just such a role, becoming an alternative communal space, counterbalancing both workplace and household.

In this chapter, I will examine a dual set of connections—those to India and those among the different spheres in the immigrant community—in order to understand the paradoxes of the Kerala Christian immigration story. I begin with the sending community of Kerala and how it has reacted to the emigration of nurses, before turning to the process of immigration itself—how it has accorded women greater economic power and changed the division of labor in the home but at the same time upheld the stigma associated with nursing. Whereas men are forced to change and compromise in the domestic sphere, the religious congregation becomes an ideal space where they can reclaim status losses suffered as a result of immigration. Yet, in asserting male privilege within the church, they also reinforce their own gender- and class-based stigmatization because of their connection to nurses.

NURSES IN KERALA: FROM BURDENS TO ASSETS

The story of the Kerala nurses and their immigration is connected to another story about the transformation of women's worth in Kerala. The discourse around the female child in Kerala was one that equated her with a liability. As one of my female respondents put it, investing money in a girl's welfare and education was seen as "watering the fruit trees in your neighbor's garden." In a society where arranged marriage is still the norm, daughters were often seen as "burdens," since the family was obliged to provide a dowry or "streedhanam" for the marriage of daughters, whereas they would receive a "streedhanam" upon the marriage of sons.[9] As the anthropologist Susan Visvanathan elaborates, "It [streedhanam] expresses the fundamental severing of economic ties for a woman from her natal home, and her incorporation into the conjugal household."[10]

As nursing opened up a window of opportunity for young women to earn money and contribute to the family income, there was a concurrent change in their position within the family. From being burdens and liabilities, they became transformed into financial assets. But this transformation was not without its contradictions. Nursing remained a low-status profession due to " . . . existing cultural norms deeply rooted in Hindu philosophy" that relegated nursing to the realm of the polluting and the impure.[11] Indeed, as the opportunities for nurses increased, their stigmatization, far from diminishing, actually increased.

One community, however, proved to be a partial exception to this rule, namely, the Christian communities of Kerala.[12] Their relative openness to nursing had much to do with the active role that English missionaries and mission hospitals took in representing nursing as noble Christian service. But here it was mostly young women from the less prosperous families who responded to the recruitment efforts of the nursing schools. Many nursing schools provided free education and a monthly stipend to the students they recruited in return for an allotted time of bonded service by the nursing graduate after the completion of her education. A number of women I interviewed admitted that they really wanted to go to medical school but because their families were not able to afford the expense nursing became a substitute.

Often it became a family project to scrape up enough money to send the aspiring nurse to begin her training. In my interviews with the immigrant nurses, many recounted how a father or a brother made the initial long train journeys to register them at the nursing school. As a result, the typical family eagerly awaited the day when their daughter's training would be over and she would find a job that would contribute to the family income. In order to help their natal families for as long as possible, many nurses dutifully delayed marriage. In interviews, some women told me how they postponed their marriage to help their family build a home or to help siblings complete their education.

Conversely, aspiring nurses from families not under economic duress met with resistance, as was the case for Mrs. Philip:

> Well, in those days, nursing was associated with the option for the poor, who would send their eldest girl to help save the rest of the family. But I was not in that category, so the family said, "No way." . . . Then a friend of mine decided to go to nursing school. She was real secretive about it. . . . I found out that this friend got the address for the nursing school from the local doctor, so I ran to him and said that I was interested in going to nursing school. He insisted that I not go, pointing out that my friend was the eldest child of many and how she was doing this to save the family. . . .

In addition to being identified as low-status work for poor families, entering the nursing profession had other consequences for young women. Being away from home and having to make choices for themselves made them relatively more independent. Whether or not the nurses abided by family dictates, their increased independence and earning capacity gave them new means to negotiate control over their incomes and their lives. But their independence and professional choice were also cause for gendered social stigma.

Enrollment in a nursing program required that many of the aspiring nurses leave Kerala and study and work in cities far away from home. Consequently, there was a loss of control over young women's mobility and sexuality. Before marriage, a young woman was expected to live under the control of her father and older brothers, and after marriage control over her life was transferred to her husband and his family. The nurses had clearly transgressed these social conventions.

Furthermore, the profession of nursing requires constant physical contact with unknown male patients and doctors. Traditionally, in Kerala society, it was not appropriate for young women to speak in the presence of males who were not relatives. As Mrs. Philip explained, "I could speak to my mother and even my brothers, but not when other men were around. I was not even allowed to go in the front room when other men were around, like my brother's friends." The working requirements of nursing, which put the women in direct contact with men who were not kin, gave rise to allegations of sexual immorality against nurses in general. Nurses who opted for late marriage were especially vulnerable to suspicions about the purity of their sexual status.

Even for the Christian community in Kerala, it was very rare for young women to work outside the home to make a living. All of the mothers of the fifty-eight immigrant men and women whom I interviewed, with the exception of one, were exclusively homemakers and did not work outside the home.[13] For the families of these nurses, the wage-earning woman was entirely novel. While the young women and their families worked out the implications of this new earning power, the cultural reverberations of these negotiations earmarked nursing professionals as deviants with respect to the customary gender norms in the Kerala Christian community.

Control over the new income often caused conflict between parents and their nurse daughters. As Mrs. Thomas explained to me, her family did not want her to get married because they assumed that her financial contribution would be cut off when she entered the husband's family. She complained that they wanted to extract as much money as they could from her, and they are angry with her to this day even though since her marriage she has sponsored all her siblings to go to the United States. In some cases, control over income led to spousal conflict, as with Mrs. John, who tearfully told me about her husband's betrayal of a pact she had made with him before their marriage. She claims to have extracted an agreement from her husband before their marriage that she would continue to help her family. The fact that she had to negotiate this explicitly points to the cultural expectation that a woman once married belongs to her husband's family and her natal family no longer has any rights over her. Mrs. John was of course aware of this expectation, but she felt that this tradition should apply only when women were not working outside the home. As the eldest of her siblings, one of her main purposes in entering the nursing profession was to help her family. Her husband, however, did not keep his word, and this became one of the causes for their severe marital problems. She bitterly observed that he probably assented to her condition before marriage because she was his ticket to the United States. Conflicts such as these, between parents and daughters and husbands and wives, became the grounds for the social evaluation of nurses as too independent, stigmatizing them as deviant.

Nurse money is no longer something new in today's Kerala. Major changes have taken place over the last thirty years. First, nursing education has undergone extended institutionalization, with increasing numbers of nursing schools and the increasing rigor of admission and accreditation requirements. Nursing is one of the few professions in Kerala with the guarantee of a job upon graduation and opportunities to make money abroad. Indeed, admission to nursing programs is so much in demand that, much as with engineering and medical school admission, the prospective applicant now has to pay a capitation fee of thousands of rupees instead of receiving a stipend to attend as in the past. The four-year Bachelor of Science degree (B.Sc.) and the Master of Science degree (M.Sc.) in nursing are now widely available in India, and applicants need high marks in science subjects to qualify for admission.

The second major change concerns the much wider social-class range from which women are recruited to the nursing profession. As one woman in Kerala described the changes, "In the old days . . . only those people with financial difficulties would send their daughters for this job. Nowadays everyone is interested—those who want to go to America, the financially well-off, and even the Muslims. After you study nursing, you can get a job right away."

The third important shift in Kerala is the greater power of nurses to negotiate control over their income. For instance, they have more bargaining power in the transnational marriage market, where it is known that men who marry nurses cannot expect a dowry. Since nurses are in high demand in most places, it is understood that they will more than make up for the unpaid dowry by their earnings and job security. In fact, nurses with degrees and a "good family background" are in such demand that they get "booked up" while still in school.

While nurses are a sought-after commodity in the job and marriage markets, the ambivalence toward nurses in Kerala is stronger than ever. In focus group interviews that I conducted with nurses currently working there, the consensus was that nurses were treated much worse in Kerala than anywhere else—both inside and outside India. One nurse with a lot of work experience outside Kerala explained how they are still saddled with the label of sexual looseness: "Here, if a nurse speaks to a patient too much, they say that they are having an affair. Outside Kerala they would think that it is a friendship. . . . Even now it is just like it was in the fifties. There is not much change." Mr. Babu, whom I interviewed in Kerala, explained the attitude toward nurses as follows: "It is a sexual kind of thinking. You can get them for anything. They are loose. . . . This is the general talk in our society. 'Oh, she is a nurse from the Gulf—that is how she got her money.' That's how they say it—contemptuously."

Despite their having come from more diverse social origins, despite the greater demand for their professional skills, and despite their transformation from a burden into an asset, nurses are still heavily stigmatized. In Kerala they are still labeled as uneducated, uncouth women from poor family backgrounds, as bossy and ostentatious with their new wealth, or simply as women with questionable sexual standards. Nonetheless, as we have seen, such stigma has not prevented Kerala nurses from continuing to supply their labor to the rest of India and from there to the rest of the world. In the next section, I will look at the factors that shape the demand for this transnational labor force, especially in the United States. I show how the immigration process inverts the occupational status of women and men, nurses and their husbands.

IMMIGRATION AND ITS GENDER EFFECTS

The incorporation of Kerala Christian nurses into the Indian labor force created a reservoir of migrant workers for a global market.[14] As families began to depend on the incomes of their pioneering daughters, many Kerala nurses accepted financially lucrative nursing opportunities in other countries. No sooner did they occupy their new immigrant jobs than they became stepping stones to further migration for the family members they sponsored.

Specifically, in the mid-sixties, the expanding oil economies in the Middle East opened up new opportunities for foreign labor, especially in the service, health, and other professional sectors. Indian nurses were part of such immigrant work forces. Among the women I interviewed in Central City, many had worked in countries such as Kuwait, Saudi Arabia, and Dubai. Others had spent years working in African countries such as Zambia and Nigeria before coming to the United States. They had become part of a process of global step-migration.[15]

In the United States, a number of factors contributed to the demand for foreign nurses. The post-World War II expansion of Medicare and Medicaid programs created a greater need for health care professionals. However, there was a decline in the domestic labor pool, as this was a period in which American-born women had attractive alternative career choices open to them. More importantly, as Paul Ong and Tania Azores explain, "the endemic and recurring shortage of nurses" in the United States " . . . is tied to wages that have remained below market level because hospitals, which employ 70 percent of nurses, have colluded to set rates."[16] They blame sex-based occupational discrimination, along with poor working conditions, for the high exit rate of those already in the profession as well for the shortage of new nurses.

The liberalization of immigration, specifically the Immigration and Nationality Act of 1965, was an attempt to respond to such labor shortages. The third preference category in this act allowed for the entry of skilled professionals who were needed in the United States. Because this act also increased immigration quotas for formerly restricted areas, it helped to induce increasing immigration of nurses from Asia, and in particular from India. By the late 1970s, immigration of Indian nurses to the United States was only exceeded by that of Filipina nurses, closely followed by Korean nurses. From 1975 to 1979, while 11.9 percent of the nurses admitted to the United States as permanent residents were from India, 11.2 percent were from Korea, and 27.6 percent were from the Philippines.[17]

Continuing shortages in the supply of nurses led to congressional hearings on the subject and to the passage of the Immigration Nursing Relief Act of 1989. Although immigrant nurses make up only a small percentage of the nursing work force (4 percent in 1984), they are a critical source of labor, particularly for inner-city hospitals that have difficulty attracting and retaining native nurses. These hospitals have actively conducted recruitment campaigns in countries such as India, leading to what some have characterized as a "brain drain" and others call a "skill drain."[18]

Kerala nurses find opportunities abroad especially attractive because working conditions at home are so deplorable. In a focus group interview, nurses talked about the high nursing vacancy rates in Kerala hospitals, leading to a disproportionately low nurse-to-patient ratio and poor quality of patient care. In one hospital, nurses told me that for every forty-five patients they had only two staff nurses. As a result, Keralites who could afford it were seeking health care outside the state. Furthermore, many of the nurses who had worked outside Kerala talked about the markedly different treatment they received from doctors and hospital administrations inside Kerala. Instead of being treated as equals and colleagues, they complained of being shouted at and treated like inferiors in Kerala hospitals.

Along with relatively poor working conditions, Kerala nurses are also unique for their lack of collective organization. As one nurse who had worked outside Kerala explained:

Here they won't strike—they won't open their mouths. The problem is that the people working here either need their bond or they have returned from abroad and they don't want to just sit at home. Low salary is not a botheration to them. So only we juniors are here for the salary and most are only here for the time being. Most of us are here on a one-year contract. This is just a temporary thing since most of us are planning to go to different places.

Despite the continuous stream of nurses going abroad, hospital administrations do not have to improve conditions to retain a minimal nursing workforce. Kerala hospitals rely on the compulsory bond that requires newly graduated nurses to serve up to a three-year period in the particular hospital designated by the nursing school. Consequently, as long as the nursing schools are filled with students, Kerala hospitals have access to fresh batches of low-paid apprentice labor. One nurse summed up the reasons why she wants to immigrate: "Why struggle here and get no money? We can go abroad, make some money, and come back. Staying here, we don't get any respect and we don't get any money." The result is a transitory transnational workforce with little motivation to fight for better conditions.

Spurned at home but in high demand abroad, nurses found themselves caught up in an unusual immigration process. Whereas for most immigrant groups to the United States the men come first, in the case of Kerala nurses it was the women who arrived first and only later sponsored their husbands and families. Typically, the men waited in India with their children until they were allowed to join their wives, who were already working in the United States and supporting the household through remittances. In some cases, single women went back to India with their green cards and found husbands with whom they could return. In this immigration experience, conventional roles were reversed for men and women.[19] The immigrant men experienced loss of status in two ways: both in terms of their relations to their wives and in relation to their positions before immigration.

While their nurse-wives and sisters experienced upward economic mobility and increased status, Kerala immigrant men faced the prospect of perhaps never making as much money or gaining equivalent professional standing. Although many of the women had worked in India and had contributed financially to the household income, they had not been the primary breadwinners they became in the United States.

Immigrant men also lost status with respect to their previous social and economic positions. As immigrants they had limited access to the political and social structures of the wider American society. Low incomes and unstable employment in secondary labor market jobs left men with few opportunities for civic participation and access to leadership positions. The difficulty in transferring Indian academic degrees, credentials, work skills, and experience to the United States often meant that men had to start their careers all over again.

They typically had to relocate to suit their wives' nursing careers and re-educate themselves in new trades and professions. Raymond Williams, in his study of immigrant groups from India and Pakistan, reports that most

Kerala Christian men "who followed their wives took positions in machine shops or factories, or used the connections their wives had in the hospitals to get training as medical technicians."[20] In both an informal survey and in interviews I conducted at St. George's, many men were hesitant to disclose the exact nature of their employment, and used such vague terms as "business" or "office."

Since the women were the primary agents of immigration, their husbands and male kin were dependent on them when they joined them. The dependence of the men on the women often went beyond the financial aspect to include all manner of adjustments to American society. The downward mobility of the men raises questions about what happens in the domestic sphere and how men compensate for their loss of status. In the next section, I will deal with the domestic division of labor in the immigrant households, and in the following section with men's use of the church to compensate for their losses.

TRANSFORMATION OF THE DOMESTIC DIVISION OF LABOR

In order to assess the degree to which the domestic division of labor had changed as a result of immigration, I first asked each of the thirty couples I interviewed to describe the gender division of labor in the households of their parents. It turned out that, with one exception, all their mothers were homemakers, so that women performed exclusively household chores, cooking, and childcare, whereas financial affairs, breadwinning, and the disciplining of children fell within the paternal realm. I next asked them about the gender division of labor in their own households. While their responses fell across a spectrum, nonetheless in all cases the men were forced to adapt by doing at least some household chores and childcare while also sharing financial decision-making with their wives.

Housework and Cooking

In most of the households, the women were still primarily responsible for the daily cooking. Some men, however, who had lived away from home in their bachelor days had some experience fending for themselves and even admitted to enjoy cooking. For example, Mr. Thomas, who left home at sixteen for technical training in north India, maintained that he does all the cooking in the house. Mr. Samuel, who has a similar story, asserted that he enjoys cooking and entertaining so much that his wife has trouble resting before her night shift because there are too many people around. Mr. Thomas and Mr. Samuel, however, are exceptional.

Most men appeared uncomfortable when talking about their contributions to household work. For instance, Mr. Eapen talked about the tension of the lifestyle, especially in relation to housework. As he explained, "Here

I had to do cooking. I had to do the cleaning—I don't mind doing that. I know some Indian men are thinking they shouldn't do this work. I do it. . . . If she will end up having to do everything, she cannot do it, right?" Here, he expresses his discomfort at being caught between the prescription that "Indian men shouldn't do this work" and the practical reality of the limitations of his wife's time and energy after working nights. His wife elaborated on the "tension" that her husband experienced as follows: "Here life is more frustration, more tension. He came in 1979 and we had a baby in 1980, so more tension developed. . . . Because my husband had three sisters and he was the one son, I think he found it more difficult here. He said he made a mistake. He should have never come here."

While the large majority of the men I interviewed aligned themselves around Mr. Eapen's position, their wives had varying responses to the changes in the male immigrant's role in the household. For instance, Mrs. Eapen's assessment of the conditions of work in the United States led her to have very democratic expectations for the division of housework. As she put it,

> In India, you leave the dishes in the sink, the lady comes and washes. Here you can't do that. Because you work—everybody works, so everybody has to help. Before I go to work, I leave everything neat and tidy so I expect the same thing when I come back from work too. The floor where I work, it is so damn busy. Sometimes I don't get out even [at] midnight, sometimes only [at] two o'clock in the morning. So I don't want to come at two o'clock in the morning to find the whole sink is full of dishes.

In a similar vein, Mrs. Philip describes the initial shock and consequent adjustment in her household around the issue of housework.

> I came first, and after eleven months my kids and my husband came. O God! That was the time I was studying for the psychiatric courses [for the licensing exams] and we had little kids. My husband did not do any work. By 4 A.M. I had to get ready, get the milk ready. At that time, I had a newborn baby. Then I went to work. At noon I needed to go to classes at [the] hospital. I took the bus there. By 10 P.M., I would come home and see all the dishes, the kids sleeping in dirty clothes. My husband then was not used [to it] and did not know how to do the work. I managed for about two weeks and then burst out crying. I was like a mad woman. I told him that I get up at 4 A.M. and between work and school get back at 10 P.M. . . . . If I have to cook and clean till 12:30 A.M. at night, how long do I have to sleep? This is when he realized how I was doing all the work. So he slowly started to help and do the chores around the house. Things started to get better after a month.

In contrast to the position taken by Mrs. Eapen and Mrs. Philip, there were some women who voiced their disapproval of the male contributions in the domestic realm. For example, Mrs. Papi explained why she did not like her husband cooking: "If I am sick, he will cook. Otherwise, I will do everything. I don't like him to do on a daily basis. . . . When I am not here, for the kids he makes [meals]. This is not the way men in our country do. . . ." She believes that to keep up tradition she must not let her husband cook. Given the lack of auxiliary support from relatives or servants, even Mrs. Papi is sometimes forced to ask her husband for help, and he has no alternative but to acquiesce.

Childcare

While a few of the families immigrated at a stage when their children were older and could take care of themselves, the vast majority had to solve the problem of babysitting for their infants. The most popular solution was to juggle their work schedules to make sure one of the parents was always home. Because shift work was available to nurses, many women I interviewed worked evening or night shifts while their husbands worked during the day.

A few families opted to take their infant children to India where grandparents or other relatives took care of them until they were ready to attend school. A number of people said that relatives they had sponsored had helped out with childcare.[21] A majority of the couples, and especially the men, complained about the difficulty of dealing with childcare issues. Couples lived like strangers for years—hardly seeing each other as they handed off the childcare baton to each other between their work shifts. The men I interviewed talked about their involvement in childcare as one of the major changes relative to their own fathers' roles in the household. Mr. Elias exemplified this view when he bemoaned the loss of a past where mothers were the exclusive caretakers of children.

> Back home taking care of the kids means, when they get back from the school, ask them to go and study. That is it. Here you have to change diapers, give them bath[s], help them dress, and the day is gone. Back home, even if the father and mother are there, mother stays at home and father works outside. Mother takes care of the kids. Mother is the one who forms the character of the kids. Here, the mother works outside the home and so that is left to the father. That is the biggest difference here. Back home it is the mother's sole responsibility. Isn't it? Mother gives baths, and tells them to study, since she is the one at home. Here it is the opposite.

Additionally, in Kerala, the role of the disciplinarian was the jurisdiction of the father. It appears that the mother has now taken this over. In an informal discussion with four immigrant nurses, disciplining children became a topic of discussion. All the women agreed that the kids came to them for permission to do things, causing conflict with husbands who were consistently more conservative, especially when it came to daughters. One woman thought that perhaps mothers were better able to relate to their American-

born children because they had studied American psychology for their reg-
istered-nurse licensing exams. Mrs. Simon described the dynamics of the
erosion of paternal authority:

> Actually, my husband is very strict with the children. See, he was disciplined
> such that if his father had said to him, "You stop right there!" he would stop.
> He was scared to stand in front of his father. That is the way it was in his fam-
> ily. . . . So the same way he tells my children too [she corrects herself]—our
> children. "Do this and do that." Of course, the children who live here don't lis-
> ten all the time. . . . I tell him, "Don't be so strict with them. With them you
> can't get too strict." And then he gets angry and says, "You are the one who
> spoils them."

At the same time that they face greater responsibilities for childcare, Mr.
Simon and his contemporaries discover that they have lost their prerogatives as patriarchal disciplinarians.

Financial Decision-Making

In addition to housework and childcare, I asked the couples about how they
divided up the work around financial decision-making. Couples typically fell
into one of two camps. First, there were those who professed an egalitarian
approach to dealing with their finances. For example, Mr. Varkey claimed
that "Both of us take part in making decisions. Sometimes she will say something. I may or may not agree. She has no problem with that. Both of us take
part in making decisions. When she disagrees, then I have to convince her,
showing the reasons. The same way she will also do to me."

Then there were other couples who staunchly claimed that the husband
was in charge of all the finances. Both husbands and wives in this category
independently made statements such as the following: "She doesn't even
sign her own paycheck," or "I [wife] don't even know how much I make." In
this respect Mrs. Thambi is typical:

> *Mrs. Thambi:* He does not know the ABCDs of cooking. On the other hand, I
> don't know anything about billing.
>
> *S.G.:* You don't know?
>
> *Mrs. Thambi:* No.
>
> *S.G.:* Is that by choice?
>
> *Mrs. Thambi:* Maybe I don't want to learn.
>
> *S.G.:* Why not?
>
> *Mrs. Thambi:* I don't like it.
>
> *S.G.:* You don't want to learn about it?

Mrs. Thambi: I just go to work and get my paycheck. I don't even know how much I make a year. I don't want to know anything about money. . . .

Later on in the interview, as we discussed the different experiences of men and women in the immigration process, Mrs. Thambi explained her cultivated ignorance regarding money matters.

Mrs. Thambi: . . . I think they [the men] feel a little insecure when they don't have jobs. If they don't have jobs—If they have jobs, I don't know . . . If he [her husband] makes much less money, he may [feel insecure]. I never give him a chance to feel that way.

S.G.: How do you think you do this?

Mrs. Thambi: I mean—I don't know—in the first place, I don't talk about salary—"You make this much?" or "I make this much."

S.G.: He takes care of all the money issues?

Mrs. Thambi: Yah, I don't ask him about that. I don't tell him about that. When the income tax comes, I ask, "So how much did I make?" I don't know exactly how much I make. I don't know where the bank accounts are. Like sometimes I say, "If something were to happen, I don't even know where the bank is." I don't think he feels that way [insecure].

S.G.: You consciously make an effort to not make him feel that way?

Mrs. Thambi: Yes.

Despite Mrs. Thambi's concerted effort to leave financial matters to her husband, he and most of the other men whom I interviewed were all too aware that the fact that their wives worked outside the home changed the balance of power. As Mr. Cherian, who claimed to take care of all financial matters in his household, put it, "Here both husband and wife work. Over there, the ladies stay home, so they don't know what the hell is up. So here we have to discuss with them. Otherwise, they don't feel equal." Unlike their fathers, men like Mr. Cherian had to recognize their wives' financial contributions and take their opinions into consideration even if their wives chose not to sign their own paychecks.

In addition to their knowing "what's up," there are additional factors which require women to participate in financial decision-making. Mrs. Punoose gave one such example when she explained why she argued and fought with her husband in a way very unlike her mother.

Mrs. Punoose: My father deals with everything. My mother does not know anything. She knows just cooking only. My father, whatever he does, he does not even tell my mother. . . . Yes, she never argued. But here we have to. Here you can't do anything yourself. If you buy, both of you have to sign. Both are working and both are responsible for the payment. Everything should not be in one person's name. It won't happen anyway. Everything is shared.

S.G.: Do you think that's better?

Mrs. Punoose: I think that's better. If everything goes to one person, you end up with nothing. Everything is not controlled by one person. Everything is equal. Equal responsibility. If I need money, I have money. If he needs money, he has money.

Financial transactions require the participation of both husband and wife. While a woman may choose not to sign her own paycheck, she has to participate in all major credit-based transactions, such as the purchase of a home or a car. Since her salary may be the larger and the more stable of the two, her husband usually needs her signature on all major loan applications. Thus, Mrs. Punoose confidently asserted, "Everything should not be in one person's name. It won't happen anyway." In the United States both members of the couple are responsible for payments. Another factor leading to female participation in financial matters is the greater facility that some women have with English. One such example is Mrs. Thomas, who talked about how she was still in charge of finances in their household:

> . . . Most of the things are still under my name—it did not change—phone bill, credit cards, and all other things. He is not good at checking and writing but he used to do it when it was necessary. He managed. When he had some problem and he could not do it, he would give it to me. I am better at talking in English. When you come from a rural area of India, there is a problem in talking. There was only Hindi in that part of the country where he was working. So I took the responsibility of dealing with all kinds of matters.

In summary, immigration has brought in its wake changes in the household division of labor. In a way their fathers would never have imagined, Kerala Christian men contribute to housework, cooking, and childcare, while at the same time sharing financial decision-making with their wives. While there is no space to examine this question here, I observed different compromises between husbands and wives, all the way from reassertion of a strict patriarchal order to radical egalitarianism.[22] The specific balance depended on a number of factors, including the relative earning power of men and women, the constraints of the specific jobs, and the availability of childcare—whether from visiting kin or by sending children home to Kerala. Whatever the variation, all the immigrant men faced a loss of both patriarchal authority within the family and of social and economic status in the wider society. The question we must tackle next is how men attempted to compensate for this profoundly difficult change in their lives.

REASSERTION OF MALE PREROGATIVES IN THE CHURCH

When the immigration literature considers the relations among spheres—work, household, and community—it assumes that changes in one sphere, such as the gender reversal in employment status, will translate into parallel changes in other spheres. We have just seen that this is indeed the case: the rising labor market fortunes of nurses relative to their husbands lead to a more egalitarian domestic division of labor. In the sphere of community, specifically the religious congregation, however, we find the opposite tendency. Instead of changes parallel to those in household and work, there is a "reactive compensation." Here, Kerala Christian men seek out opportunities for participation and leadership that counterbalance their diminished powers at work and at home.

With limited opportunities for civic participation in the wider American society, the religious congregation becomes the ideal place for immigrant men to recover their lost status. In the first place, back home in Kerala leadership roles in the church are reserved for socially and economically prominent male members of the community, so that lay leadership is associated with high status. Mr. Lukos, for example, was proud to be from a family that could trace its active role back to the first churches of Indian Orthodoxy in the seventh century.[23] Just as it is for Indian Syrian Christians in Kerala, so the church in the United States is the umbrella under which family and individual identities are formed and reputations are won or lost: for Syrian Christians in Central City, St. George's became a venue for status claims.

Second, many immigrant congregations endeavor to forge a social and religious space in the new setting that reproduces what has been left behind in the imagined homeland.[24] In many ways, St. George's attempts to create an untainted "little Kerala"—an "extended family" for its members who are experiencing alienation in the wider American society. During both happy and sad times, individual members share the events of their lives with the church family. Beaming parents bring huge birthday cakes for the whole church to celebrate the important first birthday of their child. The housewarming party is usually a communal celebration that takes place after the house-blessing ceremony conducted by the priest. Death or illness—even of relatives in Kerala—summons an immediate network of support: church members gather together at the home of the bereaved or sick member to offer spiritual consolation and material aid.

Mrs. Simon's complaint about her husband explains the importance of church participation for immigrant men. "As for me," she said, "I told my husband, 'Don't join all these [political] parties and groups in the church. Just go to church, pray, and come back. Why go for these parties? I don't like that.' My husband replied, 'I have to have a niche here somehow. At least I have three to four people with whom I can talk now.'" Without extended family or friends, and often without a satisfying job, "having a niche" becomes crucial for the men.

The congregation offers leadership to some men and a sense of community to others. More generally, and this is the third compensatory role, the congregation has always been a place of male privilege. The gender roles and ideology in the Orthodox Church are starkly delineated. Men and women are physically separated during the three-hour-long Sunday morning service, and women have no official role other than joining in communal responses and hymns. Women and girls must cover their heads during the service, and they receive communion and final blessings only after all the men and boys have taken their turn. After they have been consecrated as deacons or acolytes, only men and boys can be altar helpers or assistants to the priest. Because they are polluting by nature, the women in the church cannot enter the altar area or touch the garments of the priest. Their menstruation is defiling and they are therefore barred from contact with all that is holy.[25] Women are excluded from positions of leadership. Only men over the age of twenty-one can vote in the meetings of the General Body. Women only organize the more peripheral activities: child education, food preparation, and their own groups. Even in the women's own service and prayer groups, such as the Martha Maria Samajam, the local priest presides over their meetings. Women can become Sunday school teachers, but they cannot be elected to the managing committee of the congregation.

Thus, the immigrant congregation offers a unique setting for men to restore their lost identity, and their self-esteem. To compensate for demotion in the labor market and the family, they use the church in three significant ways: to assert their leadership, to develop a sense of belonging, and to secure their exclusiveness. The congregation does not merely reproduce gendered patterns found in Kerala; it appropriates those patterns in order to deepen and extend male prerogatives. This "reactive intensification" can be found in the three areas referred to: the search for leadership leads to the phenomenon of church splitting, and the creation of new congregations; the need for communal belonging calls for new activities for men, such as preparing and serving food on public occasions; and the claim to exclusiveness is displayed, for example, in the organization of caroling. Let me deal with each in turn.

One way of expanding the opportunities for leadership is to multiply the number of congregations.[26] While not conventionally understood as a response to the devaluation of men in work and family life, church splitting, as it is called, certainly caters to this need.[27] Because the split-off congregations tend to be small, the vigorous participation of male members becomes crucial to their survival. Mrs. Simon told me that the reason her family had left their first congregation to join a splinter group was because her husband was given the chance to serve at the altar there.[28] Her husband was not getting along with the priest at their home congregation, and so it was not difficult to persuade him to join a newly formed congregation where he could realize his ambitions more easily.

If forming new congregations provides new leadership opportunities, the creation of new roles within the congregation fosters a sense of belonging.

In Kerala there is a tradition of low-status men cooking for wedding ban-
quets and other communal social events. This, however, does not extend to
the serving of food in the congregational setting. The typically large congregations in Kerala do not have weekly refreshments after the service. At
St. George's, on the other hand, eating and drinking after service is the
norm not only because members often travel great distances to attend
church, but also because the social aspects of congregational life are central
to the immigrant community. Mr. Elias puts it well:

> Back home, if someone is visiting, your relatives will invite you. If there is
> death, your relatives will invite you. . . . For the death anniversary of a loved
> one, you would invite your relatives to your home and serve food. Here, since
> you don't have relatives, the church members become your relatives. So
> church is the center of social events. Cooking, serving, cleaning, and every-
> thing—we are like one family.

What is striking about these communal gatherings is that they are controlled from start to finish by men—from the planning, to the collective
preparation, to the serving of food. At St. George's, men take over what are
typically female responsibilities and derive much satisfaction from their
public contribution even though it involves menial labor. As Mr. Samuel
explained:

> I never did anything in India, you know—cooking and things like that. . . .
> Members of the church—poor people—are there to do it. It kind of looks
> small. The tradition over there is that if you go and cook for the church, you
> will look—you are cheap or small in the society. They look down on that. Here
> also, maybe people think about it, but I don't care . . . .

For the men, therefore, their participation in this regular public ritual gave
them a collective identity that outweighed in importance any misgivings
about the low status of cooking and serving.

If splitting congregations propagates new leadership roles, while cooking
and feeding the congregation creates a sense of belonging, caroling is a way
of establishing the church as male territory. Immigrant congregations, like
St. George's, form caroling groups, which go to the homes of both members
and nonmembers, including those of Hindus in the Kerala immigrant community. These groups bring the "good news" in the form of carols, often
written to the tunes of Malayalam film songs.[29] The expectation is that each
home they visit will make a monetary contribution to the congregation.
Because donations from caroling are an important source of income, the
caroling groups put in long hours to cover wide areas of the city.[30]

Besides providing an opportunity for sharing the gospel and fundraising,
caroling at St. George's promotes exclusive male participation and cama-
raderie. Whereas in Kerala the caroling groups of the Orthodox congregation tend to be made up of young people chaperoned by Sunday school

teachers, the same groups at St. George's were limited to adult men. Mr. Samuel considered singing as part of the Kerala Christmas: "It is an old tradition. During Christmas time everybody expects caroling to happen. If there is no caroling, you don't feel like it is Christmas." However, when the teenagers of the church voiced their desire to participate, men put up a great deal of resistance.[31] In making caroling an exclusively adult male activity, the men of St. George's were serving the community but they were also carving out a terrain of male exclusivity.

We have so far considered the church from the standpoint of men, but how do women regard their own exclusion? First, and most obviously, irregular schedules imposed by nursing work make it difficult for most of the women to attend church consistently and participate in its affiliated activities. Still, there are a number who would like more active roles and a voice in church-related, decision-making processes. Mrs. Philip explains why she curtails her own inclination to vocally participate in the meetings of the General Body.

> *Mrs. Philip:* In fact, I have felt like talking at times, but I know that they [the men] are going to talk about me.
>
> *S.G.:* Whom do they talk about? You or your husband?
>
> *Mrs. Philip:* You know what. They will talk to the husband and say, "See how your wife is." This leads to a fight at home. But when they [the women] are at work, they argue and talk, but because they don't want to fight with their husbands or have people talking, they just keep quiet [in church].

Here potential public censure and domestic discord are the cause of Mrs. Philip's silence.

Because nursing is a marker of deviant femininity, it is even more important for the "dirty" nurses to stay otherwise within gendered boundaries, guarding their carefully forged respectability in the public forum of the church. Women police their own bodies when they choose clothing, when they decide where to stand in the church. Mrs. Mani, whom I met at a national church conference, told me how she agonizes over what to wear for her visits to the home of the bishop. Whereas she usually wore a skirt and blouse to her nursing job, on the days that she had to stop by the bishop's home, she would either wear an Indian outfit or take a change of Indian clothing with her to work. She then related an incident in her church that indicated just how sensitive she was to questions of body surveillance. Once, when her daughter wore a nice, dressy pair of pants to church, the priest's wife pulled Mrs. Mani aside and asked her why her daughter wore pants to church. Mrs. Mani's answer drew on conventional norms and highlighted the detailed patrolling of the female body: "Yes, my daughter tucked her shirt in her pants. But wearing a skirt with your blouse tucked in and wearing pants—both ways your behind is visible to the same extent."

Mrs. Mathai, who left home at the age of sixteen for nursing, explains how easy it is for women to have their reputations besmirched.

> If some girl was sent for nursing, the feeling was that she was lost. But people just made up those things. Even now, our people are like that. If I speak to somebody, even though I am married, our people will make up things to say. They don't look at age. They will say whatever they want, especially our men. Even if we smile at somebody or say "Hi," immediately that information goes to the Indian store and they start talking about you. It is just like in Kerala— that's how our people are. There are many stories like that around here. This is why I don't send my daughters anywhere without their father. I am actually scared.

The need to guard her reputation against the stories that people make up "even now" about "lost" nurses defines Mrs. Mathai's behavior no less within the immigrant community than in Kerala. Even her daughters' mobility has to be monitored to prevent disrepute to the whole family.

Fear of a soiled reputation and of unwelcome gossip are important reasons for the nurse's subservience in church. This fear inspires voluntary compliance. Like her husband, she too is reacting against gender reversals at work and in the home. She too seeks to compensate for her husband's loss of status by making sure she does not cause him to lose face by transgressing acceptable behavior. She knows that she can be stigmatized as a "dirty nurse" and is therefore that much more careful to uphold expected gender norms in public spaces. In this way she becomes an accomplice in the consolidation and extension of male prerogatives.

THE PARADOX OF "MEN AT PLAY"

Ironically, the male attempt to gain back status in the community turns out to be self-defeating. If the splitting of congregations opens up new positions in the church hierarchy, at the same time—by making them more common and mundane—it also devalues those positions and thus the men who occupy them. Their increased participation only attracts the resentment and disdain of displaced onlookers, who talk of them as children "playing" in the church.

The most profound element in this entire dynamic remains the wives' independence in their role as nurses. Try as they might to elude it, nursing operates as a marker to undermine the status of the husbands. The shift in power in the domestic sphere comes back to haunt the men in the communal sphere, where their connection to nurses becomes the most salient feature of their identity. Recall what Mr. Mathen, whose wife is not a nurse, had to say in the vignette that opened this chapter, dismissing the status claims of husbands in the church as mere "play." Because of their secondary role in the immigration process, because their wives immigrate first and then send for them, the husbands initially lose much of their personal identity. They become known as "Annie's husband" or "Molly's husband" when they first arrive in Central City.

Within the community, the husbands of nurses are frequently identified as "frustrated men" while "nurses are the bosses." Mrs. Itoop, herself not a nurse, referred to the common perception that "It is the men, who are not allowed to say anything at home or at work, who come and shout at church." Mr. Itoop elaborated:

> There [in the church] the wife will not say anything. At home she might, but not in church. . . . It is considered very bad to be a controlling wife back home [in India] because men are the bosses. If it is the opposite, it is a very bad thing. . . . The wives won't try to control openly. His masculinity is shown inside the church. The idea is to show the wife and others. He may be able to get rid of what is inside. "Even though I am insignificant, I am not bad"—he wants to show that to others.

Thus, the deviant femininity attributed to their wives turns into the emasculated stereotype of the "nurse-husband" who is forced to put on a show in church.

Mr. Mathen claimed that even the husbands recognized their participation in the church as, in part, a compensation for their loss of status in the domestic sphere, as witnessed by their domination of the congregation's management committee.

> *Mr. Mathen:* You take any church [in America]—you take anywhere, it is a fact. I will tell you right now—in our church, the trustee—Mr. Varkey—his wife is a nurse; the secretary—Mr. Paul—his wife is a nurse. . . . [He went on to name all of St. George's committee members.] See where it stands—eight of them already out of ten. There are [only] two more.

> *S.G.:* I see your point.

> *Mr. Mathen:* It is not my point. Even Varkey, Patrose, Paul—they all say the same thing. Oh, I am not saying this behind their backs or anything. This is the fact.

> *S.G.:* Do they say that at home, that their wives are in control?

> *Mr. Mathen:* No. I am not saying these men have problems in the homes. They are all happily married, and they are my friends too. If you take a church, this is what you see. Kunju—his wife is not a nurse. He was never on a committee.

More concretely, as I recounted in the previous section, one of the ways husbands attempted to use the church to reclaim status was to develop a sense of collective belonging by preparing and serving food on ritual occasions. But this reactive compensation through "female work" identified them even more closely with their stigmatized wives.

Interestingly, it is not only their gender status but also their class status that is denigrated by their connection to nurses. In the absence of class identifiers that operate in Kerala, nursing is transformed into an explicit marker of class in Central City, tying husbands to the presumed pre-immigration lower-class origins of their wives. To understand this process we need to turn back to India. In Kerala, caste, class, and religion are all important indicators of identity. There, Christians are themselves separated into different denominations, castes, and classes. Most Keralite Syrian Christians choose to separate themselves from the "lower castes" by claiming that they are directly descended from the Brahmin caste, although Christian theology does not even allow for internal caste differentiation. And while Syrian Christian churches began accepting lower-caste converts in the late nineteenth century, almost all the churches maintain separate places of worship, separate congregations, and separate cemeteries for their few lower-caste converts. Keralite Syrian Christians are a strictly endogamous pseudo-caste group, in that marriages and other affiliations are limited to their own kind. Class differences within this group are therefore an important means of social differentiation. While marriages take place among members of different Syrian Christian denominations, as between Catholics and the Orthodox, class differences are critical to the regulation of these alliances.[32]

I will consider three markers of class in Kerala—material wealth, family name, and community leadership—and show how they recede in importance and in some cases disappear altogether in Central City. Let us begin with material wealth. Immigration and the resulting enrichment for most families homogenizes consumption patterns, rendering differences in material wealth less visible. Whereas in India it is only the rich who own large homes or cars, in Central City almost every nurse and her family can afford these items. Mr. Cherian, whose wife is not a nurse, explained how "nurse money" makes it difficult to distinguish between the rich and the poor.

> *Mr. C:* Here the difference between the rich and the poor is much less. In India, you can differentiate the rich and the poor much quicker.
>
> *S.G.:* Can you still recognize who is rich and poor?
>
> *Mr. C:* No, here you can't tell. Nurses make good money, so they can buy the stuff to look rich. So you can't tell who is rich. In India, the rich have a good education—you know, doctors, engineers, and lawyers. They don't marry nurses; they marry from good families, only the educated. . . . That is what we see in our church at least. Do you see any doctors working in our kitchen?

The nurse's income allows immigrants to "buy the stuff to look rich." Although you cannot tell the rich from the poor in Central City, Mr. Cherian is suggesting that you do know who is married to a nurse. Men from wealthy "good families" would not marry nurses and would not be working in the church kitchen. Thus, despite fancy cars and big homes, their marital affiliation with nurses ties the immigrant men to a lower-class background.

Family name is another indicator of social class in Kerala. In Central City it is not necessarily recognized because members of the immigrant community are not from the same parts of Kerala. Family name seemed to be an issue for those who claimed to possess a prestigious heritage. For example, Mr. Lukos claimed he knew all the top people in his community, because he himself came from one of the top families. "You ask anyone if they know this family and they should know us." Mr. Varkey similarly claimed that his family was one of the original Brahmin families to be converted to Christianity by St. Thomas about two thousand years ago. He boasted about his high standing in his natal village. When he was studying at the engineering school in Kerala, his fellow villagers referred to him as the engineer from "so and so" family. In Central City it is less likely that Mr. Lukos or Mr. Varkey would get the type of "recognition" to which they are accustomed in their home communities.

In the absence of recognition through "family name," nursing once more steps into the breach as the stamp of class origin. Both the husbands and the children of nurses are tied to the putative class status of nursing. Mr. Lukos observed:

> So many of my cousins—they are all trying to find a proper match for their boys, and they all tell me that they do not want the marriage if there is a nurse in that family. That is what is called class consciousness. They said, "Can you find a match for my son? He is a doctor, so we are looking for a doctor, and her parents should not be nurses for any reason."

Even if they are doctors in the United States, daughters of nurses are not eligible for high-class husbands from Kerala. The stigma against nursing is transmitted directly to the immigrant community, where it affects not just nurses and their husbands but their children too.

Given that his wife is a nurse, I asked Mr. Lukos if his children would have qualified as marital options for people like his cousins in Kerala. He responded: "Then again, they [my cousins] are all rich, and they are all well placed in society, and because I was the oldest [child], I married a nurse. I am very inferior to them because I married a nurse and two of my sisters are nurses. The feelings are still there." Despite his own high-class origins, Mr. Lukos was not sure that his children could climb back up because their mother and aunts were nurses. In requiring that the prospective bride not be the child of a nurse, the cousins of Mr. Lukos were employing the only class-control measure at their disposal. We see here how connections back to Kerala reconstruct, within the immigrant community, patterns of class around the marker of nursing.

Finally, leadership positions in the church and community represent another symbol of upper-class status in Kerala. In the immigrant community, at least at St. George's, leadership is linked to the disreputable nurses and their putative lower-class origins. Men from upper-class families are either crowded out or hold themselves aloof from the politics of the immigrant congregation. Mr. Cherian explained: "Here, people who are well-off do not do church politics. Look at all the committee members: they are all nurses' husbands. Professionals do not get involved. In India, it is the opposite."

In Kerala, material wealth, family name, and community leadership are the symbols of class. In the immigrant community, it is difficult to tell the difference between the rich and the poor, family names do not elicit "recognition," and leadership in the church is no longer the preserve of the upper class. In this context, nursing becomes the telltale signifier that undermines the husbands' effort to gain back the status they lose after immigration.

GENDER AND CLASS IN THE CONTEXT OF TRANSNATIONALISM

The incorporation of Kerala Christian women into the Indian labor market as nurses was the catalyst for tremendous changes in the Christian community in Kerala. The new earning power for women not only translated into trickle-down prosperity for many around them, but it also challenged the gender norms existing in Kerala, leading to the discursive construction of the "lost" and "dirty" nurse.

In an era of global demand for nurses, these pioneering women took the opportunities that came their way to become the tickets for international migration for entire families and even villages. On the face of it, this is a story of economic mobility and professional achievement. It tells of men and women who overcame many obstacles to build new communities in the United States as well as to help their families left behind. Gauging by the fairly affluent immigrant community in Central City, they represent the quintessential American success story.

A closer look, however, reveals that behind the success story lies another story about the complex reconfiguration of gender and class relations, showing how gender and class are inseparable. As they lost gender power in the immigration process, male immigrants attempted to gain back status in the only place available to them. Because their participation in the wider American society is constricted, they created new roles for themselves at St. George's. Because of their implicit identification with their wives, these men experienced a de-classing effect. Similarly, the nurses' upward mobility had immediate effects on their gender status. They became known as "bosses" and therefore had to surveil their bodies, movement, and speech ever more carefully in such communal spheres as the church.

At first it seems that the separate spheres of family, work, and community are reconfigured to help maintain equilibrium in gender relations. It appears that the church is a space where the men successfully compensate for their diminished status at work and at home. In the case of the nurses, their increased professional status and upward economic mobility seem to give them greater power in the household. However, paradoxically, the gender relations in these spheres end up undermining each other. For the men, identification with their spouses and their low-status positions in the labor market return to haunt them in their assertion of male domination in the church. Similarly, policing their bodies and their behavior in church translates into nurses' sensitivity to the predicament of their husbands. Nurses themselves make great sacrifices to bolster the self-esteem of their husbands by minimizing adjustments in the household. In other words, for both men and women the attempt to compensate within spheres is severely constrained by influences across spheres.

Finally, it is the connections to Kerala that re-create the old oppressive gender and class relations in the immigrant community. It is on her visit to Kerala that the specter of the "dirty" nurse becomes resurrected for Mrs. Thomas in her interactions with her well-educated sister-in-law. Mr. Lukos feels that his children would be excluded from marrying into the circle of his high-class cousins in India because their mother and aunts were nurses. In the immigrant community, these meanings of nursing are the ever-present backdrop that informs ongoing negotiations of gender and class relations within and among different spheres.

NOTES

I am deeply indebted to the members and the priest at St. George's, who welcomed me into their church and homes and generously shared their lives with me. I thank Raka Ray, Leslie Salzinger, and R. Stephen Warner for their insightful comments on multiple versions of this chapter. There are many people in the Berkeley community who have read and commented on this chapter. They are too many to name individually but I am grateful to them. I would be remiss in not thanking my family members, who have encouraged and inspired me throughout this process. I was supported by the New Ethnic and Immigrant Congregations Project, the American Institute for Indian Studies, The Louisville Institute, and the Sloan Center for Working Families during the course of my research. A version of this paper won the 1999 Cheryl Miller Award, for outstanding contributions to the field of women and work, from SWS (Sociologists for Women in Society).

1. All the names of individuals, cities, and institutions have been changed.

2. While I contacted thirty couples, I interviewed only fifty-eight people, since one woman's husband had died and one man refused to be interviewed.

3. See Nina Glick Schiller, Linda Basch, and Cristina Szanton Blanc, *Towards a Transnational Perspective on Migration: Race, Class, Ethnicity and Nationalism Reconsidered;* Michael Kearney, "The Local and the Global: The Anthropology of Globalization and Transnationalism"; and Michael P. Smith and Luis E. Guarnizo, eds., *Transnationalism from Below.*

4. Sarah Mahler, "Theoretical and Empirical Contributions toward a Research Agenda for Transnationalism," p. 92.

5. Pierrette Hondagneu-Sotelo, *Gendered Transitions: Mexican Experiences of Immigration.*

6. Patricia Pessar, "The Linkage between the Household and the Workplace in the Experience of Dominican Women in the U.S."

7. Yen Le Espiritu, *Asian American Women and Men: Labor, Laws and Love.*

8. Ibid., p. 62.

9. Although the Indian government in 1961 officially banned the practice of giving and receiving dowries, it is still widely practiced in Kerala and among immigrants in the United States.

10. In "Marriage, Birth and Death: Property Rights and Domestic Relationships of the Orthodox/Jacobite Syrian Christians of Kerala," Susan Visvanathan argues that whereas "streedhanam" was ideally viewed as a premortem inheritance, it has become a means of contracting marriages into desirable families, with different rates for each economic class. In addition to the economic status of the families, the educational and employment qualifications of the bride and groom as well as the woman's complexion are important factors in the negotiation (p. 1341).

11. Ranjana Ragavachari, *Conflict and Adjustments: Indian Nurses in an Urban Milieu,* p. 15.

12. This religious distinction continues to shape immigration to the United States. A directory of Keralite immigrants in the United States shows that 85 percent are Christian. See Kunnuparampil Punnoose Andrews, *Keralites in America: Community Reference Book.* A survey of the Kerala Christian community in Dallas found that 49 percent of adults reported nursing as their occupation. See T. J. Thomas, "The Shepherding Perspective of Seward Hiltner on Pastoral Care and Its Application in the Organizing of a Congregation in Dallas of East Indian Immigrants from the Mar Thoma Syrian Church of India."

13. It is quite possible that some of the mothers may have participated in an informal economy, such as helping out in the homes of more affluent community members, although this was not reported to me.

14. Saskia Sassen-Koob captures the dynamics of this process in "Notes on the Incorporation of Third World Women into Wage-Labor through Immigration and Off-Shore Production," where she notes that the large-scale entry of women into the labor market may have the effect of disrupting unwaged work structures in a community, minimizing the possibilities for women to return to their communities of origin and consequently creating a pool of migrant workers.

15. While there is a global demand for health professionals, the global distribution of nurses to meet the demand is far from equitable. In *Physician and Nurse Migration: Analysis and Policy Implications,* a study conducted for the World Health Organization, Alonso Mejia and his colleagues report that of 3.6 million nurses worldwide, 3.1 million (85 percent) are in "developed" countries which contain only a third of the world's population. Furthermore, developed countries continue to receive 92 percent of migrant nurses.

16. In "The Migration and Incorporation of Filipino Nurses," Paul Ong and Tania Azores state that since the economic crisis of the late 1970s hospitals have been under tremendous pressure to cut costs, including efforts to keep nurses' wages low (p. 167).

17. Tomoji Ishi, "Class Conflict, the State and Linkage: The International Migration of Nurses from the Philippines," p. 288.

18. See Keiko Yamanaka and Kent McClelland, "Earning the Model-Minority Image: Diverse Strategies of Economic Adaptation by Asian American Women," p. 86; Mejia et al., *Physician and Nurse Migration.*

19. A feminist critique of the conceptual use of "sex roles" argues that functionalist assumptions are inherent in the language of roles. See Barrie Thorne and Marilyn Yalom, *Rethinking the Family: Some Feminist Questions,* and R.W. Connell, *Gender and Power.* As my analysis will show, I am very aware of the power differences between men and women and the conflict that can result from such differences. I do not use "roles" here as descriptive of social reality but as indicators of social expectations— similar to social scripts.

20. Raymond Williams, *Religions of Immigrants from India and Pakistan: New Threads in the American Tapestry,* p. 108.

21. Of the thirty couples I interviewed in Central City, ten couples left their children for varying amounts of time in Kerala with family members or in boarding schools under the supervision of family members. Four couples received some help with childcare from family members they sponsored to the United States.

22. I examine the household division of labor in these families at length in "Gendered Ideologies and Strategies: The Negotiation of the Household Division of Labor among Middle-Class South Asian American Families." I also elaborate on this topic in my dissertation titled "Gendered Spheres in a Transnational Context: The Interaction of Work, Home, and Church among Indian Christian Immigrants."

23. Most of the Kerala nurses in the United States are Syrian Christians who claim their descent from the early converts of the apostle Thomas, who, tradition has it, was martyred in southern India in 72 A.D. These Christians of Kerala are called Syrian not because they have Syrian ancestry but rather because they use Syrian liturgy. Syrian missionary influences, starting in the seventh century, led to the establishment of the church under the patriarch of Antioch with a liturgy that still retains some Syriac. Over the centuries the Syrian Christians became divided into different denominations. There are Catholics and Eastern Orthodox as well as Protestants of every stripe who claim a Syrian Christian ancestry. The Orthodox Syrian Christian church of India is one such denomination in this tradition. It broke ties with Antioch in 1912 and is currently led by a patriarch from Kerala. For an in-depth description of the history and organization of various Christian groups in Kerala as well as the immigrant congregations in the United States, see Raymond Williams, *Christian Pluralism in the U.S: The Indian Immigrant Experience.*

24. Will Herberg, *Protestant-Catholic-Jew: An Essay in American Religious Sociology.*

25. In 1987, the church synod revised the constitution to permit girls under the age of five to be brought to kiss the altar along with male children during the baptism ceremony. That the church chose the age of five is not accidental. Females under the age of five are seen as nonsexual.

26. The tendency for congregations to split over nondoctrinal issues is a growing concern among many church leaders. While I do not have the exact numbers of congregations that have formed from splits, informed church members at national meetings indicate that it is a common pattern in most metropolitan areas where there is more than one congregation.

27. According to immigration scholars, schisms are prevalent in Korean immi-

grant congregations as well. Furthermore, it appears that male competition for status-enhancing staff positions in the face of postimmigration loss of status is one of the major reasons for the prevalence of such schisms. See Won Moo Hurh and Kwang Chung Kim, "Religious Participation of Korean Immigrants in the United States"; and Eui Hang Shin and Hyung Park, "An Analysis of Causes of Schisms in Ethnic Churches: The Case of Korean-American Churches."

28. While "parish" is the official designation for these immigrant religious gatherings, I am using the term "congregation" because I believe that this is a case of what the sociologist R. Stephen Warner calls the "de facto congregationalism" that is prevalent in the American religious open market. In "Work in Progress toward a New Paradigm for the Sociological Study of Religion in the United States," Warner argues that religious organizations in the United States favor the face-to-face, locally controlled congregational form over geographically based units—such as parishes—designated by higher ecclesiastical authorities. In Kerala, membership in a parish is determined by where the member lives. In the United States, immigrant Orthodox churches seem to be organized around the congregational model, since churchgoers like Mr. Simon choose among different options.

29. These songs are sometimes written by members of the community in the United States using the tunes of secular film songs from Kerala. Additionally, songs from the growing Christian popular music scene in Kerala are also used. Having songs set to the latest tunes, with instrumental accompaniment, becomes a matter of pride among the caroling groups from the different congregations, as they try to outdo each other in the caroling and in the annual Christmas ecumenical program, where the Kerala Christian congregations in the area have the opportunity to represent their respective singing talents.

30. For example, in 1994, the donations from caroling made up one-third of St. George's total income for the year (1994 year-end financial report presented at the General Body meeting).

31. I analyze this incident at length in "Caroling with the Keralites: The Negotiation of Gendered Space in an Indian Immigrant Congregation."

32. See note 10 for an example of how class differences play a part in potential marital alliances via the different rates of dowry for each class.

SIX

Net-Working for a Living

Irish Software Developers
in the Global Workplace

Seán Ó Riain

In 1992, I took the path followed by many young Irish people at that time and emigrated to the United States. In my case I left Dublin for Berkeley, California, to get a Ph.D. in sociology. Within a year or two I found myself beginning to study the Irish software industry from six thousand miles away in Silicon Valley. Through interviews with managers in Silicon Valley companies with operations in Ireland, I investigated the dynamics of foreign investment in the Irish software industry. E-mail correspondence with managers of Irish companies in Dublin directed me to their Silicon Valley offices, where I learned the basic history of the emergence of an Irish-owned software industry which was now itself becoming increasingly globalized. These contacts and other Irish people I knew in California put me in touch with Irish software developers working in the Silicon Valley area.

In the mid-1990s many of the young emigrants of the late 1980s and early 1990s were returning home, encouraged by the booming "Celtic Tiger" economy. In early 1997 I followed these global connections and returned to Ireland to carry out more detailed research. It was time to live for a while inside one of the global workplaces that constituted the industry I was studying. I spent twelve weeks as a technical writer and sometime tester on a software development team in USTech, a United States transnational corporation well established in Ireland. During this time I participated fully in the work of the team and wrote a user guide for our product which was installed on the system as on-line help for users of the system. I sat in the same cubicle as the rest of the team, attended team meetings, and interacted closely with them on a regular basis on decisions regarding the user guide. After an initial period of suspicion of my motives, which may return once they read this chapter, the team members were very welcoming and helpful to me. Indeed, the regular flow of contract personnel in and out of the team meant that I became a relatively well-established team member.

By the time I came to work at USTech in Ireland I had made many of the connections and followed many of the transnational career paths which were such a big part of my coworkers' experience. The five long-term members of the team were employees of USTech but were working on a contract designing a product for Womble Software, a spin-off from USTech headquarters in the United States. My own life in the social sciences had mirrored the experiences of my friends on the Womble team—educated on different sides of the same college campuses, working at home and abroad on emerging meanings and logics, one foot in local culture, the other in the global economy. Software had seemed like a distant world until my ethnography revealed the many aspects already familiar to me from life in the Irish knowledge-worker diaspora.

During the time I spent with the Womble team, I uncovered a characteristic set of structures and dynamics of this global workplace. Although we sat at the center of a wide array of local and global connections and of multiple career trajectories, the cubicle space we shared came to dominate our lives. The experience of local space was intensified for us, even as we sat in a global workplace. Time too was intensified as the project deadline became the defining element of our work and, to some extent, social lives. Out of this intensification of time and space emerged cooperation, innovation, and career success, but also burnout, individualism, inequality, and pressures on family. It is these dilemmas and tradeoffs that constitute the "contested terrain" of the global informational workplace.

It is 4:15 in the afternoon. On the wall of the software test group in the Irish offices of USTech, a prominent Silicon Valley computer company, there are four clocks. At the moment they show that it is 8:15 A.M. in Silicon Valley, California, 10:15 in Austin and Fort Worth, Texas, and 11:15 in Montreal, Canada. Silicon Valley has just "opened for business," and the software developers and managers in Ireland begin a hectic few hours of discussion with their American counterparts. The row of clocks evokes a smoothly working global economy, held back only by time zones, and a software operation which seamlessly manages a variety of trans-national connections.

I hurry downstairs, as I have a conference call to the United States at 4:30 P.M. Irish time (8:30 A.M. their time in Silicon Valley). Thirty minutes later I am sitting in an open-plan cubicle, along with five members of a software development team. Employed by USTech, they are developing a software product for a Silicon Valley start-up company called Womble Software. I have been writing a user guide for the product and am deep in discussion with Jane, the technical-writing editor in Silicon Valley, and Ramesh, an immigrant to the United States from India and the "chief architect" of the program, who is in St. Louis in the heart of middle-America. As my manager comes into the team area, I put the conference call on the speaker phone. Now the whole "Womble team" can hear the conversation.

As the conversation unfolds, so does the mime drama around me, as the team reacts to the flow of global communication into this cubicled "local" space. When Ramesh suggests adding new features (creating more work for the developers around me), there is an explosion of displeased sign lan-. guage, including a variety of abusive gestures directed at the speaker phone. Since Ramesh can hear everything on our end, this pantomime is con-ducted in complete silence. I have a hard time not bursting out laughing. When Jane points out to Ramesh that it is difficult to write a user guide when the final screen designs for the software program have not been decided upon (a common complaint within the development team two weeks before the product is released), there is an explosion of mimed cheering and barely controlled laughter around me.

This is just another day in the global informational workplace, a work-place which is home to increasing numbers of employees around the world. The dominant image of these workplaces is that of places lifted out of time and space, places where communication and innovation are free from the drag of local cultures and practices and untainted by power relations. Robert Reich argues that new information and communication technolo-gies make it possible and even necessary to reorganize firms into "global webs" and employees into global telecommuters.[1] For Reich these webs operate smoothly, destroying constraints of space and social structure, mov-ing in conjunction with the ever-circling hands of the clocks on the USTech wall. The global workplace is "lifted out" of its temporal and spatial contexts and becomes a "pure" space for communication based on shared rules of interaction and understanding.[2]

Others argue that this perspective is too benign. The speeding up of the global economy destroys local space—the fact that Ramesh and the Womble team can participate in the same conversation at the same time means that they essentially share the same social and economic space, despite the physical distance between them. Time annihilates space, melting away "solid" local places into the "air" of the global economy.[3] This is not a neutral process, however, as the once autonomous local space of the worker is increasingly dominated by global corporations and the ever more rapid pace of economic life under capitalism.[4] Ramesh's presence—a phone call, e-mail message, or plane trip away—undermines the autonomy provided these workers by their local space.

The Womble team is certainly connected to other global workplaces—including Silicon Valley and St. Louis on this particular afternoon. They also experience the pressure of the global economy through the demands of Ramesh for new features. However, local space is not destroyed by these global connections. The Womble cubicle takes on a culture of its own, manifested in the mimed hostility to Ramesh's suggestions, but also in the information-sharing, problem-solving, and solidarity-building within the team on an everyday basis. In fact, the demands of the global economy for increased flexibility and specialized learning actually make the local context and interactions of the global workplace even more critical. Efficient production and constant innovation require the construction of shared physical spaces where workers can interact and communicate on a face-to-face basis and where shared goals and meanings can be created and maintained.[5]

Global connections bring the pressures of the world economy into the heart of workplaces such as the Womble team cubicle. However, these pressures actually make local space and social context all the more important. The speed-up of time and the extension of social space across physical distance in the global economy do not destroy space but in fact intensify the impact of space in constituting successful global workplaces.

However, this does not herald a return to an era of workplaces dominated by localized social relations. This is because the importance of local social relations to innovation creates a dilemma for the global corporations that rely on this innovation. The local character of their work teams is essential to their efficiency but also poses a problem of regulating such localized relations from a distance. Ramesh may be aware that his proposals are not meeting with happy grins on the other end of the phone, but he is also unable to directly regulate the team's behavior because of his distance from the team and his only partial incorporation into the social space of the team. The typical managerial answer to this dilemma of control in the global workplace is to attempt to control the instrument of speed-up and pressure within the global economy—time itself. The politics of the contemporary workplace is increasingly the politics of time.[6]

The most important instrument used to control time in the global workplace is the project deadline. Although Ramesh cannot control the everyday behavior of the Womble team, the parameters within which the team can operate are set by the demands of the deadline: the team members have a great deal of autonomy in how they work, but the supervisor looking over their shoulder is time itself, with every decision measured against its impact on meeting the deadline. Ramesh's requests for new features are not considered on their technical merits but on the basis of their impact on the team's ability to meet the deadline. Even as the importance of space is intensified in the global workplace, so too is time, in its manifestation as the dominant mode of control in these workplaces. Global workplaces are subject to a process of what I call time-space intensification.

This chapter explores in detail the characteristic structures and dynamics of the global workplace under conditions of time-space intensification. The first part of the analysis shows the dilemmas posed for innovation in the global workplace due to the pressures placed on it by the intersection of the high-mobility careers of software developers and highly mobile software firms. It documents how intense cooperation in localized workplaces makes it possible for such highly mobile workers and firms to forge an alliance in the pursuit of innovation and profit. A tension persists within this structure, however—a tension between place-bound cooperation based on group solidarity and individual careers based on high rates of mobility between firms and places. This tension is reconciled through the dynamics of the workplace, which are analyzed in the second part of the chapter. The period prior to the project deadline is one of team solidarity and cohesion, while the post-deadline phase is characterized by the fragmentation of the team as they use their social networks to position themselves for the next moves in their careers. The globalization of the information technology (IT) industry is seen to result not in a virtual economy but in a global industry organized around and through certain key places and regions. Within these global workplaces, relations among workers constantly cycle through phases of cohesion and fragmentation, as worker solidarity is mobilized for purposes of innovation but disarmed by the structure of careers in the labor market. The globalization of knowledge workplaces becomes an object of tension and conflict in those workplaces; globalization is neither simply an ever-expanding process of increasingly pure communication and innovation nor an inexorable advance of the dominance of capital. Power relations in these workplaces are forged out of the interplay of mobility and place and of time and space, forms of interplay that are examined through the rest of this chapter.

This chapter argues, therefore, that as the workplace stretches out across national borders local spaces such as the Womble team cubicle become all the more crucial to the operation of the global economy. Overcoming the constraints of international time differences allows organization across time and space, but poses new problems of control from a distance—problems which are solved by the intensification of time through work-team deadlines. Global informational workplaces are characterized not by the disappearance of time and space as realities of work life, but by their increasing importance and intensification.

DILEMMAS OF THE GLOBAL WORKPLACE

Neither do these workplaces emerge tabula rasa onto the global stage, as a response to the prompting of the global market. In fact, the Womble team is the outcome of state development strategies, changing corporate structures and strategies, and the emergence of new industries organized around knowledge creation. Indeed, the routine phone and e-mail arguments between Ramesh and the Womble team would bring a glow to the heart of many industrial development agency officials in Ireland. The formation of connections to the global economy by attracting foreign high-technology investment has been the cornerstone of Ireland's industrial policy since the late 1950s. The connection to the United States has been particularly crucial—over four hundred United States companies have located in Ireland, and some three-quarters of jobs in electronics and software in Ireland are in foreign-owned companies. Through the 1970s and 1980s, transnational electronics and computer hardware firms located primarily low-level functions in Ireland and developed few links to the local economy.[7] Many of the transnational corporations used Ireland as an "export processing zone" within the European market, taking advantage of low tax and wage rates and Ireland's position within European Union tariff barriers. Irish plants were at best weakly integrated into the core activities of the corporate parents, as the typical Irish operation's activities were routine and relations with the parent hierarchical.

However, the past five to ten years have seen a shift in the nature of the activities and the character of some of the foreign investment in Ireland.[8] Encouraged by the state industrial development agencies, many hardware operations began to grow software development centers as the information technology industry moved toward a focus on software and software became the strategic technology for these corporations. Local managers, usually Irish-born, were able to carve out strategic positions for their operations within the parent companies, although their position always remained precarious. In cases such as USTech, local managers often developed relationships with customers well before discussing these new lines of business with their colleagues at headquarters. In recent years, subcontracting and business partnership relationships between United States and Irish firms have expanded and the two economies have become increasingly closely integrated. Indeed, the apparent shortage of computer skills in Silicon Valley was one of the reasons why the Womble software contract went to the USTech Ireland office. Companies such as USTech Ireland were still limited by their place in the international corporate structure and often still concentrated on testing, support, and consulting software work rather than on the strategic software development tasks. However, many were able to develop small- to medium-sized software development teams, closely integrated with the parent's operations.

USTech is well established in Ireland, having located there over fifteen years ago and becoming one of the early success stories of Irish industrial policy. For many years it was one of Ireland's primary computer hardware production operations, with a reputation for high quality. The hardware manufacturing operations of USTech Ireland were dismantled, with massive layoffs, in the early 1990s, leaving local management scrambling for the operation's survival and turning to a complete reliance on the local pool of software skills. Their links to the global economy have subsequently diversified, with a proliferation of customers, partners, and internal corporate sponsors replacing their previous model of reporting directly to a single office in the United States. The software development contract for Womble reflects this change, as there was little opportunity within the previous corporate structure for such arrangements.

Womble Software itself is a perfect example of the "global web" corporate structure, which Reich argues is becoming the norm. Formed as a spin-off from a large hierarchical corporation, the company is partly owned by the four founders, partly by USTech itself, partly by a major customer, and the rest by a venture capital fund in Silicon Valley. It has no more than fifteen employees of its own. The development team is based in Ireland and is officially contracted to provide software development services to Womble. The screens for the program are conceptualized by Ramesh, but all the development work necessary to turn them into computer graphics is done in a small graphic-design house just outside San Francisco. The helpdesk staff, which users reach if they call with a problem, is staffed by the trained employees of a helpdesk contracting company. The technical writers who write the on-screen help for users are all hired on a contract basis. In place of more rigid, hierarchical organizational structures, we have a shifting web of connections forged into a relatively fleeting alliance.

Mobility and Connections in the Global Labor Market

Womble is not only, however, the prototype of the "global web" organization but also conforms to a new model of computer-industry careers. In this model, the dominant metaphor of IBM's promise of lifetime employment has been replaced by the image of the freewheeling Silicon Valley engineers who expect little from their employers and will jump ship for more money or more challenging work at the drop of a hat.[9] Both of course are stereotypes, but there is more than a grain of truth in the emergence of cross-firm careers as the dominant pattern in software companies in Silicon Valley and in Ireland.[10] These trends are intensified by a shortage of experienced personnel in most countries' software industries.[11] Certain skills are in particularly high demand—including the Unix, C++, database, and Java skills of the employees in the Womble team. The variety of local and global connections of the team reinforces the tendency toward mobility by providing the channels of information about new opportunities and the social contacts for facilitating moves to those emerging areas. Negotiating the commitment of highly mobile employees becomes the critical dilemma facing software firms, a dilemma which is addressed in the following sections of this chapter.

In industries such as software, the typical career pattern now involves a number of moves between organizations, and there has been a clear shift from internal labor markets to job-hopping between firms. When employees stay with the same firm, their tasks and level of responsibility change on a regular basis. Furthermore, professional migration into both the United States and Ireland has been increasing, with transnational intrafirm and interfirm careers expanding. As can be seen from the career histories described above, the high mobility career pattern, with employees feeling little attachment to the employer (or, conversely, the firm to the employee) has become a reality for these particular software developers. Even in a still "semiperipheral" region like Ireland, the careers of such software developers have converged quite significantly with those of their counterparts in the leading high-technology regions such as Silicon Valley or global cities such as New York and London. A survey of 250 software firms in Ireland in 1997 revealed that a quarter of the firms had had employee turnover of 25 percent or more in the previous year.[12]

These trends were evident in the experience of the Womble software team members. Including myself, the team consisted of six people during the time I was there. Séamus, the team leader, had been at USTech for seven years. In that time he had held four completely different positions—working as a computer test engineer, software systems test engineer, information systems support, and software development team leader. The rest of the team had been assembled over the prior six to eighteen months. Conor, six months out of college, still received job postings from his college career-counseling service every two weeks. If he follows the industry pattern he will most likely leave USTech after eighteen months or so, when another software company will be glad to pay him well for his skills and experience.

Jim and Paul were employed on a contract basis. Dan had also been a contractor and took a pay cut of almost 50 percent when he accepted a permanent post in order to get a mortgage from the bank. Paul's history is one of a "software cowboy," using a series of lucrative short-term contracts to see the world without being tied down by business, social, or personal obligation. Jim and Dan have pursued a different path, having at times been employees, contractors, entrepreneurs, or several of these at the same time. The lines between employer, self-employed, and employee begin to blur in such careers.

Transnational experience is a major part of the developers' careers. Dan is originally from Hong Kong and came to Ireland to study, subsequently pursuing a career in software. Almost all the contractors who worked with the team while I was there had emigrated at one point or spent a significant amount of time working on contracts abroad. Indeed, it is the contractors who are most openly dependent on mobility for their career advancement. They are usually brought in for their quite specialized skills and are often given tasks working on relatively self-contained parts of the system being designed. Their need to communicate with other team members may be minimal, although their ability to do so remains a critical part of their effectiveness. Sometimes, contractors stay with a team for a relatively long time. Jim, a contractor, had been with the team for longer than the two permanent staff and had successfully resisted efforts to make him take a permanent position. Indeed, he was the *de facto* deputy team leader. Mobility across organizational, employer/employee, and national boundaries has therefore been central to these workers' careers and is understood by all to be the background to workplace interactions and relationships.

Mobility is also the team members' key bargaining chip with their employers. One lunchtime, Conor, Michael, the group manager, and I ended up sitting together. We had somehow got onto the topic of the difficulty of getting people for the jobs that were available within USTech. Conor went into great detail on the job offers he had received on leaving college and on the ever-improving job market for graduates, until Michael quietly finished his lunch and left. Conor turned to me and asked: "What did you make of that? I wanted him to know there are plenty of other jobs out there. What I didn't say is that I've been getting job offers every two weeks through the college."

Mobility is the dominant career strategy within the software industry as a whole and within the Womble software team. There are also, however, constraints on the mobility system for both the firm and the employee. The firm will sometimes try to get contractors with crucial product knowledge to become permanent employees so that their knowledge is kept within the organization. In the Womble team, Dan had gone permanent because he had to get a mortgage, whereas Jim, already having a mortgage, was able to resist the efforts of the project managers to have him become a permanent employee. Nor are employees completely free to exercise their mobility. Companies are reluctant to pay employees if they threaten to leave, as they are likely to set a series of threats in train which may spiral out of control. However, companies will make exceptions on occasion as long as they can avoid having other employees learn about them. In general, the threat of mobility serves as a latent possibility, which keeps the company's attention focused on getting training for key employees, increasing their pay, and so on, in order to forestall ideas of leaving.

Employees must also be careful not to get a reputation for being unlikely to stay at a company. "If you look at a CV and see that someone has moved every nine months or so, you have to wonder if they'll stay here any longer than that. But if they stay two or three years, then you know they will contribute something" (Séamus). The degree of demand for a developer's particular skills is the critical factor that affects his or her bargaining power through mobility. "When I was in Belfast, you would be on contract if you couldn't get a permanent job. Here, you would be permanent if you couldn't go on contract. It's just a question of how many jobs there are" (Paul). This can even override the threat of lost reputation if the demand is high enough: "They mightn't think you'll stay, but if they need you badly enough they'll hire you anyway!" (Paul). Industry norms have developed around the "proper" forms of mobility—mobility between jobs is not unlimited but requires a strategy that must be carefully managed.

Mobility is therefore taken for granted as an element of the composition of software teams such as the Womble team. Relations with coworkers develop in the context of a constant awareness that the members of the team might be dispersed at short notice. This can happen either by corporate decision (the team beside us was disbanded overnight when USTech in Silicon Valley halted development of the product on which they were working) or through the decision of individuals to leave the team. Mobility, then, is a double-edged sword—the advantage to employees of being able to leave with few repercussions is balanced against the lack of constraints on companies' changing employees' responsibilities and even getting rid of them (within the bounds of the law). Indeed, the Womble team was itself largely disbanded when development work was moved back to the United States and fully disbanded when Womble itself went out of business. These advantages and dangers are all the more significant for contract employees, given their complete lack of formal job security. These highly fluid conditions threaten the ability of software developers to work together in a cohesive way on a common project. The intensification of space in the global workplace provides some of the critical elements of the answer to this organizational dilemma.

Putting Work in Its Place

While software developers may move quite regularly from job to job, they have an intense relationship with each other once in a particular job. In informational and design work, the labor process is usually organized in the form of teams working closely together on specific projects. Some see these as "virtual" teams interacting purely through cybertechnologies—the process of generating cooperation among employees is assumed to be unproblematic.[13] Indeed, Ramesh himself subscribed to the theory of the virtual economy in a "Thank You" e-mail message he sent to the contract graphic-design firm in California:

> Our project team was truly an international virtual-team, with up to 8 hours of time-zone difference among the different team members. We expected you to work at such a hectic pace, yet, we also demanded extreme flexibility from you in all respects. It is very rare that anybody of your caliber would be able to excel on both these fronts.

However, Ramesh had misread his own organization. Members of such teams are usually located in close proximity to one another, as this allows the team to handle the complex interdependencies among them through easy and constant communication and allows them to build a coherent collective identity, which becomes the basis of cooperation within the team.

The sheer volumes of information and the dependence of each member of the team on the design decisions of the others makes the easy interaction of the team members critical. As Jim at USTech worked on the user interface screens he would intermittently call over to Paul two desks away: "What did you call the course number variable, Paul? I can't find it," "Are you working on the database at the moment? It's a bit slow," "Who's doing the security screens?" The questions and answers are discussed on the way to and from breakfast and lunch, although by common consent rarely during the meal itself.

By contrast, information flows to the United States can be patchy and tend to be limited to broad strategic decisions. A developer in Silicon Valley would have great difficulty in developing this product with the team around me in Ireland. Indeed, my own easy ability to ask the developers around me for information fifteen times a day contrasts with the difficulties I have sharing information with Jane in Silicon Valley, a process that sometimes left me idle for mornings or afternoons as I waited to be able to call her in the United States to clear up some minor misunderstandings. Where such transnational "virtual" relationships work, they are constantly supplemented by travel to meet the team or teams in the other country. Ramesh was a regular visitor to the USTech Ireland office. Distance also clearly limits how much employees can learn from their colleagues. The experience of working in close physical proximity with the more experienced and skilled developers teaches others the skills and tricks that turn a computer science graduate into an effective and innovative programmer.[14]

The accountability of team members to one another is also much more easily sustained in face-to-face interactions than in "virtual" communications. Problems can arise even in the most apparently "flat" and nonhierarchical of organizations. I was caught in a bind during the conference call when Ramesh asked me, an untrained technical writer with a long and largely irrelevant training in sociology, "Seán, are you happy with the proposal to put the toolbar in the help box?" While I was being formally asked to participate in a design decision, the social structure of this global organization made me think first not of the implications of my decision for the system itself but of my loyalties to the fuming developers around me. Even the periodical visits of Ramesh to Ireland did not solve the problems of miscommunication and alienation felt by the Irish team. As Michael, the business manager of the group, said, "Having a remote manager has made getting a process of communication in place a lot more difficult." Problems which would require solution in a face-to-face context can be swept under the carpet or become a figure of fun in a context where communication is by phone and the Internet.

The issues that can be resolved in a daily phone call to the United States are those relating to the strategic technical decisions, which were hotly debated with Ramesh every day by Séamus, the team leader, and even by the other members of the team. E-mail was generally used within the team to pass on relatively routine information to one another—whether that was between the team members or between Séamus, the team leader, and Ramesh. On one occasion, although we sat fewer than ten feet apart, Conor and I exchanged a series of e-mails about problems I had found with the program and the fixes he had made—without ever turning around to speak to one another. Only when it became clear that one of the problems was more complex than it appeared did we discuss the issue face to face. E-mail also appeared to be a valuable tool for allowing the team members to stay in touch with their friends throughout the industry. I was able to combine my membership in the "global ethnography group" with participation in the Womble team, largely unbeknownst to anyone else on the team. Other team members seemed to use e-mail similarly—every now and then someone would read out a joke they had been sent by a friend or tell us about the bonuses being offered at other companies for recruiting a new employee. Overall, while face-to-face interactions were critical to conveying complex information or to building and sustaining trust, computer-supported communication seemed "especially suited to maintaining intermediate-strength ties between people who cannot see each other frequently."[15]

USTech is situated in one of the areas best known for information technology in Ireland. In a city that is attractive to the young people who dominate the software industry, USTech also benefits from access to a large pool of local skilled labor and from the connections of the Womble team members to the broader "culture of innovation" within the region. The Womble team members, especially those who have had more mobile career patterns, have many connections to people throughout the local industry and often recount stories of people they know in common, people who could be hired by the team, other developers they met around the city and discussed their work with, and so on. Their high-mobility careers are also sustained through social ties to others in the industry who can provide the team members with information on job opportunities and can provide formal or informal recommendations to employers regarding the team members' competence. It turns out that both the high-mobility careers and the face-to-face interactions which mitigate the corrosive effect of that mobility on workplace cohesion are supported by the emergence of this regional "innovative milieu."[16]

Face-to-face interaction, localized social relations, and electronic networks each structure the global workplace in important but different ways. Clearly face-to-face interaction does not guarantee good communication or cooperative working relationships. However, it makes it a lot easier than trying to achieve these across eight time zones and numerous digital interactions. Ease of communication and mutual accountability at "work" ensure that spaces defined by face-to-face interaction remain a critical component of the global workplace, even as virtual spaces proliferate.

A Globalized Local Culture

These globalized workplaces also take on a distinct culture, which reinforces the cooperation and cohesion produced by the organization of work itself. In many ways even these human paradigms of the global economy are "global locals" bringing distinct "local" cultures to the global stage and remaking both global and local social relations in the process. This small open-plan team area may be a globalized space but it is one that has a clearly defined local identity and that interacts with the global economy with caution and at times with difficulty. Some have argued that such tensions between the local and the global are born out of a traditionalist resistance by the local to the cosmopolitanism of the global.[17] However, the Womble team does not resist the global in and of itself but contests how the global should operate, showing disdain for the mismanagement of the global by the remote managers.

This can be seen most clearly in their perceptions of American software developers and managers. As an Irish manager at USTech told me:

> The test group here was the best in the corporation and they were really saving USTech with their customers in the field. So we had all these American managers coming over telling them they were the greatest and how they were the best thing since sliced pan. That's OK the first time, but after a while the people here started saying among themselves "Quit the bullshit—if you think we're so great, give us a raise or at least buy us a few pints."

This disjunction was shown up dramatically after one particular bout of complaining about the United States managers of the team. Séamus, the team leader, summed up the relationship to the United States parent ironically:

> *Séamus:* It's not as if there's "us and them" or anything. . . . It's not even that, it's just "them" really!
>
> *Jim (wearily):* Yep, they're the enemy!

Nonetheless, the Irish managers and developers tended to work very successfully with their American counterparts, accepting some aspects of United States corporate culture while maintaining a clear rejection of many aspects of the Americanized environment in which they find themselves.

The developers themselves regard their team culture as homogenous, despite the fact that Dan is from Hong Kong:

Jim: What would we do if a black guy joined the group? Who would we pick on?

Conor: Or a woman?

Jim: Séamus, you can't ever hire a black woman!

Seán: There's always Americans to pick on. . . .

Séamus: Yeah, but they're too easy. There's no challenge in that. [Laughter.]

The mention of a "black guy" was largely rhetorical, as I never heard any comment within the team directed against "black guys." The team culture was clearly masculine, and there is no doubt that this culture could be self-perpetuating.[18] "American" is also somewhat ambiguous in this context, as Ramesh, the "American" with whom the Womble team members have the most interaction, is originally from India. On a different occasion, three members of a different team discussed their Indian boss in the United States with Conor and me:

Pat: We have one too—Ranjit.

Conor: Ranjit—that sounds like something out of Aladdin.

Peter: [Says something imitating Ramesh's accent.] That's racist, that is. [Criticizing himself, very serious about it.]

Bob: Yeah, that's an "ism," that is. That's racism.

Pat: They're [Indian software developers] probably over there saying "those bloody Micks."

Aidan: Yeah, saying "drinking pints of Guinness over their computers."

"Difference" on a global scale is an everyday part of these software developers' milieu, although it is negotiated within a strong, homogenous local culture. This was evident in the team's relationship to Dan (from Hong Kong). In fact, while the culture of the team was strongly male and Irish, members of the team were highly aware of this global culture, and most would criticize racism and sexism that they saw elsewhere. On one occasion, two other team members and I were both shocked and amused on hearing Dan racially slander a visiting technical trainer who was Pakistani. "The other" was accepted as an everyday part of life for Irish software developers and helped to define the team identity. When Dan revealed his own criticisms of another Asian ethnic group, this disrupted our assumption of a single "other" and was both surprising and funny to Dan's team members. It revealed that Dan's behavior and attitudes regarding race were subject to different rules than those of the Irish-born team members.

While the team members worked relatively easily with people of a variety of national, ethnic, and racial backgrounds, they consciously maintained a strong local team culture. Operating in the global workplace required them to work with and around "difference" but, by the same token, the less hierarchical forms of economic domination in the global workplace allowed them to maintain their local culture within these global connections. There is also a strong pragmatic element in this ability of people from different backgrounds to work together in the global workplace. One of the Womble Software managers took us out for a meal when she was visiting from the United States. Halfway through the evening I commented to Pat, a contractor, "She seems OK, decent enough," to which Pat replied, "Well, when you come to discover the jungle you have to play with the natives."

Not only are the Womble developers "global locals," but they also think of themselves as such. Their highly mobile careers and relatively fleeting association with one another in the workplace demand an intense experience of a shared space and culture in order for them to create a cohesive work team. The team members use elements of a shared culture from outside the team to create this solidarity but are also able to accommodate aspects such as Dan's non-Irish racial and ethnic background into the team through the overriding emphasis on work and technical competence. While these local team cultures can be exclusionary of women and other ethnic groups, as indicated in the quotes above, they are also flexible enough to accommodate the presence of such others within the dominant team culture when necessary. Place, mobility, and the global workplace are not necessarily in tension with one another, as they might appear to be on first glance, but are in fact symbiotic, underpinning one another's importance and sustainability.

In short, globalization does not mean the end of place. Instead, it creates places which are increasingly "between" other places and have ever-deepening connections to other places. The high-mobility career pattern that is typical of the software industry poses a threat to the work team cooperation, commitment, and cohesion necessary for innovation. What I have called the intensification of space through the dense social networks of the team and the region provides a solution of sorts to this dilemma. However, local networks also serve to reproduce mobility, as developers use their connections to engineer their next career moves. Mobility and place sustain one another but also remain in tension within the structure of the global workplace. In order to understand how this tension is resolved, we need to go beyond the intensification of space in the structure of the global workplace to an analysis of the dynamics of that workplace, dynamics that are set in motion by the control, regulation, and intensification of time.

THE DYNAMICS OF THE GLOBAL WORKPLACE

The mechanism for controlling the software development team is the project deadline. As it is impossible for the final design specifications to provide solutions to every issue faced by the team, and as the actual work done by the team is difficult for management to supervise directly, the deadline becomes the focus of both management and team efforts. "Do what needs to be done to get this specification working by the deadline" is the broad task of the team. The deadline represents the first point in the development process when both team and management will be able to examine the entire working product. The deadline is the mechanism by which management brings the intensification of time into the heart of the team. It is also an attractive mechanism of control, since direct management authority over the work process is undermined by the employees' superior expertise and by their need for rapid communication and cooperation. In contrast, time can be regulated through the use of the deadline, with only a limited local managerial presence, and with relatively little ongoing exercise of managerial authority. This deadline becomes the stimulus that sets the dynamics of time-space intensification in motion in the global workplace—leading to a pre-deadline phase of team introversion and a post-deadline phase of extroversion.

The Womble team schedule had three main phases—a beginning period of "normal work," a hectic middle period before releasing the product at the deadline, and a final period of rest and negotiation after the deadline and the release had passed. The character of the team and the issues it faced changed as the team members went through these stages of the cycle together. I joined the team in the hectic pre-release phase and left them as the post-release phase wound down.

Introversion before the Deadline: A Team against the World

In the weeks before March 1, the release date for our product, life in the Womble cubicle becomes busier and busier. The team works longer hours and becomes more and more isolated from the life of the company around it. Internally, the team becomes more cohesive, communication becomes more urgent, technical arguments take on a new edge, and any delay or new instruction from outside the team is met with a barrage of criticism. The graphics for the screens of the system (what the user sees when using the system) are delayed in coming in from the graphic-design house outside San Francisco. The Womble developers grow more and more impatient, furiously criticizing management and the graphic designers for their incompetence. The time allotted for particular development tasks is counted first in weeks and then in days. From time to time, a particular problem is put aside, to be dealt with in the period set aside for fixing the initial bugs in the system, a period between March 1 and March 10. Such postponements create some dissatisfaction among the developers:

> *Conor:* We're all tired. We've been at it for two months really. It's a lot of pressure. Something every day. There's no time to take a day and research something. We need a week to go over some of the bigger issues, have some meetings, go over things, you know. There's some dodgy code in there too.

While not as long as the hours worked by some other software development firms in Ireland, the work hours do start to creep up toward sixty a
week. Séamus, the team leader, works constantly, often late into the evening
and the night.

Weeks earlier, Conor had told me:

> I've a feeling this is the calm before the storm. My attitude when it's calm is get
> out of here at 4 or 5, 'cause when it gets busy. . . . You have to draw the line
> yourself as far as hours go, you have to say once in a while "Sorry I have some-
> thing on tonight, I can't stay." You have to keep your standard hours around
> thirty-nine/forty. If you let your standard hours go up to forty-five, then they'll
> still come to you and ask you to do a few extra hours that evening. They won't
> think about that extra six hours you're doing as part of your standard. It's up
> to yourself to draw the line.

As the deadline nears, however, he ends up staying late and coming in two
weekends in a row. While not pleased by having to work these long hours,
they are largely accepted as the industry norm. In the Irish economy as a
whole managerial and professional workers, especially in small firms, tend
to work the longest hours and work a great deal of unremunerated overtime, according to a recent study: "Ireland may be a long way from the
Japanese or North American patterns of executive working time, which
involve managers working particularly long hours . . . as a normal feature of
managerial careers, but the trajectory of change is in this direction." The
authors of this study argue that the same findings apply to professional
workers, although the trend is somewhat weaker.[19] Among the team members, proposed legislation limiting working hours is discussed ironically:

> *Séamus:* I wonder does Ramesh know about the European Social Charter lim-
> iting the working week? Forty-three hours per week or something.
>
> *Conor:* Great!
>
> *Jim:* It's forty-eight.
>
> *Conor:* Fuck, that long?
>
> *Jim:* Yeah, forty-eight for each company, forty-eight for Womble, and forty-
> eight for USTech!

Such hours and constant pressure take their toll—the week after the release
I bumped into Paul on our way in to work:

> *Paul:* I was feeling crap lately 'cause I've been under a lot of pressure and
> everything. But now I feel great after having that day off.

The impact on the developers' personal lives is also clear from a conversation weeks later before Ramesh arrived in Ireland to take us to a promised
celebration dinner:

Jim: Maybe we'll all meet up. I hope he doesn't meet my wife. She has it in for him.

Séamus: Herself and Linda should get together so. They have a lot in common actually—they're both vegetarians too.

Seán: Except when it comes to Ramesh! [Laughter.]

Jim: I see you've met my wife!

However, what appeared to be deep antagonism to Ramesh during the pre-release stage faded away in the post-release phase. While the developers' complaints about management's making their life more difficult persisted, their intensity waned so that when Ramesh came on a visit to Ireland after the release he was quite warmly welcomed (he was also quite well liked by the team members on a personal basis). Apparently, however, the complaints did not fade as quickly for the developers' families, who experienced only the long hours and intense demands on their personal lives without sharing in the collective team "buzz" of getting the product out in time and of working well together.

While attempting (with little success) to limit their hours, the developers also tried to protect themselves against the follies of management in other ways. The team responded to the pressures from Ramesh and the outside world by turning in on themselves, by becoming increasingly introverted. Having a manager on the other side of the world allowed the team, including the team leader, to screen information from management in order to let the team balance the technical and time demands to their own satisfaction. Having encountered a particularly thorny problem, the team finally found a solution:

Jim: So we're going to do that then. Ramesh never needs to know about it. So we can have it set up the way we want it, and he'll have it the way he wants too.

Paul: So we're going to do it the sneaky bastard way.

Séamus: I like the sneaky bastard way!

Paul: And Ramesh never needs to know.

Séamus: No, no. Well done, gentlemen!

Jim: Just don't say anything about this on Monday when Ramesh is here!

In many cases the reason for this screening of information was to avoid Ramesh's interference with a solution which the team considered to be the most technically effective. At other times, the goal was to avoid any extra tasks being given to the team before the deadline. On one occasion, Ramesh sent an e-mail about a problem in the database they were using. Not realizing that Dan had been working on this issue for a while now, Ramesh set aside a day the week before the release for Dan to work on it.

Jim: Dan will have that done today.

Seán: So what about the day Ramesh is setting aside for it next week?

Jim: Oh God, I'm not going to tell him we already have a solution. He's already expecting it to slip a bit, so if we get it in on time he'll be really happy. I think we're a little bit ahead of schedule, but he thinks we're a bit behind, so that suits us.

In general, team members were careful to protect themselves from undue interference from headquarters in the United States and left the negotiation of deadlines and larger technical issues to Séamus, the team leader. As Conor advised me when I had sent an e-mail to Ramesh about a problem in the "help" screens:

> Be careful what you send to Ramesh. Cc it to Séamus, or, better yet, send it to Séamus first; let him decide. That's what I do. You have to look after your own behind first, you know. I try to get involved as little as possible with Silicon Valley; I give it to Séamus. That way I have a buffer between me and the United States.

The team could also use the Product Technical Specification (PTS) as a rhetorical device with which they could, if necessary, justify not doing certain tasks. The technical specification for the product was a detailed document outlining the technical basis and logic of the system and supposedly defining the key aspects of the actual development process. However, in contrast to the expectations of formal models of software engineering, the specification document was necessarily vague in places and could not capture all the technical dilemmas that arose during the development process.

Dan, sitting beside me, constantly justified his resistance to certain new tasks that arrived before the deadline with the refrain "If it's not in the specs, I'm not doing it." On one occasion, Jim and Paul discussed a new requirement for the system that had come from Ramesh in an e-mail that morning:

Jim: Is it in the specs?

Paul: No.

Jim: Well, screw it then; we don't need to do it.

However, they later came up with a solution to the problem, which they knew was not strictly compatible with the technical requirements of the PTS but which would solve the problem satisfactorily. In this case they were willing to drop their apparent dedication to following the specs in order to try to slip a different solution past Ramesh:

> *Paul:* I have a feeling we're going to get screwed on this. I think the thing to do is to keep our mouths shut, do this what I'm doing now, present it to them

without saying anything, and then if they come back saying "We're not supporting that," then OK. 'Cause if I just say it to him, he'll just say "Noooo. . . ."

Jim: Yeah, he does that.

At times the dissatisfaction extended into banter about collective action
among the employees. When new changes to the computer graphics for the
screens arrived one week before the deadline, the team was furious:

Conor: I'm going on strike.

Seán: That'll make history, the first strike in the software industry.

[Dan laughs ironically.]

Conor: You know what last minute changes means: it means you work your arse
off.

Dan: If it's something we've agreed already, I'll work my ass off. But if it's last
minute changes I won't. It has to be reasonable, or else it's "See you later."

Later, at breakfast, Conor brought up the issue again:

Conor: I'm going on strike. I say, "In with the union!"

Jim: Well if it's minor changes to what we still have to do, then we'll do it. But
if it's changing stuff we've done already, then we're not doing it.

The others on the team agreed. Conor's view was that the developers themselves were not an elite, as it was the companies that were making the real
money. Of course, software developers are generally relatively well paid:

Jim: Maybe we should join SIPTU [the largest national union] and get union
rates. But who wants that kind of pay cut?

Conor was, however, the only team member who put the complaints of the
team in the language of collective action. Despite the close ties between the
team members and the generous cooperation and help they gave to one
another, the solidarity of the team was cast almost entirely in negative terms,
terms that grew out of their need to protect themselves from the interference of management and less competent designers and developers, in
order to get a technically good job done under reasonable conditions. This
was achieved largely by controlling the flow of information out of the team
as best they can. Collective efforts to negotiate what such reasonable conditions might be were not on the agenda, as industry norms around hours,
unreasonable deadlines, and so on were rarely challenged. However, as the
team comes together to resist the pressures of time intensification, they created the team cohesion and work intensity that allowed them to meet the
challenges of innovation in the global economy. Ironically, it was the team's
resistance to corporate interference that created the conditions under
which the team managed to meet corporate innovation goals.

Extroversion after the Deadline: A Team in the World

After the release, the team goes into temporary collapse, with the work pace slowing dramatically. As work starts to pick up again, I notice that the solidarity of the team in the pre-deadline, introverted phase has fractured somewhat. During the period after the release, individual team members begin to negotiate their roles in the next phase of product development. The team begins to fragment as the focus of the team members shifts from getting the work done to building their careers: the team members become extroverted, looking outward to their future opportunities within and beyond the team.

The next deadline is three to four months away and requires the implementation of the system in the Java programming language. This move to Java is critical for the product, although difficult because it is a new language. People with Java development skills are in short supply and many products with which the Irish teams work do not have Java "drivers," which are needed in order to work with a system designed in Java. From the team members' point of view, this is a great opportunity: training in Java and experience in developing a complex product in the language will greatly enhance their appeal in the labor market.

However, the distribution of such opportunities for training and for valuable experience is not determined by the technical requirements of the product. It is an object of negotiation within the team, negotiation that takes place through the social networks among team members and between team members and the team leader and managers. The issue is rarely mentioned publicly, let alone discussed collectively. Furthermore, the move to Java is a gradual one and each stage produces different sets of conflicts.

The move to Java represents an opportunity for the Irish team, but also a threat. As the team moves to a new technical phase in the development, an opportunity opens for Womble Software to relocate the development work. Despite the Irish team's advantages of knowledge and experience of the system, there is still a danger that development work could move back to the United States. One team meeting discussing the move to Java produced the following exchange:

> *Michael (Business Manager):* We have to get a Java person in Ireland. Ramesh has someone in the United States, but we can't let that happen. We can't let it go there.

> *Paul:* Yeah, you don't want to let the development stuff leak back to the United States. If it starts it'll all end up back there eventually.

The Irish team scrambles to gather together Java skills and to give Ramesh the impression that we have more skills than we do. Later it is my clear impression that Ramesh is aware of the limited level of skills in the Irish team but that he has developed a trust in the Irish team's ability to get up to speed on Java in time.

Of course, merely keeping the Java work in Ireland does not solve the issue of how exactly the need for Java knowledge will be solved for the team. This issue arises first in relation to a totally different problem. The system with which we work needs to be able to run on computers with Apple's Macintosh operating system. At present, our system cannot do that. One quick way to achieve this is to buy a particular software product. However, this will add two thousand pounds to the cost of each copy of our product for Mac. Instead, it is decided to adjust some parts of our system using Java, which will achieve two goals: make the system work on Mac and begin the process of implementing the system in Java. The team must look for a contract developer who can do this work before the release date.

> *Michael:* I think we'll have to get a contractor. Pat is up there with the porting team at the moment. He should be able to do it.
>
> *Jim:* Yeah, Pat is very good.
>
> *Michael:* Under normal circumstances we'd put that 2,000 into training somebody on the team so that they could do it, but we don't have the time at the moment because of the release date coming up. So I think we should get Pat.

There are usually multiple ways to incorporate new skills and sources of knowledge into the team. The strategy of buying a product made by another company, a product that embodies that knowledge, is rejected in this case due to its cost. Training current employees is always an option but is often overlooked in the hectic development schedule. No one can be spared for a week-long course with the deadline hanging over the team. The team also missed out on other training opportunities while I was there due to this pressure of time. Finally, bringing in someone with the necessary knowledge is chosen as the strategy, less than satisfactory in the long-term but necessary given the time constraints.

The issue of hiring contractors versus training employees is of course a sensitive one:

> *Conor:* Be careful we don't keep getting contractors to do Java stuff and none of us get to go to the training on it.
>
> *Jim:* Sure, I know. I'm thinking if we get someone on Java he'll have lots of ideas about things to do in Java, and that'll create lots of work for us to do in Java.

This strategy poses a particular danger to the team: while contractors may come only for a short while, they often stay longer as they develop knowledge of a particular piece of the product or become valuable to the team in a particular area. Even I, as a novice technical writer, become valuable: having developed a knowledge of the system, I will be able to write the help materials for future editions more quickly than some professional "tech writers" with no knowledge of the product.

This tension between contract and permanent employees becomes clear in the negotiation of team members' roles around opportunities for working with Java. It is in this internal competition for Java work that the fragmentation of team solidarity and the shift from an introverted to an extroverted orientation within the team is clearest. When Paul, a contractor, declares that he is starting to teach himself Java and wants to do a Java implementation of his part of the system, this meets with some (private) concern from some other members of the team: "I thought he was just here to do that section of the system and not to do this Java stuff." Dan is particularly worried about the involvement of contractors in Java work to the exclusion of permanent employees:

> *Dan:* The three contract people are doing Java and the two permanent people are doing everything else. It is not right. Conor and myself were told in our one-on-one reviews with Michael that the permanent people would get Java training. They would get priority over the contractors. Michael said that they didn't want to give it to the contractors first 'cause they could just leave and take it somewhere else. But that's not how it's going to be—over the next few months they will be doing Java, and we will be doing everything else. I was talking to Conor about it yesterday. He is aware of it.
>
> *Seán:* Will you say anything about it?
>
> *Dan:* What can I say? My attitude is if something is wrong and I can't change it, then I just leave and go somewhere else. It's as simple as that. It doesn't make sense from USTech's point of view. They are paying all this money for contractors, and they are not paying for training for permanent staff. In the end they just pile up the costs for themselves. It's crazy from USTech's point of view. And from my point of view. [Laughs ironically.]

Dan did eventually talk to Séamus, the team leader, about this and received assurances that he would be doing Java work. Paul's growing interest in other advanced technical areas also helped defuse the situation to some extent. However, the negotiations continued as I left. Indeed, on Ramesh's second visit he treated the whole team to a dinner and a night out on the town. Each one of us, as we sat over dinner and wound our way through the city streets, discussed our future roles with Ramesh. I talked over the possibility of doing some further technical writing on a contract basis once my fieldwork was over. Paul discussed his hopes to do some field consulting on the product, Jim and Paul their plans to work on a new technical area of the product, and Conor his desire to do work with Java in a particular application of our system. Indeed, we also put in a good word with Ramesh for each other where the different roles seemed complementary.

Even while competing over certain areas of the work, the team members helped each other out in others.

The team solidarity of the pre-release phase becomes more fractured as opportunities for training and learning become a focus of conflict within the team. However, the conflict is submerged and operates through a complex set of social networks and shifting alliances among team members. These ties interact with the formal categories of permanent and contract employees to produce a politics of learning and skills within the team. These local dynamics are intimately connected to the nature of the opportunities in the global market for knowledge embodied (in this case) in the skills of United States developers and the products (software tools) available to carry out certain tasks.

The pre-release phase reveals the nature of the local and global solidarities of the team, with local solidarities increasingly pitted against global interference, as the local team fights for the space to achieve the "global" goal of releasing a good product in the way that they see fit. The post-release phase reveals more schisms within the team and shows how the local team is forged out of a range of alliances among local and global employees and managers. The mobility of team members through various learning paths, both within the team and outside it, is negotiated in this phase, laying the foundation for the next pre-release phase, which is three to four months away.

TIME-SPACE INTENSIFICATION

The emergence of a global information economy has transformed the character of the workplace for many employees, including those within informational industries such as software. Many authors argue that the globalization of work destroys place and locality, creating placeless "virtual" work. Against this view, this chapter has argued for a concept of globalization that emphasizes the organization of the global economy through particular places and regions and the critical importance of patterns of mobility of people, information, and resources within and between these regions. These changes in the territorial organization of capitalism interact with an organizational restructuring characterized by the decentralization of work and firms. While some authors argue that these organizational changes will bring relative equality and a rough and ready economic democracy, this chapter has shown that new forms of power operate within these new organizational forms. Ethnography reveals that we cannot simply deduce concrete social practices and power relations from a particular organizational and territorial work structure. Instead, we find that a new ground is emerging upon which the struggles of the global informational economy will be waged—a new set of social identities, resources, interests, and issues is created, which will be the basis of the politics of the global workplace in the years to come.

This new "contested terrain" of the global workplace is a system of time-space intensification where workers experience not the "end of time and space" but their ascent to a new level of intensity. Space is intensified by the necessity of local cooperation and the increased use of project teams in the face of the challenges posed by the global economy. Time becomes an ever more pressing reality in the deadline-driven workplace. This time-space intensification shapes the structure of both work and careers in the global workplace. Careers are built using mobility between firms to bargain for improved wages and access to technical learning, and these mobile careers only increase the importance of close interactions and strong local cooperation while working on any particular project. Out of these underlying structures emerges a set of dynamics, organized around the project deadline, which give the global workplace its dynamism but also generate certain costs and dilemmas for the participants. Conflicts over these dilemmas of time-space intensification constitute the new politics of the globalization of knowledge work.

What will be the central controversies on this new contested terrain? The two phases of time-space intensification create characteristic advantages and dilemmas for knowledge workers such as the software developers in this chapter, for firms such as USTech and Womble Software, and for workers' families, software users, and the other (largely invisible) social actors beyond the industry with an interest in its social organization. While these dynamics and dilemmas have been recognized for some time in the information industries, globalization intensifies them.[20]

Certain characteristic organizational problems are likely to emerge: these are the internal organizational dilemmas of time-space intensification. In the pre-release phase, the introversion of the team, the intensification of time, and the pressures imposed by the deadline create the conditions that lead to employee burnout—manifested in the case I have described in the exhaustion of the team members up to and after the deadline and also in the decision made by Ramesh (some five months after I left the team) to resign due to overwork. This creates problems for the organization, as the team's introversion cuts it off from the rest of the organization and raises the danger of organizational involution and the distancing of teams from one another, even teams working on related technical or business issues. For the Womble team this can be seen in the antagonistic attitude to the graphics team in California, a set of relationships which, if more cooperative, could have been very valuable in improving the product under development.

In the post-deadline phase, the solidarity fragments and team members begin to look elsewhere for future opportunities. The extroverted phase is when employees can turn to the labor market to gain the rewards of their new-found expertise and the organization can assemble a new group of employees with new sets of skills and resources into a project team for the next phase of the development effort. However, there is also a significant cost associated with the high levels of employee turnover within the industry. The accumulated knowledge derived from the development of the Womble software product, which has built up within the team, is now dissipated throughout the industry. This constitutes a significant loss of firm-specific knowledge from Womble's point of view and also a loss of the effort put into developing effective working relationships within the team. There are therefore clear organizational costs attached to failure to address these internal dilemmas.[21]

Time-space intensification also causes certain external social dilemmas. The pressure and introverted character of the pre-deadline phase, and the resulting insulation of workers and the organization of their work from any kind of broader social accountability make it difficult to reconcile the team structure and team culture with broader social concerns. This is manifested in at least two areas. The most directly obvious is the work-family nexus, where work demands come to dominate family life, leaving very little space for workers to negotiate alternative work and family time arrangements. Secondly, as technology increasingly penetrates our everyday social practices, the involvement of users in decisions regarding these technologies becomes more and more crucial. But the isolation and insulation of the developers during their most creative and innovative phase militates strongly against any meaningful interaction with prospective users of the product from outside the team. To the extent that we might fear the arrival of the Weberian "iron cage" in the form of a society dominated by large, centralized organizations, there is some promise in the decentralized organizational forms compatible with this high-mobility system. However, although organizations no longer have the same rigid bureaucratic structures insulating them from social accountability, the intensification of time ultimately results in a similar outcome.

The post-deadline phase of high mobility creates a very high degree of volatility and insecurity in the labor market so that employees lack strong employment guarantees. This is not currently a major issue in the Irish industry, given the generally very high demand for software skills. Even in the current tight labor market, "employment security" gives way to "employability security."[22] However, when career gains are based on the threat of mobility, this seems inevitably to lead to increased labor market inequality, as the threat to leave is only effective when replacing the employee is difficult. As it is inherently based on scarcity, the limits of mobility as a universal career strategy are clear. This seems likely to be a contributing factor to the spiraling wage inequality in Ireland over the past ten years.[23]

These internal and external dilemmas of time-space intensification are all the more crucial given that the economic success of the Republic of Ireland over the past ten years has been built upon the success of industries such as software.[24] The politics of the conference call became the new politics of the global workplace—distant yet closely integrated into operations in the core, less hierarchical but nonetheless subject to new forms of power relations. As these global workplaces spread through economies such as Ireland's, the dilemmas of time-space intensification will become central economic and social issues for societies incorporated into new, deeper processes of globalization. The value of global ethnography is its ability to reveal these dilemmas as aspects of a "contested terrain" of globalization, rather than as inevitable outcomes of an apolitical process.

NOTES

My thanks to my comrades at USTech for letting me pry into their lives for three months. Thanks to Becky King for comments and for going to Dublin. I received helpful comments at presentations of earlier versions of this paper at the Economic and Social Research Institute (ESRI), Dublin; the Center for Work, Technology, and Organizing, Stanford University; Braverman Memorial Conference on the Labor Process, State University of New York, Binghamton; and the Department of Sociology, University of California, Berkeley. Mike Hout and Anno Saxenian provided incisive comments and great encouragement. Material support was provided by the ESRI, Forfás, and Forbairt in Ireland. This research was assisted by a grant from the Joint Committee on Western Europe of the American Council of Learned Societies and the Social Science Research Council, with funds provided by the Ford and Mellon Foundations.

1. Robert Reich, *The Work of Nations.*

2. Anthony Giddens, *The Consequences of Modernity.* Giddens argues that globalization occurs in a process of *time-space distanciation,* as space and time are "distanciated" from (lifted out of) their local contexts. There are two main mechanisms through which this happens: the use of *symbolic tokens* (universal media of exchange/interaction such as money) and of *expert systems* (shared bodies of technical knowledge that can be applied in a wide variety of contexts).

3. See Marshall Berman, *All That Is Solid Melts Into Air;* David Harvey, *The Condition of Postmodernity;* and Manuel Castells, *The Rise of the Network Society.* Harvey argues that globalization is characterized by a process of *time-space compression,* in which the speed-up of time in the global economy also serves to compress the autonomy of local space and social context, as different places are integrated into an increasingly universal capitalist economy.

4. See Barry Bluestone and Bennett Harrison, *The Deindustrialization of America;* Michael Burawoy, *The Politics of Production;* and Harley Shaiken, *Mexico in the Global Economy.*

5. We might refer to this perspective as *time-space embedding,* as embeddedness of workplaces in their local social contexts appears to provide a solution to the speed-up of the global economy, giving the successful workplaces some insulation from these pressures and perhaps even re-embedding time itself in local contexts. See

Michael Piore and Charles Sabel, *The Second Industrial Divide;* AnnaLee Saxenian, *Regional Advantage;* and Michael Storper, *The Regional World.*

6. See Leslie Perlow, *Finding Time,* and "Boundary Control," for detailed empirical analyses of these issues in a software workplace.

7. Eoin O'Malley, *Industry and Economic Development.*

8. For a more detailed analysis of this process, see Seán Ó Riain, "The Birth of a Celtic Tiger?," "An Offshore Silicon Valley?," and "Remaking the Developmental State."

9. IBM's employment guarantee collapsed with a reduction of 140,000 in a workforce of 400,000 between 1986 and 1993. For an analysis of "corporate culture" in such workplaces, see Gideon Kunda, *Engineering Culture.*

10. See Saxenian, *Regional Advantage,* and Baron, Burton, and Hannon, "The Road Taken."

11. Office of Technology Policy, *America's New Deficit.*

12. Seán Ó Riain, "Remaking the Developmental State." See also Saskia Sassen, *The Global City,* and Saxenian, op. cit., for discussion of labor markets in agglomerated industries in core regions.

13. Reich, *The Work of Nations.*

14. Much of this learning, especially in a team context, derives from what Jean Lave and Etienne Wenger call "situated learning." See Lave and Wenger, *Situated Learning.*

15. Barry Wellman et al., "Computer Networks as Social Networks," p. 231.

16. For a discussion of this concept and a review of a variety of examples, see Manuel Castells and Peter Hall, *Technopoles of the World.*

17. See, for example, Rosabeth Moss Kanter, *World Class,* and Manuel Castells, *The Rise of the Network Society.*

18. For a more detailed analysis of these processes, based on a case study of a software company in Ireland in the mid-1980s, see Margaret Tierney, "Negotiating a Software Career."

19. Brian Fynes et al., *Flexible Working Lives,* p. 138.

20. For a classic account of these dynamics in a computer design workplace in the 1970s, see Tracy Kidder, *The Soul of a New Machine.*

21. For an organizational and management theory perspective, see Brown and Eisenhardt, "The Art of Continuous Change."

22. See Kanter, *World Class,* for a discussion of this concept as developed in a study of a software company in Massachusetts.

23. For a detailed analysis of trends from 1987 to 1994, see Alan Barrett, Tim Callan, and Brian Nolan, "Rising Wage Inequality, Returns to Education and Labour Market Institutions."

24. For a more detailed analysis of the growth of the Irish software industry, with particular reference to its potential and to the limits of state-society alliances in shaping the industry's development and impact, see Ó Riain, "Remaking the Developmental State."

SEVEN

Traveling Feminisms

From Embodied Women to Gendered Citizenship

Millie Thayer

My project began with a feminist health organization in Recife, a coastal city in the northeastern region of Brazil. My goal was to study globalization—not the inexorable spread of capital and commercialized culture throughout the world, but the construction of a transnational social movement and the complex network of relationships that sustained it. As a point of entry, I chose a feminist nongovernmental organization known as SOS Corpo (SOS Body), which had a long history, global connections, and broad influence inside and outside Brazil. My research, which took place during three five-week trips to the country followed by ten months of fieldwork, combined interviews, archival work, and participant observation as a volunteer for the organization. I translated grant proposals and brochures, catalogued English-language library materials, attended meetings, seminars, and international conferences, drank cachaça, danced, and went to the beach with members and former members of the organization, as well as with activists from a wide variety of women's groups in the region. In between I interviewed many of them, as well as representatives of key institutions with which Recife feminists engaged.

But, for some time, the global eluded me. It was everywhere in organizational practice and discourse, and nowhere that I could pin down to study. E-mails winged silently across borders, SOS members flew off to international conferences, visiting researchers and activists appeared from abroad, the fax machine churned out a steady stream of global correspondence, and the daily mail produced bushels of feminist publications from everywhere imaginable. Early on I had thought I could delimit my subject by researching the links between SOS and a particular feminist institution in the United States, but I discovered that there was no single, prototypical relationship that incorporated the meanings of globalization for Brazilian feminism. Instead, there was a variegated web of transnational relations between SOS and international development agencies, foundations, academic feminists, women's organizations, and other social movements around the world.

Frustrated with the difficulties of drawing boundaries around the field, and unwilling to spend my time simply cataloging the multiple mechanisms of global connection, I began to listen to the ways SOS members talked about their work, the key meanings around which their practice was organized. Tracing the paths these discourses had followed in their travels led me back "home" to Boston, the city where I grew up, and where one of the earliest and best-known organizations in the United States-based women's health movement was located. As a teenager in 1970, I had joined a pro-choice guerrilla theater group led by a member of the Boston Women's Health Book Collective, the first edition of whose health manual, *Our Bodies, Our Selves,* had just hit the streets. As the decade wore on, the Collective's book became a best seller and its influence spread around the world. In Brazil, a group of women heard and appropriated its message about women's right to their own bodies, founding an organization called SOS Corpo: Grupo de Saúde da Mulher (SOS Body: Women's Health Group).

But, as these Brazilian feminists struggled and negotiated with institutions in their environment, the imported discourses of "women" and "body" took on distinctive meanings. In time, SOS's evolving practices outgrew their discursive foundations and "women's bodies" were eclipsed by reconstructed conceptions of "gender" and "citizenship," the former with roots in the United States academy, the latter a creation of Brazilian social movements. The two new discourses were linked by feminists in a way that politicized gender struggles, locating them in the context of broader efforts for social transformation.

Many years after my first contact with the Boston Collective I went back, curious about how the United States-based organization had changed and what shape its discourses and practices had taken. I

wondered whether any of the discursive innovations I had seen in
Brazil had traveled north and how they had been received. I found
an organization which though its practices had touched the lives of
nearly every woman I knew, and whose influence reached Congress
and the Food and Drug Administration as well as movements around
the world, had a discourse remarkably similar to that with which it
was founded. "Gender" and "citizenship" were nowhere to be found;
discursive travel, at least in this case, was a one-way affair.

During my time in Brazil, like most ethnographers, I felt permanently liminal—neither definitively outside, nor categorically inside
the organization I was studying—a status that was simultaneously
painful and privileged, humiliating and exhilarating. In my case,
this unsteady location gave me useful insight into the very disjunc-
tures in communications between people rooted in different sets
of global and local hegemonies that I was writing about: I, within
the orbit of the United States academy, engaged in specific funding
relations, part of a particular kind of feminist political community,
and SOS members, in their relationships with the state, international
funders, local social movements, and women's health movements
around the world. Like the traveling discourses I was studying, my
questions and their answers often threatened to pass each other,
without connection, in midair—though, as time went by, they
increasingly swerved to meet awkwardly in some negotiated equiva-
lence. Just as the members of SOS Corpo transposed and translated
the discourses of the Boston Women's Health Book Collective and
other Northern feminists in their own context, I have done my best
to translate and transpose Brazilian feminist conceptions in mine,
while recognizing that meanings never arrive quite intact from their
global journeys.

In 1980, a small group of feminists in the city of Recife, in the northeast corner of Brazil, founded a women's health organization and gave it the name
SOS Corpo—SOS Body. For a decade, women's bodies had been situated at
the focal point of feminist movements in Europe and the United States.[1]
The Boston Women's Health Course Collective, founded in 1969 in the hey-
day of the women's liberation movement, was one of the earliest advocates
in the United States of women's empowerment through knowledge of their
own bodies.[2] "The information [about women's anatomy and physiology] is
a weapon without which we cannot begin the collective struggle for control
over our own bodies and lives," the group wrote in its book, *Our Bodies, Our
Selves,* first published in 1970.[3] The health manual sought to demystify

medicine by equipping women with the tools to make informed choices about their medical care. At a time when knowledge about the female body was still seen as the province of male experts, topics such as sexuality, contraception, pregnancy, and childbirth, as well as women's feelings about them, were discussed openly in accessible language. The Boston Collective made the revolutionary claim that women themselves were the best source of knowledge about their own bodies, as well as the agents of change, through both individual empowerment and a collective process in which personal problems were transformed into political issues.

It was not long before this feminist approach to the politicization of women's bodies began to travel. In the latter half of the 1970s, Collective members began to take a leadership role in the incipient international women's health movement and to make contact with the many organizations that were beginning to emerge around the world. By 1976, *Our Bodies, Ourselves* had made the United States best-seller list, and, by 1980, it had been adapted and translated by local women's groups from English into eleven other languages and had sold more than two million copies.[4] The book was read and its influence felt on every continent. However, though feminists around the world seized on the message that knowledge of and control over the body were central to the project of women's liberation, this conception took distinctive forms in different places.

The discourses of women and the body reached Recife sometime in the mid- to late 1970s. A number of the women who founded SOS Corpo had read *Our Bodies, Ourselves* and others had participated in the feminist self-help movement as exiles in France. In the early 1980s, discourses of "women's bodies," similar to those of the women's health movement in Boston, predominated within SOS, and gynecological self-exams and discussions of their own sexuality gave internal coherence to the group. By the 1990s, however, a striking shift had occurred in the organization's discourses and practices. The privileged place of "women" had been seized by "gender relations," and the view had shifted outward from "the body" to "citizenship," while still remaining focused on health questions. Rather than practicing self-help, the organization engaged directly with the state in a quest for bodily rights.

How did these discursive changes come about, and how were they linked both to local institutions and to the global connections forged by groups such as SOS? What were the relations between traveling theories and discourses, and between movement discourses and the on-the-ground practices that expressed and were articulated by them? And, finally, how did global power relations constrain or facilitate theoretical and discursive migration?

Though the feminists of SOS Corpo participated in the conferences, networks, and alliances of the transnational feminist movement, the shifts in the discursive landscape in northeast Brazil were not a simple matter of one-way transmission from the North and passive absorption in the South, but reflected significant departures from European and North American models.[5] Nor were these discourses and the practices related to them locked together in one to one correspondence, but rather operated in semi-autonomous relation to one another. The discourses of women and body "imported" in 1980 brought with them a certain set of practices based in feminist self-help movements in the United States and Europe. However, while the discourses remained essentially the same over the next decade, the practices quickly began to change, ultimately undermining a language and conception that could no longer make sense of them. After a decade, new discourses, this time with roots in academic theory, supplanted the old. Finally, while dramatic changes occurred in the discourse and practice of feminist movements in northeast Brazil, the same was not true for the women's health movement in Boston, where a discourse of women and the body persisted nearly three decades after its initial appearance.

TRAVELING FEMINISMS

There is a growing body of academic literature on "traveling theories," much of this work by feminists interested in untangling the complex and often disjunctive connections among feminisms in different geographical locations.[6] These authors treat theory as what Grewal and Kaplan call an "object of exchange," part of the transnational cultural flows in an increasingly globalized world.[7] It is a literature acutely aware of the significance of context, which looks at the way meanings meet resistance and shift as they cross different kinds of borders. John, who studied relations between feminist theorizing in the United States and India, argues that theory is a "composite," "geological" construction whose sedimentations reflect the locations in which it was created or through which it has passed. Relocation and assimilation are not smooth processes, given the ways that fundamental assumptions embedded in the theory reflect its origins in different circumstances.

A number of these scholars call attention to the structural inequalities among the differently situated nodes of theoretical travel. As John comments, "The power of the West is manifested . . . in its ability to project its influence beyond its own geo-national borders—to render selectively permeable the boundaries of *other* states and nations."[8] What were initially conceptions *local* to the richer, more developed countries, become, with the benefit of the material power at their points of origin, *global* forces as they travel to, and embed themselves in, the so-called "Third World."[9]

But this body of literature lacks a concrete analysis of the dynamics involved in these relationships of unequal conceptual exchange. In part, this is because most of these theorists focus their attention on how academics transmit and receive new conceptions, rather than on how social movements selectively appropriate and transform global meanings, and materialize them in local practices.[10] The concern of the authors referred to here is with the transfer of theories— *intellectual systems of thought that are both coherent and explicit, and that have no necessary connection to concrete practices.* Through my study of SOS Corpo, I argue that, while social movements at times incorporate theories, more commonly it is discourses—*ways of conceiving of and talking about social experience that are often fragmentary, sometimes contradictory, and frequently founded on only partially conscious assumptions—* that movements draw on and that come to shape their thinking and action. Discourses are a much more flexible and easily assimilable weapon for tactical maneuver and improvisation in the face of obstacles. When movements do call on more formal theories, they often dismantle and reconstruct them as discourses, which can then be linked, not only to other discourses, but to a variety of practices.

As means of conceptualizing the world, both theories and discourses can have important consequences for institutional and movement action. Unlike theories, however, discourses are always linked to a set of practices. But the practices inspired by a given discourse are not inextricably bound up with it in a seamless package; the two are semi-autonomous with respect to one another, change at different rhythms, and are capable of mutual influence, even as they present an apparently unified front. To understand the fate of traveling feminisms as they are transposed by movements outside their places of origin, discourses and practices must be pried apart and the relation of their respective rhythms revealed. Beyond that, analysis requires understanding the ways activist discourses and practices are shaped by the configuration of global and local institutions that constitute any particular movement's field of action.[11]

Theories and discourses are constructed and travel differently, as I have argued here, and they are appropriated by social movements at different points in their development, in the context of shifting fields of action and contrasting sets of power relations between local political actors and global influences. The relationship of social movements in the South to globally mobile meanings from the North is neither a matter of simple imposition of alien conceptions, nor of totally autonomous local innovation, but rather an ongoing process of negotiation with distinctive moments.

In the case described here, the first moment occurred in 1980, around the founding of SOS Corpo, at a time when both the organization itself and the larger Brazilian feminist movement were still relatively new, lacking formal structures and established practices. "Women's bodies" initially entered Brazil and reached SOS in Recife as a set of European and North American discourses linked to particular kinds of feminist practices. At this juncture, for a brief period, Northern feminism gone global imposed its outlines on feminism in northeast Brazil. But, as Recife women's health activists engaged with the forces around them—the state, international funding agencies, and local social movements—their practices developed in different directions from those initially imported, and ultimately outgrew the old discourses.

At a second moment, traveling feminisms once again played a catalyzing role, but this time SOS leaders drew, not on movement discourses, but on academic theory, to at least partially fill the discursive gap left by the obsolescence of "women" and "the body." Theories of "gender relations" had become pervasive in Northern academic feminist circles in the late 1980s and began to circulate as well among Brazilian intellectuals in the academy and in nongovernmental organizations. In 1990, SOS Corpo, now fully institutionalized, with a history of innovating its own practices, and a leadership role in the Brazilian feminist movement, as well as in international women's networks, organized discussions of Joan Scott's work on gender. At this historical juncture, Recife feminists negotiated with Northern theoretical conceptions from a position of relative strength and organizational maturity. Rather than simply adopting the language of gender, SOS members made a conscious choice to incorporate Scott's approach into their work, reconstructing the theory as discourse and linking its disaggregated elements to other local discursive constructions. The fact that the theory migrated South direct from the academy, unencumbered with activist methodology, facilitated the process of articulating "gender relations" to SOS's pre-existing organizational practices. In the process, responding to the particular institutional configuration within which SOS carried out its work, like "women" and "the body" before it, the discourse of gender evolved differently in its new surroundings than it did in the United States.

The differences were crystallized in the links made by SOS between "gender" and another discourse, that of "citizenship." Brazilian feminist understandings of citizenship had a historical trajectory much more rooted in the local context than that of gender relations discourse. A product of social movements born in the struggle against dictatorship, "citizenship" became a rallying cry as the process of democratization unfolded. By coupling "gender" with demands for new kinds of rights, what had originated as academic theory became politicized as discourse in Brazil, becoming an organizing tool as well as an analytical category.

EMBODYING WOMEN, 1980–1982

But why this silence? Why does the woman's body remain so unknown, so mysterious, so forbidden for the very owner of this body? Could it be that we never had the curiosity to know ourselves? How is that possible, if knowing oneself is an elementary right of human beings? Could it be that this right has always been denied to us?
SOS CORPO, *SOS: Corpo de Mulher,* 5.[12]

The founders of SOS Corpo were, for the most part, white, well-educated, middle-class women with links to or sympathies with the left opposition to the dictatorship then in place.[13] The majority had international connections or experiences: three had lived in France, one had traveled in the United States and Mexico, another was from Switzerland. A number of them had read and been influenced by *Our Bodies, Ourselves,* and some had had contact with gynecological self-help practices in France. Most had participated in an earlier feminist consciousness-raising group, Ação Mulher, which disbanded in 1980 as members' interests and strategic visions diverged. Those who conceived SOS were united by their concern with sexuality and women's health.

The state of Pernambuco, where they launched their project, is located in the poorest region of a semiperipheral country. But, even there, state-led economic development made itself felt in the 1960s and 1970s, stimulating urbanization and migration from rural areas to Recife and the new industrial centers in the southern part of the country, creating greater social and economic polarization, drawing women into the labor force in growing numbers, and offering new educational opportunities to women of the upper and middle classes who would become the social base of incipient feminism in Recife and around the country.[14]

In 1980, a dictatorship still ruled Brazil, but a gradual political opening begun five years earlier had loosened the regime's grip.[15] What had been a dichotomous political field of state and opposition was breaking down, and new political subjects were beginning to appear. In the mid- to late 1970s the hegemony of class discourses in the opposition was eroding, as movements around race, gender, and sexuality began to challenge social, as well as political, authoritarianism.[16]

Feminist movements in Brazil were galvanized by the activities around the United Nations World Conference of the International Women's Year in Mexico in 1975, whose ripple effects were felt throughout the Third World, but particularly in Latin America. A seminar held in Rio de Janeiro that year led to the formation of a number of Brazilian groups in southern cities. Most of these were consciousness-raising groups; to the extent that they took political action during the 1970s, their struggles were articulated with the broader movement for democratization and what Molyneux called "strategic gender interests"[17] were kept out of the public sphere.[18]

SOS was one of a number of new groups to take a different approach, putting the focus directly on women's specificity. In a December 1980 fundraising letter written to a woman in France, its founders stated their goals:

> Knowledge of our bodies, of our sexuality, of possible maladies, of their cure and prevention, in order to diminish the dependence which has tied us to doctors and allopathic medicines; to make this new knowledge known . . . [and], in the medium term, to form other groups of the same kind. . . . [19]

Initially, like the Boston collective, their objectives were to educate themselves and to help other women develop the knowledge that they felt would change doctor-patient relations. Though they had ambitions to transform the institutions which affected women's lives, they were not, at first, oriented toward pressuring the state, not least because of the dictatorship's continuing power.

For ten months the group concentrated on conducting self-exams together and experimenting with herbs and other alternative cures. By the second meeting everyone had bought speculums and begun to explore the terrain of their own bodies. Their new knowledge represented a "great discovery" for SOS members, according to one participant, one which they were eager to share, particularly with women in poor neighborhoods who had little access to such information and faced wretched health conditions.[20]

With this in mind, they produced a booklet, *SOS: Corpo de Mulher* (*SOS: Woman's Body*)—a Brazilian version of *Our Bodies, Ourselves,* written in popularized form—and began doing outreach in low-income areas where some members had contacts, using a theater piece designed to stimulate discussions about women's lives and reproductive issues, offering workshops on sexuality, female anatomy, and the use of herbal remedies, and participating in a weekly radio call-in program.

The enthusiastic response from the *bairros* confirmed their sense that those who claimed that "this business of the body is a middle-class women's thing" were entirely wrong. However, their plan to encourage low-income women to conduct their own gynecological self-exams fell flat, because, explained one SOS member, of the "cultural abyss" between the middle-class activists and their constituency.

As a means of making further contact with women in the *bairros,* and of better understanding their experiences, individuals in SOS acquired funding to conduct research, based largely on interviews with women, about sterilization, the causes and consequences of abortion, and the quality of medical attention they received. Their plan was to use the data to improve their organizing strategies and to disseminate the results in popularized form to the research subjects. Though the SOS founders considered setting up a women's clinic in a marginalized community, the idea was ultimately rejected as too restrictive in terms of the constituency that they would have the resources to serve.

Central to SOS's work in these early years was a discourse of the body, expressed also in the content of their practices. As one founder put it, " . . . the question of [the slogan] 'Our Bodies Belong to Us!' and of the body as a physical reality, as a metaphor, of the body as a symbol, . . . as personal existence, was a very powerful thing which was emerging in the debate." Empowerment for women, SOS members believed, would come through knowledge of their own bodies. Their first publication urged women to "get to know this body better, and to love it," and both their internal practices and their educational work in the poor communities on the periphery of the city reflected this exhortation.[21]

This attention to matters of the body reflected, in large part, the long reach of feminism in the industrialized North. "We drank from that fountain," said one of Recife's early feminists, referring to the local influence of European and United States movements.[22] The transnationalized experiences and connections of many SOS founders had put them into contact with European and North American radical feminisms which focused on the body and on reproductive health, discourses to which they were especially receptive because these conceptions reached them at a time in their lives when sexuality and the bodily experience of reproduction were key personal issues, as they were for many other women.[23] But global feminism was only one of the institutions with which feminists in Recife were entangled: their relationships to the state, other social movements, and international funding agencies also played a part in the course of the organization's discursive development.

SOS members' literal inward turn toward their own bodies came at a time when the state was beginning to open up, and democratization of some sort had begun to seem inevitable, if not yet a reality. Unified opposition to and focus on the state no longer seemed imperative, and women, along with other social actors throughout Brazil, had begun to assert their own identities. Self-help for one's own body was a discourse and tactic that befitted this brief moment of transition, when the regime still clung to power, new possibilities for intervention in the state had not yet solidified, and the class-based movements which had dominated the opposition struggled to adjust to the new political conjuncture. Then too, as the dictatorship sputtered to an end, the focus on the body by a political generation which had seen many of its members physically "disappeared" may have also served as a means of reasserting ownership over their corporeal selves and their right to exist in the world.

The feminists of SOS defended women's rights to make informed decisions about their own fertility and were openly critical of both the government's official pronatalist position in the early 1980s and the neo-Malthusian politics of population control being fomented by certain sectors of the Brazilian elite in alliance with USAID and other international interests.[24] At the time that SOS founders launched their project and chose to structure their practices around a discourse of the body, there was little to suggest that their approach might win the approval of international funders. However, it was not long before international agencies, such as the Ford Foundation, which funded SOS's first research project in 1982, offered support for this orientation.[25] Subsequently, the decision to focus on women's health issues was consistently rewarded with funding, making possible institutional consolidation and expansion, as well as SOS's growing hegemony within the local and national women's movements.[26]

Similar factors influenced the appropriation of the discourse of "women" by SOS, as well as many other Brazilian feminists of the time. The 1980 letter describes the purpose of the group's proposed research as follows: "[T]he research aims to know the voice of women . . . to understand how to describe their lived experience . . . to make known their testimonies . . . to try to let women speak. . . ."[27] Women, in SOS discourse, were both victims of patriarchy and potential carriers of their own liberation through knowledge and self-awareness.

This was a discourse that reflected that of *Our Bodies, Ourselves* and other Euro-American feminisms with which SOS founders had had contact, but, given the Brazilian political and social context, "women" came to have a particular meaning. For Recife activists, it meant, not women in general, but the poor women of the urban periphery and their allies of the middle class. Rejecting "militancy for me," SOS members saw themselves as sharing the knowledge that privilege had granted them.[28] As one woman explained, unlike what she had seen in the United States, in Brazil the links between middle-class and low-income women

> . . . occurred immediately because there were women [in the group] who came from participating in the movement for direct elections, and for amnesty. So, there was already a concern with the democratization of the country and of information and a clarity that the majority of women lived in conditions of poverty and didn't have access to what we were experiencing.

SOS's discourse reflected the influence of the Marxist world view dominant in the opposition in other ways as well. "Women" was a category parallel to that of "working class" for the left; both represented groups whose oppression was seen as fundamental to the social structure and who were the potential carriers of transformation. Unlike "class," however, the discourse of "women" (and of "the body") offered a bridge across the "cultural abyss," as well as across the stark economic differences that separated the SOS founders from the women they sought to reach. Both groups of women shared, at least apparently, fundamental concerns about sexuality and reproductive health.

The state participated as well, though indirectly, in the construction of the discourse of "women." Alvarez argues that its own machismo caused the dictatorial regime to conceive of women's organizing as nonpolitical and therefore unthreatening. By tolerating women's activism around the cost of living, political prisoners, exiles, and other issues, the state allowed "women" as a category to consolidate itself in public discourse. Within a few years of SOS's founding, international funders too began to offer support for projects framed within this category.

During this first moment, the incipient Recife women's health movement looked abroad for discursive models, adopting a set of discourses and, along with them, particular practices, from movements in Europe and the United States whose early development and location in the Northern centers of power gave their conceptual frameworks global reach. But the ties between these imported discourses and the practices that had accompanied them soon began to unravel.

INDIGENIZING PRACTICES, 1983–1989

Between 1983 and the end of the decade, though SOS discourse remained centered primarily on women and the body, the organization's practices began to shift as it engaged with a web of local and global institutions and expanded its arenas of action. Changes occurred in four areas: themes of organizing, tactics and strategy, constituency, and institutional structure. In each, the new forms of practice ultimately came to outgrow the discourses with which the organization was founded and to pose new kinds of risks and challenges.

In terms of broad themes, over the decade SOS moved from an initial emphasis on sexuality to questions of reproductive health, from pleasure to survival. One current staff member explained:

> . . . [T]he door of entry was sexuality, and from sexuality you passed immediately to health issues or to issues of violence. Given that this NGO [nongovernmental organization] works in Brazil, if you put a foot down in the field of health, you have no way to leave because health conditions are really very dramatic. . . . [S]o we practically stopped working on sexuality . . . [and] health occupied a greater and greater place. . . .

Working in the marginal *bairros* brought SOS members into contact with women's urgent health needs and the incapacity or unwillingness of the state to address them. Reproductive health conditions, in particular, were alarming. As economic development and urbanization restructured the labor market and changed values, many women entered the labor force and large families became economically disadvantageous. The state, meanwhile, maintained an official pronatalist policy until the early 1980s, while allowing private family planning programs to operate without oversight and fostering sales of the pill through its pharmaceutical policy.[29]

This attitude of planned omission meant that contraceptives were distributed indiscriminately with little or no education or medical supervision. SOS's research found that women, discouraged by the side effects and ineffectiveness of available methods, increasingly turned to clandestine abortion and sterilization promoted by "philanthropic" physicians. The result was a 50 percent drop in Brazilian fertility rates between 1970 and 1990;[30] by the mid-1980s 18 to 20 percent of women under twenty-five in the state of Pernambuco had been sterilized, according to an SOS estimate.[31] Conditions such as these increasingly led SOS toward basic reproductive health concerns, an arena that was simultaneously becoming the object of interest for international funders concerned more with lowering birth rates than with the right of women in the Third World to sexual pleasure.

At the same time, the organization made another transition, from an emphasis on practices of self-help and the autonomous development of knowledge in local communities to a growing engagement with the state at a national level, both from outside and from inside. One of the first tentative contacts occurred in 1984, in the twilight of the old regime, when a health ministry official sympathetic to feminism came to Recife. An SOS founder described the interaction:

> . . . [H]e was Coordinator General of the Ministry, and he asked to visit SOS. We received him with a lot of interest . . . somewhat fearful of that invasion, all of us suspicious. We received him, but not very well. . . . In the afternoon, there was a big debate here in a [state] government agency, the Pernambuco Development Council, . . . and we were invited. SOS was there, but there were other people, from the union. It was the period when those moments of dialogue were beginning . . . and there was representation of civil society, but more as observers. [The Coordinator General] spoke about the importance of dialogue and said that it gave him enormous pleasure . . . to see seated there "my associates of SOS Corpo." He said that and we panicked. We left running to SOS and had an urgent meeting where we said that he had stated publicly that SOS was an associate [of the Ministry]. Girl, it was something. It caused chaos . . . [and people said] that we had to undo it. Earlier, [in the debate itself], during the period for comments, the other two pushed me—they said, "You have to speak." And I was very delicate. . . . I spoke nicely, but I clarified that the partnership did not exist, and then ran to shelter myself among my autonomous comrades.

Despite their early misgivings, SOS became involved in designing a new, comprehensive women's health program, initiated by feminists within the health ministry, and in training groups of state health professionals to increase their sensitivity to women's needs. Unlike the earlier maternal-infant care models, in which women were seen as no more than a "reproductive apparatus," the new Program for the Integral Protection of Women's Health (PAISM) treated women as "citizens possessing rights and as whole beings, where the body's history is linked to the life history . . ." according to an analysis published by SOS.[32] Approving of this framework, and seeing an opportunity to influence the medical care provided to the poor majority in the public health system, SOS members and other autonomous feminists put aside their doubts and launched into a collaborative relationship with the state.

In 1985, an activist from the organization was invited, as a representative of the broader feminist movement, to join the National Council for Women's Rights, created by the newly elected government to channel demands from civil society. Again, SOS debated the issue, but again accepted the invitation, swayed by the urgings of other women's organizations whose members saw it as important to counteract the influence of the church on government policies. Three years later, the Recife women's health organization, along with most of Brazil's feminist movement, participated in a national effort to lobby for the inclusion of feminist concerns in the new national constitution. In the process, as with its involvement on the women's council, SOS was drawn into debates on issues, such as the rights of domestic workers and of female agricultural laborers, outside the more limited sphere of health. The move to the political arena in the context of democratization required developing proposals for change that went beyond knowledge of the body to claims for rights to citizenship.

The third process of realignment revolved around the nature of the group's constituency. Initially, SOS, in the tradition of radical feminism, was an organization explicitly devoted to working with women and fostering their identity and sense of power as women, as distinct from men.[33] But, over the years, they increasingly found themselves working with mixed groups of men and women, as they began training state health professionals, holding workshops for other NGOs, working with women's organizations affiliated with mixed unions and neighborhood associations, and encountering the personal and familial networks in which their female constituents were embedded. All of this was a long way from SOS's beginnings when, as one staff member put it, "it was unthinkable for you to have feminists, both in the governmental and the nongovernmental spheres, training men."

In one final transition, over the decade, what had been a collective of eight volunteers working out of their homes became a formal institution with a sizable office, some twenty-five staff members and a budget of several hundred thousand dollars a year. At the beginning, the group studied feminist theory and practiced self-exams together, everyone participated in all projects, and all administrative tasks were rotated. There was an implicit philosophy of what one person called "spontaneous horizontality." But growing public demands and personal differences led to painful internal strife:

> You cannot imagine the level of internal conflict. . . . It [had] become the close house of the sisters, with the tensions deriving from . . . personal idiosyncrasies, deep conflicts . . . you bring from your previous life . . . , and the conflict with this original imaginary that women are good—we are the *bon sauvage* from the twentieth century, which is not exactly the case. So, we [had] that kind of mobilizing ideology from the beginning and we were struggling with the [drama] of internal conflict and being challenged by the fact that we were already very public.

For a time, tensions were so high that paralysis set in and the group brought in a psychoanalyst to help them repair their relationships and move forward.

But, by the late 1980s, in an effort to respond to the growing demands on their time, the group had begun a process of professionalization and institutionalization. Members specialized in certain tasks, group self-help practices were abandoned, and general discussions of theory became more sporadic. One participant explained her pragmatic view of collective decision-making:

> It works when you don't have so many responsibilities. But you have to define priorities. . . . Institutions are complex and have a division of labor and . . . hierarchy, not because they love power, but because it is necessary to make things work.

The process of institutionalization was both facilitated and demanded by the United States and European funding agencies that increasingly supported SOS's work. The first significant funding came from the Ford Foundation in 1982, in the form of a grant to one individual to carry out research. In the mid-1980s, European agencies, inspired by the 1985 United Nations Conference on the Decade for Women in Nairobi, began funding women's organizations in Brazil, including SOS. It was one of them, a German institution, that insisted in 1989 that SOS put an end to administrative chaos in order to provide better financial accountability:

> It was very clear. I went to Germany in '89 and they told me. They made a huge request about accounting. . . . They demanded . . . a full report for the three years of projects and this was real conditionality. It was, either you do it, [or] you won't have the money. When I got back, I came to Rio and I called [SOS] . . . and for three days I kept hearing screaming on the phone that I have submitted myself to the Germans, to the men, to whoever . . . and I said, OK, it is up to you. You decide. If you want to say no, for me that is OK. Just remember that seven people from this organization are getting their salaries from that [grant].

This incident led to the creation of a new, more professionalized structure with a specialized administrative department; what was once a collective of volunteers had become an institution. The move both ratified and facilitated SOS's increasing involvement with state agencies, international funders, and the broader transnational network of allied feminist organizations.

These changes in SOS's practices both allowed the organization to extend its field of influence and put new perils in the path of a group of feminists who had set their sights on deep social changes—the perils of co-optation, bureaucratization, and loss of radical vision. At the same time, their evolving practices began to put questions on the table that could not be addressed by the discourses of women and body alone. Increasingly their work revolved implicitly around notions of corporal citizenship, rather than bodily knowledge, and around the creation of and participation in a new kind of polity as gendered beings, rather than as women per se. New discourses ultimately made this subterranean shift in conceptions explicit and gave SOS tools to confront the dangers that faced them as an expanding movement.

ENGENDERING FEMINISM, 1990–1997

Gender is a useful concept to explain many of the behaviors of men and women in our society, helping us to understand a large part of the problems and difficulties that women confront at work, in political life, in their sexual and reproductive lives, in the family. That is why the women's movement discusses gender so much.

CAMURÇA AND GOUVEIA, *O Que É Gênero?*
Um Novo Desafio para a Ação das Mulheres Trabalhadoras Rurais, 5.

In 1990, SOS Corpo: Grupo de Saúde da Mulher (SOS Body: Women's Health Group) became SOS Corpo: Gênero e Cidadania (SOS Body: Gender and Citizenship), reflecting the incorporation of new discourses that had a better fit with the institution's modified practices and with its increasingly political vision. "Gender" had appeared in SOS documents some years earlier, soon after the 1985 United Nations Conference in Nairobi, where the term was already being used. It came into broader circulation among Brazilian feminists during the mobilization around the new national constitution in 1988, when they sought, through their proposals, to articulate women's concerns with broader social changes.

Though some feminists had begun to incorporate a gender analysis, in 1990 there was still little or no bibliography on or discussion of gender in the local universities in Pernambuco,[34] and debate on the concept was just beginning within the national social science association.[35] "Gender" was starting to make its way into the language of mainstream development and funding agencies, but, with a few exceptions, had not yet been widely institutionalized or clearly theorized.

One SOS founding member read Gayle Rubin's "The Traffic in Women" in 1980, but the concept of gender was not integrated into organizational discourse until 1990 when she read and translated Joan Scott's article "Gender: A Useful Category of Historical Analysis" into Portuguese. SOS subsequently organized both internal discussions and public debates for the Recife feminist community on Scott's theory.

The initial reaction to gender as an analytical category among participants in these discussions was mixed. One woman expressed the source of her frustration at the time:

I thought ["gender"] was very strange and it took me a long time to incorporate this concept. Since it was very complex, with different interpretations from different authors, . . . for me, not being a theoretician, this discussion was very complicated and I didn't identify much with it. And I was a little exasperated because in reality people began to use the term without knowing what they were talking about. . . .

According to another SOS member, there were also political objections:

> People didn't want to abandon the old categories—subordination and patri-
> archy—and . . . they were not convinced. The reaction was that this is much
> too abstract. It does not talk about women's suffering. . . . I think that femi-
> nists [were] more nervous about gender . . . [because] they had to start think-
> ing about men again. . . . You cannot think of gender . . . without having to
> pay attention to men. And feminists reacted very quickly.

But, for reasons discussed below, the concept was compelling, and the
theory, reconstituted as discourse and linked to other discourses on gender,
was increasingly integrated into the work of SOS, as well as that of many
other feminist organizations around Brazil, in a way and to a degree
unprecedented among feminist movements in the discourse's country of
origin where "women" continued to dominate the field.

SOS staff members brought "gender" to constituencies as far removed
as peasant women and international funders. In 1995, they wrote a pamphlet for and with the Rural Women Workers' Movement (MMTR) entitled
O Que É Gênero? (What Is Gender?),[36] which required what they described as a
very difficult process of translating Joan Scott for the realities of the
Brazilian countryside. The MMTR supplemented the material with workshops in which male and female agricultural workers analyzed the way gender relations were played out in institutions such as the union, family agriculture, and the Catholic Church.

In that same year, SOS organized a seminar which brought together
Brazilian feminists and representatives of European, United States, and
United Nations funding agencies to discuss the relationship between development funding and gender politics. The organization also launched a new
"Gender and Development Project" aimed at working with women involved
in mixed community-based urban movements, and, in 1997, SOS members
planned a project to analyze the gender content of government communications on health issues. Throughout the 1990s, the Recife women's health
organization conducted "gender training" workshops and seminars for a
wide variety of groups in Pernambuco and around the country, including
mixed (male and female) NGOs oriented toward social change, feminist
institutions, and grassroots women's organizations.

Beyond the programs explicitly addressing the new conception, rather
than signaling dramatic changes in practice, for the most part the move to
"gender" facilitated those that were already occurring. By 1990, SOS was
already working with mixed groups of men and women in workshops and
other settings, though all of its work was intended to benefit women, and
most projects continued to be directed at them. But gender offered a new
tool for approaching these groups. Whereas, in the 1980s, health workers
were trained to be more sensitive to women, in the 1990s, they were edu-

cated about the nature of gender relations and the ways they structured all aspects of life, including health care.

SOS had already begun working within the state before the discursive transition, but the language and meanings of gender gave the organization added legitimacy vis-à-vis government institutions, as one staff member explained:

> Going to the government health service or any other area of social policies and saying, "Listen, if you don't deal with this question, you aren't going to be doing anything. . . . [I]f you don't take into account that the impacts of policies are differentiated for men and women, that policy won't work." And for you to say that and be heard . . . I think that owes a lot both to the introduction of the concept and to the adoption of this perspective within Brazil in the form that it was adopted. . . . [H]ere in Brazil the impression I have is that we took . . . the gender perspective and used it to broaden political action.

In the 1980s, SOS had already expanded from its initial focus on sexuality to the broader field of health and reproductive rights. With the introduction of gender discourse, the institution moved into the arena of gender and development, while maintaining its central concern with health. This more encompassing approach gave legitimacy and greater capacity for negotiation with a wide variety of institutional counterparts—including funding agencies and other NGOs, as well as the state. Given the widespread prejudices against feminism, the adoption of new language also created the potential for deepening alliances with other social movements, such as unions and community organizations, which had seen the pursuit of "women's" interests as parochial and divisive.

Some feminist activists have critiqued "gender" as a technocratic discourse linked to the professionalization of feminism, as well as to the development industry.[37] In the case of SOS, by 1990, when the new conception was adopted, the Recife organization had already begun to move away from "spontaneous horizontality" toward institutionalization and to extend its sphere of influence. However, the arrival of "gender" helped to further consolidate this process by giving the organization expanded access to a development establishment alert to the latest trends in discourse.

Gender is a contested concept and the meanings associated with it in the academic literature as well as in activist practice are diverse. Joan Scott was cited repeatedly by SOS staff as the inspiration for their interpretation of "gender":

> SOS understands gender as a social relation of power, developed at the level of representations, and . . . produced and reproduced through norms, laws, customs, institutions, [and] the ways individual action is structured. It therefore adopts Joan Scott's perspective.[38]

Shifting their discourse from "women" to this particular approach to "gender" had a number of important theoretical implications for SOS. Whereas the earlier discourse, and the practices initially associated with it, implicitly placed both problem (patriarchy/women's oppression) and solution (women's knowledge of and control over their bodies) in the hands of one sex, "gender," as the institution interpreted it in much of its work, focused on social relations as the problem and their transformation as the solution. Society as a whole, rather than women alone, was depicted as both object and agent of change. Women's health and bodily knowledge became vehicles for promoting broader changes, as well as ends in themselves.

Just as the category of "women" had earlier been to feminism what "working class" was to Marxist analysis, in the 1990s "gender" paralleled "class" in its theoretical power and ability to embrace all of society. From the new discourse, groups like SOS drew theoretical justification for a much more ambitious political project than that originally constructed around "women." Executive director Silvia Camurça described the universe they saw opened up by the new conception: "Working with gender requires us to act at the level of social contradictions, in the subjective arena, the field of politics, relationships, institutions, norms, laws."[39]

By stressing that gender relations were socially constructed, SOS moved away from an ahistorical conception of patriarchy as an entrenched system to an understanding of gender as potentially infinitely malleable. This allowed a shift in how men were conceived; from villains, they became victims and potential allies, albeit with power over women under current gender arrangements:

> In our work with mixed NGOs, it gives a certain tranquillity to people . . . to show a . . . possibility that men—concrete men—are not the villains and that gender relations also create certain difficulties for them. It's very interesting when we start to talk about norms: that men don't cry . . . that men are violent, that men always have to be ready for sex. . . . [P]eople feel relieved, because it seems like we are going to accuse them and suddenly we show that everything is a cultural construction.

Finally, in contrast to the universal quality that had been bestowed on "women," Scott's conception of gender relations created the possibility of recognizing differences among women through acknowledging the ways gender was inflected by other experiences, such as class, race, and sexuality. Indeed, SOS pamphlets and workshops made reference to the "great web of differences" among women, as well as between women and men. But, in practice, SOS mainly addressed differences of class and gender, leaving others unexplored. None of their projects explicitly addressed either race or sexual preference, for example. One longtime SOS member commented:

> . . . SOS Corpo never discussed lesbianism adequately, at least in the same depth that it discussed other themes, never. . . . I think that it is really a resistance . . . a prejudice. . . . I think that race also was never discussed, though at

certain moments there were certain choices of staff members to be contracted, choosing the black woman because it was necessary, it was good to have black people in the picture, but the issue of race . . . was never debated.

In the 1990s, these omissions were increasingly critiqued by black women and lesbians, as they began the process of constructing their own movements. Though some black and lesbian activists kept their distance from white feminism, others maintained a dialogue with SOS, seeking to expand the institution's practices around gender. One Afro-Brazilian activist and SOS ally remarked, "I think that the organization should be looking more closely at this racial question. . . . You can't work on things in an isolated way. The gender relation isn't so simple. There is something that differentiates a black woman and a white woman. What is this something? What can we do so that we advance as a group, as black, white, and indigenous women?"

Though Scott's was their dominant interpretation of "gender," SOS members at times drew strategically on other sources of meanings for the term, based on the work of feminists from Latin America, as well as the United States and Europe. Moser's operational approach to "gender planning"[40] was used in their workshops with development professionals eager for ways to implement their new understandings. The conception of gender as a variable by which the impact of government policies could be measured surfaced in their work directed toward the state. In the context of SOS's organizing with grassroots constituencies, the work of Castro and Saffioti along with that of other Brazilian feminists, on the intersection of class and gender, was an important influence.[41]

The process of theoretical appropriation and conversion to discourse took place in the context of SOS's relationships with three other dominant forces in their field of action at that particular historical moment, two of them "local" and one "global." The characteristics of the existing social movement field in Pernambuco played an important part in shaping feminist discourses. In particular, the early dominance of class-based movements in the struggle against dictatorship meant that SOS feminists who came of age in that period had absorbed radical inclinations toward social transformation and, when "gender" came on the scene, were receptive to Scott's approach. One group member explained:

I think that ideas reach a certain place [from elsewhere], but they find a political, theoretical and cultural base where they either settle in or they don't. . . . I think Joan Scott caught on so much here because feminists . . . , in general, have a Marxist heritage. Even though . . . radical feminism was very strong in Brazil . . . it didn't lose the commitment to a historical perspective on social transformation. . . .

This perspective, along with the social inequalities in Brazil, led SOS to direct its message toward the popular majority from the beginning, and, later, to give class content to "gender." At the same time, the absence of movements around sexual preference and the weakness of black women's organizing in the region in the early 1990s meant that there was little pressure to incorporate these other differences among women more actively.

The shifting nature of the Brazilian state also influenced SOS's discourse. The lack of resources for health in a context of political democratization drew SOS's attention back to the state, after a brief period of withdrawal into civil society. Simultaneously, the infiltration of the Ministry of Health, in the last years of the dictatorship, by a number of feminist bureaucrats, offered opportunities not available to feminists working on other issues for the women's health organization to intervene in state policies. With feminist pressure from outside, other niches were created, such as the National Council on Women's Rights, and the struggle to shape the new national constitution, in both of which SOS participated. Taking advantage of these openings meant working with both men and women, creating alliances, and developing proposals for broader social change. Scott's notion of gender offered a theoretical means of making sense of this new political context.

Finally, international funding agencies also had a role in the emergence of a particular set of meanings around "gender." The early support they gave for SOS's focus on women's health made possible and accelerated institutionalization and professionalization. These developments, in turn, allowed SOS to maintain and expand its transnational connections through participation in global networks, attendance at international conferences, growing access to and use of the Internet, and so on, connections through which gender theories and discourse were propagated and reached Recife. Subsequently, international grants made possible SOS's visibility around gender issues and its capacity to respond to a new demand for gender training created by the pressure of funding agencies on all grant recipients for proposals with a gender component.

In the process, through its ability to use its legitimacy with each institution to strengthen its position with the others, SOS itself became a hegemonic force in its own right. It had begun to play a leadership role in feminist networks in Latin America and was much sought after to participate in transnational projects around health and reproductive rights coordinated in the North. Funding agencies increasingly looked to SOS to coordinate exchanges among foreign donors and their grantee organizations, and state institutions continued to invite the feminist health organization to collaborate on a variety of programs. This national and global networking gave the women's health organization the resources to hegemonize local women's movements. Not only did SOS act as translator of transnational feminist discourses and as broker for women's groups in Recife in dealing with international funding agencies, but it played a key role in setting the agenda for local feminist activity, a role not always appreciated by those, like some of the black and working-class activists, who felt their perspective was sometimes marginalized in coalition efforts. Locally, then, SOS's global connections were a double-edged sword—both conferring and undermining its legitimacy.

In 1990, faced with the inadequacy of the organization's original discourse to articulate its evolving practices, SOS once again drew on feminism from the North as a resource. But, at this juncture in its history, as an established institution with a leadership role at the national and international levels, SOS negotiated with foreign influences from a position of strength. Rather than borrowing both discourses and practices directly from Northern feminist movements, the organization's leaders selectively appropriated academic theories of gender, rearticulating them as a set of activist discourses and integrating them with their own pre-existing practices, as well as with other more locally based discursive constructions.

EXPANDING CITIZENSHIP, 1990–1997

[O]ne of the fundamental elements in transformations of gender inequalities is precisely the recognition that by struggling to improve the concrete conditions of their lives, women [are] exercising their citizenship on a daily basis; they are acting in the political sphere and, beyond that, constructing through these actions a bridge between the public and the private. . . .

CAMURÇA AND GOUVEIA,
Cidade, Cidadania: Um Olhar a partir das Mulheres, 33.

Gender did not stand alone in SOS discourse, but was closely linked to a much more indigenous idiom—that of citizenship. Placing gender in the context of this local discourse had a politicizing effect that opened up the possibility of navigating the treacherous shoals of success and maintaining commitments to social transformation.

Unlike "gender," "citizenship" made no sudden, dramatic appearance among the feminists of SOS Corpo; rather it seemed to seep into their discourse, as if part of the surrounding air, its ensconcing in the organization's name the first clear signal of its arrival. Though it appeared frequently in writings and political slogans, grant proposals, and seminars, the concept was not often the explicit focus of efforts aimed at demystification; instead, "citizenship" was incorporated as a broad framework, though one associated with certain practices.

The first practice was the dissemination of knowledge. In the 1990s, SOS grouped its documentation center, media liaison, and video distribution projects under the rubric "Information for Citizenship." Knowledge of the body and health practices took on new meaning; no longer only a vehicle for women's autonomy and empowerment, now they were also a means to full participation in a new social order.

At the end of the decade of the 1980s, as political openings were closed and the national state retreated from earlier commitments, SOS, like other Brazilian feminist groups, also shifted its efforts from fighting for the formal recognition of social rights, to struggling for the implementation of those rights it had won in the previous decade. At the same time, its locus of political action moved away from direct involvement with the state on a national level, and toward, on the one hand, greater engagement with local government and, on the other, more concerted efforts to influence the national and local states through transnational organizing.

Thanks to changes in the laws which gave them greater autonomy and resources, "Municipalities become . . . the basic political setting in which the daily construction of democracy and citizenship takes place, through negotiation and local agreements among groups with diverse interests," according to a publication edited by SOS in 1997.[42] With this understanding, the institution sent a representative to the Municipal Development Council, began working with women in neighborhood associations, and launched a newsletter, *De Olho na Cidade* (*With an Eye on the City*).

But it was also in the 1990s that SOS's global involvement accelerated. By the end of the previous decade they were already participating in a raft of transnational feminist articulations and had attended manifold international events. In the 1990s, they assumed leadership of several networks and played an important role in the local, national, and international preparations for the 1995 United Nations women's conference, using the latter as an opportunity to strengthen a local alliance among women's organizations and articulate their demands. In the aftermath of Beijing, SOS worked with the Pernambuco Women's Forum to publicize the Platform of Action and use it as a means to lobby for concrete legislative and policy changes at a municipal level, as well as participating in a similar effort at a national level through the Brazilian Women's Network. Global participation became a vehicle for expanding women's citizenship in Recife, as well as in the nation-state as a whole.

SOS's conception of citizenship included both elements common to feminist analysis elsewhere and contributions particular to the Brazilian context. Its overall concern was with pushing the boundaries of citizenship outward to incorporate rights that would allow women equal participation in both society and polity. In particular, the Recife organization, like feminist movements in the United States and Europe, sought the inclusion of reproductive rights in a broader definition of citizenship, a move that would "make the sphere of reproduction a site of the constitution of political subjects," and contribute to the dissolution of boundaries between public and private.[43]

Beyond a set of particular rights, for SOS:

. . . [C]itizenship [was] also a "conflictive practice linked to power, which reflects struggles about who can say what in defining what are common problems and how they will be treated" [Jelin 1994]. In other words, the conquest of rights necessarily passes through the recognition and action of political subjects, male or female, and the "right to have rights" [Arendt, cited in Jelin 1994].[44]

In this sense, the concept was closely linked to overall struggles for democratization being carried on by a wide variety of social movements in Brazil at the time.

Finally, "citizenship" involved not only guaranteeing the right of women and other vulnerable groups to make decisions affecting their lives, but also ensuring the social conditions to guarantee their ability to take advantage of this right. Women who faced the dramatic conditions of poverty, illiteracy, poor health, and racism in Brazil, and in the Northeast in particular, would not have access to "free" political and reproductive choices without sweeping changes in social relations. In an article published in the academic journal, *Revista Estudos Feministas,* SOS coordinator Maria Betânia Ávila wrote: "Feminism . . . should constitute itself as a permanent site of redefinition and insertion of these [reproductive] rights in the broader dynamic of the transformation of social inequalities."[45]

In this context, SOS's discourse on citizenship implied firm opposition to the dominant economic and political model whose effects in terms of misery and marginalization were increasingly felt in the 1990s among the women with whom they worked. In Ávila's words:

. . . [L]iberalism, . . . where the market is perceived as the institution that promotes possibilities for choice, and accumulation and competition are basic values that support it, . . . could never incorporate the implicit issues in the notion of reproductive rights in an integral way.[46]

Full citizenship and the competitive market economy being championed by successive Brazilian states were fundamentally incompatible.

The shift in SOS discourse from "the body" to the kind of "citizenship" described above had important theoretical and strategic implications. The discourse of the body had first been linked to practices based on an inward turn toward oneself as an autonomous being. As organizational practice evolved, however, the body was constituted as the carrier of (reproductive) rights and, therefore, a subject of politics. In both cases, the focus was on female specificity and the struggle was defined as the province of women.

The move to citizenship, which grew out of this change in practices, established a broader framework in which bodily rights were to be claimed. It implied, in fact required, the negotiation of alliances with diverse groups, both inside and outside Brazil, that shared an interest in this inclusive vision. And it meant understanding how, not only women, but men and women, and the reconstructed relations between them might be part of this vision. As with "the body," the emphasis was on gender difference, rather than sameness, but, in this case, it was on the particular rights required to ensure that women, particularly poor women, had equal status as political subjects.

The new discourse of citizenship came, not from abroad, but from Brazilian movements struggling to push democratization beyond the narrow confines conceived by the elite. It began to circulate among the opposition in the 1980s, as defeat for the old regime became inevitable and formal democratic political institutions were established, and became a vehicle for a wide diversity of heretofore suppressed aspirations for social rights, from employment and land, to racial pride and culture, to health and sexual pleasure. As an SOS staff person explained, it was also a means of rejecting old "clientelistic" practices:

> Citizenship, in the general discussion, means this: I am a person full of rights, that might not be recognized, but I have the right to be happy, to earn money, to study, . . . to have fun, to be healthy. I don't owe favors to anyone. I have to win this right for myself. To do that I have to have the right to participate, to express myself, to organize freely, to march, to carry out political pressure. . . .

It was not surprising that the conception of citizenship constructed by an opposition with a Marxist legacy would also reject liberal policies and emphasize the importance of social transformation as a necessary condition of political participation.

But despite the indigenous origins of citizenship as an oppositional discourse, transnational feminism—and the international funding agencies that facilitated access to it—also played a part by shaping the specific content that feminists gave to citizenship. Both SOS founders' experiences with movements around reproductive issues in Europe and the United States, and their participation in the international women's health movement during the 1980s, contributed to their conception of rights. Early struggles in the Northern countries around abortion and birth control as fundamental to women's right to sexuality were broadened and reframed as reproductive rights in a 1984 International Tribunal in Amsterdam. According to Ávila, "In this new perspective, conception, birth, contraception and abortion are seen as interlinked events where the impossibility of access to any one of them puts the woman in a submissive position."[47] This approach, which defends the right of women to have, as well as not to have, children, is the one reflected in the meanings SOS gave to citizenship.

Finally, feminists' relationship to the state played a part in constructing the discourse of citizenship. During the 1980s, openings for feminist movements led SOS and other organizations to occupy spaces in the state and to participate in struggles for the formal recognition of social rights. Despite a series of victories, however, many of the programs that were won, including the women's health program, PAISM, were never effectively implemented. According to SOS analyses, this reflected intervention by the Church and private family planning agencies, political corruption, and a lack of political will to address women's needs, as well as structural ties between the state and economic elites whose interest lay in restrictions on social spending.[48]

Meanwhile, an accelerating economic crisis deepened the reproductive health crisis. By 1992, one study found that 64.39 percent of those using a contraceptive method in the Northeast used sterilization, an increase of 16.49 percent over 1986.[49] This was one factor in what has been called the "demographic transition" expressed in plunging fertility rates. At the same time, maternal mortality showed a dramatic increase. Given their political commitments, the combination of worsening health conditions, the closing of doors to feminists at the national level, and the clear inadequacy of a democratization process that remained at the level of formal political institutions led SOS to adopt a conception of citizenship that embraced substantive social rights and that rested on an inclusive political vision.

Gender, as a discourse with academic roots far from Recife, offered much to local feminists. But it was only by fusing it with homegrown concepts of citizenship that its radical implications could be fully explored. By calling for the extension of democratization, citizenship tempered to some degree the disequilibria fostered by unequal access to global connections and provided a framework for alliances among movements based on class, race, sexual orientation, and gender, among others. Whether these alliances could be forged, however, remained a subject of ongoing struggle and negotiation.

DISLOCATED TRAVEL

The experience of SOS clearly shows that feminist theories and discourses sometimes follow trajectories from North to South, where they are selectively appropriated and idiosyncratically implemented in the context of new institutional configurations. But do they travel the other direction? Did "gender" linked to "citizenship" survive the journey North to be adapted and incorporated by activists in the United States, just as "women's bodies" and "gender" had earlier traveled South and been appropriated and transformed by feminists in Recife?

Revisiting the Boston Women's Health Book Collective (BWHBC) nearly thirty years after its emergence revealed an organization quite changed in some respects, but, at the same time, quite faithful to its original discursive orientation. Women's bodies remained central to its project; neither gender nor citizenship were anywhere apparent in its discourse. Where SOS used the language of "gender," the Boston Collective continued to speak of "women"; where SOS fought social exclusion and targeted the state, BWHBC continued to struggle against the social control of women's bodies and took aim at the institution of medicine; where SOS demanded citizenship and the right to have rights, the Boston Collective continued to seek consumer empowerment and the right to control one's own body.

The experience of the BWHBC does not stand alone. Across the United States, few nonacademic feminist activists have given discourses of gender and citizenship the central place in their work and thinking that SOS Corpo and many other Brazilian feminists have.[50] Discursive and theoretical travel between women's health activists in different parts of the globe has a dislocated quality, with flows from North to South occurring far more easily than in the reverse direction. On the one hand, it is clear that activists in different locations engage with different kinds of institutions. Organizing in the context of a newly democratizing state, for example, calls for distinctive discursive strategies, unlike those called for by organizing in the context of a vast private medical industry. On the other hand, despite these kinds of differences, Brazilian feminists were able to make use of discourses from the United States and European women's health movements, as well as theories from the Northern academy, even while adapting them to their own local conditions. How, then, is it that the reverse did not occur?

Here enter those dominant global forces that have the power to close borders and exclude, or to ensure their porosity to cultural imports. The barriers to South-North conceptual migration are both economic and discursive. On the one hand, the periphery and its intellectual products are constructed as both exotic and specific, while the center and its discourses and theories enjoy all-embracing, universal status. On the other, economic inequalities ensure that distribution networks for Brazilian academic—and activist—theorizing do not operate with the same insistence and power as those that disseminate Euro-American discourses and theories.[51] Despite its impressive accomplishments, the transnational feminist movement has only begun the process of constructing a social space where horizontal discursive travel could replace the fundamental asymmetries in global cultural flows, a space where women's movements in the North could benefit fully from the rich experience of feminists in the South.

NOTES

I would like to thank Sonia Alvarez, Maria Betânia Ávila, Caren Kaplan, Leslie Salzinger, Maria Cecilia dos Santos, and Hulda Stadtler for their encouragement and thoughtful insights on various incarnations of this paper, as well as my transcribers, Tiana Arruda, Regina Camargo, Cida Fernandez, and Ana Nery dos Santos, for their painstaking labors. Finally, I am especially grateful to the members of SOS Corpo and the Boston Women's Health Book Collective for their willingness to be the subjects of this ethnographic endeavor, and for their generosity with their time and accumulated wisdom. My work was supported in part by the Andrew W. Mellon Foundation, the University of California, Berkeley, Vice Chancellor's Research Fund, and by a University of California, Berkeley, Humanities Graduate Research Grant.

1. See Deborah A. Gerson, "Speculums and Small Groups," for a discussion of the body politics of early United States second-wave feminism.

2. The group, which started by offering a women's health class, later changed its title to the Boston Women's Health Book Collective as their raison d'être shifted.

3. Boston Women's Health Course Collective, *Our Bodies, Our Selves*, p. 4. The initial printing in 1970 was entitled *Women and their Bodies*, but the book was renamed the following year. In subsequent printings "*Our Selves*" became "*Ourselves.*"

4. By 1996, it had sold over four million copies in fifteen languages, including Braille (Madaline Feinberg, "The Boston Women's Health Book Collective Celebrates Its 25th Anniversary!").

5. Although, along with capital, social movements of many kinds are stretching around the globe, the feminist movement is one of the most transnationalized, in part because of the United Nations conferences on women, which, beginning in Mexico in 1975, brought activists together at parallel gatherings. Out of these contacts have grown multiple feminist networks, global action campaigns, and transnational alliances—a "subaltern public" in which meanings are articulated, transmitted, contested, and reconstituted (Nancy Fraser, "Rethinking the Public Sphere"). See Margaret E. Keck and Kathryn Sikkink, *Activists beyond Borders*, for a description of how what they call "transnational advocacy networks" were built around issues of women and violence.

6. See James Clifford, "Notes on Travel and Theory"; Claudia Lima Costa, "Being There and Writing Here"; Inderpal Grewal and Caren Kaplan, "Introduction"; Mary E. John, *Discrepant Dislocations;* Lata Mani, "Multiple Mediations"; and Edward W. Said, "Traveling Theory."

7. Grewal and Kaplan, "Introduction," p. 16.

8. John, *Discrepant Dislocations*, p. 3.

9. I recognize that much of the terminology available to characterize the differences in power and wealth among countries (*First World/ Third World, center* or *core/ periphery, developed/underdeveloped, industrialized/agricultural*) is laden with implicit hierarchies, as well as dichotomies that seem increasingly inadequate to describe the complexities of contemporary societies. Geographical labels are also problematic, but perhaps less value-ridden. While some authors refer to the "West," in this paper, writing from the perspective of Latin America, I have chosen to use the term "North" to describe the economically dominant Euro-American states/cultures from which feminists in countries of the "South," including Brazil, appropriated theories and discourses.

10. While many academics, both North and South, identify with and participate in feminist movements, the literature on traveling theories does not analyze the ways theories/discourses are integrated into and shape the strategies and tactics of these movements.

11. Grewal and Kaplan, in a critique of universalist conceptions of women's oppression, refer to the diverse array of dominant forces with which different movements engage as "scattered hegemonies."

12. All passages originally in Portuguese have been translated by the author.

13. They were a doctor, a body movement teacher, a sociologist, an architect, a photographer, two social workers, and a student (Maria Betânia Ávila, in Estela de Aquino and Dina C. Costa, "Entrevista Realizada com Betânia").

14. Sonia E. Alvarez, *Engendering Democracy in Brazil.*

15. Maria Helena Moreira Alves, *State and Opposition in Military Brazil;* and Thomas E. Skidmore, *"Brazil's Slow Road to Democratization."*

16. Sonia E. Alvarez and Evelina Dagnino, "Para Além da 'Democracia Realmente Existente.'"

17. Maxine Molyneux, "Mobilization without Emancipation?"

18. Alvarez, *Engendering Democracy in Brazil;* Elizabeth Lobo, "Mulheres, Feminismo e Novas Práticas Sociais."

19. Ação Mulher/Brasil Mulher, Letter, p. 4.

20. Unless otherwise noted, all cited material is from the author's interviews conducted in March and April 1997 and between February and December 1998.

21. SOS Corpo, *SOS,* p. 7.

22. Though feminism in the cities of southern Brazil also had an influence in Recife, in the interview I conducted with her, this woman argued that, to some degree, feminists in northeast Brazil looked abroad for inspiration as a means to assert the independence and innovative capacity of a region often disparaged by intellectuals in the more developed southern region of the country.

23. Perhaps because of their roots in the left, SOS members were less responsive to the liberal feminism which predominated in the United States and which was influential among development workers in the 1970s who became advocates of "Women in Development" (WID). This approach, which focused on women in production, rather than on reproductive or welfare issues, was reflected in USAID programs as well as in United Nations conferences and projects during the United Nations Decade for Women (Eva M. Rathgeber, "WID, WAD, GAD"; Shahrashoub Razavi and Carol Miller, "From WID to GAD").

24. Sonia Corrêa, "Uma Recusa da Maternidade?" and "Direitos Reprodutivos como Direitos Humanos"; Betsy Hartmann, *Reproductive Rights and Wrongs.*

25. Ford had funded international population-control research and activities since the early 1950s and made a transition to supporting "reproductive health" programs in the mid-1980s; Elizabeth Coleman, "From Population Control to Reproductive Health"; Hartmann, *Reproductive Rights and Wrongs.*

26. SOS's success contrasted with the experience of feminist projects around other issues, such as violence and income generation, which reported greater difficulty generating funding. On this issue, see Maria Cecilia MacDowell dos Santos, "The Battle for a Feminist State within a Context of Globalization," p. 12.

27. Ação Mulher/Brasil Mulher, Letter, p. 5.

28. Ávila in Aquino and Costa, "Entrevista Realizada com Betânia," p. 16.

29. The "private" programs were often largely funded by foreign government agencies such as USAID, which thereby avoided accusations of imperialist interference. In the 1970s, half of the budget of the International Planned Parenthood Federation (IPPF) came from USAID (Hartmann, *Reproductive Rights and Wrongs*). Bemfam, the Brazilian IPPF affiliate, was one of the largest agencies operating in the Northeast.

30. George Martine, cited in Ana Paula Portella et al., "'Not Like Our Mothers,'" p. 13.

31. Corrêa, "Direitos Reprodutivos como Direitos Humanos," p. 6.

32. Maria Betânia Ávila, "PAISM," p. 7.

33. The value placed on being an all-women's institution was such that there was even controversy when a proposal was made to hire a man to guard the building at night.

34. Universities in the region suffered from lack of resources and the "brain drain" of academics who had had opportunities for study abroad to more prestigious and better-endowed institutions in Rio de Janeiro and São Paulo. In the Northeast, NGOs produce as much, if not more, theory than the local academy, given that they frequently have greater resources and more international contacts than the university, and staff members are often intellectuals whose political commitments, developed in the opposition to dictatorship, have led them into community-oriented work.

35. Mary Garcia Castro and Lena Lavinas, "Do Feminino ao Gênero." The first women's studies program was founded in Rio de Janeiro in 1980. After 1990, when gender "arrived" in local theorizing, there was a dramatic increase in the numbers of programs established, mainly in the southern part of the country. Six were created in one year, all with "gender," rather than "women," in the title. Gender work groups were created in eight different professional organizations, and the Ford Foundation began funding scholarships for "gender studies" (Ana Alice A. Costa and Cecilia M. B. Sardenberg, "Teoria e Praxis Feministas na Academia" p. 6).

36. Silvia Camurça and Taciana Gouveia, *O Que É Gênero?*

37. See Sally Baden and Anne Marie Goetz, "Who Needs [Sex] When You Can Have [Gender]?"

38. Cida Fernandez and Silvia Camurça, *Relações de Cooperação ao Desenvolvimento e a Política de Gênero*, p. 41. This interpretation of gender offered far more possibilities from a feminist perspective than the one being implemented in the development world, where gender came to represent an inert, depoliticized category, rather than a power relation reproduced through a wide variety of institutions. In the context of development work, "gender" was often disconnected from the feminist transformatory project and became a static variable used to measure policy impacts (Baden and Goetz, "Who Needs [Sex] When You Can Have [Gender]?"; Caroline O. Moser, *Gender Planning and Development*). Moser reported in 1993 that, where Gender and Development (GAD) units had been established, "gender" had all too often merely replaced "women" without any change in substance from the efficiency-based approach of earlier Women in Development (WID) programs. A similar process occurred in the Brazilian academy, where, according to Costa and Sardenberg, gender lost its initial meaning, often becoming a synonym for "women" that functioned to make feminist work seem more respectable and scientific. The result was growing distance between the academy and women's movements, with some activists giving the pejorative label of "*genericas*" to those academics who tried to hide their politics behind a "gender" shield and some *genericas* criticizing the feminist scholars who sought to maintain their activist commitments (Costa and Sardenberg, "Teoria e Praxis Feministas na Academia"). See Costa, "Being There and Writing Here," for a discussion of the factors that made it difficult for Brazilian feminist academics to develop a gender analysis with more radical implications as well as for references to those who did.

39. Cited in Fernandez and Camurça, *Relações de Cooperação ao Desenvolvimento e a Política de Gênero*, p. 41.

40. Moser, *Gender Planning and Development*.

41. See, for example, Mary Garcia Castro, "A Dinâmica entre Classe e Gênero na América Latina," and Heleieth I. B. Saffioti, "Rearticulando Gênero e Classe Social." Other authors cited by SOS members were: Teresa Barbieri (Mexico), Françoise Collin (France), Elizabeth Lobo (Brazil), and Gayle Rubin (United States).

42. SOS Corpo, *O Que as Mulheres de Pernambuco Querem como Políticas Públicas Municipais de 1997 ao Ano 2000.*

43. Maria Betânia Ávila, "Modernidade e Cidadania Reprodutiva," p. 392.

44. Camurça and Gouveia, *Cidade, Cidadania,* p. 7.

45. Ávila, "Modernidade e Cidadania Reprodutiva," p. 391.

46. Ibid., p. 387.

47. Ibid., p. 383.

48. Ávila, "PAISM"; Sonia Corrêa, "PAISM."

49. DSH/Bemfam, cited in Corrêa, "PAISM," p. 5.

50. The situation in the United States academy is, of course, quite different, with gender theories and discourses pervading many disciplines and debates around citizenship proliferating. The fact that these trends are not reflected among feminist activists in the United States is testimony to the gap in this country between the academy and women's movements, a gap that is, for historical reasons, far less significant in Brazil and elsewhere in Latin America.

51. Costa, "Being There and Writing Here."

Global Imaginations

Introduction to Part Three

Part 1 of this volume examines the rise of new global forces and their destructive effects on individuals and communities once protected by hegemonic institutions. Part 2 explores the character of new global connections that function within, define, and reorganize an expanding transnational social space. In Part 3, we examine how the construction and deployment of "global imaginations" have become central to new political projects and controversies.

In the era of postwar globalization, nation states created protected enclaves in various spheres of economic, social, and political life. In the United States and Western Europe, postwar class compromises guaranteed manufacturing workers a privileged position in the global economy. In the United States institutions like the American medical establishment monopolized information, made decisions for patients, and delivered medical care through practices that individualized, isolated, and (in the case of breast cancer patients) stigmatized. On the other side of the political world socialist enterprises were largely protected from the ups and downs of international markets but also from public accountability for environmental pollution. At the same time an extensive welfare state gave citizens material security. These enclaving institutions benefited some at the expense of others: in general the prosperity of industrial workers and the distribution of social benefits in the wealthy "core" of the world system were directly related to inequality, poverty, oppression, and immobility in the dependent periphery and semiperiphery.

In the contemporary period, many of these systems of industrial, political, and social hegemony that once operated at the core have dissolved, collapsed, or become subject to external challenges. As Part 1 shows, these changes have been disastrous for once-protected industrial workers and populations, whose former positions, identities, and lives depended on the viability of now-vanished institutions. As a result, they now find themselves uprooted, cast out, their worlds torn apart, their work degraded if they still have work, their claims denied if they still make claims. Stuck in the old order, they decline along with it. To them, the global surely is a destructive whirlwind of forces that has wreaked havoc on former ways of life.

For others, however, the reorganization of the global has had a different effect. Part 2 demonstrates that at least some groups in newly industrializing countries and other semiperipheral regions have taken advantage of the new cross-border flows of people, culture, and technology that have marked the crumbling or transformation of old national-level hegemonies. As a result, they find themselves more able than before to forge new identities, follow new opportunities, and pursue social transformations. For such groups, the old global order was not enclaving and protecting but more usually marginalizing or constraining. The increased transnational flows that accompanied the dissolution or transformation of old hegemonies have enabled such groups as Indian nurses, Irish software developers, and Brazilian feminists to launch themselves into an emerging transnational social space rather than sinking with the wreckage of the old order.

But there is a third position as well: the position of those whose relation to the old global order was originally more ambiguous. Such groups may have been sheltered or marginalized by old regimes, but they were neither completely dependent on those regimes nor capable of transcending them. As a result, they are neither destroyed by new global forces nor completely comfortable with them. They may see new connections, but these connections do not induce them to completely give up old identities, solidarities, values, or activities. Like the groups considered in Parts 1 and 2, they must also relate to the global, but unlike the others their situation is not sink or swim. They are neither drowning in the global's tsunami nor swimming in its currents: instead, the relative autonomy of their structural locations allows them to try to channel and control the global tide. Like people who live uncomfortably on low ground near the sea, they can try to build protective dikes or harness the power of the tides in service of their own projects. For them, to be sure, the global may imply threatening forces or promise potentially liberating connections. But unlike those who sink with the inundation of old orders or who swim in new global seas, groups in this third category find some niche in the new order from which they can collectively contest the global.

For these groups, the collapse or transformation of old orders has allowed the hidden to become visible: where global forces and connections were once difficult to perceive, the global has new relevance. New conflicts emerge, with conceptions of the global—global imaginations, if you will—at their center. It is not clear what sorts of hegemony (or what scattered hegemonies) will take shape from these new conflicts, but our chapters explore how contemporary struggles are being fought over the power to define, refuse, create, join, or appeal to global forces and global connections. Thus, Steve Lopez shows how the dislocations that rapidly destroyed the lives of steelworkers in Pittsburgh did not affect Pittsburgh's unionized public service workers so directly. Public service workers are now threatened by the drive to make Pittsburgh more attractive to global investment by cutting local taxes and privatizing services, but they are able to respond by appealing to universal principles of justice superimposed on local images of vulnerable nursing home residents. Zsuzsa Gille's chapter studies Hungarian villagers and environmental activists who were once marginalized by the socialist state's protection of Hungarian industry, which shielded industrial hazards from public view. The disappearance of the socialist state does not allow these villagers to escape the pollution by swimming freely in the seas of global connections, but neither does it necessarily doom them to life in a cesspool. Instead, they reach out to the global environmental movement or bargain for morsels of profits from the global incinerator industry. Maren Klawiter shows how American breast cancer patients, once marginalized, individualized, and stigmatized by American medicine, politicize breast cancer by reversing its stigma, by attacking medical authority, and finally by linking breast cancer to global pollution. The breast cancer activists of the Toxic Links Coalition—like Hungarian villagers and Pittsburgh's public service workers—do experience the global as a threat but they are also able to mobilize successfully around it, in response to it.

Our studies of global imaginations are of course not intended as representative of all structural positions from which challenges to the global can emerge and take root, nor are they an exhaustive catalog of the ways in which global imaginations can become central to collective actors. Imaginations of the global can be organized around conceptions of global-as-forces or global-as-connections, and they can be deployed on behalf of (or against) political projects of widely divergent character. But whatever their content, and whatever the project in whose service they are mobilized, global imaginations must resonate locally in order to succeed as a discursive strategy. Indeed, one way to challenge global forces that seem to float freely above the horizon of local communities of workers, consumers, nursing home residents, and cancer patients and activists is precisely to counterpose and appeal to local solidarities, identities, images, and interests. Finally, we happen to study three movements located in the United States and Hungary. We thus ignore, for example, the possibility of challenges and conflicts over the global incorporation of former peripheral areas. These studies are intended to explore some of the ways in which the meaning and reality of "the global" are now being—and may be in the future—contested through collective action.

Zsuzsa Gille, Maren Klawiter, and Steven H. Lopez

EIGHT

Cognitive Cartography in a European Wasteland

Multinational Capital and Greens Vie for Village Allegiance

Zsuzsa Gille

Between my case and me it was a love at first "site." This occurred in 1993 when I first read of the Garé dump in a Hungarian weekly. The case, to put it simply, is a controversy over the siting of a hazardous waste incinerator that would burn the wastes dumped in Garé since 1978. It immediately struck me as such a fascinating combination of elements familiar from Western cases of environmental racism and of distinctly postsocialist economic and political issues, yet a case that violated so many of our assumptions about how environmental destruction occurred in former socialist countries, that I soon decided to make this study an entry point into the history of the concepts of waste in Hungary—a dissertation topic I had already settled on.

Since the case had already generated much hostility among villages and primarily between those villages that opposed the incinerator and the chemical firm that proposed to build it, I knew that I had to tread a fine line. Even before I actually started my year of fieldwork I made a point of hanging out with villagers and partaking in their routine afternoon chat on the wooden benches outside their houses, talking about everyday issues with them on the crowded buses they took to and from the nearest large town. I felt I needed to gain more confidence from my subjects than ordinary ethnographic topics would require, because soon they would see me in company with leaders they did not necessarily agree with, or even feared, and with their opponents on the incinerator issue. However, the most painful thing for me was not gaining their trust but keeping my views on the incinerator to myself. On occasions when women with children would approach me and, whispering, ask for my opinion on the incinerator's health effects, about which I was by no means an expert, I felt truly torn between my roles, on the one hand, as an observer worried about biasing the responses in my interviews, anxious not to encourage the rumor that I was there to "subvert," and, on the other hand, as a mother myself, conscious of environmental effects on children's health.

It was one thing to gain the confidence of villagers and another to gain that of the chemical firm's management, of village leaders, and of the Greens. My greatest fear was that either side would think of me as a spy for the opponents or as interested in only a very biased account of the conflict, which would have cut me off from important sources of information. That is why from the very beginning I made myself very visible and open to both sides, and made sure that on public occasions, such as public hearings, I spent about equal amounts of time with both parties. Although I was successful inasmuch as I found open doors everywhere, I still found myself charged with being an American spy and publicly threatened to be killed by one of my interviewees if I revealed his name.

While I was preoccupied with gaining entry, maintaining my trustworthiness, and staying alive, my fieldwork did not stop posing serious methodological questions. It became clear that this case had so many links with the past and with near and distant locations that my research would not be able to rely on a simple traditional type of ethnography. If I was to understand the conflict over the meaning of the piece of land on which the dump was created, it was imperative to go beyond observing in the present. In addition to observing this conflict in its most obvious forms on occasions such as environmental public hearings and press conferences, and in addition to relying on interviews about the conflict itself, I had to apply the ethnographic method to data available from the past. What that meant is that I had to locate this case in a broader social, political, economic, and ethnic history of this region because villagers' collective memory, often manipulated by leaders, significantly affected the terms of the debate in the present. Applying the ethnographic method to this history required that, instead of synthesizing the complex accounts of villagers and enterprise managers into one history,

I unpack the meanings of that piece of land and the attitudes of certain social actors toward others from archival documents and from interviews I conducted with people with firsthand knowledge of these histories.

As a result, I ended up relying more on what the Comaroffs call "historical imagination" than on "hard" participant observation data from the ethnographic present. This shift to historical sources, however, was still ethnographic, inasmuch as I made it following my informants' explicit or, at times, implicit suggestions. Having concluded my ethnohistorical research, I am convinced that crossing ethnography's forbidden borders of time and space allowed me to give a more comprehensive and "inside" account of this case (because it is written from the viewpoints of many insiders). Long after the first sight my love for the site endures.

In the periodical publication of a Hungarian activist group that concentrates on waste issues, a photo cartoon portrays a donkey stumbling toward an "EU" (European Union) sign. The donkey pulls a trash can from which piles of Coca-Cola cans and bottles have spilled; the caption reads: "We're heading to Europe. We are taking all we have." This cartoon ridicules the belief that one can become European/Western by accepting and generating Western waste.

By illustrating the Western perspective that Hungary has nothing to offer but waste, the cartoon also speaks to an enduring representation of Eastern Europe as a wasteland. State socialism, as it existed, was commonly described as a wasteland both figuratively and literally. In the figurative sense, socialist countries were characterized as a dull region of out-of-date, faulty, awkward, and unappealing products. They were portrayed as a gray, gloomy landscape populated by inefficient people leading squalid lives. In literal terms, mostly Western observers have made much of the fact that planned economies produced much higher amounts of waste per Gross Domestic Product (GDP) and a much higher percentage of rejects than did market economies.[1] The image of Eastern Europe as a figurative and literal wasteland still holds firm, but now the juxtaposition of that image with images of the neatness, naturalness, and purity of capitalism creates the impression that Westernization—that is, the "rationalization" of the economy—will reduce the amount of waste and thus benefit both the economy and the environment.[2] My case study, on the contrary, shows that certain Western agents help reinforce the old image by exporting toxic wastes as well as toxic waste treatment facilities to Eastern Europe. The revival of certain local identities and histories plays a crucial role in perpetuating the region as a literal wasteland.

To understand this role, my story will largely be told from a local, or, more precisely, from several local perspectives. There are, however, some other pressing reasons to assume such a focus. Many scholars have feared that, as globalization proceeds, "social meaning evaporates from places" and only returns in the form of regressive politics.[3] Students of the transition in Eastern Europe have been speaking in especially alarming terms about the future of political identity in formerly socialist countries. Scholars argue that political actions are limited to "symbolic gestures" without "directly acting on the behavior of institutions,"[4] that they lack real (economic) interests,[5] that they are grounded in residual—that is, religious and ethnic—conflicts, and, as such, are somehow irrational.[6] There are fears of the returning left,[7] fears of "movements of rage,"[8] and warnings that there may be too much remembering going on in those countries, which is also deemed dangerous.[9] Overall, observers tend to limit the outcome of competing political identities to two choices: nationalist totalitarianism and cosmopolitan democracy. In terms of geographical identities, the alternatives translate respectively into a closure to the West or an openness to it.

In contrast, localities, with newly found independence from the state and with new struggles for resources, face choices that are far more complicated and that do not map easily onto these mega-scenarios and mega-identities. Furthermore, it is often Western agents who foment discourses and political actions that fit the negative characterization of postsocialist politics quoted and characterized above. Through a case study of a siting controversy around a toxic waste incinerator, I will show how the postsocialist transition, as well as the insertion of former socialist countries into global economic, political, and cultural fields, dovetails with local identities and with the wasteland image of the region.

Beginning in 1978, the Budapest Chemical Works dumped about 17,500 tons of tetra-chlorobenzene—a highly toxic substance generated in pesticide production—in the vicinity of Garé, a small agricultural village in Baranya county, a relatively underdeveloped and multiethnic region of southern Hungary. For decades, residents complained that the dump caused cancers in villagers, contaminated groundwater and soil, caused excessive numbers of diseases and deaths among domestic animals, and produced a constant foul odor. As the leaking toxic waste started to threaten the nearby spring and the health and livelihood of an entire region, the Budapest Chemical Works was ordered to eliminate this dump site. The company made plans to do this by incinerating the accumulated waste in a facility that would also be built in Garé, the imminent construction of which has, however, sharpened divisions among the surrounding villages. Many fear that the facility would be perilous to their health. The incinerator would be financed with mostly French capital and thus many also worry that it would soon begin to burn toxic wastes imported from abroad. As I write this, in 1999, it has been seven years since the controversy began its path through numerous public hearings, demonstrations, petitions, resignations, and lawsuits. The siting controversy has become Hungary's most publicized and most divisive environmental pollution case.

I will, first, introduce the key global player in this case, namely, the global incinerator industry; then I will show the industry's dependence on local histories and identities as well as on certain discourses about the economic and political transition taking place in Hungary. Then I will delve into the local-global connections being forged and the cognitive maps that are made in challenging this global force. Finally, I will reflect upon the connection of local identities and images of Eastern Europe as a wasteland.

THE GLOBAL WASTE INCINERATION INDUSTRY

The world produces an estimated 338 million tons of hazardous waste per year. Experts argue that between 180 and 250 million tons are generated in the United States, between 30 and 45 million by European OECD countries, between 25 and 30 million by the former Soviet Union, and about six million by Central and Eastern Europe. This amount keeps increasing: the European OECD (Organization for Economic Cooperation and Development) countries alone add an additional 3 percent, that is about 9 million tons, to their industrial waste output each year. Most hazardous wastes are still landfilled; in the European Community countries about 70 percent, while 10 percent are recovered, 10 percent treated, and 8 percent incinerated.[10] But due to rising public resistance to landfilling and subsequent tightening of environmental regulation, there was a major shift toward incineration of hazardous wastes in the 1980s. (This is also the trend for municipal waste,[11] of which 19 percent in OECD countries is incinerated.)[12] In the United States, the quantity of hazardous waste burned increased by at least 20 percent in 1988 and 1989.[13] Individual records of chemical plants also suggest a turn toward incineration.

The increase of incinerator capacity led to a slower rate of cost increase for incineration relative to that for other waste treatment methods, primarily landfilling, which provided further incentive to burn. Incineration is now a highly profitable business. With charges of $1,500 for burning one ton of hazardous waste, a medium-sized facility (50,000 tons per year) can earn its investment costs (about $50 or $60 million) within a year. In 1988, in the United States, revenues from the manufacture and sale of incineration equipment were estimated "at $1.6 billion, while income from 'incineration services' was estimated at $370 million."[14] Between 1977 and 1988 the growth in each of these two sectors' revenue averaged more than 30 percent per year, while projected growth through 1993 was 20 percent per year for both sectors.[15]

Costs, however, are not universal; they depend on the stringency of emission standards in individual countries—hence the geographical element in the tug-of-war between the waste incinerator business and environmental regulation. Wastes are transported for treatment to those countries that have the loosest emission standards, until the regulations "catch up" with those of others.[16] The gap in regulatory standards is a key cause of hazardous waste exports from Western Europe to developing countries and to Eastern Europe.[17] The flipside of capital's increasing mobility is the mobility of hazardous waste.

Incineration of wastes, despite the alleged constant increase in safety, is still a menace to public health and the environment. Incinerators decrease the volume of waste (some by only 60 percent), but whether they actually reduce its toxicity depends on the composition of the burned wastes. Incineration itself has its waste products (such as bottom ash and fly ash), which are still considered toxic and which thus have to be screened from the air and landfilled. Incinerator emissions of dioxins and furans, the most toxic substances ever known, account for 80 percent of all such emissions in industrialized countries. Health impacts of incineration have triggered resistance to incinerators in Western countries, forcing the state to raise emission standards but ultimately also making it practically impossible to site new facilities.[18]

With West European incinerators facing a saturated and environmentally more conscious domestic market, a surplus capacity of incinerator manufacturing facilities and know-how has been built up, which forces investors to create a demand outside Western countries. What better market than Central and Eastern Europe, a main producer of hazardous wastes (see data above), which had practically no domestic incinerator capacity until the end of the 1980s.[19] According to the Greens, however, the facilities built by Western investors, such as that proposed for Garé, would burn not only domestic wastes but also wastes imported from the West. Central and Eastern Europe is attractive to Western Europe and the United States because it is lagging behind both in the regulation of emissions and in incineration capacity. The relative scarcity of existing facilities makes it possible to keep incineration costs high, so that even if Western exporters have to grant soft loans to Eastern Europeans for the purchase of their technology, the region's market still promises great profitability. Western exporters can also rely on the economic desperation of both the state and local communities, as well as on the weakness of newly formed democratic institutions. Transition aid packages as well as an explicit policy of the European Union encourage the movement of waste-to-energy facilities to the Eastern half of the continent.[20]

Since 1988, there has been an estimated annual minimum of 18 million tons of incinerator capacity proposed just in Russia, the Baltics, Hungary, Poland, the Czech Republic, and Slovakia, with about 93 percent of that offered for export by Western countries.[21] Put another way, by 1996 about 187 facilities had been proposed in the region. Germany is leading the way with participation in 30 projects, Austria in 29, Denmark in 14, and the United States in 10.

It would be easy to argue that the Western incineration industry is simply seeking to annex Central and Eastern Europe; however, there is more to this trend than is implied by the data and arguments above. The incinerator industry is being fought all the way, and in this battle its potential victims have successfully appealed to another global force, the international environmental movement. In the past few years, seventy waste incinerator projects have been stopped by Greens and affected residents or have been withdrawn by their proponents before realization[22]—a magnitude suggesting that the doom and gloom observations that civil society is dying in postsocialist countries should be revised in light of *local* political actions. The expansion of this industry across national and regional borders depends on and takes the form of local struggles, which grow out of local histories and which mobilize local identities. This is what I address next.

PRELUDE TO THE ENTRY OF THE GLOBAL INCINERATOR INDUSTRY

In this section, I will analyze the global, national, and local contexts of the Garé dump. The history of the dump did not start when the first barrels arrived in Garé's woods. First, this waste had to be produced, and, second, Garé had to emerge as a possible repository for this waste.

In order to understand the global context of producing this waste, we must understand that the manufacturing of tetrachlorobenzene (TCB) has a high waste-to-final-product ratio. The amount of waste produced is almost equal to the amount of the intended final product (45 percent). It was exactly for this reason, according to a former high-ranking employee of Budapest Chemical Works (BCW), that by the 1970s most West European countries ceased the production of TCB and passed its production down to less developed ones.[23] Austria secured a barter deal with its neighbor Hungary.

Hungary, however, besides its proximity, had other reasons for being a good candidate. It was a key pesticide supplier for COMECON, the agency for economic integration among socialist countries, even though its domestic production did not cover its own rapidly growing needs for agricultural chemicals. This role and the shortage of hard currency compelled Hungary, first, to find barter deals in which such articles could be imported without spending hard currency; and, second, to increase its leverage with its socialist trading partners by demonstrating its ability to trade and compete with Western chemical producers.

BCW has been a prominent chemical manufacturer in Hungary since the early 1960s, known both for its products, which filled a large portion of Hungary's pesticide and artificial fertilizer needs, and for its top managers, who maintained an unorthodox attitude toward production organization and foreign trade. The firm's longtime reform-minded president earned little support in the most influential party circles: BCW was denied the extra funds and loans that other large socialist enterprises acquired on a regular basis. This created a further incentive for the management to search for foreign cooperation.

Among the first such deals between a Hungarian and a Western firm (the first involving chemical companies) was the one BCW struck with the Austrian firm ÖSW in 1967. BCW delivered paradichlorobenzene and tetrachlorobenzene (TCB) in exchange for Trifanox (a herbicide made out of the compounds BCW delivered) and pesticides that BCW sold to Hungarian agriculture in forints, nonconvertible Hungarian currency. The Austrian firm paid with hard currency for the difference in value between the Hungarian TCB and the Austrian products. The low price to BCW of the raw materials (chlorine and benzene) made the deal look very advantageous; however, a few middle-level managers in the company warned against the deal because of the high ratio of waste to final product. The pressures on the company to sustain itself relatively independently and to bring in hard currency for the country won out, leaving the waste problems unresolved for a decade after production started.

While the Hungarian state reaped most of the benefits of this deal, when it came to assisting BCW in solving its waste problems, the state threw up its hands. BCW started its quest for a way to reuse or to safely dispose of the toxic byproduct in the year it signed the contract with the Austrian firm. By 1969, that is, within a year of signing the contract, BCW had approached two ministerial departments, seven land- and water-use and public health authorities, three scientific institutes, and five state-owned enterprises.[24] BCW also suggested that the ministry work out an action plan to deal with the wastes of the entire chemical industry. While these efforts resulted in several concrete proposals for reuse and disposal, they all met with obstacles, which forced BCW to resort to delivering the waste barrels for storage to its newly acquired branch plant in Baranya county. In the long run, this proved to be convenient because it allowed BCW to present its waste as if it were produced locally, in the Baranya branch plant, entitling BCW to dump its barrels in a nearby dump that was being established in the mid-seventies.[25] This was the dump at Garé.

Why Garé? Long before Garé became a literal wasteland, it became a figurative one, and the processes leading to that point must be sought in the policies of socialist regional development.

In the earlier decades, the Party's development policy aimed at the "emaciation" (elsorvasztás) of small settlements, by neglecting their infrastructural development, in hopes of encouraging rural populations to migrate to the cities, where they could relieve the labor shortage. Later, the government's policy was to fuse agricultural cooperatives, withdrawing their lands from production and finally merging the villages themselves. These mergers implied a joint administrative body (the council), with funds effectively under the control of the dominant villages.

Baranya's villages were not merged at a greater rate than those of other counties, but, because of the area's historical pattern of small but densely located settlements, the amalgamations had a particularly emaciating effect in Baranya.[26] By the end of 1978, a meager 4 percent of all the villages in Baranya county had their own councils, while the national average (of nineteen counties) was 32 percent. Only the neighboring Zala and Somogy counties had a lower ratio. From the beginning of state socialism, Baranya's tiny settlements were regarded as bastions of small-scale production, which did not conform to the utopia of large-scale collectivized and nationalized farming. Indeed, the performance of the region's agricultural collectives lagged behind others, partly for geographic and demographic (aging population) reasons. The aging of Baranya's villages was intensified by the state's unwillingness to develop industry so close to Yugoslavia, and possibly also by the ethnic heterogeneity of the county. In the 1960s, plans were drawn up to harmonize the geographic distribution of industry and infrastructure with what policy-makers called the intensive path of development. These policies, under the slogans of efficiency and rationality, led to the termination of cultivation on lands that were not fit for mechanization, such as the hilly plots in Baranya county, and to the fusing of agricultural cooperatives. The loss of economic autonomy, even though it had been relative, justified and was quickly followed by the loss of administrative autonomy as well.

The socialist history of Garé, now a village of 340 inhabitants, is typical in many respects. But Garé had not always been a victim of history. Because its soil was good, Garé used to house the richest landlords; in fact, it was a religious and cultural center (a substantial town in the fifteenth century), with both a Protestant and a Catholic church. Garé's nobility employed the peasants of surrounding villages, primarily those of Szalánta, who could not own land because of their Croatian origin. Garé, according to the local teacher and chronicler, was in a leading position ("it was a trendy place") until the formation of the agricultural cooperative in 1960. That was when the peasants of Szalánta, Garé's former cotters, started their ascendance to become its masters, and when Garé's distinguished historical path merged with the typical paths of other small villages of the region, outlined above: the path to a figurative wasteland. Garé's agricultural cooperative was fused with that of Szalánta in 1975; its council was closed and its administration was put in the hands of Szalánta in 1978.

Garéans lost their veterinarian and their bank office; most of the small businesses closed, construction permits were banned, and infrastructural development came to a halt. Garéans also suffered discrimination in the now fused cooperative, in terms of labor tasks and remuneration. Similar circumstances in other villages in Baranya led to their becoming completely deserted. After becoming a figurative wasteland in this way, Garé greatly improved its chances, of course unknown to its residents, of becoming a literal wasteland.

Garéans thought they had seen the worst, and slowly resigned themselves to having their lives managed by Szalánta. When an unfamiliar bad odor began entering their gardens and their houses in the early eighties, they started wondering whether their fate was governed from further away than the neighboring village. As it turned out, in 1979, the councils of the county and Szalánta had struck a deal with the Budapest Chemical Works in which BCW had been given a permit to establish a toxic waste dump in Garé's borderlands in return for extra funds channeled to the councils.

In fact, many other villages had achieved this "literal wasteland" status. Baranya is one of those counties whose small villages have been very popular as destinations for various kinds of waste consignments. In Ófalu, about twenty kilometers away, for example, the state planned the country's first radioactive waste dump. In 1986, there were sixty-two industrial waste dump sites registered in Baranya county; among these, twenty-seven were storing industrial hazardous wastes. In comparison, the two neighboring counties, Tolna and Somogy, housed six and one hazardous toxic waste dumps, respectively.[27] Given that Baranya is very densely populated, the rationality behind such a specialization is rather questionable. Scientists might point to the county's extensive bed of clay that, due to its supposed impermeability, was believed to prevent toxins from seeping into the groundwater. However, the claybed in Garé did not prevent the leaking of TCB waste to deeper layers of the soil.

Why has Baranya been such a likely destination of industrial wastes, given that clay can be found in abundance elsewhere in the country? The answer lies partially in the fact that decision-makers had the most data available from test drills for this region because Baranya was the only place in Hungary where uranium had been found. The sheer abundance of geological data and the region's huge geological research apparatus thus made Baranya a very likely target for waste, especially given the fact that it was known to have the necessary clay soil conditions.

Beyond these scientific-institutional factors, however, social reasons were just as important, such as Baranya's relative underdevelopment, its aging and ethnically heterogeneous population, and the relatively large number of administratively paralyzed settlements such as Garé. The direct interests involved in the Garé dump are difficult to decipher. According to a local resident, when the president of the joint council protested the idea of the dump sites, he was threatened. Many interviewees report that the money Szalánta received in return for accommodating the dump helped that village to build its new road. In addition to this carrot and stick operation, certain informal relations must also have contributed to the making of the deal. For no apparent reason, Garé and Szalánta were switched to the administrative district (consisting of about ten villages) of Pécs, the county seat, just for the short period (from April 1, 1977, to December 31, 1978) in which the permits were issued not just for BCW but for two other firms in Pécs.[28] They were subsequently returned to the jurisdiction of the Siklós district, where they had always belonged.

Thus, Garé as a wasteland has to be seen as the sour fruit partly of Hungary's position in the international division of labor structured by the country's political dependence on its socialist trading partners and partly of its economic dependence on the West.[29] While BCW also benefited from this division of labor, especially by externalizing and passing on the ecological costs of its TCB production to an unknowing rural population, its choices were very limited by the state. The state's imperative of "produce-and-dump or be punished," which in BCW's case was a real threat, and its ignorance of BCW's plea for an action plan to deal with the wastes of the entire chemical sector have to be seen as entries in the dictionary with which global political and economic forces were translated into Hungarian. The state's agility, however, did not exhaust itself in generating the 63,000 barrels of toxic waste; as we have seen, its ideology and practice of regional development also played a key, although less direct, role in making it possible for this waste to be dumped in Garé. The global context of my case study is thus best characterized by the East-West politics of Cold War and détente and by core-semiperiphery economic relations mediated by a state that owned and controlled the means of production and that was free from democratic restraint. For the state, for BCW, and especially for the village where the material by-products of these international politics spoiled the quality of life irreversibly, this global context appeared very much like an external, out-of-reach, impinging force. The leaking toxic waste contaminated the soil in a large radius around the dump, making animals and people sick, making it very difficult for Garéans to sell their produce on the market, and considerably reducing real estate value in the village.[30]

THE GLOBAL INCINERATOR INDUSTRY FROM BELOW

Garé could be deprived of its own cooperative, of its council, its small businesses, its bank, its veterinarian, even its clean environment, but it could never be deprived of the collective memory of its "good old days." The landmarks of its two churches served as constant reminders, helping to maintain the villagers' sense of pride, especially vis-à-vis Szalánta, which never had a church, and whose residents were forced to keep coming to Garé for weddings, baptisms, funeral services, and religious holidays. The mistreatment Garé's residents had to suffer while under Szalánta's domination is a key ingredient of this collective memory. When Garé regained its autonomy in 1990, the first thing the village did was to take the dump business and, with it, the village's fate into its own hands. In the ensuing debates about the incinerator, village leaders have cleverly mobilized this collective memory.

Garéans wanted a cleanup, but the state had been unable to force BCW to do anything other than paying fines for delaying cleanup. What's more, under the general amnesty of 1989, the state had dropped criminal charges against BCW for polluting the environment and endangering public health, a decision which the still joint council of Szalánta had appealed with no success. Garé's new and independent leadership did not fail to draw the lesson: relying on the state to get the waste out of their backyards was futile. The new local government approached BCW and invited it to build the incinerator in the dump's location. The management of BCW had already been thinking in terms of incineration because its profits offered the only likely source to cover the dump's cleanup costs. However, there were two problems: 1) BCW did not have money to invest in a new facility, and 2) everywhere in the country communities were banning dumps and incinerators one after the other. Garé's and BCW's interests now matched as they never had before: they both wanted to survive in an increasingly volatile economic situation *and* get the cleanup done. Fortuitously, there existed a third party the goals of which were not only the same, but which also had the capital and the technology to achieve them—the French state firm, EMC Services. BCW formed a joint venture with EMC, called Hungaropec.[31]

The novelty of this triumvirate resides not so much in its unlikelihood (a victim with its victimizer—the village with its polluter) as in its direct, unmediated relations between a village and an industrial firm, on the one hand, and between a small, disempowered village and a relatively powerful Western company, on the other. It is in stark contrast to the past in which the state held the remote control of Garé's life. Garé had not known of BCW. The councils of Szalánta and of the county, and other agents of the party-state, stood between them. For a decade after the dump was put in operation, Garéans had no direct contact with anyone from BCW: for them, the company's presence was limited to the odor its waste barrels perspired in the heat of the summer. To make sense out of the smell and the slowly leaking pieces of information about the dump and its dangers, the villagers conjured up this absent Other. When animals died, BCW had killed them; when red snow fell, BCW had colored it; when Szalánta got a new road, BCW had paid for it; when trees dried out, BCW had desiccated them; when fruit tasted badly, BCW's poison had spoiled it; when the candle went out in the basement, BCW's gases had put it out. After 1990, in contrast, the residents of Garé could reach BCW for comment without having to go through Szalánta or other extralocal representatives, and the company, the absent cause of their miseries, suddenly materialized; it was brought near to them, and its representatives sat down to negotiate with them. Since then, its presence has been made permanent by an office maintained for its French joint venture, Hungaropec, in the town hall. Adding further weight to its presence, Hungaropec has organized exhibitions with the aim of popularizing the idea of the incinerator and has been publishing a locally circulated (in ten villages) paper whose title, *Between Ourselves,* expresses rather clearly the intent of BCW and Hungaropec to portray themselves as "one of the villagers."[32] The void created by the state's disappearance from Garé's life, both in financial and administrative terms, was quickly filled by global forces and discourses that the new elite successfully utilized in its own interests under the slogan of cleanup. Such a direct connection between local and global could not have emerged under socialism, as the state's umbrella shielded localities from global weathers, rain or shine.

If Garé and BCW were to successfully deploy the global incineration industry in their own survival struggles, they first had to sell the idea of "cleanup-via-incineration" to authorities and, most importantly, to those other villages that now, thanks to democratization, had a say in such investments. Interestingly, the pro-incinerator language typically applied in the West was much less utilized in this case. In its place was a customized discourse about Garé's "insertion into the bloodstream of Europe." The public relations campaign has thus drafted a "cognitive map" that located Hungary and Garé in particular ways vis-à-vis Western Europe.[33] The best visual representation of this cognitive map is the photo on the cover page of the brochure of Hungaropec Ltd. In the top portion you have a close-up of the problem: the barrels—filling, through the technique of photomontage, the map of the district. In the bottom, partially superimposed on the upper photo, you see a bird's-eye view of one of EMC's plants, the incinerator in Saint Vulbas, France. You could not find a more didactic illustration for the story that the Budapest Chemical Works wants to tell, which is "We have a global solution for a local problem."

The narrative part of the eight-page brochure elaborates on this theme: the first paragraph talks about "the present situation," the second about the "experiences from abroad," and the third simply draws the obvious conclusion that the solution consists in the application of experiences from abroad to the present, local situation. The first paragraph ignores the history of the dump, fails to identify its creator, and underestimates its ecological dangers, thereby wiping out any traces of the past controversy between Garé and BCW.

> In the vicinity of Garé, there was a significant amount of industrial waste deposited in accordance with the designation of location and prescriptions of the authorities. The long-term presence of these wastes *may endanger* the soil, the flora and fauna, agricultural production, the ground- and drinking-water supplies, and indirectly people's health. For this reason it is justified and nec-

essary to eliminate and neutralize the wastes stored here, and to re-establish the cleanliness of the environment in the long run.[34]

The next paragraph, anticipating the reader's sense of something missing, imaginatively substitutes global histories for the missing local history, and immediately suggests the progressive nature of the solution to be offered in the third paragraph.

Hungary, like her Eastern neighbors, was characterized by the dumping of the hazardous by-products of industry, that is by "sweeping the problem under the rug" due to the incorrect industrial policy of the past decades, while in Western European countries with a developed industry and with an ever higher concern about the environment the *most widely accepted solution* has become the *utilization* of industrial wastes *by incineration*, which is already applied in numerous densely populated areas of Western Europe (Switzerland, the Ruhr, the vicinity of Lyon, Strasbourg, etc.).[35]

The third paragraph makes two unsupported claims: that incineration of the wastes in Garé is the only technologically rational solution and that the solution must be "entrepreneurial."[36] The paragraph concludes by saying that Hungaropec Ltd. offers a solution that satisfies both of the above rational requirements, the technological and the economical.

In the East/West dichotomy applied in Hungaropec's cognitive map, the "East" is synonymous with the past; it is a wasteland that produces so much waste that it threatens residents with "suffocating in garbage," but it is not even credited with having a developed industry.[37] According to Hungaropec's brochure, all the East has is an "incorrect industrial policy," industrial by-products (the two thus tacitly connected in a causal relation), and authorities who designate locations and prescribe the technological parameters of waste treatment. What emerges from this portrayal is more than just the invitation to the "European" road, the staple of postcommunist ideology: it implicitly portrays BCW as a victim at the hands of socialist state authorities when dumping, and as a hero when burning the waste that it produced, a hero that will thus take Garé to Europe. Indeed, in 1993, Hungaropec literally took villagers, environmentalists, and journalists for a visit to model plants in Western Europe. Autobiographies told in the form of similar conversions from victim to hero have been the key source of moral and political capital in Central and Eastern Europe since 1989.[38]

THE GLOBAL INCINERATOR INDUSTRY CHALLENGED: THE GREEN PERSPECTIVE

Building moral capital on either side of the case has been a critical strategy. The incinerator is viewed by most Garéans as an opportunity for revenge against Szalánta. Garéans think that, since administration was in Szalánta's hands at the time the permit was issued for the dump, and since it was

Szalánta that reaped all of its benefits, Szalánta's residents, more or less collectively, are responsible for the present situation. As a consequence, Garéans believe Szalántans have no moral right to have a say in the decision about the incinerator. Szalánta, however, has been quite successful in presenting itself as the guardian of the district's physical and moral health. In doing so, it has been able to redefine the terms of its leadership in the vicinity, which was shaken first by the 1990 decentralization, and then by Hungaropec's plan to build the incinerator, a project that would make Garé economically the most powerful settlement in the district.

In resisting the incinerator, local villages, under the leadership of Szalánta, have mobilized surrounding towns, whose existence depends on thermal-water-related tourism and wine production, and whose reputations might easily be ruined by the incinerator. They have recruited a competing Swiss-Hungarian joint venture and a French incinerator in Dorog into their ranks by positing them as alternatives to the incinerator in Garé.[39] In addition, they have formed an alliance with Hungarian Greens, who provide the villages with information, contacts, suggestions for action, equipment, and publicity.

There are two environmentalist entities active in the case. One, which has advocated against the incinerator since 1989, is the main Green group in the county seat, the Green Circle of Pécs. The Green Alternative Party (GAP), based in Budapest, was established in 1993, and for them the Garé case was a formative issue. Szalánta needed their resources—contacts, information, techniques of political action—and in return, GAP needed Garé as a salient issue around which it could rally publicity before the 1994 elections. Both Green Circle and GAP suggest various alternatives to the Garé incinerator. Most villagers outside Garé support burning the barrels in the already existing incinerator at Dorog; other residents and environmentalists would go along with a mobile incinerator that could be disassembled and moved elsewhere after cleanup is completed; still others talk about trying the biodegradation method; and a few people, such as members of Green Circle, might even prefer the Swiss-Hungarian incinerator planned nearby, for reasons given below.

Both Green organizations cultivate extensive relations with foreign environmental movements and organizations. Several of their members had attended the Rio Summit in 1992; they often travel to meetings in other countries and host environmentalists from abroad. GAP and Green Circle ask for information and assistance from Greens in other countries, including the Green fraction of the European Parliament and Greenpeace. The former provided them with updates on the European Union's incinerator policy and arranged a showing in several villages of the video on incinerators made by Greenpeace. Green Circle received United States Peace Corps volunteers, who enriched their technical repertoire and made English-language grants more accessible, one of which, a Dutch grant, the Greens in

Pécs used specifically for organizing around Garé. The Austrian Greens are often invited by both environmental organizations to talks on the Garé incinerator, both as experts and as fellow-countrymen of ÖSW (the partner of BCW in the TCB contract). The Environmental Management and Law Association (EMLA), which is the Hungarian affiliate of a United States nonprofit environmental law consulting agency, has been gratuitously managing several of the lawsuits that have emerged from this case, and has kept the Green alliance up to date on the legal tactics foreign corporations use against environmental activists. In sum, the Hungarian anti-incinerator agents have been very successful in inserting themselves into and benefiting from the international environmental movement, which is a key pillar of what some call the global civil society.[40]

Under socialism, environmental issues functioned as a relatively safe terrain for expressing political dissent, and in many countries (especially in Hungary and Lithuania) the environmental movements were instrumental in bringing down the system. While these fledgling groups and initiatives were certainly informed by Western environmental movements, they developed without much of their assistance until the late 1980s. After 1989, even though environmentalism was losing its appeal as a political agenda, various Western agencies became more active in building cooperation and providing help in many forms to postsocialist environmental organizations.[41]

However, it is not only funds, people, and information that cross borders in this greening civil society, but also discourses. The Green alliance thus draws on one mainstream, global, environmental discourse—NIMBY-ism—and other, less mainstream, but still global, discourses—namely, those of ecological colonization and environmental racism. The charge of environmental racism is raised primarily in relation to the entire district, if not the whole county, which has an ethnically very heterogeneous population, consisting primarily of Croats, Germans, and Romanis (Gypsies). This charge gains particular significance in relation to Bosta, the village that is, after Garé, second-closest to the dump and the incinerator site. Bosta has a population that is 80 percent Romani and has historically been one of the most disadvantaged villages in the county; like Garé, it also used to be economically and administratively fused with Szalánta. Initially, Bosta took Garé's side in the incinerator-siting debate, but when in 1994 the present mayor took her seat, a referendum quickly revealed that the large majority of Bosta's residents opposed the incinerator.

The Greens' insistent efforts to educate Bosta's residents and government played a major role in this change, as did economic and social pressures by Szalánta. During the past decades, Bosta's livelihood had grown so dependent on this larger village that the prospect of Szalánta's severing its links because of Bosta's support for the incinerator had an impact on Bosta's residents. They told me of hostile exchanges, including Szalántans' refusal to continue lending agricultural machines to them.

In 1995, Hungaropec published a social-economic impact assessment study, as part of a general environmental impact study.[42] The racist undertones of this document were taken by Bosta's residents as demeaning and helped renew their alliance with Szalánta.

The impact study tries to scare the small villages into approval. It argues that their populations have consistently decreased since 1949 and that they will be "Gypsified" ("elcigányosodnak") unless there is a boost to their economic development, such as the incinerator at Garé would provide. The analysis ignores Romani immigration and thus suggests that Bosta, as well as other villages, face extinction. The report treats the Romanis not as a population that can keep the village alive but as yet another force rushing the village to its demise. The report's deceptive language and use of statistics were powerfully confronted in the 1995 Bosta public hearing. The villagers said that, first, eight new families had moved in since the prior year; second, that it was not their fault that they had not developed and grown; and third, that they were all one people—Hungarian, whether Gypsy or not. While the impact study views the incinerator as a way to "keep Gypsies out" of the district, the Romani Civil Rights Foundation credits the large Romani population with attracting such dubious investments.

By treating the Garé case in terms of economic and ethnic relations, with their claims about ecological colonization and environmental racism, the Greens offer a global cognitive map that presents quite a different picture of the West from that advanced by the incinerator's supporters. They go to great efforts to discredit the "expert systems" in Hungaropec's references, such as the EU or the Basel Convention, exposing them as players in the toxic waste export game.[43] They argue that the EU, however high the environmental standards it may have for itself, encourages the transfer of waste-to-energy facilities to the Eastern half of Europe. They also point out that the Basel Convention simply requires that toxic wastes be imported and exported with the mutual agreement of both countries, which, they imply, is not likely to be an obstacle in BCW's case.

The villagers and some Greens think especially badly of France, partly because of its alleged competition with the famous Villányi wine produced nearby, and because of France's bad historical record in Hungary's past. A speaker at a public hearing on the incinerator said:

> We have not received anything especially good from the French since Rákóczi's war of independence.[44] Until they regain their credit, I don't feel [we can believe them], since so far they only helped to sever two-thirds of our country's territory.[45] Let them leave at least our air for us, and let us live in peace in this country in a manner suitable to a Hungarian.[46]

What about the Greens' image of the East or the past? Opponents of the incinerator try to expose Hungaropec and BCW as representing not a break with, but rather a continuation of socialism. Greens like to point out that the decision to have a permanent dump in Garé was made under socialism. As one pamphlet said, "a decision made by the State Committee of Planning in 1980 cannot be put into effect against the will of the region's taxpaying citizens."[47] They also see a parallel between the process of decision-making about the waste dump and that about the incinerator. "Once already there was a bad decision made without us; let's not let another bad decision be made again. . . . I hope . . . we can make a decision based on consensus."[48]

Democracy and especially local autonomy are the key arguments of the Greens in the debate; furthermore, such values represent the only positive connotation of "Europe" that they acknowledge. This value preference is so strong that it may even take precedence over their environmental principles. Some Greens, for example, would welcome the rival Swiss-Hungarian incinerator in nearby Kökény because that would be built at least partiallly with local capital and it would incinerate only local (county-wide) wastes. One activist stressed to me her opinion that the head of the plant in Switzerland that served as the model for this incinerator was a lot more "open and more democratic" in his dealings with the local population than were Garé's local leaders and the management of BCW and Hungaropec.

Locals are also listening closely to the undertone of Hungaropec's self-praise, which celebrates industrialization. As a participant in the Szalánta public hearing exclaimed, "Socialism is over, and it's not clear that we should be a chemical superpower." This is a tacit reference to the Hungarian communist slogan of the 1960s, "Let's chemicalize!" which came, in turn, after the failure of the 1950s strategy celebrated in the prophecy "We will be the country of iron and steel." Most Hungarian Greens do not reject industrialization in itself, but they do so when it is planned in primarily agricultural areas and otherwise still relatively clean natural environments. They see Garé's incinerator as the implicit continuation of socialist regional development policy that favored distributing industry more or less equally throughout the country in the name of geographical and social equality.[49]

In sum, the Greens' cognitive map shows a different picture: rather than transporting Garé and its region to a paradise-like Europe, Western firms propose to bring Europe to the local backyards, but this Europe is different—it embodies regressive and even criminal forces. For the opponents of the incinerator, Western European firms do not export solutions to local problems but export their wastes and *their* local problems—in particular, the lack of domestic demand for their waste-treatment technologies—and thus make these problems global. This is the counter-vision so expressively illustrated in the cartoon described in my opening vignette. The same group, criticizing Western products for causing so much waste, writes:

The strategy of the [Coca-Cola] company is thus summarized by the chief of Coca-Cola Corp., Roberto Goizueta: "By the year 2000 we'll establish a distribution network in which all the six billion inhabitants of the Earth will simply need to reach out their hands if they want a taste of Coca-Cola." In the Third World countries of the Earth there are already many hundreds of millions of people reaching out their hands. It's as if there were more and more in the Hungarian subways, as well. We're not sure that what they desire is exactly Coke. . . . [50]

So, according to the Greens, becoming European or Western, in the dictionary of agents like EMC and Hungaropec, does not mean cleaning up; it means importing waste in the form of Western, high waste-ratio goods and in the form of actual waste to be treated in state-of-the-art Western facilities. Having an ample supply of waste treatment facilities, which usually means incinerators, has indeed been treated as a condition of joining the European Union. As an American banker investing in the export of waste treatment facilities says: "If they [East Europeans] want to become part of the greater European community, I don't see they have much of a choice."[51] Hungarians might tacitly agree that they live in a wasteland in need of a cleanup, but by accepting Western waste in order to run the incinerator facilities bought from the West for the benefit of Western investors, they really end up, as one local doctor put it, as "the cesspool of Europe," and thus reinforce their wasteland image. This Catch-22, endorsing development-via-waste-treatment and joining-Europe-via-waste-incineration, is thus exposed by the Greens as a false transition consciousness.

LOCAL VISIONS OF THE TRANSITION

Rather than being about "joining Europe," whose positive meaning is uncontested, this debate is about local transitions, about the future path of local development. Garé sees the incinerator as a way back into its trend-setting historical path, derailed sometime under socialism. As its leaders say, Garé could become a "little Paradise," or "a model village," where Westerners would come to study the incinerator and its effects at the site of EMC Services' most up-to-date plant. They argue that Garé's population has changed, that there is no hope for developing agriculture on a private small-scale basis, because nobody has domestic animals, or machines to cultivate the land, the elderly are not capable of working enough, and youth do not have enough experience to make that happen. Indeed, most people I talked to who had owned land before collectivization have left their plot in the cooperative or rented it back to the cooperative. Garéans feel that if they are to survive and rid their village of its roles as literal *and* figurative wasteland, they simply have no choice other than what their opponents call "building a castle out of shit."[52]

Let's see what this castle looks like. Garé, like all other communities since 1990, receives a budget from the state based on its population size, which has to be spent on maintaining infrastructure and institutions, such as schools or clubs, and on organizing local events. This amount, which is derived in part from personal income taxes paid by local residents, is about 7.2 million forints (about $48,000) per year.[53] For health services Garé receives 2.9 million fts ($19,300) from social security funds, and it raises about 2.3 million ($15,300) from interests, rent, and service fees.[54] Thus, the basic annual budget of the village is about 12 to 13 million fts ($80,000 to $87,000), compared to which Hungaropec has offered 80 million fts ($530,000)—that is, about six years' budget—in compensation for the land-use permit, an amount that certainly appeals to the local elite and, in fact, to all local residents. In 1994, Garé's government requested, and received, an advance of 40 percent of that amount to pay for infrastructural developments. By postponing some of the development, the village government was able to distribute a total of 2.6 million fts ($17,000) to individual households just before the 1994 November elections, which led to accusations of vote-buying.

If supporting the cause of the incinerator seemed financially advantageous even before starting construction, the long-term benefits after incineration starts promise to be even greater. Garé will receive a share of the plant's profits. Villagers anticipate building new houses and creating new infrastructural developments; construction promises an ample demand for physical labor to be recruited from the village's unemployed. It is hoped that these developments, besides lowering or canceling local taxes, will also spur local entrepreneurial activity.

A handful of the local elite has benefited greatly from their cooperation with Hungaropec. They have used the compensation for maintaining their political power, in part, as villagers told me, by distributing local development contracts to "their people." They also seek to influence the siting of the incinerator so that Hungaropec will have to buy the land from them. The village's increased leverage over other villages and its government's good bargaining position with a Western company have enabled the elite to silence dissent and thus diminish public control over issues other than the incinerator, as well. No wonder that those interviewees who fall outside the circle of the local government's beneficiaries complained about abuses which, according to them, were unheard of under socialism.

While Garé searches in the realm of novel economic activities for a viable economic road, Szalánta's path of transition relies on the development of more traditional economic activities, primarily agriculture. Szalánta's rate of individual entrepreneurs is hardly higher (8 percent of the population) than Garé's (7 percent), but entrepreneurs in Garé tend to be less able to make a living from agriculture (4.5 percent against 7 percent in Szalánta). In Garé, only 29 percent of the employed work in agriculture, while in Szalánta 37 percent do. With the latter figures, Garé is the second lowest in the district, while Szalánta is the first.[55]

Greens and especially the villagers who are against the Garé incinerator are not anticapitalist; they simply reject the "to-the-future-via-waste-business" path of transition. As the mayor of Szalánta said of his position in the public hearing, "I am a capitalist, too, but not to the disadvantage of others." Others likened the waste industry to prostitution: "Here Hungarian men will only be good for pushing trashcans, and women can go . . . tie a red light on their backs." They clearly consider incineration a dirty business, and they regard this dirtiness not only and not even primarily in the sense of environmental pollution: they reject what they consider its moral dirtiness. They compare bringing in waste to their backyards for profit to individual citizens throwing garbage over into their neighbors' yards, and they question the cleanliness of the money from the revenues of incineration or waste treatment in general. Several people opposing the incinerator told me that what repelled them the most was the compensation offered by Hungaropec, which they defined as bribery, and they found it offensive that after Garé was "bribed," Garé's elite and Hungaropec would think that other villagers, including them, could be bought off as well. An industry that is willing to pay them "for nothing" can only be evil.

This sensitivity around money-related issues triggers charges, on an almost daily basis and on both sides, that people have been bribed or are not acting according to professional etiquette. The charges have resulted in a couple of libel suits already. The roots of what might be called the ethical problem, however, reach beyond the district's boundaries. Hungary is a country where corruption is routine, where it is difficult to get anything done without bribes or connections; but it is also a country that desperately wants to get rid of its "socialist legacy" and become "European." To become European in Hungary has become synonymous with national self-purification. Thus, consorting with a European firm that not only pollutes nature but itself perpetuates corruption is, as the opponents of the incinerator see it, equivalent to telling a four-year-old that Santa Claus does not really exist. The disappointment with this "European road" has encouraged calls for a separate path of transition, based on local needs and resources, such as village tourism, agriculture, and thermal-water tourism, possibilities that the Greens have been active in exploring along with plans for helping the district modernize its infrastructure in order to boost local development. It is important to note, however, that this seeming closure to the West still holds dear a certain, idealized, meaning of Europeanness, its democratic values, its "environmentalism," and its resistance to any form of racism.

There has never been a debate about the future of the country on the national level. As a consequence, the discussion got pushed back to the local level, where, due to the small-scale nature of the issues that bring it forth, it inevitably turns into a nasty, name-calling quarrel, ultimately, in the eyes of many citizens, discrediting democracy. People on both sides speak very dubiously about the gains of democracy. In general, they agree that democratization has made it possible to talk about the dump and its dangers for the first time, but they also complain that the public hearings and other deliberation processes have grown way too long and complicated. Thus, ironically, some people in Garé have found themselves nostalgic for the past, because, they suggest, if state socialism had not collapsed the state would by now have built the incinerator and completed the cleanup. Citing Edward Teller as his source, a local intellectual even argued that "democracy is dangerous because in democracy a few clever individuals have to convince a lot of stupid ones." Those in Szalánta also cast the discussion in terms of expertise and democracy, but they draw a different conclusion. Although they feel they have educated themselves in order to enter the debate fully informed, they are determined to enforce their majority view through actions. As the former mayor of Szalánta said, "neither I nor the members of the local government can decide what is more dangerous: this [waste] staying here without treatment or the incinerator. . . . But one thing is clear. The citizens [of Szalánta] have declared that, if necessary, they will lie down on the highway and will not let this incinerator be built."

In its new global context, the situation in Garé is the story of global forces that are less constraining and more enabling than they once were, a story in which the local actors can use their imaginations to put those global forces to work on their behalf. There are four factors that have the potential for liberating their political imagination and hijacking global forces, the last three of which are entirely ignored in the literature about the prodigious transformations under way in Eastern Europe: 1) the disappearance of an omnipresent state; 2) a powerful sense of local history; 3) the immediate connections between localities and global forces; and 4) the nature of the issue, namely, environmental destruction.

In Hungary in general, and in Garé in particular, the national government has not only ceased to be the most important economic and political agent, but has practically dropped out of the picture altogether. Various state authorities keep waffling on the incinerator issue, suggesting that the state is only following the lead of others—the residents, the firms, the environmentalists.[56] According to many of my interviewees, public officials still influence the outcome of this controversy on both sides, but only to advance their own interests and not to represent the interests of the state per se.[57] Neither do they claim to do so. Instead they present their arguments in terms of local needs, privatization, democracy, or environmental protection. In this light, the focus of the bulk of the transition literature on the state, the often repeated argument of a "weak civil society," and the reprimand of the public for placing an "excessive faith . . . in what can be achieved by the state"[58] is baffling.[59]

The strong sense of local history is also related to the disappearance of the state. The one-party state suppressed local identities in the name of socialist equality and attempted to force the realization of its utopia of a "New Man." Especially those villages that suffered a lot as a result of regional development policies and that have now regained their autonomy, such as Garé, find that they need to revive their local identities in order to establish and legitimate new local governments.

Globalization, with the collapse of the state as a mediating force, allows localities to have independent access to the outside world (the West) and to consider carefully which of its features to embrace and which to reject. As we have seen, both the global incinerator industry and the global environmental movement are prepared to work very closely with the villages.

Finally, the cause of the environment, which has always functioned as a veiled social critique in Central and Eastern Europe, and which has achieved such a discursive salience in economic and political decision-making practically all over the world, now allows the questioning of certain authorities and certain development visions.

Taken together, these four factors have the effect of expanding space for local action even in the face of globalization that might otherwise have made that space contract.

POLITICAL REGENERATION OR DEGENERATION?

I have described how both sides of the siting controversy use or try to use global forces as resources. Garé or, more precisely, its elite tries to ally with the global incinerator industry and take advantage of what Greenpeace calls the global "rush to burn" trend. Opponents of the incinerator ally themselves with Western Greens, using their information and discourses. I have also argued that it is only by reference to the future path of development of the region, as well as to its local history, that either side can use the global as a resource, and I have referred to this practice as "cognitive cartography." Defining the opposing agents as "cognitive mapmakers" emphasizes the fact that both sides wage their struggles with distinct images of the world and with categorical views of the global and the local in their minds. Furthermore, this approach has the effect of emphasizing the role of the citizens as agents, rather than that of the discourses imported from the respective global contexts, locating the necessary imagination and "mapmaking" right in the center of political action.

This conflict is thus in large part a debate about the postsocialist transition: it is about who has the power to define the economic value of a region, and who has the power to determine the meaning of powerful symbols in the transition discourse, such as "Europe" and "democracy." Pro-incinerator actors promote an image of Hungary as a wasteland that needs cleanup; only after achieving certain standards of cleanliness can she be welcome into the European family. Greens and villagers who are against the incinerator in Garé, in contrast, seem to care more about the lack of moral cleanliness that is implied in such toxic-waste-for-money swaps between the

Western and the Eastern parts of Europe, and what they appreciate in Europe are not its alleged standards of state-of-the-art-cleanliness but rather its assumed democratic, civic, antiracist, and environmentalist values. The choice is not between rejecting the West or following it. "Openness to the West" and adopting the model of market democracies have different, if not contradictory, meanings to actors on opposite sides of the siting controversy.

On the surface this controversy appears as symbolic politics obsessed with purity and pollution, not reflecting economic interests and with no impact on institutions. A more historical and sociological analysis, however, reveals that this is indeed a struggle for resources that could ensure a viable economic future for the region. Local actors were able not only to put the economic issues on the agenda but were also able to affect various authorities without the state's assistance. It was the Western partner that initiated this symbolic politics by branding the state socialist past as dirty, morally and physically, and marking the West as clean and pure. Thus, the heightened concern about the physical and moral cleanliness of the Hungarian people that manifests itself in this struggle cannot simply be brushed aside as irrational symbolic politics, as a mere legacy of state socialism.[60] Garé's story is about the regeneration of politics, especially about the regeneration of politics on the local level. The degeneration of politics, that is, the failure of new environmental politics to solve the problem of Garé's dump, even as of the end of 1999, however, has more to do with certain Western agendas than with the East's legacy.

NOTES

Research for this paper has been supported by the International Research and Exchanges Board, the Joint Committee on Eastern Europe of the American Council of Learned Societies and the Social Science Research Council, the Wenner-Gren Foundation for Anthropological Research, and the Project on European Environmental History, Sociology, and Policy at the University of California, Santa Cruz. I am grateful to the residents of Garé, Szalánta, and Bosta, to the many activists, and to the enterprise representatives for their time and kindness. An earlier version of this paper won the Marvin E. Olsen Award from the Environment and Technology Section of the American Sociological Association.

1. Cornelius Castoriadis, "The Social Regime in Russia"; Marshall I. Goldman, *The Spoils of Progress: Environmental Pollution in the Soviet Union;* Donald Filtzer, *Soviet Workers and Stalinist Industrialization: The Formation of Modern Soviet Production Relations* and *Soviet Workers and De-Stalinization: The Consolidation of the Modern System of Soviet Production Relations 1953–1964;* János Kornai, *Economics of Shortage;* Roger Manser, *The Squandered Dividend: The Free Market and the Environment in Eastern Europe;* Alec Nove, *The Soviet Economic System;* Róbert Reiniger, "Veszélyes hulladékok" [Hazardous Wastes]; Mihály Simai, "Környezetbarát fejlödésünk" (Our Environment-Friendly Development); János Szlávik, "Piacosítható-e a környezetvédelem?" [Is Environ-

mental Protection Marketable?]; Hillel Ticktin, "The Contradictions of Soviet Society and Professor Bettelheim" and *Origins of the Crisis in the USSR: Essays on the Political Economy of a Disintegrating System.*

2. Roger Manser, *The Squandered Dividend,* and János Szlávik, "Piacosítható-e a környezetvédelem?"

3. Manuel Castells, *The Informational City,* p. 349.

4. George Schöpflin, "Post-Communism: A Profile."

5. Valerie Bunce and Mária Csanádi, "Uncertainty in the Transition: Post-Communism in Hungary"; Jadwiga Staniszkis, *The Dynamics of the Breakthrough in Eastern Europe: The Polish Experience.*

6. George Schöpflin, "Post-Communism: A Profile."

7. Martin Malia, "Leninist Endgame."

8. Ken Jowitt, *New World Disorder: The Leninist Extinction.*

9. Tony Judt, "The Past Is Another Country: Myth and Memory in Postwar Europe."

10. David Stanners and Philippe Bourdeau, *Europe's Environment: The Dobris Assessment.*

11. Matthew Gandy, *Recycling and the Politics of Urban Waste.*

12. David Stanners and Philippe Bourdeau, *Europe's Environment: The Dobris Assessment.*

13. Pat Costner and Joe Thornton, *Playing with Fire: Hazardous Waste Incineration,* p. 46.

14. Ibid.

15. Ibid.

16. This is why, for example, the eighties saw a massive increase in hazardous waste imports to the United Kingdom, where standards were less stringent than in other West European countries.

17. The reported amount exported to developing countries was 120,000 tons annually in the early 1990s, but according to the Dobris Assessment, a study by the European Environment Agency, there is "increasing evidence that the magnitude of these transfrontier movements is far larger than recorded" (David Stanners and Philippe Bourdeau, *Europe's Environment: The Dobris Assessment,* p. 352). No data exist for the total amount exported to Eastern Europe, but the fact that Western Europe exported 1 million tons of hazardous wastes just to the German Democratic Republic (East Germany) in 1988 gives some idea of the magnitude.

18. In 1993, in the United States, the Environmental Protection Agency (EPA) actually put an eighteen-month moratorium on incinerator construction, partly because of resistance, partly because an overcapacity had been created.

19. In 1993, in Europe, France and Germany led in incinerator capacity, with an annual 9.5 and 8.7 million tons respectively; the United States had an annual capacity of about 3.9 *billion* tons; while four reported East European countries had a combined annual capacity of little over 2 million tons (Stanners and Bourdeau).

20. Letter from Gérard Monnier-Besombes, member of the French delegation of the Green fraction of the European Parliament, to Zöld Kör (Green Circle), June 10, 1993, p. 3, archives of Zöld Kör, Pécs.

21. My calculation is based on Greenpeace data from Pawel Gluszynski and Iza Kruszewska, *Western Pyromania Moves East: A Case Study in Hazardous Technology Transfer.*

22. Ibid.

23. Data on the production of individual chemical compounds are incredibly scarce. I have not found data for European countries; but according to United States government data, which rely on voluntary reporting, the United States did not produce TCB after 1982, five years before BCW itself terminated the production of TCB.

24. Archives of Budapest Chemical Works (Letter, April 4, 1968, from President of Budapest Chemical Works to Ministry of Heavy Industries, p. 1; Minutes, Operative Meeting of Management—June 12, 1968; August 7, 1972; and July 14, 1975).

25. Similar requests of other companies from outside Baranya were turned down by the county council on the grounds that their wastes were not locally produced (letter by Baranya Megyei KÖJÁL, March 14, 1978).

26. Mostly due to its hilliness, but maybe also due to its ethnic heterogeneity, Baranya had developed small but closely located settlements and farms, rather than larger and more distant ones more characteristic of the rest of Hungary. Baranya had a large proportion of Croats and Germans for a long time, and the socialist state's efforts to solve the "Gypsy problem" by settling Romanis in abandoned village houses further colored the ethnic palette.

27. In 1986 there were nineteen counties in Hungary, of which only three, each with much higher industrial activity than Baranya, had more industrial waste dumps (MTESZ-MÁFI, *Waste Dump Survey;* data from three counties were missing or were compiled in a way that precludes comparison).

28. BCW actually got its permit in 1979, but the first negotiation was held in Szalánta in June 1978.

29. Jadwiga Staniszkis, *The Ontology of Socialism;* József Böröcz, "Dual Dependency and Property Vacuum: Social Change on the State Socialist Semiperiphery."

30. Of course, there is no agreement on what sicknesses are caused by the dump and there are no surveys that would show a connection.

31. BCW's share in Hungaropec's capital stock is 26 percent; this is the minimum allowable, according to Hungarian laws, for BCW to retain a say in the increase of the capital stock.

32. The importance of the paper is enhanced by the fact that this district never had its own newspaper, and that nowadays very few people can afford to buy the large-circulation regional daily that covers issues in their villages.

33. My use of the term "cognitive map" is closest to Fredric Jameson's (*Postmodernism, or, the Cultural Logic of Late Capitalism*). He argues that political action requires cognitive mapping—"nam[ing] the system" (p. 418), that is, a spatial imagining of the self in relation to an increasingly globalized social reality.

34. Hungaropec, *Tájékoztató a Garéban tervezett ipari hulladékégetöröl* [Information on the Incinerator Planned in Garé], p. 1. Emphasis in the original. All translations are the author's.

35. Ibid. Emphasis in the original.

36. The term "entrepreneur" (vállalkozó) had a very positive connotation in the years immediately preceding and following the collapse of state socialism. Its primary meaning was not "business for profit" as much as "working on one's own initiative," independently from the state. This positive connotation is here exploited to hide the fact that the proposal is actually about a profit-making venture.

37. The quoted phrase is from a 1995 study of the social impact of the proposed incinerator (Fact Betéti-társaság, *A Garé térségében építendö hulladékégetö társadalmi hatástanulmánya*).

38. Katherine Verdery, *What Was Socialism, and What Comes Next?*

39. The Swiss-Hungarian joint venture is building an incinerator just a few kilometers away, while the Dorog incinerator is an already functioning facility about two hundred kilometers north, much closer to Budapest.

40. I am referring to Lipschutz's use of the term (Ronnie D. Lipschutz with Judith Mayer, *Global Civil Society and Global Environmental Governance: The Politics of Nature from Place to Planet*). The estimated number of nongovernmental organizations (NGOs), as well as their financial resources, has been steadily increasing since the 1970s, with a real take-off in the 1980s. It is practically impossible to know the exact number of environmental NGOs, partly because environmental and developmental or other issues are often tackled together in the same organizations and partly because of their independence. Some NGOs are not accounted for in registries, such as those maintained by the United Nations or other international associations, partly because of their often temporary existence—that is, because they transform themselves with relative ease as projects dictate. We know that there were five thousand NGOs registered at the Rio Summit in 1992, but the United Nations reports that just in India there were twelve thousand such organizations at the beginning of the nineties, which should help us imagine their magnitude and salience.

41. Ibid.

42. Fact Betéti-társaság, *A Garé. . . .*

43. "Expert systems" is Anthony Giddens's term. In *The Consequences of Modernity*, he claims that in the age of global "disembedding," expert systems, institutions that produce and "guarantee" knowledge, provide a key link for individuals to distant sources of knowledge.

44. In this long war for Hungarian independence from Austria (1703–1711), the French king Louis XIV failed to establish formal diplomatic relations with the new Hungarian government, which badly needed to overcome its international isolation, although he had a tacit alliance with Rákóczi, the Hungarian leader.

45. Reference to the peace treaty of Trianon in 1920.

46. Speaker at the Baranya county public hearing on the Garé incinerator, Pécs, June 1996.

47. Pécsi Zöld Kör Environmental Affairs Team, *A király meztelen* [The Emperor Has No Clothes], p. 4. In fact, a plan from 1988 went beyond building a regional toxic waste dump in Garé and proposed an incinerator.

48. Ibid., p. 5.

49. One key aim was to undermine peasant majorities in rural areas.

50. Hulladék Munkaszövetség, No title, p. 19.

51. John Schwartz, Carla Koehl, and Karen Breslau, "Cleaning Up by Cleaning Up," p. 41.

52. This refers to a traditional Hungarian saying: "One cannot build a castle out of shit."

53. Data, as provided by the mayor of Garé, and currency rate from 1996.

54. Garé could afford not to collect local taxes for the past few years, thanks to

the compensation (more precisely the interest on it) it received from Hungaropec. This would have been a meager amount anyway (120,000 fts).

55. Data from the economic-social impact study (Fact Betéti-társaság, *A Garé . . .*).

56. The first decision, made by the regional environmental authority, denied the permission; the second, made at the national level, gave the permit; and the third, which was the result of a successful civil lawsuit charging the national authority with endangering the public health and the environment, obliged the previous authorities to start the process of impact studies and public hearings all over. Presently, this decision is being appealed.

57. The fact that a prominent employee of the regional environmental authority resigned the day the permit was denied to Hungaropec, and the fact that the head of the national authority resigned a few days after giving the permit raised suspicions that these decisions represented more individual, or at the most departmental, interests.

58. George Schöpflin, "Post-Communism: A Profile," p. 65.

59. Zygmunt Bauman, "Hol az osztályérdek mostanában?" [Where Is Class Interest These Days?]; Ken Jowitt, *New World Disorder: The Leninist Extinction.*

60. George Schöpflin, "Post-Communism: A Profile."

NINE

Contesting the Global City

Pittsburgh's Public Service Unions Confront a Neoliberal Agenda

Steven H. Lopez

In early June of 1997 I began working as an intern for Local 9876 of the Service Employees International Union in Pittsburgh, Pennsylvania. I had come to Pittsburgh to compare that city's response to globalization and de-industrialization with the experience of the German Ruhr. Both regions faced declining steel industries; both regions had been industrial heartlands of postwar economic expansion. But I found Pittsburgh so absorbing in its own right that I soon dropped the Ruhr. If in Germany the old labor regime was sufficiently durable to steer a gradual change, Pittsburgh was experiencing a veritable revolution. Its once mighty steel mills had become museum pieces along the Monongahela Valley and its unions seemed headed for the dustbin of history, as Pittsburgh's elites busily tried to reinvent the city as a center of finance, health services, and informational and biomedical technologies. I wanted to know how the labor movement was dealing with this dramatic transition from Steel City to Global City, from the ideology of class collaboration to a neoliberal offensive. Could this be soil for the restoration of labor? Could it take root in the burgeoning service economy?

I gravitated to the SEIU's Local 9876 because, amidst the historic collapse of industrial unionism in Pittsburgh, it had built a remarkable record of successfully organizing low-wage nursing home workers, often using confrontational tactics of grassroots public protest. Taking me on as an apprentice organizer, the union put me to work on an "internal" organizing project aimed at helping its unit of

1,500 Allegheny County workers (mostly clerical workers and clerks, with a few janitors and jail guards thrown in) win new contracts. Initially I was disappointed not to be working on new organizing campaigns, but I contented myself with the thought that successfully defending existing union members was just as important. My two fellow interns and I thus set about holding meetings with worksite stewards and leaders, planning a series of lunchtime worksite union meetings, and recruiting county workers' participation in a series of public protests.

Right from the beginning it was clear that Local 9876's Allegheny County chapter was struggling to adapt to a new labor relations climate. The local was being pushed by circumstances to innovate, to apply the lessons of private-sector organizing to its base in the formerly hospitable public sector, now under attack by a new Republican county administration. As the contract campaign unfolded it was very clear that the organizational legacies of a vanished labor-relations regime were making it difficult to mount a sustained grass-roots campaign. Workers demanded action, but did not want to plan it or lead it. Workers also understood that the bureaucratic procedures through which paid union staff had traditionally resolved their grievances and negotiated new contracts were not working—but they lacked any vision of a more participatory, social-movement-oriented unionism based on collective struggle and solidarity. On the other side, the union staff was itself divided between those who saw the campaign as a jumping-off point for a thorough organizational reform and those who, unable to envision a different role for themselves, preferred to view mobilization as a short-term means to an end.

But if the importance of the union's organizational legacies was clear from the outset, what was not clear was the significance of the contract campaign itself. Perhaps because of my continuing involvement as an organizer, perhaps because I needed a longer time horizon, I kept vacillating about how to understand the campaign—especially since, despite its problems, it did lead to the successful negotiation of new contracts in the fall of 1997. Was the campaign a success because it won new contracts, or was it a failure because it did not immediately transform the organizational structure of the union's Allegheny County chapter? Indeed, it was not until early 1999, when the union decided to begin earnestly building a functioning structure of worksite stewards in its Allegheny County unit, that I could fully appreciate the positive long-term effects of the campaign.

Nor could I immediately understand how it had even accomplished its victory. While it had organized a number of successful public actions, including one large rally involving more than five hundred workers from several dozen worksites, I was puzzled as to why these few rallies so easily induced the county administration to drop its demands for concessions. The Republican majority on the county Board of Commissioners had come to office, after all, promising to vanquish the county unions once and for all, to eliminate bloated budgets and payrolls, and to put the county's fiscal house in order. Why should a few demonstrations and informational pickets have caused them to change course so abruptly?

This second set of questions led me outside of my experience as a participant observer, back to the union's earlier campaign against privatization of the county's four public nursing homes, the Kane Regional Centers. In the winter of 1997–1998 I conducted interviews with Kane workers, union staff, and other participants; I studied news reports and watched several videotapes of television news coverage that union staff had compiled. Slowly I began to grasp the importance of an oppositional ideology that crystallized in the Kane struggle, an ideology that pitted the human rights of elderly and disabled nursing home residents against the market imperatives of efficiency and competitiveness. This humanitarian vision proved crucial to the union's ability to mobilize a broad coalition of actors to defeat privatization—and crucial for the success of the contract campaign as well, since defeat on the privatization issue created fiscal pressures undermining the county administration's ability to engage in a lengthy contract stalemate.

In the end, I concluded that for labor the very real pressures of globalization demanded not only a new set of tactics, not only new organizational forms overriding legacies of the past, but also new imaginations with which to challenge the assumptions of neoliberal ideology.

I had just returned to the union office from one of the informational picket sites I had helped organize for the day. As part of its three-month-old effort to win new contracts for 1,500 workers employed by Allegheny County, the

union had organized a wave of pickets dubbed "rolling thunder week."
Workers at various departments around the county picketed and leafleted at
lunchtime; each day was a different department or set of departments.
Interns delivered picket signs, union tee shirts, and union buttons to the
worksites ahead of time, and gave a schedule of picket locations, days, and
times to the television news departments. Several television stations sent out
news crews each day of the week to do live coverage for the noon news. On
this day, August 25, 1997, the picketing was taking place during workers'
lunch breaks at Allegheny County's four publicly owned regional geriatric
hospitals, the Kane Regional Centers.

I had taken some pictures of Allegheny County workers at one of the
Kane Centers as a handful picketed and leafleted, and I gave a brief pep
talk. Now, back at the office, I was about to receive bad news in the form of
voice-mail messages from workers at two of the Kanes, where the scheduled
picketing had not materialized. At one of the sites, the picketing simply did
not materialize and no one could say why. At the other location, two union
stewards had at the last minute scuttled the action by refusing to participate.
Despite the presence of the media (a mobile news unit from one of the local
television channels had been setting up in the parking lot since mid-
morning), the two women had driven off to lunch together in a car containing all the picket signs and materials for the action. Leaderless and without picket signs, the other workers had stayed inside. Worst of all, the news
crew had done a bewildered live report from the parking lot, saying they
had been told picketing was supposed to have occurred but that no one had
shown up.

I was stunned by this information, not only because all of the stewards
had assured me earlier in the day that they would lead the picketing at their
sites, but also because I knew that months earlier, they and other Kane workers had eagerly participated in a whole series of informational picketing and
protests during a union campaign to prevent the privatization of the four
Kane centers. They had descended en masse on the county courthouse and
had disrupted weekly meetings of the County Board of Commissioners. Why
were these same workers, earlier so eager to protest against privatization,
now so reluctant to protest on behalf of new contracts?

Part of the answer was organizational. The earlier protests had all been
organized and led by the union; worksite stewards and other rank and file
workers had been asked to turn up to union-orchestrated events. The
"rolling thunder" actions, however, depended on stewards and worksite
leaders to take responsibility for organizing, directing, and leading the
actions themselves. Historically, the union had relied on paid staff representatives and bureaucratic procedures, rather than rank-and-file-led collective action, to deal with worksite problems. Stewards were volunteers, not

paid union staff, and their activities had traditionally been limited to serving as contacts for their worksites. They were not accustomed to organizing or supervising collective actions, particularly within the context of a tense contract situation, and they had not received any training as organizers. Thus, the union's historic orientation toward bureaucratic "servicing" rather than collective struggle constituted a set of organizational *legacies*, which now constrained its ability to mount worker-led collective actions without direct supervision from union staff.

A second piece of the puzzle had to do with *ideology*. My interviews with union staff and Kane workers indicated that even in union-led actions and protests, Kane workers had been much easier to mobilize in the earlier struggle against privatization than in the contract campaign because they perceived the two struggles very differently. Kane workers immediately perceived privatization as a threat, not only to themselves, but also to the aged and disabled residents they cared for. They viewed privatization as something they had a moral duty to struggle against, in order to safeguard the dignity and safety of their residents. Against the ideology of market efficiency which privatization would supposedly introduce, Kane workers counterposed a humanitarian vision of their residents' needs, which called them to action. On the contract issue, however, Kane workers had no such counter-ideology. They bitterly opposed the county's demands for greater scheduling flexibility, new management rights, and wage and benefit concessions, but lacked a mobilizing vision which would call them to action in their own self-defense.

Initially I did not see the significance of ideology and legacies in the story of the two Kane workers who, in driving off to lunch, had chosen bread over struggle. It was tempting to see their abdications as their own individual failures of responsibility, or, conversely, as the fault of the union for not adequately preparing them for the action they were asked to lead. But as I reflected further, it became clear that in trying to decide whom to blame, I had missed the point completely. The real significance of the story is that the two dilemmas it highlights are in fact central problems, not just of the two interconnected union campaigns examined here, but also of the American labor movement as a whole.

NEW UNIONISM: TACTICS, LEGACIES, AND IDEOLOGY

Recent scholarship on new forms of union struggle emphasizes how participatory, disruptive, and confrontational tactics—like those Local 9876 attempted to use in its privatization and contract struggles—allow unions more effectively to exploit employer weaknesses and build workers' power. The literature emphasizes the importance of building lasting labor-community coalitions;[1] revitalizing local labor councils as organizational hubs of local labor-movement activity;[2] organizing collective action campaigns emphasizing public protest and disruptive tactics;[3] and using "rank-and-file intensive" grassroots approaches to organizing, utilizing the talents of union member volunteers to connect one-on-one with potential new union members.[4]

A few writers have gone beyond the emphasis on tactics. Some have raised the issue of organizational legacies, pointing out that for local unions, using new tactics means embarking on a difficult process of organizational transformation. The structures of bureaucratic-servicing unionism have long discouraged worker participation and channeled workers' grievances into demobilizing bureaucratic procedures.[5] Moving from an approach that sought to manipulate bureaucratic procedures to service existing union members, toward one in which the collective *mobilization* of workers is paramount both to winning new members and defending existing ones, means shifting resources away from traditional representational activities.[6] The organizational legacies of business unionism are composed not only of the entrenched positions of many union staff, who remain wedded to traditional bureaucratic representation functions and identities, but also to deeply ingrained dispositions of rank and file members—who have been well taught not to see their union as a participatory social movement organization but rather as a sort of insurance company from which they purchase representational services with their dues.[7]

Other scholars have drawn attention to the problem of ideology, arguing that unions must create an appealing vision of society capable of mobilizing workers and their community allies: a "labor ideology" which "unabashedly champions class-unifying themes" such as universal rights to decent jobs, housing, publicly funded health care, education, day care, paid family leave, and vacations.[8] Such attempts are necessary to counter the ascendant neoliberal ideology of the contemporary period, which presents market forces as universal, natural, inevitable, and irresistible—suggesting that, at best, unions may make futile and backward attempts to protect their members from harsh economic "reality," while, at worst, they may actually hinder the functioning of competitive markets.[9] Moreover, some have noted, this challenge is all the greater in the contemporary period because economic globalization extends and deepens market ideology. The apparent unmanageability and universality of the global economy undercuts local or even national attempts to curb the destructive social effects of unregulated market competition. Globalization has become its own ideology, according to which the desperate competition of all regions and localities in an unregulated global economy is also natural, inevitable, and irresistible. Therefore a revitalized labor movement must ultimately construct and deploy persuasive new visions and ideologies, not only to counter the neoliberal view of market supremacy, but also against the naturalization of globalization itself.[10]

However, while labor movement scholars have noted the existence of both ideology and organizational legacies as challenges unions must over-come, they have not studied *how* ideology and legacies are, or are not, dealt with in union campaigns. Case studies of union campaigns have, in the main, presented successful cases as strategic and tactical exemplars, as success sto-ries illustrating the effectiveness of particular tactics. But as the anecdote with which this chapter began illustrates, union victories do not result merely from the mechanical application of new tactics; they reflect unions' abilities to somehow deal with the dilemmas of ideology and organizational legacies. When union campaigns succeed, in other words, it is not because they typify the use of new tactics, but because in using new tactics, they have been (per-haps uniquely) creative and clever enough to find ways of overcoming or bypassing these central dilemmas. Rather than simply noting their exis-tence, we need to understand how, through what concrete processes, unions have struggled with ideology and legacies in actual campaigns.

This chapter examines the relation of ideology and legacies in the two campaigns introduced in the opening anecdote. First, I show how the increased salience of the global led to a neoliberal turn in Pittsburgh's local politics, underpinning both the privatization initiative and the county's demands for contract concessions from its employees. Second, I argue that the union's campaign against Kane privatization succeeded because it was able to deploy a humanitarian discourse emphasizing the dark side of mar-ket efficiency, transforming privatization into a synonym for cutbacks that would needlessly victimize the Kanes' innocent elderly and disabled resi-dents. This union discourse mobilized diverse constituencies against priva-tization, allowing the union to *bypass* (rather than confront) its organiza-tional legacies. The third part of this chapter argues that in its contract campaign, the union was forced to confront its organizational legacies more directly, because it could *not* generate an appealing ideological alter-native and could not mobilize external allies. As a result, the union found contract mobilization a much more difficult task. Finally, I argue that mov-ing beyond local successes like these will require the construction of a coherent ideological response to globalization—a task that will itself be complicated by the movement's organizational legacies.

GLOBALIZATION AND NEOLIBERAL IDEOLOGY

Pittsburgh presents an archetypal example of two distinct periods of glob-alization, each conforming to a quite different pattern. During the extended period of postwar United States hegemony, Pittsburgh was at the center of a global steel industry. Southwestern Pennsylvania headquartered a half-dozen large steel firms, and the Monongahela Valley was one of the world's most heavily industrialized regions. Pittsburgh's industrial products found global markets—but most Pittsburghers thought little about the global economy, which remained hidden behind ideas about American industrial superiority. Pittsburgh's broad-based prosperity (indeed, its identity as the "Steel City") was perceived instead as part of the natural order of the world, even as it was underpinned by the steel industry's historic but temporary acceptance of unions and collective bargaining. Industry-wide pattern bargaining ensured, for a time, that global steel profits were spread to a prosperous local industrial working class.

In the 1980s, everything changed. Foreign steel producers, once scorned, were suddenly producing higher-quality products more efficiently. The tables were turned on union leaders who had thought themselves securely part of the institutional apparatus of American industry. Now they found capital's consent being relentlessly withdrawn. Pattern bargaining collapsed as steel and other industrial firms lined up to exact painful concessions with the threat of plant closures, then closed the plants anyway. During a remarkably brief span, southwestern Pennsylvania lost over 150,000 industrial jobs. In a few short years, Pittsburgh was transformed from the large United States city with the highest proportion of manufacturing jobs to that with the lowest.[11]

Ironically, it was only now that Pittsburgh was being displaced from the center of the global economy—and hence now *less* globalized—that ideas about globalization and the global economy began to dominate the local political landscape. The question of how to transform Pittsburgh in order to meet the requirements of the new global economy now consumed business and political leaders and informed local public debate. In the 1990s, with less than 10 percent of Pittsburgh's work force remaining in manufacturing, it is public service workers, not manufacturing workers, who are most affected by the new salience of the global.

This can be seen in the way that, even as the tax base has shrunk, numerous projects aimed at making Pittsburgh more attractive to investors, visitors, and tourists have siphoned funds away from public services in favor of corporate subsidies. The city of Pittsburgh has committed millions in subsidies toward construction of a new downtown convention center; new ballparks for the Pittsburgh Pirates and Steelers; new upscale retail space and apartments downtown; a new regional history center; trolleys for a "tourist transportation" business; and a pedestrian walkway over the Allegheny River linking Point State Park with the replacement to Three Rivers Stadium.[12] All of these projects have been justified with reference to the necessity of making Pittsburgh a more attractive location for global investment.

Efforts to shrink county government and cut taxes have also been underway throughout the 1990s. Democratic administrations reduced the number of employees on Allegheny County's payroll from over ten thousand in the late 1980s to seven thousand by the mid-1990s.[13] A Democratic administration cut county tax rates by 16 percent (from 37.5 mills to 31.5 mills) in 1994 and enacted another cut of nearly 10 percent (to 28.5 mills) in late 1995.[14] Republicans upped the ante, however, during the 1995 county election campaign, promising a further across-the-board property tax cut of 20 percent, to be paid for with privatization initiatives and contract concessions from eleven unions representing county employees. The Democrats announced that they intended to match the Republicans' promise of a 20 percent property tax cut, but argued that it should be phased in gradually over four years instead of introduced all at once. Like the Republicans, the Democrats also promised to further streamline county departments and eliminate "unnecessary" jobs.[15]

Both parties also framed the issue of tax cuts in terms of the demands of interurban competition in a global economy. During the 1995 commissioners' race, for example, Democratic candidate Vuono argued that Allegheny County needed a 20 percent property tax reduction because it would make the county more competitive in attracting people and capital to the region, saying, "Part of the reason we're losing residents and losing business is because of the taxes."[16] The views of the Republican candidates were the same. In a letter to the *Pittsburgh Post-Gazette* published two days before the election, Larry Dunn and Bob Cranmer wrote, "We believe that an immediate 20 percent cut in property taxes is the only sure way to send the message to the world that Allegheny County is open for business. We want to compete with other cities and counties for new jobs." The letter added that "by totally changing the economic atmosphere (with a taxpayer-friendly property tax rate) businesses and jobs will come to Allegheny County."[17]

Republican victory in the county elections of November 1995 thus meant only the acceleration of a neoliberal agenda that had already been defining county politics throughout the decade. On their first day in office, Dunn and Cranmer instituted the promised tax cut. Shortly afterward they sacked the county's in-house labor negotiator, replacing him with a high-profile law firm known for union-busting. The county's new labor counsel demanded a variety of givebacks and concessions from the unions, and insisted that all negotiations begin with a set of completely new documents erasing existing contract language on seniority rights, scheduling, and numerous other issues. Publicly, the county's new negotiators portrayed county employees as overpaid and underworked, and blamed the county's fiscal dilemma on a bloated county payroll. (Not mentioned was the fact that most unionized county workers earned only around $20,000 annually, or that upper-level managers had received large bonuses and raises since Dunn and Cranmer took office.) Finally, the county repeatedly told the unions that no substantive discussions were possible until the unions agreed to a new, two-page "management's-rights" clause. The county's proposal would have given it the right to privatize or contract out any county function without bargaining with the unions, and to unilaterally change workers' schedules and job assignments—or lay them off—without notice.[18] Not surprisingly, contract negotiations made no progress in 1996.

In September of the same year, the Republicans floated their detailed plan to lease the four regional John J. Kane Centers to a private entity, Alleco, specially created for that purpose. Alleco would lease the Kanes for $23 million annually and be responsible for all operating costs—although the long-term debt burden remaining from the centers' construction in the early 1980s would still be borne by the county. Alleco and the Republican commissioners publicly warned the unions that if they did not agree to concessionary contracts with the county before privatization took place, Alleco would not honor the expired contracts.[19] Alleco's business plan promised not to slash existing Kane workers' wages and benefits, but reserved the right to downsize. New hires would be brought in at lower wages and with fewer benefits.

The commissioners' arguments on behalf of Kane privatization illuminate the symbiotic relation between globalization and neoliberal ideology. While the global competition for jobs and investment can be directly invoked in support of tax cuts and business subsidies, proposals to dismantle public provision of needed services require specific rationales. Therefore, to justify their proposal to privatize the Kane Regional Centers, Republicans deployed neoliberal ideas about the superiority of private markets over public administration. Alleco, they claimed, could do the job more efficiently than county administrators, without harming Kane residents in any way.[20] The Kanes were overstaffed, they argued, relative to private-sector nursing homes—particularly in departments other than nursing (maintenance, housekeeping, dietary, and laundry). Kane management was burdened with arcane and inflexible work-rules that stood in the way of efficiency. And worst of all, they claimed, the Kanes were beginning to lose money—a problem that would only worsen in coming years because of recent changes in state reimbursement rules. In sum, privatization would allow the county to more efficiently meet its legal obligations to provide for the elderly and disabled—by getting rid of unnecessary staff, negotiating better deals with contractors, and using staff more flexibly.[21]

Here we see how, on the one hand, the necessity of competing for global investment and jobs seems to make public provision of services unsustainable, too expensive, and noncompetitive; while, on the other, the ideology of market efficiency provides ready-made "solutions" and plans for dismantling public provision. During debates over such "solutions," globalization recedes into the background, where it remains as an unspoken, unquestioned context for neoliberal arguments. The unstated presence of the global makes it more difficult to counter neoliberal claims because the threat of disinvestment and capital flight looms over everything. As we will see, however, this nested relationship between discourses about globalization and neoliberal ideology is not invulnerable to counterattack, for where fundamental questions of justice and human rights can be raised, neoliberal ideology becomes vulnerable. In this case, Local 9876 was certainly not in a position to mount an attack on ideas about the global competition for jobs and investment (it could not and did not challenge the Republicans' tax cut). But the commissioners' specific claims about the virtues of privatization were ripe for contestation. The union's strategy, therefore, would be to mobilize a grassroots coalition around the idea that "efficiency" really meant cutbacks, and that cutbacks would unacceptably harm the Kanes' elderly and infirm residents. Even if the global could not be directly contested, the union hoped that public sympathy for these innocents would neutralize the Republicans' arguments about costs and efficiency.

"SAVE OUR KANES": FIGHTING PRIVATIZATION

In building a grassroots coalition against privatization, Local 9876 faced serious organizational obstacles related to the history of business unionism. Organized in more labor-friendly times in the early 1970s, the union's county chapter had evolved a fairly traditional bureaucratic-servicing model of unionism. Workers generally reported grievances directly to their union staff representative, bypassing worksite stewards. Staff representatives tended not to educate workers about the contract, preferring instead to play the role of "expert" over whether issues were grievable or not. Many of Local 9876's worksites and departments had not bothered to elect union stewards. In some worksites, only a few of the workers actually joined the union. Local 9876's clerical units at the Kanes were no exception: they did not have a functioning worksite-steward structure, with well-trained stewards capable of organizing and carrying out a strategy of grassroots protest.

Complicating matters was the fact that most Kane workers were represented by another union, the Laborers' Local X. Local X was even more firmly wedded to its tradition of business-union organization, and extremely wary of involvement in a public antiprivatization campaign.[22] While the leadership of Local X agreed to allow Local 9876 to try to mobilize Kane workers, Local X did not want to be publicly identified with the campaign or to participate directly in the mobilization effort. Therefore, Local 9876 would have to mobilize Kane workers without the benefit of any kind of effective worksite infrastructure.

Local 9876 could not directly overcome these business union legacies, particularly those involving Local X. But the union was able successfully to *bypass* these problems of internal union organization, because of the special appeal this particular issue held for three constituencies: Kane workers, an older generation of Kane activists, and Pittsburgh's progressive religious community. As we will see, each of these constituencies had its own reasons for seeing Kane privatization in humanitarian—rather than economic—terms, and each group brought a different sort of credibility to the campaign to stop privatization.

Kane Workers: Defending Our Residents

Kane workers themselves were acutely aware of the privatization plan. They were particularly concerned about the possibility of staff cuts because staffing had already been affected by a countywide early-retirement plan enacted in the spring of 1996. Many Kane workers had taken the buyout, but these workers had not been replaced. As a result, Kane units were now working shorthanded more often.[23] Kane workers paid very close attention to the Republican commissioners' public claims that the Kanes were overstaffed, that its workers were overpaid, and that they enjoyed benefits and perks unheard of in the private sector. They understood very clearly that privatization would likely lead to further cutbacks in staffing, wages, and benefits. They were outraged by the commissioners' attack on the Kanes because, they felt, the Kanes' staffing patterns (one nurses' aide for every ten residents on the day shift) and relatively good wages and benefits (about $10 an hour for starting nurses' aides) were key ingredients of the facilities' low employee turnover and generally good care. As one Kane worker said:

> I get to take care of the same people every day, so I know them and their needs very well. And most of our workers have been at the Kanes for a long time. There's very little turnover. If you cut people down to six dollars an hour, a lot of people will leave. For six dollars an hour, it would be a lot easier to flip hamburgers, and not be dealing with the emotional stress of taking care of very sick people.

Kane workers were particularly worried about the effects of future cutbacks on residents. Dozens of workers I spoke with were visibly upset about the effects of the buyouts, the likely effects of future cutbacks, and the effect of talk of privatization on residents' morale. One worker's bitter comments captured a theme I heard often:

> The residents wonder why we can't spend as much time with them as we used to. They ask us, "What did I do to make you not love me anymore?" They think it's something they did wrong. It's heartbreaking. And all you can do is tell them it's not their fault and go on to the next patient. They deserve better.

Because of Kane workers' level of anger over privatization and the strength of their emotional ties to residents, Local 9876 was able to mobilize them in opposition to privatization even without an easily activated internal union structure. When the union began announcing rallies, workers turned up in fairly large numbers, with very little organizational effort on the part of the union. In late September 1996, about seventy-five Kane workers from both locals turned out on short notice to an anti-privatization rally. Several weeks later, hundreds of workers responded to Local 9876's call to attend a Wednesday night meeting of the county Board of Commissioners. In January of 1997, Local 9876 successfully organized three days of rallies and marches; noisy crowds of workers descended on the Allegheny County courthouse each day. In between these large events, several dozen workers turned out for each biweekly county commissioners' meeting—to harass the county administration and to use the portion of the meetings designated for "public comment" as a platform to denounce Kane privatization.

The mobilization of Kane workers contributed a crucial piece to the overall response to the Republicans' assault on the Kanes. The sheer scale of workers' rallies and protests, combined with careful attention to media outreach, resulted in extensive coverage by all local television networks and both of Pittsburgh's daily newspapers. The *Post-Gazette*, which editorially favored Kane privatization, described the scene at one rally as a "buzz-saw of opposition," during which the crowd "chanted slogans like 'Hey hey, ho ho, Dunn and Cranmer got to go.'"[24] The workers' protests—and the resulting media coverage—also emphasized workers' concern for their residents in addition to their own opposition as workers. Local television coverage of one meeting, for example, featured a Kane worker saying, "I'm very opposed to [privatization] because we're very dedicated workers and I don't feel we should be put out in the streets. And our patients, our poor patients, some of them are asking questions about where we're gonna go, and where they're gonna go." Another gave an emotional statement to the cameras, with tears in her eyes as she referred to the Kane centers' historical mission: "The [Kane] hospitals used to have a motto that said, 'we'll take the poor and we'll take the indigent.' Now they want to run [the homes] as a business. . . . Well, businesses don't take in the poor." Television coverage of another rally gave a Kane worker the last word: "[Kane residents] have become family—when they hurt, you hurt."

But the two Republican commissioners' responses illustrate the limitations of mobilization by Kane workers alone and the importance of the union's decision to build a broader community coalition: they portrayed the workers and unions as motivated purely by self-interest in the face of difficult but necessary change. In response to one early protest, Commissioner Dunn said, "They're concerned about their jobs, and that's understandable." Cranmer added, "We want a positive relationship with the unions, but times are changing." As the campaign developed, the commissioners took a harder line, portraying the unions as obstructionist. "If the unions stand back and don't negotiate, then as far as I'm concerned, we turn this thing over to Alleco," Dunn threatened in January 1997. "The employees have had their chance. If their leaders don't do the right thing, then we're going to turn it over to Alleco and let Alleco negotiate with them."[25] Further, the Republican commissioners and the county's law firm began pointedly attacking "wasteful" labor agreements as the source of inefficiency at the Kanes, slamming Kane workers' free cafeteria lunches and differential rates ($0.25 an hour) for assignments off their normal units. "You'll find no counterpart to that in the private sector," complained John Lyncheski, the county's chief negotiator to local television news cameras. "It's just inefficient and wasteful, frankly." To the union's chagrin, despite its efforts to respond to these charges, the commissioners clearly scored major points with these attacks.[26]

Elderly Advocates: Independent Credibility

Fortunately, however, union leaders had anticipated that mobilizing Kane workers would not be enough. Right from the beginning of the campaign the union had enlisted a group called the Alliance for Progressive Action (APA) to help organize an effective labor-community coalition.[27] One way APA staff broadened the base of antiprivatization opposition was to begin meeting with a number of activists who had spearheaded a reform effort at the old Kane Hospital nearly two decades earlier. These activists were former workers at Kane Hospital who had gone public in the late 1970s with a damning report called "Kane: A Place to Die." Their central contention then was that low wages, understaffing, and high employee turnover at Kane Hospital led to low worker morale, patient neglect, and patient abuse. Their exposé had received national attention, had led to changes in federal government regulation of county nursing homes across the country, and had ultimately resulted in the demolition of Kane Hospital and the construction of the four regional Kane Centers in the early 1980s. These activists were justifiably proud of their reform efforts and of the new Kanes' continuing record of quality care; like Kane workers, they understood that the Kanes' vastly improved reputation was the result of their good staffing ratios, decent wages and benefits, and low staff turnover. The old Kane activists were thus very concerned about the commissioners' plans to privatize the Kanes, fearing that a private operator would undo precisely the improvements in staffing, wages and benefits, and turnover they had fought so hard for two decades ago. One of the original Kane activists who now led the group's efforts against privatization later related, "I ran into [another old Kane activist] at the supermarket, and we said, you know, we should really do something. So we called the union." APA and Local 9876 staff began meeting with these activists in September of 1996. Together, they formed a new group called the Committee to Save Kane, and began planning to organize residents' family members and to circulate petitions.

The members of the Committee to Save Kane played on their former positions as courageous whistleblowers at the old Kane Hospital and current identities as elderly advocates, garnering an aura of impartiality that current Kane workers could not command. When the Committee to Save Kane held a press conference announcing its opposition to privatization and outlining its concern that any attempt to cut costs would necessarily rely on reduced staffing, wages, and benefits, press reports were respectful, treating its members as independent advocates for the elderly.[28] Coverage noted that Committee members included a regional director of the National Council for Senior Citizens and the president of the local chapter of the Steelworkers Organization of Active Retirees.[29]

In responding to the Committee to Save Kane, the Republicans continued to try to blame all opposition on the unions, saying that privatization foes had been "'sold a bill of goods' by union leaders with a stake in [Kane jobs]."[30] But claiming that advocates for the elderly and retired had somehow been duped by the Kane unions was not nearly as effective as being able to blast the unions directly. As a result, the commissioners were forced to respond more substantively to the committee's arguments. Sounding defensive, the Republicans denied that there would be any job cuts directly involving patient care, but their denial acknowledged that in fact job reductions were likely through attrition and possibly even layoffs.[31]

The Committee to Save Kane also contributed to the campaign in other ways. When committee members independently discovered that the Kanes were busing nurses' aides from one facility to another to beef up staffing during a state inspection—thus casting doubt on claims of overstaffing— they went public with the information. The Laborers' Local X, which represented these nurse aides, had known about the practice, but had chosen not to go public or even communicate this knowledge to Local 9876. Committee members spent hours discussing these discoveries and their analysis of privatization with several television reporters, and this paid off in the form of an in-depth television news report on staffing changes at the Kanes since the Republicans had taken office.

But perhaps the most important Committee to Save Kane activity was its effort to contact and organize the family members of Kane residents. Through its organizing efforts, the committee was able to turn out a contingent of residents' family members to protest at the commissioners' biweekly public meetings and at union rallies. The family members were extremely effective and enthusiastic advocates for the Kanes. At commissioners' meetings I attended, dozens of family members—mostly middle-aged and elderly women—formed a rowdy caucus. At every opportunity, they yelled at the commissioners, saying, for example, "Shame on you! How can you do this to my mother?" At one meeting, Commissioner Cranmer inadvertently stepped on their toes when he criticized Kane workers. The family members were outraged. "[Kane workers] are the nicest people anywhere!" one white-haired lady shouted angrily. "They take care of my sister every day and she loves them dearly! Don't you say anything bad about them!" Cranmer was clearly flustered by all this, and neither Republican commissioner ever figured out how to respond effectively to the family members' vocal opposition: they simply could not dismiss family members' concerns as "selfish."

Religious Leaders: Moral Authority

In addition to its work with the Committee to Save Kane, the APA also helped coordinate opposition from progressive church leaders. The APA had already been in the process of organizing the Pittsburgh Area Religious Task Force on the Economy, recruiting church leaders who had historically supported labor causes and issues, and who were generally concerned about problems of economic inequality and injustice. When the commissioners announced their plans to privatize the Kanes, the APA and Local 9876 suggested Kane privatization as the Religious Task Force's first major project. "They needed something to get started on, they needed something concrete to work around," says the APA's Newman. The union put together a fact sheet on privatization emphasizing how Alleco's plan would likely affect the quality of care, and Newman and Janet Zimmerman, the president of Local 9876, presented the issue to the Task Force. They proposed that the Task Force convene public hearings on the issue, take testimony, and then issue an opinion.

The Catholic, Presbyterian, Baptist, and Jewish clergy who comprised the Religious Task Force responded enthusiastically to this proposal. The idea of holding public hearings was particularly attractive because, rather than being asked automatically to side with the unions with knee-jerk support, the clergy were being asked to form their own independent view and issue a thoughtful opinion. Clearly, though, the sympathies of this progressive group of clergy were with workers and residents from the outset. As the Reverend Phil Wilson, a Task Force member, later said, "You know, a lot of us visit parishioners at the Kanes on a regular basis. I have always been impressed with the staff there, and whenever I am visiting, they always seem to be working very hard. So to me, and to a number of other clergy, the things the commissioners were saying about the Kanes being overstaffed just didn't make sense." Also, Wilson added, "Some of us have been around long enough to remember the old Kane Hospital—and we didn't want to see a return to those kinds of conditions."

The hearings held by the Religious Task Force on March 5, and their subsequent opinion statement, added a crucial final piece to the strategy of resistance. The hearings themselves offered another opportunity to mobilize "disinterested" expert opinion. Written testimony from Linda Rhodes, former Pennsylvania Secretary of Aging, was introduced, emphasizing the Kanes' record of providing high-quality care to a vulnerable population. She wrote of having received many calls, as Secretary of Aging, "from Pitts-burghers who asked if there was anything I could do to get their family members into one of the Kane Regional Centers because they knew that the care was so good but the waiting lists were so long." MIT-trained economist Stephen Herzenberg warned that nursing home markets and reimburse-ment schemes did not reward care quality in the private sector, contributing to understaffing and the spread of a low-wage, high-turnover model of labor relations. Finally, widely respected Democratic county controller Frank Lucchino testified that short-term budget considerations rather than concern for quality were driving the privatization plan. Lucchino noted that the Republican commissioners were eager to receive a $23 million lease pay-ment from Alleco to help ease the county's self-imposed budget crisis. Moreover, Lucchino testified, in order to come up with the lease money, Alleco would necessarily have to cut jobs, wages, and services at the Kanes.

Again, the Republicans had difficulty responding effectively to these claims. *Post-Gazette* coverage of the Religious Task Force hearings gave exten-sive play to Lucchino's financial analysis of the privatization proposal, which James Roddey, Alleco's chairman, was not able to convincingly refute.[32] Roddey and Commissioner Cranmer repeated their denials that privatiza-tion would lead to cuts in the medical staff at the Kanes, but they now seemed to be outnumbered by a myriad of experts claiming the opposite.

On March 24, 1997, the Religious Task Force on the Economy issued its opinion on Kane privatization and its appeal to the Board of Commissioners to reconsider the plan. Its statement, quoted in the *Post-Gazette*, expressed concern about "increased social costs, the loss of public accountability, the stripping of public assets, the potential for corruption, the jobs of Kane workers and the undercutting of union organization."[33] The statement went on to say that "We are deeply concerned about reductions in the quality and availability of patient care. As religious people, we believe society has a duty toward the poor, the elderly, the infirm and the isolated."[34] Sister Mary Carol Bennett, of the Peace and Justice Office of the Sisters of Mercy, also com-mented that "[Privatization] is a dollar move to cut the bottom line figure. And the only way you're going to do that is to cut services and to cut jobs."[35] The press conference concluded with a call for parishioners and the general public to contact the commissioners to oppose privatization.

According to the APA's Wendy Newman, the Religious Task Force's con-tribution to the campaign was, organizationally speaking, "frankly, some-what smoke and mirrors. But it ended up being a very important piece, because [the clergy] had a certain moral authority that had a very real impact." Indeed, the extensive publicity surrounding the appeal by the Religious Task Force on the Economy seemed the final straw for Commissioner Larry Dunn. Dunn had been quiet throughout the month of March, but decided several hours after the Task Force made its appeal—six days before his original deadline for a final decision on Kane privatization—to quash privatization at least until the end of the year.

The timing of Dunn's reversal confirms the success of the union's three-pronged mobilization strategy—but more importantly it highlights the fact that the antiprivatization campaign's success was not rooted in the mere *fact* of grassroots mobilization tactics but rather in the union's careful attention to *whose* voices were raised and *what* they said. Together, Kane workers, old Kane activists (and the residents' family members they organized), and the religious community had articulated an emergent, still inchoate ideology, a vision of human dignity that ultimately made the commissioners' bottom-line arguments about efficiency and cost-savings seem not only heartless and insupportable, but beside the point. Ultimately, by helping the union *change the subject* from the costs of operating the Kanes to the importance of maintaining high-quality care for Allegheny County's most vulnerable citizens, the credibility of family members, old Kane activists, and religious leaders accomplished what worker mobilization alone could not.

We have thus seen how the union, unable to challenge either the reality or the ideology of globalization, astutely attacked the specific market-oriented arguments for privatization instead. The union's next campaign, aimed at winning new contracts for all its county workers (including Kane employees) was quite different in this respect. In its contract struggle, Local 9876 could not construct *any* issue of similarly broad-based appeal, capable of mobilizing credible allies and neutralizing neoliberal assumptions and discourse. The union's contract campaign also used grassroots, social-movement-style organizing and protest—but here, the absence of an attractive ideological alternative forced the union to more directly confront the historical legacies of its business-union structure in order to mobilize its workers. Moreover, as we will see, worker mobilization around the contract issue ultimately yielded fruit only because of the Republican commissioners' fiscal and political weakness in the wake of their defeat on Kane privatization.

WINNING FAIR CONTRACTS

Even though public opposition had put Kane privatization on hold by the spring of 1997, 3,500 workers represented by eleven county unions were still working under the terms of expired contracts, with no thaw in negotiations looming anywhere on the horizon. And despite the success of Local 9876's public organizing efforts in defeating Kane privatization, leaders of the other county unions favored returning to a strategy of quiet lobbying and behind-the-scenes pressure in order to settle the county contracts. Janet Zimmerman, president of Local 9876, saw clearly that such a strategy would not lead to a successful conclusion to county bargaining; she believed that the commissioners would need a stronger push.

The issue of contracts for county workers, however, did not inspire the same sort of community activism that Kane privatization had done. The activists and religious leaders who had helped generate a groundswell of opposition to privatization were not only less interested in county workers' contract situations, they were also in a weaker position for issuing morally charged public statements on the issue. Kane privatization had offered the specter of cruelty to innocent old people; the county's demands for contract concessions on seniority rights, scheduling, and contracting-out, on the other hand, simply did not appeal in the same way to a ready-made social justice constituency. County workers' stalled contract negotiations did not seem to portend human suffering of the same magnitude as nursing home privatization and cutbacks. Even though county workers stood to lose important seniority and educational benefits, not to mention their legal right to bargain over privatization and contracting-out, the union was not able to construct an appealing public discourse about the commissioners' attack or generate the same kind of emotional punch that the specter of Kane privatization had offered. As a result, the union could not rely primarily on external linkages with progressive organizations in its contract battle, and was forced to rely on leverage from within.

But without a ready-made counter-ideology to deploy, mobilizing county workers to fight for fair contracts required more intensive organizing than mobilizing angry Kane workers had done. Kane workers had been keenly aware of the privatization issue and its potential effects on themselves and Kane residents, and were eager to show their anger publicly. Kane and other county workers alike, in contrast, generally did not understand the bargaining situation at the outset of the union's internal organizing effort. Indeed, while many workers were angry about having to work under expired contracts, their anger usually took the form of blaming the union for "taking so long" to settle the contract. In contrast to the Kane struggle, therefore, contract mobilization would not happen so spontaneously. Here the union was forced to struggle with three central organizational legacies that the Kane campaign had been able to bypass: bureaucratic inertia, rank and file repertoires, and a worksite leadership vacuum. These legacies did not *prevent* the union from mobilizing workers around the contract issue, but they limited and constrained mobilization. The contract campaign did not solve any of these problems but rather temporarily overcame them or simply operated within the constraints they defined.

Bureaucratic Inertia

Right from the start, the union's bureaucratic-servicing history shaped the development of the contract campaign. Of the three staff representatives responsible for the 1,500 Allegheny county workers represented by Local 9876, the most senior, Fred Jones, was firmly entrenched in the bureaucratic proceduralism that had served him well over the years, and he had little talent or inclination for organizing. Part of the reason the union had hired three college-student interns to carry out the internal organizing campaign was that Jones could not be induced to fully support the campaign. Jones may have recognized that a pressure-campaign was necessary to move the contract negotiations forward, but he clearly wanted as little to do with it as possible, and he hoped to return to his standard representational activities as soon as the campaign ended.

Jones's response was not universal among the staff. Unlike Jones, staff representative Art Lazarra believed that the new context of Allegheny County labor relations demanded a radical response from the union. In Lazarra's view, the organizing campaign should not seek merely to temporarily mobilize workers in pursuit of contract agreements, only to return to the status quo; rather, he believed that the campaign should be a first step toward organizational reform and restructuring. Lazarra wanted to introduce a functioning worksite steward structure so that future mobilizations could be accomplished without having to start from scratch every time. But as consistently as Lazarra tried to introduce the issue of organizational reform into discussions about the campaign, Jones just as consistently tried to focus the campaign purely on short-term mobilization, member recruitment, and member donations to COPE, the local's political fund.

At one early planning meeting, for example, Lazzara criticized the agenda for the lunchtime worksite meetings, arguing that they focused only on short-term mobilization and ignored the underlying organizational problems of the county unit. Lazzara suggested mounting a program of stewards' training, which would be aimed at increasing the capacities of worksite stewards to organize their worksites more effectively. This proposal was tabled after vehement objections from a group of union staff led by Jones, who claimed that we would "not have time" to implement such a program, and that the worksite meetings themselves already represented "a pretty heavy schedule." Later in the summer, after privately lobbying the president of Local 9876, Lazarra and another staff person were given permission to hold a stewards' training session for county workers from Allegheny, Butler, Beaver, and Washington counties—but by that time, it was too late to make stewards' training a major focus of the Allegheny county contract campaign. The training session, held on a Saturday in early September, was indeed poorly attended by Allegheny County stewards, because only a few departments were contacted.

The competing agendas of Lazzara and Jones ran right through the organizing activities I carried out along with the other interns, the staff representatives, and the volunteer member organizers. The central organizing strategy of the contract campaign was a series of lunchtime worksite meetings at several dozen county departments and locations, representing about

900 of the local's 1,500 Allegheny County workers, during late June and early July of 1997. These worksite meetings were used to bring workers up to date on the status of negotiations, to convey the need for collective action to put pressure on the commissioners, and to encourage workers to sign up for specific actions the union was planning. But the lunchtime worksite meetings ended up being infused with conflicting elements from both Lazarra's and Jones's agendas.

Anticipating bitterness on the part of workers who felt the union had not been doing enough to get them a new contract, Local 9876 staff director Joe Reilly encouraged us to tell workers that the union recognized its past failure to be sufficiently organized, and that the present internal organizing effort represented the union's commitment to change. "We need to change our image of what a union is," Reilly told us as we practiced giving the rap. "You can say that. Instead of seeing it as a sort of insurance company, where we buy a kind of policy with our dues, we need to involve all the workers in rebuilding the union." Along with the other interns, I incorporated this kind of talk into the rap. Buoyed by our own visions of a more participatory model of unionism, we naively promised workers that the union was firmly committed to a fundamental change in how their unit functioned.

This kind of talk made promises that Jones was clearly not very interested in fulfilling. Responsible for delivering a bargaining report to the worksites he represented, Jones would continually turn up late at meetings and then leave early. Workers were simultaneously presented with enthusiastic young interns telling them that with their help the union was committed to rebuilding itself, and with their staff representative who looked on in boredom and left early—not exactly a convincing combination. It was never clear whether Jones really thought of the meetings as a waste of time or whether, as a fellow intern argued, he was simply uncomfortable with this kind of interaction with the membership. Jones was obviously accustomed to playing the role of "expert" and took pride in being able to solve county workers' problems. In the current context—in which Jones's bureaucratic skills were useless—he may have felt embarrassed by the need to turn to the members for help. Either way, the absence of firm staff commitment to the new model of unionism we were promising was clear to rank and file members.

Rank and File Repertoires

Despite the mixed messages from the union, most workers were fairly enthusiastic about the union's decision to pursue a collective action strategy in order to win new contracts. They understood that embarrassing the commissioners, drawing media attention to the contract stalemate, and publicly demonstrating the union's resolve were worthwhile activities. Therefore, substantial percentages of the workers we approached signed up for participation in the rallies, button days, and other activities we were organizing. However, workers' willingness to participate in the union's contract campaign did *not* imply that they were eager for a more participatory, grassroots model of day-to-day unionism. Years of experience with a traditional model of bureaucratic unionism had taught workers to view the union not as the sum of their collective participation, not as something that they created through their mutual support of one another, but rather as something outside themselves, an external service to call on whenever there was a problem. These ingrained dispositions persisted even in the context of the contract campaign.

This could be plainly seen at meetings involving Art Lazarra's worksites. Lazarra took the opposite approach from Jones: rather than trying to undercut the idea of worksite participation, he tried very hard to convince workers that they could and should respond directly and collectively to worksite problems instead of just filing grievances and waiting for a procedural resolution. Lazzara always stressed the idea that direct worksite actions were particularly important now that grievances were piling up instead of being resolved in an orderly fashion. He used several examples to show how effective this sort of response can be.

In one of his favorite stories, Lazarra told of a hot, muggy day in late June when the air conditioning in one of the county offices broke down. The workers asked their supervisor if they could remove their ties because of the heat, but the supervisor said no. One of the stewards called Art, who, instead of filing a grievance (which would not have resulted in immediate relief in any case), suggested that all the workers should march down to the row officer's office, give him their ties, an explanation of the problem, and tell him that they were prepared to alert the media to the working conditions if they were forced to continue wearing their ties in ninety-degree heat. The strategy was successful—faced with collective protest, the row officer overruled the workers' supervisor and allowed the workers to remove their ties. In fact, for the rest of the week, until the air conditioning was fixed, the workers were allowed to report to work in shorts and tee-shirts.

This story never had the intended effect in any of the meetings Art attended. Workers invariably responded not with enthusiasm but with baffled incomprehension, as if he were missing the point. Every time Art would make his pitch and give an example, workers would counter with a grievance, and ask when the union was going to do something about it. They always seemed both puzzled and annoyed by Art's responses. As I watched this on numerous occasions, I could almost hear the workers thinking, "What's going on here? Why isn't he listening to us? We keep telling him about these problems and instead of promising to take care of it, he keeps trying to push them off on us." Often, workers actually said in frustration things like "Why am I paying dues if the union isn't going to help me with these problems?" These exchanges always ended with Art and the workers exasperated and annoyed at one another. Lazarra interpreted their responses as an inability to understand their situation, what they were up against, and what they needed to do about it; workers in turn interpreted Lazarra's suggestion that they rely on their collective power to solve worksite problems as an abdication of responsibility by the union.

Why did workers approve of and participate in the union's collective-action strategy on the contract campaign, but respond so negatively to Art Lazarra's suggestion that they apply the same principles to worksite grievances? The answer is that these were two very different ideas. Unlike spontaneous worksite resistance, the protests we organized were relatively easy to participate in precisely because they took place *outside* the workplace—on the steps of the county courthouse, for example, or at commissioners' meetings. Acting up *in* the workplace, on the other hand, implies a potentially tense confrontation with the boss, which is an entirely different matter. Moreover, our public rallies and activities offered safety in numbers, almost an anonymity of participation. In contrast, asking a few isolated workers to stand up to the boss requires someone to go out on a limb in hopes that other workers will back him or her up. My point is certainly not that a more participatory model of worksite unionism is not possible. Rather, it should be understood that rank and file workers accustomed to a servicing approach will not embrace such threatening new ideas as Lazarra's without a great deal more support, leadership, and encouragement than was forthcoming in this campaign.

Worksite Leadership Vacuum

If the union's bureaucratic history made both ordinary workers and union staff ambivalent about the relationship between the contract campaign and a new model of worker participation, this was also true of the union's volunteer worksite leadership. As one staff person said, "You've got to understand that for years and years, the position of steward was basically meaningless. The steward was just a figurehead with no real function." As a result, many stewards had become accustomed to viewing the position as essentially symbolic. These stewards often resisted the idea or suggestion that they take responsibility for organizing. Understandably, they saw organizing and mobilizing as "the union's job" and often refused to do it. When we visited one steward as part of the planning for a worksite meeting for her department, she was taken aback by our request that she circulate "Contract Now!" petitions and flyers about the meeting, and post notices about the meeting at her worksite. She reluctantly agreed but added, "I can tell you right now that these workers here won't do anything. They just won't get involved." This turned out to be a self-fulfilling prophecy. Like many other stewards, she was not prepared to take on organizing responsibilities, primarily because the union had not provided the necessary training and support.

The traditional organizational irrelevance of the worksite steward, the lack of training, and the lack of real responsibility the position entailed also had the unfortunate effect of making the position attractive to the wrong people for the wrong reasons. In many worksites the only workers willing to volunteer for the position did so not because they wanted to represent their fellow workers, but because it was a way of being "in the know," of having something over co-workers, or even because they hoped it would give them a platform from which to harass union staff or other workers. In these departments, a kind of "crowding out" took place, a process in which workers with good leadership potential were kept from getting involved by the presence of self-serving volunteers who bullied, harassed, and intimidated them into staying uninvolved. Conversely, genuinely good leaders who held the position of steward with the best of intentions found the position extremely frustrating. Lacking any clearly defined role, lacking support from the union's staff representative for plans to organize worksites and departments, such stewards found themselves simply the unfortunate lightning rod for the frustrations of fellow workers. As one such steward commented, "I have no authority, no real purpose. I'm not able to do anything for the workers in my department. I'm just the guy who puts stuff up on the bulletin board. The people in this department either laugh at me, or they bitch at me for everything that's wrong with the union. And I can't change a damn thing."

The union's inability or unwillingness to clearly define a meaningful role for volunteer worksite stewards, to provide training and support, and to establish standards of performance for which stewards would be accountable meant that the union depended entirely on top-down organization in order to mobilize workers during the contract campaign. This ultimately limited the union to actions that paid union staff could directly organize and supervise—such as a series of rallies held at evening commissioners' meetings and a large day-long rally and protest at the courthouse dubbed "Solidarity Day." These events were successful and generated generally positive media coverage of the workers' fight for fair contracts (between fifty and one hundred workers protested at each of the committee meetings, and more than five hundred turned out for Solidarity Day)—but unlike the earlier Kane rallies, these actions required an enormous amount of logistical and organizing effort to create. The union could not simply call a contract rally and expect county workers to show up; indeed, it did not even have reliable means of communication with many county worksites. The contract rallies therefore had to be carefully planned ahead of time. Interns and member organizers had to set up and carry out dozens of worksite meetings in order to educate the membership about the bargaining situation and the need for rank and file involvement in the contract campaign, and to recruit workers' participation in the planned rallies. Workers who signed up for these events were then systematically phone-banked in the days leading up to them. The one initiative in which the union tried to rely on worksite stewards to directly organize a series of actions, the "rolling thunder week" described in the opening anecdote, led to decidedly mixed results.

The reliance on top-down organization also constrained the union's ability to mount a *sustained* campaign. By the end of August 1997, two of the three interns had returned to graduate school, and the union had exhausted its small supply of "member organizers" willing to take two weeks off work, paid by the union, to work on the campaign. Though the commissioners could not have known it, the union could not have sustained the campaign at the same level beyond August without a regrouping period. Had the commissioners been able to hold firm into the fall of 1997, the outcome of the campaign might have been different. Fortunately for the union, however, time was not on the commissioners' side in the wake of their defeat over Kane privatization. The commissioners had failed to realize $23 million in immediate savings by privatizing the Kanes, and county government was still operating under the constraints of the 20 percent property-tax cut. As a result, the county's fiscal situation was spiraling out of control. Vast budget deficits loomed, as bond rating agencies, citing the mismatch between the sharp revenue reductions and the failure to find new savings, lowered Allegheny County's rating twice during the summer of 1997. The two Republican commissioners were even called to New York to receive a "scolding" from Standard and Poors in early August.[36] By that point, $76 million in county cash reserves had evaporated and the Republicans' only plan to deal with a budget deficit of $26.5 million involved the one-time sale of property tax liens. The commissioners were thus under tremendous pressure from bond rating agencies to restore some semblance of order to county finances by the end of the year.

Initially, the Republicans had hoped to realize the necessary savings— and indeed ultimately to resurrect Kane privatization—by defeating the county unions on the contract issue. If they could force the unions to accept their proposed contract language on contracting-out, they would have a free hand once again as far as the Kanes were concerned. But such a strategy depended on defeating the unions quickly. Local 9876's contract campaign, culminating with its large "Solidarity Day" rally, demonstrated that a quick union collapse was not forthcoming. As a result, there seemed to be no possibility of resurrecting Kane privatization any time soon. Therefore, Republican Commissioner Bob Cranmer backed down. In late August, he joined forces with Democratic Commissioner Mike Dawida to oust the Republican chair of the Board of Commissioners, Larry Dunn, who was not yet prepared to settle. Cranmer would be the new chairman, and Cranmer and Dawida agreed to work together to reach quick settlements with the county unions.[37] Ultimately, all the county unions but one signed nonconcessionary contracts. Local 9876's contract included raises, compensation for back raises, improved bumping and bidding rights, and no concessions on contracting-out or "management rights."

THE FUTURE OF SOCIAL-MOVEMENT UNIONISM

Each of the two interconnected union campaigns discussed here managed to find a *partial* solution to just *one* of the two central dilemmas facing the labor movement. The Kane campaign, unable to construct a counter-ideology capable of taking on globalization or the Republicans' tax cut, successfully attacked instead the specific neoliberal arguments in favor of privatization. As a result, it was able to mobilize both workers and allies against privatization—despite its inability to deal with organizational legacies. The contract campaign, unable to really solve the organizational problems of the union's county chapter, nevertheless devised short-term, ad hoc ways of dealing with them. As a result, it was able to mobilize workers (but not allies) in the struggle for new contracts—despite its inability to construct an appealing counter-ideology. The asymmetry between the two campaigns thus lies in the facts that partially overcoming the dilemma of ideology led to the mobilization of workers *and* their allies in one campaign, while partially overcoming the dilemma of organizational legacies led only to the mobilization of workers in the other. Hence the Kane campaign developed more leverage than the contract campaign—so much so that contract success ultimately depended on the aftereffects of the Kane campaign.

What conclusions are we to draw from this asymmetry of effects? Does it mean that the dilemma of ideology is more central to the labor movement's success than the dilemma of legacies? That legacies can safely be ignored while ideology must at all costs be dealt with? Quite the opposite, for several related reasons. First, in many cases the humanitarian issues are not so ready-made or appealing as in the Kane fight. The political weakness of the contract campaign, its inability to mobilize allies despite its successes in mobilizing workers themselves, is its real significance: somehow the labor movement must move beyond reliance on easy public sympathy for appealing protagonists like nursing home residents, or it will be limited to the rarest of victories. Most workers, after all, are not connected closely with such appealing clients.

But moving beyond reliance on easy public sympathy for appealing protagonists will necessitate the development of imaginative alternatives to globalization itself, to the context underwriting all manner of neoliberal attacks. As others have noted, in order to move beyond piecemeal local victories such as these, the labor movement will need to vigorously champion an analysis that exposes how the global competition for jobs and investment is not "natural" but an artifact; not the inevitable result of computer and communications technology but the political result of trade and banking policy decisions primarily advocated by the United States. It will need to replace the ideology of globalization with one of its own, emphasizing perhaps the "re-nationalization" of capital and the internationalization of labor and environmental standards. Such an ideology does not yet exist, and as the following discussion demonstrates, the very effort to create it will mean confronting the organizational legacies of the movement.

Working Families 2000, a labor initiative begun in Allegheny County in the wake of the campaigns analyzed in this chapter, may represent the kind of necessary starting point required for constructing a coherent response to globalization—but it also serves as a reminder that such efforts will be complicated by the organizational legacies of the movement itself. Working Families is a new coalition involving Local 9876, the SEIU international union, the Pennsylvania AFL-CIO, Allegheny County's Central Labor Council, and a number of other local unions. It has been constructed with the goal of developing a progressive, worker-friendly political agenda for county politics. Coalition members have donated staff and an office at the international headquarters of the United Steelworkers in downtown Pittsburgh. The campaign has been attempting to coordinate the political endorsements of local labor unions in the 1999 county elections, to support labor-friendly county politicians, and to articulate a progressive agenda for county politics around four planks: (1) support for the "living wage" campaign of the Alliance for Progressive Action, which would require recipients of local tax subsidies or government contracts to pay their workers a living wage of $8.82 an hour with benefits;[38] (2) enforcing the right to organize, so that tax subsidies or government contracts are not used to fight unionization; (3) fair taxation; and (4) no privatization or contracting-out.

Ideas such as these could represent the modest beginning of a coherent response to globalization—not so much for what they stand for in themselves but because the very attempt to construct a platform has forced Allegheny County's coalition of labor leaders to confront the context of globalization and think about ways of responding to it. But here we see how organizational legacies are themselves implicated in the search for new ideologies: Working Families 2000's efforts to create a meaningful political agenda remain complicated by the organizational history of the local labor movement. While coalition members agreed in principle to support the living wage campaign, many union locals remain uncomfortable with the idea of actually attaching living wage conditions to county contracts and subsidies. Building trades unions in particular have strongly supported the city's and county's subsidies on behalf of new stadiums, a new convention center, and downtown retail outlets, even though no living wage or job-provision conditions were attached to these projects, because they promised short-term jobs for unionized construction workers. As a result, Working Families 2000 has struggled with the issue but has not identified a single subsidy they are prepared to oppose, despite the lack of living wage or job guarantees.

The issue of taxation is similarly problematic: coalition members agreed to fair taxation as a slogan but do not have the political will to publicly oppose cuts in property tax rates or the recent creation of a highly regressive county sales tax—let alone to make concrete proposals that would address the regressiveness of local taxes. And other issues remain unaddressed by Working Families 2000 altogether: the coalition is silent on the shift of local public resources from needed social services to social control agencies because the jail guards' union resists any suggestion that there should be fewer jails, more schools, and more social services.

Building labor coalitions of this character is, we can see, very precarious—but only through such organization-building efforts, at both local and national levels, can the labor movement as a whole hope to build a coherent ideological response to globalization. Solutions to both dilemmas, ideology and organizational legacies, are thus equally important and inextricably intertwined.

NOTES

I would like to thank the Sociology Department at the University of California, Berkeley, for generous financial support of this research. Stephen Herzenberg, Daniel Kovalik, and David Turner commented on early drafts. Kim Lopez offered much feedback, insight, and encouragement. The Service Employees International Union (SEIU) made this research possible by generously allowing me to conduct participant observation research without restriction. Several staff from Local 9876 commented helpfully on this chapter, without making any requests that I change my analysis to suit the union. At the request of union staff, however, I have given the local a fictitious name. Also, all names in the chapter, except those of elected officials or candidates for public office, are pseudonyms.

1. Andy Banks, "The Power and Promise of Community Unionism"; James Craft, "The Community as a Source of Power"; Ruth Needleman, "Building Relationships for the Long Haul: Unions and Community Organizing Groups Working Together to Organize Low-Wage Workers"; Ronald Peters and Theresa Merrill, "Clergy and Religious Persons' Roles in Organizing at O'Hare Airport and St. Joseph Medical Center"; and Katherine Sciacchitano, "Finding the Community in the Union and the Union in the Community: The First-Contract Campaign at Steeltech."

2. Fernando Gapasin and Howard Wial, "The Role of Central Labor Councils in Union Organizing in the 1990s"; Philip McLewin, "The Concerted Voice of Labor and the Suburbanization of Capital: Fragmentation of the Community Labor Council"; Stewart Acuff, "Expanded Roles for the Central Labor Council: The View from Atlanta."

3. Roger Waldinger et al., "Helots No More: A Case Study of the Justice for Jan-

itors Campaign in Los Angeles"; Acuff, "Expanded Roles for the Central Labor Council"; Larry Cohen and Steve Early, "Defending Workers' Rights in the Global Economy: The CWA Experience."

4. Kate Bronfenbrenner and Tom Juravich, "The Promise of Union Organizing in the Public and Private Sectors"; Steve Early, "Membership-Based Organizing"; Janice Fine, "Moving Innovation from the Margins to the Center"; Sam Gindin, "Notes on Labor at the End of the Century: Starting Over?"; Josephine LeBeau and Kevin Lynch, "Successful Organizing at the Local Level: The Experience of AFCSME District Council 1707"; Stephen Lerner, "Taking the Offensive, Turning the Tide"; and Linda Markowitz, "Union Presentation of Self and Worker Participation in Organizing Campaigns."

5. Kate Bronfenbrenner and Tom Juravich, "It Takes More than House Calls: Organizing to Win with a Comprehensive Union-Building Strategy"; Linda Markowitz, "Union Presentation of Self and Worker Participation in Organizing Campaigns"; Kim Moody, *An Injury to All;* Moody, *Workers in a Lean World: Unions in the International Economy;* Moody, "American Labor: A Movement Again?"; Peter Rachleff, *Hard Times in the Heartland;* Rachleff, "Organizing Wall to Wall: The Independent Union of All Workers, 1933–37."

6. Bill Fletcher, Jr., and Richard Hurd, "Beyond the Organizing Model: The Transformation Process in Local Unions"; Fletcher and Hurd, "Political Will, Local Union Transformation, and the Organizing Imperative"; Kim Voss and Rachel Sherman, "Breaking the Iron Law of Oligarchy: Tactical Innovation and the Revitalization of the American Labor Movement."

7. Michael Eisenscher, "Critical Juncture: Unionism at the Crossroads"; James Craft, "Unions, Bureaucracy, and Change: Old Dogs Learn New Tricks Very Slowly."

8. Fernando Gapasin and Michael Yates, "Organizing the Unorganized: Will Promises Become Practices?"; see also Gregory Mantsios, "What Does Labor Stand For?"

9. Elaine Barnard, "Creating Democratic Communities in the Workplace."

10. Barbara Shailor and George Kourpias, "Developing and Enforcing International Labor Standards"; Héctor Figueroa, "International Labor Solidarity in an Era of Global Competition"; Ellen M. Wood, "Labor, Class, and State in Global Capitalism."

11. United States Department of Labor, *County Business Patterns.*

12. City of Pittsburgh, "Mayor's Annual Report."

13. John Bull, "County May Offer Buyout Packages: Republican Takeover Could Frighten Many to Take Money, Leave."

14. David Michelmore, "Democrats Match GOP Vow of 20% Cut in County Millage."

15. Ibid.

16. Ibid.

17. Larry Dunn and Bob Cranmer, "Our Campaign is Different."

18. The management's-rights clause was important to the county because Pennsylvania labor law requires public employers to negotiate with unions over any proposed privatization or contracting out, even if these subjects are not mentioned in collective bargaining agreements. Therefore, to gain a free hand in this area, the county hoped to force each union to accept the management's-rights clause.

19. Mark Belko, "Dunn Gives Ultimatum to Kane Unions."

20. Mark Belko, "Control of Kanes May Be Shifted."

21. These claims were developed in two reports commissioned by the Republicans: James McDonough, "John J. Kane Regional Centers: Privatization Options," and Jake Hauk, "The Case for Privatizing the Kane Regional Centers."

22. Unlike Local 9876, Local X had no previous experience with public protest campaigns. Local 9876 had been involved in a series of difficult (but ultimately successful) grassroots, social-movement style struggles against private sector nursing home operators, and it was largely this experience of struggle that led the local to conclude that a similar approach was now necessary to fight Kane privatization. The leadership of Local X had no tradition of public struggle, having relied mainly on close relations with Democratic politicians over the years. Despite the open hostility of the Republican privatizers towards the county unions, Local X feared that a public protest strategy would irreparably damage relationships with the commissioners and make it difficult to ultimately negotiate contracts.

23. According to workers, the Kanes had historically kept a day- and evening-shift ratio of one nurses' aide for every ten residents, but since the buyouts, it was more difficult to find replacements for workers who called in sick. By the fall of 1996, they say, it was common for day-shift nurses' aides to be given twelve residents to care for, and on the evening shift the ratio sometimes approached one to twenty. Workers I spoke with generally reported that while they were still able to meet the basic physical needs of their residents, as a result of the buyouts they were no longer able to take time to talk with their residents, to comfort them, read to them, or comb their hair.

24. Mark Belko, "Privatization Hits Strong Opposition: Commissioners Booed, Questioned by Crowd."

25. Mark Belko, "Dunn Gives Ultimatum to Kane Unions." This approach backfired when the unions revealed that they had been trying to set up negotiation meetings with the county's law firm for months, only to be told that the county negotiator's schedule was "virtually full."

26. According to Local 9876 staff, the free lunches had been proposed by the county in the 1970s, in lieu of a pay increase, and accepted by the unions in order to help the county save money; the modest off-unit differential was designed to reinforce the Kanes' philosophy of developing long-term relationships between residents and their primary caregivers, and to discourage managers from assigning workers to take care of residents whose needs they did not know well.

27. The Alliance for Progressive Action, founded in 1991, was an umbrella group for more than a dozen progressive and civil rights organizations in Allegheny County. Local 9876 was a founding member of APA and had contributed funding since its inception. Other APA members included the Rainbow Coalition, Act/Up, the United Electrical Workers (UE), and a number of civil rights organizations. Longtime Local 9876 organizer Wendy Newman had been involved with APA since 1991 and, at the time of the battle over the Kanes, was in the process of leaving the local to take a full-time job at APA.

28. Mark Belko, "Keep Kane Homes Public, Group Asks."

29. Ibid.

30. Ibid.

31. Ibid.

32. Mark Belko, "Lucchino: Privatization of Kanes Just a Quick Fix."

33. Mark Belko, "Dunn Halts Proposed Transfer of Kanes."

34. Ibid.

35. Joseph Crumb, "Religious Leaders Put Out Call for No Privatization."

36. *Pittsburgh Post-Gazette*, "County's Former Third Wheel Comes Full Circle."

37. Ibid.

38. The figure of $8.82 an hour was arrived at on the basis of several studies by Ralph Bangs, who analyzed more than two dozen family types and calculated the income requirements sufficient for "minimal" realistic family budgets in Pittsburgh. $8.82 is the wage required by families with two working parents and two children.

TEN

From Private Stigma to Global Assembly

Transforming the Terrain of Breast Cancer

Maren Klawiter

It was in the fall of 1994 that I began my study of breast cancer
activism in the San Francisco Bay Area, inspired by a fellow student
in a participant observation seminar—a woman who had just
finished chemotherapy treatments for breast cancer. With her
encouragement, I began observing a breast cancer support group
and, at the same time, entered a volunteer training program at the
Women's Cancer Resource Center (WCRC) in Berkeley, the first
feminist cancer community of its kind in the country. Through
WCRC, a local hub of information and cancer activities, I learned
about and became involved in a series of projects, including those
that figure prominently in this chapter—Race for the Cure, the
Women & Cancer Walk, the Toxic Tour of the Cancer Industry,
and the World Conference on Breast Cancer.

For the next three-plus years I conducted multi-sited participant
observation in a range of settings: cancer support groups, cancer
organizations, cultural events, coalitions; fund-raisers, educational
forums, environmental protests, public hearings; early detection
campaigns, street theater, and various conferences and symposia.
I supplemented this ethnographic data with interviews of cancer
activists, experts, survivors, and women living with breast cancer.
I discovered that the breast cancer movement was multiple rather
than monolithic, and my focus shifted from studying "the" breast
cancer movement to analyzing multiple mobilizations around
breast cancer. In the summer of 1997, I joined a large contingent
of activists from the Bay Area who made the historic trek to

Kingston, Canada, to participate in the first World Conference on Breast Cancer. The Kingston conference signified one of the first steps toward building a global breast cancer movement and it is written about here in that context.

Equally important, as I mapped these social movement formations, I became increasingly fascinated by the larger, historical question of movement emergence and movement-facilitating conditions. I kept wondering how a disease that had been so institutionally privatized and culturally stigmatized could have become an anchor for such dynamic and diverse mobilizations. In this chapter I outline an answer to that question by developing a sort of "ethnohistory" of the breast cancer apparatus and arguing that changes in the medical management of this disease—including the expansion of early detection technologies, the growth of treatment choices and uncertainty, the extension of treatment regimens, and the institutionalization of support groups—had important consequences for the development of social movements. I argue that these changes produced new subjects, solidarities, and sensibilities and, in so doing, laid the groundwork for the development of social movements.

My research strategy—and I think it was more intuitive than deliberate—was one of roving, multi-sited ethnography, full participation, and emotional engagement. As a result, the experiential, relational, emotional, and physical dimensions of my research have served as a central source of my own meaning-making practices and knowledge-production. In retrospect, I don't think it ever occurred to me to strive for distance or to even attempt a stance of objectivity and, in many respects, I have perhaps erred more on the side of participation than observation. Now, four years after having entered the field, as I write about the boundary-blurring transformations of breast cancer and the ways that new subjects, solidarities, and sensibilities have emerged within the Bay Area terrain, I can't help noting the unmistakable convergence of theory and theorizer. The boundaries of the field, and of breast cancer itself, have blurred for me as well. And as I write about the construction of new subjects, solidarities, and sensibilities, I note that I, too, have been caught up in and deeply transformed by the same forces and forms of resistance that I have been studying.

More than twenty years ago the acclaimed novelist and cultural critic Susan Sontag was diagnosed with breast cancer. Deeply disturbed by the reactions she received to her diagnosis, she began researching the history of cultural meanings—or metaphors—of cancer. In 1977 she published the now classic *Illness as Metaphor*. In this wide-ranging and lyrical essay Sontag described and decried the medical, social, and cultural patterns of response to this disease. She outlined the "conventions of concealment" practiced by physicians and by cancer patients themselves. Physicians concealed the truth from cancer patients, and cancer patients concealed their disease from others, not just because cancer was thought to be a death sentence but because cancer was "felt to be obscene—in the original meaning of that word: ill-omened, abominable, repugnant to the senses."[1] Cancer was a stigma and as such its bearers, in the language of Erving Goffman, were perceived as "blemished," "ritually polluted," and "dangers to the social order."[2]

In *Illness as Metaphor*, Sontag uses the metaphor of "exile to the subterranean land of the diseased" to describe the effects of a normalizing power that, in the theorizing of Michel Foucault, functions by separating, comparing, evaluating, hierarchizing, and banishing to "the external frontiers of the abnormal."[3] In the language of the poet and cancer activist Sandra Steingraber, this normalizing, or stigmatizing, power appears as "the process by which cancer victims [are forced to] adopt the status of the untouchable."[4] And in the language of medical anthropology, the effects of this stigmatizing power appear as "the disease double, . . . the layers of stigma, rejection, fear, and exclusion that attach to a particularly dreaded disease."[5] Whether exiled to subterranean lands, banished to the frontiers of the abnormal, forced to adopt the status of the untouchable, or saddled with disease doubles—these social processes, historically, have forced the cancer patient, "twice victimized, further into the cage of his or her illness: now shunned, silenced, and shamed in addition to being very sick."[6] In *Illness as Metaphor* Sontag does not describe the physical suffering and indignities imposed by cancer. Instead, she paints a picture of the social suffering endured by those who are exiled to "the kingdom of the diseased" and she argues that their suffering is immeasurably compounded by "the lurid metaphors" with which this kingdom has been landscaped by outsiders. Although Sontag vehemently rejects these stigmatizing metaphors, she makes no attempt to replace these with less stigmatizing representations. "It seems unimaginable," writes the artist in 1977, "to aestheticize the disease."

Thus, instead of creating new metaphors to displace the old, Sontag attempts to disband the invading metaphors while issuing a call for cultural silence. In the face of overwhelming stigma and in the absence of an alternative imagination, Sontag places all her hopes for physical salvation and cultural redemption in biomedical science—what she terms "real science." She argues that only scientific understanding and its translation into a medical cure will strip cancer of its lurid meanings, purify it of metaphor, and release its victims from their forced exile to the land of stigma and disease.

In Sontag's vision, medicine and science are cast as heroic forces of liberation; she believes them capable of conquering cancer and eliminating meanings and metaphors without constituting their own.

Sontag's vision of scientific medicine as a force of liberation may seem a bit fantastical, but it was hardly a flight of fancy. In fact, Sontag's dreamscape merged with what cultural historian James Patterson has referred to as "the official dream."[7] This dream achieved its greatest development in the United States—materializing institutionally during the postwar period in the expansion of biomedical research on cancer and gathering additional momentum in the 1970s with the establishment and expansion of the National Cancer Program and its officially declared "War on Cancer."[8] But research on cancer was also enthusiastically pursued by the federally subsidized and increasingly globalized pharmaceutical industry and by networks of privately and publicly funded scientists and research centers dotted across Canada and Western Europe.[9] Research was also pursued by new international formations. In 1965, for example, the International Agency for Research on Cancer (IARC) was established in Lyon, France, under the auspices of the World Health Organization. The IARC primarily concentrated on cancer epidemiology and the development of cancer tumor registries around the world, but this research agenda was supplemented with biological and chemical research carried out in IARC laboratories and, through collaborative research agreements and subcontracting, in research institutes in various other countries.[10] Indeed, during the seventies and eighties, Sontag's dream of salvationist science was lucidly materialized in a growing global network of scientists, in the expansion and proliferation of cancer-related research programs, in the production and circulation of an ever-increasing body of cancer knowledge, and in the growth of a multinational pharmaceutical industry catering to and helping constitute an ever-expanding global market for cancer treatment drugs.[11]

THE WORLD CONFERENCE ON BREAST CANCER: PROJECTING THE GLOBAL ONTO THE LOCAL

The tremendous, albeit unequal growth and expansion of cancer research and medicine was in abundant display in July 1997 as more than 650 delegates from fifty countries descended on Kingston, Canada, to attend the first World Conference on Breast Cancer. What was "first" about this conference was not the international character of its scientific discourse but a different set of border-crossings. Instead of bringing together scientists and clinicians who shared disciplinary perspectives, research programs, and conceptual paradigms, this conference sought to bring together scientists and practitioners from a broad range of cancer-related areas and specializations and combine them with health activists, policy-makers, health care professionals and health educators, public health workers, social scientists, social workers, and, most importantly, women with breast cancer histories—many of whom identified as breast cancer fighters, activists, survivors, and women living with cancer. Many participants wore multiple hats. This blurring of categories was observable, as well, in the organization of panels, plenaries, and workshops, many of which included mixed categories of presenters. But perhaps most significant of all was the fact that, unlike most conferences on cancer, this one was not sponsored by a professional organization with ties to the research establishment or clinical medicine, nor was it underwritten by contributions from the transnational pharmaceutical industry. Instead, it was organized by committed volunteers in Kingston and spearheaded by the efforts of Janet Collins, a lesbian, feminist activist from Kingston who had lost her partner to breast cancer. This organizing cadre was later joined by the resources and sponsorship of the Women's Environment and Development Organization (WEDO)—Bella Abzug's feminist, internationally-active, activist organization. With WEDO's connections and initiative, word of the conference had quickly circulated in international networks of feminist health activists and environmentalists.

The conference was organized thematically. Day One was dedicated to "Research and Medical Treatment," and it focused on biomedical research on medical treatments, as well as breast cancer screening and diagnosis. Day Two was entitled "Caring for the Whole Woman," and it included presentations and workshops on alternative and complementary therapies, social and psychological support, and issues of patient advocacy and empowerment. The theme of Day Three was "Environmental Factors and Breast Cancer," and it addressed many different dimensions of cancer and the environment. There were scientific presentations on electro-magnetic fields, radiation, pesticides, persistent organic pollutants, dioxins, and other endocrine-disrupting chemicals. Other presentations examined the limited abilities of science to address questions of synergy, history, and multiple causation. Still others presented their research on the politics of cancer and analyses of the global cancer industry. The fourth day was devoted to the presentation of testimony to an international public hearing and was conceptualized as the first step in developing and implementing "a global action plan to eradicate breast cancer"—the stated goal of the conference.

As the conference wore on, it was difficult to avoid reaching the conclusion that scientific medicine had failed miserably in its noble quest to conquer cancer. As presentation after presentation made clear, the cancer research establishment, treatment delivery systems, and pharmaceutical corporations were not the only phenomena that had been expanding during the last fifty years. So, too, had the incidence and mortality rates of breast cancer worldwide.[12] Globally, breast cancer was the most common malignancy among women and the number-one killer. The highest breast morality rates

Deaths

cancer incidence rates were reported in Northern European countries and in the United States—with women in the San Francisco Bay Area topping the list. But although the incidence rates were highest in Western, industrialized countries, the rates were rising fastest in the more recently industrializing and chemicalizing countries and among immigrant groups moving to areas with high rates of breast cancer. Although earlier detection was slowing the rise in mortality rates in some population groups, overall and among many populations, mortality rates were either holding steady or continuing to climb. Even in the United States, the country where early detection screening technologies were most extensively used and where investments in cancer research and clinical medicine had been most intense, breast cancer incidence rates continued to rise and could not be fully accounted for by the expansion of screening and early detection. And, although more American women diagnosed with breast cancer were surviving longer after their original diagnoses, the most recent statistics showed that nearly 40 percent of United States women diagnosed with breast cancer had died from the disease within twelve years.[13] This fact, it was pointed out, was conveniently hidden by standard "survival rate" statistics that defined "survival" in terms of five years. And although overall mortality rates in the United States were no longer rising, they also had not improved significantly in twenty-five years—despite the billions of dollars invested in treatment technologies. And still more alarming, breast cancer mortality rates were actually rising for some groups—especially African-American women. Clearly, Sontag's dream of cultural redemption and physical salvation had not arrived on the wings of scientific medicine.

Unlike most scientific conferences, the point of this conference was not to celebrate the development of science and medicine but to make a sober assessment and begin outlining a new direction and a global vision. This was a critical and skeptical assembly of very active participants who did not genuflect to the established cancer orthodoxies. Time and again, they sought to pry open and reconsider the thinking hidden within the black box of biomedicine, and they tirelessly pushed for a broader research vision. They demanded greater access to early detection technologies but at the same time criticized their inadequacy, challenged the dumping of high-radiation mammography machines in third world countries, and questioned the usefulness of high-tech approaches to early detection for countries that lacked the health care infrastructures to make these technologies widely available.

chemicals

And they repeatedly challenged established approaches to public health that focused exclusively on individual bodies while ignoring their toxic environments. They called for policy-makers to adopt "the precautionary principle" and act preventatively on the basis of compelling evidence to end "this uncontrolled human experiment" in which all of the earth's inhabitants were being involuntarily and repeatedly exposed to toxic chemicals and carcinogens.

Indeed, what was in evidence in Kingston, in addition to the incredible buildup of biomedical research, epidemiology, and clinical medicine, was the proliferation of political projects that had developed outside of the institutions of the cancer establishment and biomedicine yet were seeking to transform them. But how in the world did we get from Sontag to Kingston? How did we move from exile and invisibility to the beginnings of a global movement? That is the puzzle this chapter seeks to explain.

The first step toward answering this question begins with the recognition that, although the Kingston conference was a world conference, it was propelled forward by North American breast cancer activism. This does not mean that the conference lacked a global perspective. Indeed, the global vision of the conference was apparent in the attention given to the borderless circulation of dangerous chemicals and carcinogens and the conference's commitment to developing a "Global Action Plan for the Eradication of Breast Cancer." Nor did the conference lack an international perspective. Throughout the conference speakers emphasized that the conditions under which women experienced and made sense of breast cancer varied tremendously both across and within nations and communities. But whereas many North American participants were already linked into national and local movements, many of the participants from outside of North America came to the conference as isolated breast cancer activists in search of information and connections rather than as already networked participants in locally and nationally developed movements.

What became clear was that the conditions for the development of movements around breast cancer did not exist in most places. In most parts of the world, women lacked access to basic health care and faced a broad range of serious health problems exacerbated by poverty. Breast cancer, often considered a disease of old age, was not seen as a top priority. Moreover, in many "developing" countries, cervical cancer posed a far more lethal threat to women than did cancer of the breast. But the obstacles to organizing around breast cancer extended beyond poverty, the demographics of disease, and the structures of health care systems. Even in nation states with elaborate public health and medical care systems, obstacles to addressing the growing epidemic of breast cancer persisted. Beyond the demographics of disease and the political economies of health, the stigma of breast cancer consistently intensified barriers to treatment and early detection. And, although this stigma was differently inflected in different cultures and communities, it uniformly functioned to enforce a code of silence and invisibility. Thus, in addition to these other factors, the stigma of breast cancer presented overwhelming obstacles to mobilizing and globalizing a breast cancer movement.

In order to explain the movement from Sontag to Kingston we need to examine how North American breast cancer movements overcame the obstacle of stigma in order to develop within specific, local conditions.

how did it develop locally.

Indeed, the political visions and activism at the World Conference on Breast Cancer did not emerge, initially, within the context of global connections but at the grassroots level and within local fields of action. What made Kingston possible was the emergence of grassroots activism that *itself* was made possible through the restructuring of stigma. And what gave the Kingston conference its particular three-pronged agenda—biomedical research and early detection; caring for the whole woman; breast cancer and the environment—was the elaboration and crystallization of these issues in specific, largely North American, contexts.

The San Francisco Bay Area offers a unique opportunity to explore both of these dimensions—the restructuring of breast cancer stigma and the development of movements around breast cancer. For the past twenty years, the Bay Area has reported the highest rates of breast cancer in the world and has become known as "the breast cancer capital of the world."[14] In addition to its demographic infamy, however, the Bay Area is known as one of the most vibrant centers of breast cancer activism, and it is one of the first places where women with cancer first began creating the networks and forms of community and began reshaping and publicly resignifying the meanings of this disease.[15] And, although Bay Area activists did not organize the Kingston conference, it was from the Bay Area in particular, and California in general, that the World Conference on Breast Cancer drew one of its largest and most active groups of presenters and participants. Finally, if we turn to the Bay Area, we can see how the three themes that the Kingston conference was organized around have been locally elaborated into three different logics of action.

The remainder of this chapter is divided into two parts. The first part links the development of breast cancer movements to the growth of the United States cancer establishment and the medical-industrial complex. In order to understand the emergence of breast cancer activism, we need to identify and analyze the specific practices that changed the way that breast cancer was experienced and administered. I argue that historical changes in the medical management of women with breast cancer and expansion in the surveillance of healthy populations created new relationships to this disease and that these new relationships—appearing in the form of new subjects, solidarities, and sensibilities—transformed the structure of breast cancer stigma. In transforming the structure of stigma, they created the facilitating conditions for the emergence of breast cancer movements.[16]

In the second and longer part, I explore the specific ways in which these new subjects, solidarities, and sensibilities were drawn upon, reshaped, and resignified within three different Bay Area mobilizations. The first, represented by Race for the Cure®, mobilized the resources of corporate capital, scientific medicine, and the health care industry behind an individualizing biomedical discourse of research and early detection. The second, represented by the Women & Cancer Walk, mobilized a multicultural assortment of women's health organizations behind a feminist discourse that repositioned breast cancer within a broader continuum of women's health concerns, promoted social services for women with cancer, and supported treatment activism. The third, represented by the Toxic Tour of the Cancer Industry, mobilized a network of environmental justice and feminist cancer organizations behind a discourse of cancer prevention. This discourse mapped the global cancer industry as a distinct entity and, in so doing, directly challenged the biomedical focus on research and early detection. Thus, the ingredients that constituted the preconditions of the breast cancer movement reappeared, reshaped, as the foundation of different mobilizations. It was, in other words, the restructuring of stigma that made possible its resignification. I conclude by reflecting on the relationship between local and global movements and outlining two different trajectories of global breast cancer activism.

THE RESTRUCTURING OF STIGMA:
NEW SUBJECTS, SOLIDARITIES, SENSIBILITIES

Beginning in the 1970s, the way in which breast cancer was managed—both within and outside of the medical clinic—began to undergo a series of transformations. Within the medical clinic, three sets of analytically distinct, although chronologically overlapping, changes in the diagnosis, treatment, and rehabilitation of women with breast cancer redefined the role of breast cancer patient-subjects and repositioned them within the medical care system. And, within the vast expanse of terrain that lay outside the medical clinic, a fourth process expanded and accelerated into the healthy, or "asymptomatic" populations of women, changing the way that breast cancer was surveilled, administered, and anticipated. Taken together, these changes both within and outside the walls of the medical clinic transformed the structure of stigma in ways that facilitated the development of breast cancer movements. These four processes and their significance are outlined below.

Prior to the 1980s, when a woman was diagnosed with a suspicious breast lesion, she would enter the hospital for a surgical diagnostic biopsy and, if the surgeon determined with the aid of the pathologist that the lesion was malignant, the surgeon would proceed with an immediate breast amputation—a mastectomy—while the patient was still under general anesthesia. This was known as the one-step procedure, and it meant that a woman—often reassured of the implausibility of breast cancer before undergoing surgery—awoke afterwards to face not only a diagnosis of breast cancer, but an already performed radical breast amputation. During the eighties, however, this procedure began to change. Prompted by the activism of an ex-breast cancer patient, Rose Kushner, and the public testimony of others, breast cancer informed-consent legislation was proposed in twenty-two states and adopted, during the eighties, in fourteen.[17] California was the second state to adopt such legislation and did so in 1980—one year after the National Cancer Institute issued an official advisory recommending that surgical biopsies be separated from surgical treatment.[18] The separation of breast cancer diagnoses from surgical treatment within the space of the clinic helped reconstitute breast cancer patients as medical citizens. Instead of being positioned as the passive and anesthetized objects—the "docile bodies"—of the omnipotent surgeon's gaze, breast cancer patients gained the right to "gaze back" at their physicians and to participate in their treatment as conscious, speaking subjects.[19]

During the mid-eighties, the space that had opened up for patient participation continued to expand. Halsted radical mastectomies gradually gave way to less radical mastectomies and expanded further to include a variety of breast-conserving surgeries.[20] As in other things, the Bay Area was at the forefront of the trend toward breast-conserving surgeries.[21] The expansion of surgical repertoires created, for growing numbers of women, the possibility and even the obligation of making choices about their surgical treatment.

Also during the eighties, treatment shifted away from surgery alone, or surgery followed by radiation therapy, and began increasingly to incorporate chemotherapy. Although chemotherapy had long been used to treat women with advanced (metastatic) breast cancer, it was increasingly incorporated into the treatment regimens of women with earlier stage disease.[22] The increasing incorporation of adjuvant therapies—namely, radiation, chemotherapy, and hormone therapy—not only multiplied the treatment possibilities, but also prolonged the treatment experience. No longer did women enter the hospital for a single surgical procedure and leave, several days later, as officially rehabilitated ex-patients. Now, in addition to undergoing a mastectomy or breast-conserving surgery, breast cancer patients could expect to return to the medical facility for repeated follow-up sessions. Several weeks of daily radiation were often added to months and months of systemic chemotherapy. Tamoxifen, a hormone therapy developed by Zeneca Pharmaceuticals and originally used to treat women with metastatic breast cancer, was increasingly incorporated into the treatment regimens of women with earlier stage disease and prescribed, either with or without chemotherapy, for a period of between two and five years.[23] These adjuvant therapies not only involved the penetration of treatment further into women's bodies and the production of often debilitating side-effects, especially with chemotherapy, but they also further deepened the role of the breast cancer patient by prolonging it, expanding it into new terrain, and demanding its repeated re-enactment.

As the role of the breast cancer patient underwent redefinition, it also underwent a process of repositioning. The incorporation of adjuvant therapies into standard treatment regimens resulted in the multiplication of cancer specialists and health care professionals. As this occurred, breast cancer patients were repositioned at the hub of a much larger circle of activity. Now, instead of a relationship with her breast cancer surgeon alone, breast cancer patients became involved in a much larger network of relationships. Patients moved from site to site and from appointment to appointment, consulting with surgeons, hematology oncologists, and radiation oncologists. They interacted, as well, with a wider array of nurses, technicians, and even social workers. And, in the Bay Area, the proliferation of cancer specialists and health care professionals was further complicated by the rise of alternative and complementary therapies and practitioners. As a result, for growing numbers of women, being a breast cancer patient became, at least temporarily, a full-time occupation. Taken together, the proliferation of specialists and treatment modalities further undermined the omnipotence of the breast cancer surgeon and repositioned the breast cancer patient-subject within a much more complex series of linkages and flows of information. Thus, the subjectivity of the breast cancer patient, instead of being produced through brief interactions with her surgeon, was reconfigured within a broader set of relationships. The omnipotent gaze of the surgeon was replaced with a polyvalent gaze that included different specialists, but included, as well, the coordinating gaze of the breast cancer patient.

And finally, the space of patient participation, once created, continued to expand as the medical management of women with breast cancer changed in a third and perhaps even more significant dimension. In addition to the aforementioned changes in diagnosis and treatment, a significant shift occurred in approaches to patient rehabilitation. In the mid-eighties, cancer support groups began to proliferate in the San Francisco Bay Area.[24] First developed outside of and at the margins of biomedicine, support groups gradually became institutionalized as an adjuvant therapy and rehabilitative technology in the Bay Area medical care system.[25] If we think of breast cancer informed-consent legislation as establishing the rights of breast cancer patients to be informed consumers and decision-makers, then the proliferation of support groups and their institutionalization signified the actual expression of that right.

Support groups, initially resisted by physicians, marked a sea change in institutionalized approaches to breast cancer patient rehabilitation. Earlier rehabilitative programs, such as Reach to Recovery and Look Good/Feel Better, were implemented by the American Cancer Society and were dependent upon the approval of an attending physician.[26] These programs emphasized a cosmetic approach to dealing with the disease, discouraged the formation of ongoing relationships with other breast cancer patients and "mastectomees," trained women to hide the evidence of their breast cancer treatments and histories, and encouraged women to quickly return to their former identities and rejoin the "normal" population of women. Within these programs, ACS volunteers were forbidden from offering medical advice to their clients, passing on information about treatments or physicians, or sharing their opinions.[27]

During the late eighties and nineties, while the Reach to Recovery and Look Good/Feel Better programs continued to expand, support groups appeared alongside them and, without displacing them, began to disrupt certain aspects of the normalization process that these ACS programs were designed to produce. Support groups expanded and deepened the space available for the formation of patient subjectivities, but they did so in a radically new way. For the first time, spaces were created that directly challenged and reconfigured the structures of patient individualization, isolation, silence, and invisibility. They did so through the simple act of bringing patients together in a common space and time and thus facilitating the creation of multiple, ongoing, lateral ties among breast cancer patients. Support groups repositioned patients within an even larger hub of activity and further multiplied an already polyvalent gaze—changing its direction from exclusively up and down, to up and down and sideways.

Support groups pooled the knowledge and experience of their members and facilitators. Participants exchanged information about doctors and treatments, shared experiences, thoughts, feelings, and reactions; validated and affirmed one another's struggles and successes; encouraged each other to get second and third opinions, and to challenge their physicians, insurance companies, and health care providers. Through support groups, breast cancer patients learned how to navigate their way through administrative barriers and mystifying procedures. They learned about clinical trials, experimental procedures, scientific studies, medical databases, alternative treatments, and complementary therapies. They learned about cancer web sites, electronic discussion groups, and listserves. In short, what they acquired, in these spaces, was a sense of being part of a group, a body of knowledge and a set of skills for acquiring information, and a sense of entitlement as breast cancer patients.

Although support groups differed along a number of dimensions and individual women turned to them and away from them for different reasons, it would be difficult to overestimate the significance of their existence, their proliferation, and their gradual institutionalization within the Bay Area medical care system. Support groups shattered the institutionalized barriers that separated women with breast cancer from one another and replaced these with new relationships, emotional support, social connections, flows of information, the development of new languages and bodies of knowledge, a sense of "groupness," solidarity, and new sensitivities.

Unlike the practices of individually-oriented rehabilitation programs which encouraged women to dis-identify, dissociate, and distance themselves from their experience as breast cancer patients, support groups were oriented toward integration in a double sense. First, isolated patients were integrated into one space and time, but second, the experience of breast cancer was integrated into the self—or subjectivity—of the breast cancer patient. Instead of being positioned as an isolated event that was left behind, breast cancer was woven into new relationships, many of which endured beyond the space and time of treatment. And, as disavowal and dissociation were replaced with connection and integration, the institutionalization of support groups created an ever-widening circle of women with new and enduring group identities.

In addition to the transformation of the breast cancer patient-subject within the space of the clinic, an equally significant transformation occurred outside the walls of clinical medicine. In the 1970s, mammography—an X-ray technology that had been used erratically since the fifties to visualize already identified breast lesions—began being used as a technology for screening asymptomatic populations of women.[28] In 1973 the American Cancer Society (ACS) and the National Cancer Institute (NCI) launched the Breast Cancer Detection Demonstration Project (BCDDP), the first major "field campaign" in the newly declared "War on Cancer."[29] Designed as a mammography public relations and educational campaign rather than a scientific study, the "demonstration project" enrolled over 275,000 women over the age of thirty-five for five years of free clinical exams and screening mammograms at twenty-seven medical centers around the country.[30] By the time it concluded in 1978, the BCDDP had received both positive and negative publicity and it had ignited a series of public debates and controversies about mammography, some of which are still with us today.[31] But it also, and most importantly—despite the volatile debates it engendered—introduced growing segments of the female population to the concept, and increasingly the practice, of self-surveillance and mammographic screenings for breast cancer.

Although the movement of the "mammographic gaze" into the public sphere was initiated during the seventies, the mammographic screening of healthy populations expanded rapidly during the eighties and nineties.[32] A two-pronged campaign initiated by the ACS directed educational efforts to physicians, on the one hand, and women as consumers of medical services, on the other. Both prongs emphasized the holy trinity of early detection practices—breast self-exams, clinical breast exams, and screening mammograms.[33] While this was underway, private industry developed its own early detection campaigns. During the mid-eighties, mammography equipment companies such as General Electric and DuPont (manufacturers of mammography machines and the film that they use) initiated their own series of campaigns, advertising in women's magazines, newspapers, and other media.[34] And, in 1985, National Breast Cancer Awareness Month (NBCAM) was invented by Imperial Chemical Industries (ICI)—a British manufacturer of plastics, pesticides, and pharmaceutical drugs. NBCAM was later taken over by its subsidiary Zeneca Pharmaceuticals, manufacturers of tamoxifen, the best-selling breast cancer treatment drug in the world. Every October since 1984, NBCAM—which is now supported and endorsed by more than seventeen governmental, professional, and medical organizations, including the National Cancer Institute, the American College of Radiology, and the Susan G. Komen Breast Cancer Research Foundation— organizes a massive campaign and media blitz that promotes the message of mammographic screenings and early detection. Although, over the years, NBCAM and other early detection campaigns have made exaggerated claims about the benefits and dependability of mammography, used misleading slogans that substituted the language of prevention for the possibility of earlier detection, and have targeted younger women—the group for which no benefit of screening has ever been definitively established— the circulation of the discourse of early detection has been very successful in reaching an ever-widening audience of women.[35]

During the eighties, the expansion of mammography as a screening technology was particularly successful in the Bay Area and particularly among middle-class white women. As in other parts of the country, breast cancer incidence rates jumped suddenly during the mid-eighties as more women began getting screened. The rates then settled back down to a slow but consistent creep upward.[36] And between 1987 and 1994 in California, the rates of screening mammography continued to rise steadily among all racial categories.[37]

By the early 1990s, early detection campaigns had moved the possibility and even the anticipation, of breast cancer into the psyches and practices of growing numbers of women, especially middle-class white women. The expansion of early detection practices transformed normal breasts into suspect purveyors of disease, healthy women into asymptomatic patients, and entire female populations into populations "at-risk." As the imaging technology of mammography improved, it also repositioned growing numbers of screened women who received "suspicious" or "abnormal" mammograms within ambiguous categories. Some of these women watched and waited, others underwent further diagnostic procedures and biopsies of their lesions—most of which turned out to be benign. But some of these biopsies resulted in the diagnosis of conditions that were not well understood and for which clinical treatment was uncertain.[38] Increasing numbers of women thus entered into liminal sorts of "higher risk" and "precancerous" statuses in which they were forced to choose between prophylactic treatments such as mastectomy and/or hormone therapy, or years of intensified surveillance, anxiety, and waiting.[39]

Thus, the effects of mammographic screening extended far beyond the thousands of women whose breast cancers were ultimately discovered. The millions of women who received "normal" mammograms were reconstituted as always at risk and taught to practice self-surveillance and hyper-vigilance. Every suspicious mammogram and each benign breast condition and every diagnosis with an unclear prognosis created another woman *without* breast cancer but whose life—whose psyche and body—had become more deeply entangled in the breast cancer apparatus. The acceptance and practice of breast cancer screening in the Bay Area thus made more permeable and ambiguous the rigid borders that had formerly separated the relatively small numbers of women who were *inside* the medical machinery of breast cancer from the vast majority of women who remained *outside* of it. Ultimately, then, what emerged were new relationships to breast cancer: rigid separations were replaced by shifting positions on a disease continuum and the future that every woman sought to avoid was searched for and anticipated within the lived present.

Together, these new relationships carved out a space for the formation of new subjectivities. They created new flows of information, new social connections, and new forms of solidarity. And they created new sensibilities—a heightened sense of risk and vulnerability and a greater involvement in the practices of breast cancer surveillance and risk management among ostensibly cancer-free women. It was these developments that restructured the stigma of breast cancer and created fertile soil for the grassroots mobilizations that ensued. As the decade of the nineties wore on, federal and state programs were developed and implemented in California that extended early detection campaigns into populations of medically marginalized women, especially within the overlapping categories of poor and uninsured women, older women, and women of color.[40] These developments further expanded the populations of asymptomatic women incorporated into the breast cancer apparatus and reconstituted them as risky subjects.

Out of these conditions emerged dedicated activists, concerned participants, and receptive audiences. Each strand of activism in the Bay Area— represented by Race for the Cure, the Women & Cancer Walk, and the Toxic Tour of the Cancer Industry—built upon the foundation created by these changing breast cancer and breast health practices and drew upon the material and discursive resources of pre-existing industries and social movement communities. Race for the Cure drew upon the medical-industrial complex, corporate cultures, and the beauty, fitness, and fashion industries. The Women & Cancer Walk drew upon the women's health movement and AIDS activism. And the Toxic Tour drew upon feminist cancer activism and joined it to the environmental justice movement. Each form of activism sought to appeal to and reshape these emergent subjectivities, solidarities, and sensibilities, and each movement defined itself according to the different ways in which it did so.

THE SAN FRANCISCO RACE FOR THE CURE

It is a beautiful October morning in San Francisco and, over the next few hours, nine thousand individuals, families, friends, corporate running teams, and corporate sponsors will gather together and engage in a participatory public ritual that honors and celebrates the lives of women with breast cancer—from past, present, and future generations.[41] As they do so, they will raise $400,000 as a symbol of their support for scientific research and breast cancer early detection practices. By the end of 1996, more than sixty Race for the Cure events will have been held across the country. This one, like many others, falls during National Breast Cancer Awareness Month and complements the NBCAM agenda.[42]

In Golden Gate Park, the atmosphere of a carnival prevails. The sixth annual Race for the Cure, sponsored by the Susan G. Komen Breast Cancer Foundation, is coming to life. Corporate booths line the outskirts of Sharon Meadow. Inside the booths, staffers hawk their wares. Dressed in running attire, thousands of women, children, and men meander about. The crowd is about three-quarters white and three-quarters women, most of whom are towing clear plastic *Vogue* bags that contain free hair products, cosmetics, lotions, and perfumes. The bags are rapidly filling up with more free items—pins displaying the newly issued breast cancer awareness postage stamp, pink ribbons, and breast self-exam brochures. A brochure from Tropicana Orange Juice, one of the national sponsors of the Race, offers some encouraging news about how to avoid breast cancer. We're told: "Don't gamble with the odds. If you play it smart, you can beat them." Tropicana even provides a set of diet tips and orange juice recipes to help us do it. The brochure explains that being overweight and not getting enough vitamin C are "risk factors" for the development of breast cancer.

In addition to the booths of the corporate sponsors (Chevron, Genentech, J. C. Penney, American Airlines, Ford, Pacific Bell, *Vogue,* Nordstrom, Wells Fargo, BankAmerica), the medical care industry is in attendance: Kaiser Permanente, California Pacific, Davies Medical Center, UCSF (University of California, San Francisco)–Mount Zion Hospital, the UCSF Mobile Mammography Van, Marin General Hospital, and others. In an increasingly competitive industry and in the breast cancer capital of the world, breast cancer is a big-ticket item. The last few years have witnessed a whirlwind of sales, closures, and mergers, and many of the medical centers that remain have reorganized their services and repackaged their messages to better appeal to the concerns and demands of these female baby-boomer consumers. One "breast health" center distributes an eleven-page handout listing thirty-four services, groups, and programs for women with breast cancer and breast health concerns.

Last but certainly not least, the fitness, nutrition, beauty, and fashion industries are here in spades. They offer an amazing array of services and top-of-the-line accessories tailored to the special needs of women in treatment for cancer and women who have survived breast cancer treatments. There are nutrition consultants, fitness experts, and hair stylists. There are special lotions and cremes. There are special swimsuits, wigs, scarves, make-up, clothing, and vitamins. There are customized breast prostheses, beginning at $2,100, that are created from the cast of a woman's breast before it is surgically removed. There are partial prostheses for women with less radical surgeries. And, for the more active crowd, there are sports bras, biker pants, and baseball caps—with or without attached ponytails. There is a lot of sexy lingerie. And in a stroke of marketing genius, one women's fashion catalogue weds the breast cancer patient's pursuit of femininity to the baby boomers' feminist sensibilities. The cover of the catalogue features a quote attributed to Simone de Beauvoir: "One is not born a woman, one becomes one." Inside the catalogue are means of (re)becoming a woman—prostheses, lingerie, ponytails, and fitness wear.

Adding to the festive atmosphere are the shiny new automobiles parked in the middle of the meadow and adorned with balloons, courtesy of Ford and Lincoln-Mercury dealerships—national sponsors of the Race. In every direction, purple and aqua balloons dance in the air. Also bobbing about in the crowds and easily noticeable from a distance are women in bright pink visors. These visors signal a special status and are worn with pride. On each visor, below the corporate logos, the following message is stitched in black: "I'm a survivor." The visors are being distributed from a special booth, situated in the center of the meadow—the Breast Cancer Survivors' Station. Here, more than a dozen queues have formed with women standing six deep, chatting, socializing, and awaiting their turn to receive the complimentary pink visors that mark them as breast cancer survivors. As each woman dons her visor and mingles with the crowd, she proudly, voluntarily, and publicly marks herself as a breast cancer survivor. This is an act of social disobedience—a collective "coming out," a rejection of stigma and invisibility. Later, after the Race has been run and walked, there is an official ceremony during which all the breast cancer survivors who wish to be recognized are asked to ascend the main stage. They are honored for their courage in fighting breast cancer and for their willingness to demonstrate to other women, through their rejection of the cultural code of silence and invisibility, that breast cancer is not shameful, that it is survivable, and that it is not disfiguring or defeminizing.

One way of publicly remembering and honoring women with breast cancer is provided at the registration tables. Instead of the standard numbered forms pinned to the backs of the contestants, participants can choose to wear "In Honor of" and "In Memory of" forms displaying the names of women—both living and dead—whom they wish to publicly honor and acknowledge or mourn and remember. These forms are pink instead of the standard white. They mark their wearers with a particular status. In choosing to display these forms, the exhibitors identify themselves as part of the expanding circle of those whose lives have been touched by breast cancer. These moving exhibits generate powerful effects. Watching, running, or walking in the Race, one encounters the pink signs here, there, and everywhere. They are powerful visual reminders of the pervasiveness of this disease. They are symbols that generate strong emotions and solidarity. The practice of wearing a sign is a way of enacting community, including oneself in this sea of runners who have suffered, personally or vicariously, from this disease and who are working together to raise awareness of breast cancer and money for mammograms and a cure. These signs embody the public display of private triumphs and losses. Wearing them is a collective act at once painful, brave, and hopeful.

There are three more ways in which breast cancer is visually coded, packaged, and displayed. All three are stationed at one end of the meadow, apart from the booths. The first display is in the form of a large vertical cloth banner. The banner is imprinted with thousands of pink ribbons—the symbol of breast cancer awareness. Many of these ribbons are filled in with handwritten names. Everyone is invited to write a name on a ribbon. The second display is "The Breast Cancer Quilt." Modeled after the AIDS Quilt but in smaller dimensions, the project consists of many quilts—and there are several on display—each containing approximately twenty twelve-by-fourteen-inch panels. Unlike the AIDS Quilt, however, which recognizes those who have died, the Breast Cancer Quilt recognizes survival. Each panel is created by a breast cancer survivor—or by a woman who, at least at the time of the quilt-making, was a survivor. Not far from the Breast Cancer Quilt is the "Wall of Hope." This display contains a long series of panels. Each panel is comprised of fifteen eight-by-ten-inch "glamour photos" of breast cancer survivors. The survivors are photographed in full make-up and adorned in brightly colored evening gowns, sparkling jewelry, and even feather boas. Almost all of the survivors are white. Dark-skinned women stand out in a sea of light faces, their visages poorly captured by a photographer accustomed to working with lighter hues. Each woman is identified by name and by year of diagnosis or by number of years of survival. Frozen in time, all of these women are "survivors"—even those, unidentified, who are now dead.

The message of the official program, conducted on a stage by a woman in a pink visor, is clear and concise: the cure for breast cancer lies in two directions—bio-medical research and early detection. The audience is informed that the San Francisco chapter of the Komen Foundation—sponsors of this Race and sixty-six others being organized by local chapters throughout the country—has contributed more money for breast cancer research, screening, and early detection than any other private organization dedicated solely to breast cancer in the world. The audience learns that the

Susan G. Komen Breast Cancer Foundation was established in 1982 by Nancy Brinker in memory of her sister, Suzy, who died from breast cancer at age thirty-six. "Back then," says the speaker, "there was no follow-up therapy, no radiation, no chemotherapy, no pill." Those were the dark ages of medicine.

The speaker continues with her story of individual control and medical progress: Nancy Brinker learned from her sister's experience "that early detection is the key." This knowledge served her well. As a result, she was vigilant and proactive in her own "breast health practices" and was soon thereafter diagnosed with early-stage breast cancer. She is now a survivor. This is a success story. The speaker concludes: "This is what every woman here needs to know. All women should get a baseline mammogram at age thirty-five, every two years after age forty, and yearly after age fifty. And every woman should practice monthly breast self-exam." The message here is clear: bio-medical research has led to advances in breast cancer treatments that, in combination with breast self-exam and mammography, are saving a new generation of breast cancer patients and transforming them into breast cancer survivors.

This is the archetypal story of Race for the Cure and Breast Cancer Awareness Month. It is a story of individual triumph and agency. There is nothing sad or tragic about Brinker's encounter with breast cancer. Responsibility exists solely in the context of detection, not within the realm of causation. In fact, questions of causality are unspeakable within the terms of this discourse. The Brinker narrative is a story of unqualified success. It is also, of course, a story of failure, and in this sense it serves as a cautionary tale. Brinker's sister Suzy was not aware of or did not practice early detection. Suzy's breast cancer was diagnosed too late. She did not receive radiation or chemotherapy. She died. In this morality tale the proactive survive and the irresponsible and unaware die. In the discourse of the Race, survival is a matter of individual choice and responsibility. Mammograms never fail to diagnose breast cancer early and women diagnosed early never die. And for those who practice breast health, breast cancer may constitute a momentary setback, but it is no longer a debilitating, recurring, or chronic disease. In the discourse of the Race, breast cancer is part of each survivor's historical biography. A finished chapter. Thus the story told by Race for the Cure to the participants gathered together is a story of individual control and empowerment, a narrative of hope, and a declaration of faith in the steady progress of science and medicine.

THE BAY AREA WOMEN & CANCER WALK

It is a cold fall morning in San Francisco.[43] Gradually a crowd of between six and eight hundred assembles in front of a makeshift stage in Golden Gate Park. This is the fifth annual Women & Cancer Walk. Like the Race for the

Cure, this is a fund-raiser and a celebration of community and solidarity. The money raised by these walkers, however, does not go to breast cancer research or to fund the UCSF Mobile Mammography Van. Instead, the proceeds—which totaled $115,000 the previous year—are evenly divided among a multicultural set of health organizations, twelve in all, and are loosely earmarked for any project or purpose that benefits women with any type of cancer, not just cancer of the breast. Like Race for the Cure, the Women & Cancer Walk is held in Sharon Meadow. But in such an expansive meadow, eight hundred feels like a small group. At the Race, this meadow easily accommodated nine thousand participants.

But this crowd is different from the Race crowd in other respects as well. Like those at the Race, the vast majority of the participants, perhaps three-quarters, are white women. But although the Race crowd appears to draw most of its participants from the corporate sector, most of the participants of the Women & Cancer Walk do not look like middle-class married professionals. Both the Race and the Walk are dominated by white women in their forties and fifties, but the majority of the women at the Walk appear to hail from different political and cultural locations. This event has a different feel to it and a different visual impact. At the Walk, there is a strong feminist, lesbian, queer, and countercultural presence. It is signaled by styles of dress, hair, adornment, and body language, and by the decentering of emphasized Anglo heterofemininity. At the Walk, there are women with obvious disabilities, large women, women for whom walking a mile will be an effort and for whom running a race would be out of the question. There are relatively few women in brand-name fitness wear. There are women with multiple piercings and women with tattoos. There are women with dreadlocks, very short hair, and no hair at all. There are couples and some children in evidence, but the children are just as likely to be accompanied by two moms as by a mom and a dad. Unlike the Race, at the Walk women of color are visible as volunteers, performers, and participants, although their numbers are small for a city as racially and culturally diverse as San Francisco.

Several folding tables line one side of the meadow with signs crowded together that are blowing over repeatedly, each identifying one of the thirteen beneficiary organizations. The beneficiaries include three feminist cancer organizations and six women's health advocacy organizations—two Latina, two African-American, one Vietnamese, and one older women's. The beneficiaries also include three community health clinics—one lesbian, one Native American, and one serving a cross-section of poor people in San Francisco's Mission neighborhood. But, although the Walk tries to construct a multicultural and multiracial community, the links within this community are visibly weak. Several of the beneficiary organizations are present in name only.

Except for a small Kaiser Permanente table set off by itself, the health care industry is entirely absent. There is no trace of the beauty, fashion, fitness, banking, chemical, and pharmaceutical industries. Although one panel of the Breast Cancer Quilt is on display, the Wall of Hope exhibit of glamour photos is absent. Pink ribbons signifying breast cancer awareness are not in evidence, although a number of women are wearing the "Cancer Sucks" button distributed by Breast Cancer Action. There are no pink visors. What seems to be emphasized in the context of the Walk is not the specialness and separateness of women with cancer histories, but their unremarkable typicality. Nonetheless, it is possible to identify some women who have experienced cancer treatments. Beneath the T-shirts and sweatshirts of these women it is possible to discern the outline of one breast, but not two.

Even to the untrained eye, it is impossible to miss the lingering evidence of breast cancer inscribed on the body of one participant. RavenLight, a local activist who was honored last year as one of five "Walkers of Courage," moves about greeting friends and fans. She is bedecked in a tight white and black dress with a red belt, black hose, and high heels. Hardly a display of normative femininity, however, one side of her bodice is pulled down and secured in back to reveal a smooth surface traversed by a thin scar where her right breast used to be. The absence of one breast is exaggerated by the fullness of the breast that remains. She is a lesbian breast cancer activist and an ambassador of exhibitionism. In a manner quite different from the way that Race for the Cure connects breast cancer to femininity and heterosexuality, RavenLight unabashedly displays and celebrates the enduring sexuality of one-breasted women.

For the past couple of years, Walkers of Courage have been named and honored on stage. Sometimes they are women with breast cancer in their recent history. Just as often they are women currently living with advanced disease. But always, they are women who are singled out for their service and activism rather than for their survival. Last year, Gracia Buffleben, a woman then living with advanced metastatic breast cancer, was honored as a Walker of Courage. During the previous year, Buffleben and a handful of local breast cancer activists had worked with AIDS activists from ACT UP Golden Gate (AIDS Coalition to Unleash Power) to graft ACT UP tactics onto breast cancer activism.[44] In December they had organized an act of civil disobedience against Genentech, a powerful Bay Area biotech company, in order to win access, on the principle of "compassionate use," to a promising new drug then in the final phase of clinical trials. When Buffleben ascended the Women & Cancer Walk stage to accept her award, ACT UP activists, dressed in their uniform of black T-shirts, stood behind her holding signs emblazoned with rows of gravestones. The signs read: "Don't Go Quietly to the Grave. Scream for Compassionate Use!" In form and structure, this ceremony was no different from Race for the Cure's onstage recognition of breast cancer survivors. The contrast in images and meanings, however, was striking: black replaced pink; death replaced life; anger replaced gratitude.

As in previous years, the Walk's program is deliberately multicultural and multiracial—more so than the audience. Sign language interpretation is provided on stage. Music is provided by Tuck and Patti—a mixed-race couple, performers in the jazz music scene. The program is kicked off by an Afro-Brazilian dancer and masseuse who leads a pre-walk warm-up. San Francisco Mayor Willie Brown is next, and he begins by promoting the upcoming Mayor's Summit on Breast Cancer and ends by promoting prostate cancer awareness. He is followed by a speaker from the Native American Health Center—one of two main speakers. She speaks about the large Native American community in Oakland, a community that she is a part of, and she describes the lack of access to basic health and cancer support services. She then describes the uses to which the money donated to her health center by the Women & Cancer Walk has been put. These funds paid for cab fare to the hospital for a woman receiving chemotherapy who was too sick to take the bus across town to the public hospital. They paid for phone service for a woman dying of cancer so that she could talk to her family in the Southwest during her final weeks of life. They bought Christmas toys for the children of a third woman with cancer. They paid for a therapist for a fourth woman who was trying to come to terms with her imminent death. And they helped pay the burial expenses of another. Each woman's story is narrated with respect and compassion.

These are stories of desperation, complications, hardship, loss, and death. The subjects of these stories do not speak for themselves: they are spoken of by another. But they are spoken of, and discursively constituted, as women with complex lives, commitments, and responsibilities; these are women with their own needs, histories, priorities, and desires. They are individuals, but individuals embedded within particular cultures, classes, and communities. These women are not passive and they are not irresponsible—even if they are struggling with and dying from cancer. The speaker makes clear that their lives are lived in a vortex of multiple institutionalized inequalities and that cancer is just one of many obstacles they have faced. Perhaps some of these women will become long-term survivors, but this is not where the logic of the narrative leads. This is not a discourse of individual choice and responsibility. This is not a story of hope, survival, and triumph over adversity. This is a discourse of harsh realities, poverty, and medical marginalization.

Although the Women & Cancer Walk focuses on services, advocacy, and treatment activism for women with cancer, during the last three years the event has begun to emphasize the importance of the environment as a cause of deteriorating health and rising rates of cancer. The keynote address is delivered by an Italian woman, a cancer and environmental activist who tells a series of stories about real people in faraway places, weaving together the global connections between rising cancer rates, profit-driven industries, and environmental racism. She connects struggles against environmental pollution in the Bay Area to the struggles of communities in Mexico, Italy, and elsewhere. She constructs a hopeful story about a global struggle against the cancer industry. And she identifies herself as an activist with the Toxic Links Coalition.

THE TOXIC TOUR OF THE CANCER INDUSTRY

Just before noon on a crisp October day in downtown San Francisco, a boisterous crowd has gathered on Market Street in front of Chevron's corporate headquarters.[45] Metal barriers and uniformed police line the sidewalk and street, separating the courtyard and sidewalk traffic from the approximately 150 protesters who are assembling on the other side to kick off the third annual Toxic Tour of the Cancer Industry. As at the Race and the Walk, about three-quarters of the participants are women and three-quarters are white. But a majority of the speakers will be people of color and, in contrast to the Race and the Walk, men are equally positioned as speaking subjects at this event. A large banner identifies the organizers of the Toxic Tour. It reads: "Toxic Links Coalition. United for Health and Environmental Justice." Although neither the name of the coalition nor the slogan on this banner refers explicitly to cancer, the majority of the visual signs and signifiers do. The main theme of the tour—"Stop Cancer Where It Starts! Stop Corporate Pollution!"—is written across a large banner that occupies center stage.

As the Tour proceeds, each and every speaker along the way will create discursive linkages between the rising rates of cancer and the targets of the Toxic Tour—Chevron, the American Cancer Society, Pacific Gas & Electric, United States Senator Dianne Feinstein, Burson Marsteller (a public relations firm), and Bechtel (a builder of nuclear power plants). But these targets are just convenient symbols of what the Tour's organizers characterize as "the cancer industry": they are local outposts of a much larger and interlocking system. During the next hour, these activists will make repeated references to breast cancer, some of them self-referential, but they will consistently connect breast cancer to cancer in general, and to other environmentally related health problems. Within this discourse, breast cancer is positioned as the canary in the coal mine. It is one among many escalating health problems. These health problems will be redefined by the Toxic Links Coalition as human rights abuses rather than individual medical disorders, and they will be discursively linked to the cancer industry. Through the delivery of speeches, the display of signs, and the movement from site to site, the cancer industry as an entity will be physically mapped and conceptually constructed—brought to life and materialized through the performance of the Toxic Tour.

The Toxic Tour kicks off at Chevron and begins by ceremoniously replacing National Breast Cancer Awareness Month (NBCAM) with a different public relations campaign: Cancer Industry Awareness Month. NBCAM is exposed as a public relations campaign started in 1985 by Zeneca, a pharmaceutical and chemical corporation that manufacturers the pesticides that contribute to the breast cancer epidemic, produces the breast cancer drugs that treat it, and owns the cancer centers that distribute drug prescriptions. All of the speakers shift the focus from the biomedical geography of individual women's bodies that is promoted by NBCAM to the political geography of the cancer industry.[46]

Nancy Evans, a white woman who speaks on behalf of Breast Cancer Action, the Toxic Links Coalition, and the National Coalition for Health and Environmental Justice, delivers the first short speech:

> We're here because America has lost the war on cancer. Despite twenty-five years and more than thirty billion dollars, cancer incidence is up 18 percent, mortality is up 8 percent. Breast cancer is only a symptom of this larger epidemic, but every day in the Bay Area twelve women are newly diagnosed with breast cancer, and three women die of breast cancer, and every one of those is one too many. Cancer kills half a million people every year in this country. It kills somebody every minute, and by the year 2000 it's gonna be the leading cause of death. So we're here today to tell the truth about cancer—that cancer starts in the boardrooms of corporate America and in the boardrooms of PR [public relations] agencies who are paid to cover up the crimes of corporate America. If I shoot somebody and kill them, I go to jail. But if a corporation poisons a whole community, they go on doing business as usual. Cancer is a multi-billion dollar industry, and many of the same corporations who are making pesticides and herbicides and other cancer-causing chemicals are also making drugs to treat cancer. . . . It's time to take back our communities. . . . Stop the poisoning!

Interestingly enough, although Evans identifies herself with three organizations, she does not foreground her own history with breast cancer or identify herself, in this instance, as a "breast cancer survivor." Instead, like many other speakers throughout the day, she shifts attention away from her individual story in order to foreground a narrative about the cancer industry. Throughout the Tour, when speakers refer to their individual cancer histories, they do so with outrage and anger, rather than with pride and the sense of accomplishment. Instead of calling herself a survivor, for example, Essie Mormen, an African-American activist, begins her speech by explaining that it is difficult for her to step up to the speaker's platform because "it's hard to move these days since getting this disease and being tired all the time." She then continues with a narrative quite different from the Race's narrative of survival: "I'm very suspicious of pesticides because my mother died from breast cancer, I just lost my brother, . . . and I'm probably dying from it too! So let's act! . . . We ain't gonna take this anymore!" Other speakers refer to themselves as "cancer victims" and women "living with cancer," thus constructing cancer as an ongoing struggle rather than a story of triumph.

The Toxic Tour is choreographed so that each stop along the way constitutes a link in the chain of the cancer industry. Because good public images are highly valued commodities, the Toxic Tour uses the only weapon it has at its disposal: the Tour attempts to generate negative publicity and sully corporate images. This is a smear campaign, a strategy of public shaming, an attack on corporate images. At each stop along the way, a culprit is identified and its name is bellowed out over a bullhorn. Henry Clark, an African-American activist with the Richmond, California-based West County Toxics Coalition, stands in front of Chevron and condemns them for "profiting at our expense!" He explains that Chevron's incinerators spew dioxins and other toxins into his community, poisoning them, causing cancer, and destroying their health. The goal of the Tour—which is chanted over and over again—is to "Make the Link!" and Clark's narrative is representative of those that will follow. The Toxic Tour makes no attempt to engage in conversation or compromise. There are clear lines separating "us" from "them." And if there is any doubt, these lines are reinforced by the uniformed police escort and barricades. This is ritualized confrontation and condemnation. It is street theater that creates the opportunity for the mobilization and expression of oppositional identities. And it is a far cry from the rituals of corporate caring and cooperation that are enacted at the Race.

There are no freebies distributed at this event—none of the beauty products, pink ribbons, or breast health brochures that abound at the Race. There are no corporate sponsors. Although Chevron and the American Cancer Society are present at both the Race and the Tour, they are participants and sponsors of the Race, whereas they are targets of the Tour. At the American Cancer Society, for example, Judy Brady—a breast cancer activist and self-described "cancer victim"—delivers a series of withering charges which she substantiates by handing out bootleg copies of an ACS brochure and a recent internal ACS memo marked "Confidential." The memo instructs all ACS offices to suppress the distribution of an unauthorized brochure produced by a maverick ACS office. The brochure in question is entitled "Warning: The use of pesticides may be hazardous to your health!" This brochure describes the health hazards of pesticides and suggests non-toxic alternatives. Brady charges the ACS with miseducating the public, ignoring cancer prevention, refusing to take a stand against industrial pollution and agricultural poisoning, and colluding with the corporate stakeholders to hide evidence of corporate carcinogens.

The demonstrators carry signs aloft and loudly chant: "Stop Cancer Where it Starts! Stop Corporate Pollution!"—"Toxins Outside! Cancer Inside! Industry Profits! People Suffer!"—"Stop Environmental Racism!"—"Reduce it! Don't Produce it!"—and "Environmental Justice NOW!" Last year the sixty or so protesters carried handmade signs painted with slogans, miniature coffins, and gravestones emblazoned with a handwritten name, a life span, and the letters "R.I.P." This year, the coffins and gravestones are nowhere to be seen but there are other images of death and destruction. There is a show-stealing twenty-foot papier-mâché puppet representing a woman with blue skin and a mastectomy scar dripping blood where her second breast should be. In each of her gigantic moveable hands she holds a container of toxic substances, painted with a skull and crossbones. One woman holds high an exhibit of photographs of women's nude torsos. The photographs include startling images of disfigured women with double mastectomies—some of them with the concave chests characteristic of the Halsted radical mastectomy, a surgical procedure performed by American surgeons on women diagnosed with breast cancer from the 1880s until the 1980s. It is just these sorts of images that Race for the Cure seeks to banish from the fabric of the collective consciousness. But here they are, resurrected and pasted onto the sandwich boards donned by angry women who are marching through downtown San Francisco.

The Toxic Tour draws heavily upon, and seeks to promote, the public's heightened awareness of cancer and its growing sensitivity and exposure to discourses of risk. The bright orange flyers distributed along the way announce that one-third of United States women and half of United States men will be diagnosed with cancer in their lifetimes. The flyer states that the lifetime risk for breast cancer is one in eight and rising, that the Bay Area has the highest rates of breast cancer in the world, and that African-American women living in Bayview–Hunters Point (a predominantly African-American and low-income neighborhood in San Francisco) have rates of breast cancer double those of the rest of San Francisco. The orange flyer also states that "we are all exposed in increasing doses to industrial chemicals and radioactive waste *known* to cause cancer, reproductive, and developmental disorders" and that "big profits are made from the continued production of cancer-causing chemicals." It is this growing sense that cancer is everywhere and affects all of us that the Toxic Tour seeks to mobilize and redirect into demands for cancer prevention and industry regulations.

At the Toxic Tour, there is no call for more research to uncover the mysteries of tumor biology or discern the patterns of epidemiology. There are no demands for more or better science, or for more or better medical services. There is no call for women to be vigilant, to practice breast self-exam and get mammograms. Mammography *is* invoked—but as an example of false promises and corporate profit-mongering. These activists do not promote the ideology of early detection. Instead, they map the sickness and disease of the collective body onto the corporate corpus. Prevention, it is clear, requires a different kind of cartography.

PROJECTING THE LOCAL ONTO THE GLOBAL

Twenty years ago, Susan Sontag dreamed of a world in which people diagnosed with cancer would no longer be forced into exile and haunted by the lurid metaphors created by fearful and ignorant outsiders. Although she was an artist and a visionary, Sontag nonetheless considered farfetched the possibility of redeeming the stigmatized social identities of people with cancer, and she viewed as impossible the task of aestheticizing a disease so thoroughly "overlaid with mystification" and so firmly shackled to "the fantasy of inescapable fatality."[47] Impossible, that is, but for the forces of biomedicine. In Sontag's biomedical dreamscape—a dreamscape shared and institutionalized by the state, by the pharmaceutical industry, and by the scientific research and medical establishments—faith and fantasy joined hands and together mapped a future in which the stigmatizing metaphors of cancer would become obsolete as the steady march of biomedicine demystified disease and disconnected it from macabre visions of death. Drawing an example from the history of tuberculosis, Sontag reasoned that advances in the science of cancer would likewise remove it from the realm of metaphor, place it squarely in the realm of science, and then sweep it into the dustbin of history. In short, stigma would be replaced by science, meaning by medicine, and cancer by cure.

In the twenty years that have elapsed since the publication of *Illness as Metaphor,* the socially organized stigmatization of women diagnosed with breast cancer has indeed diminished. At first glance, then, it might appear that Sontag was prophetic in tying the social fortunes of people with cancer to advances in biomedicine. But closer examination reveals that the necessary conditions for this process of destigmatization were *not* produced as a result of the medical and scientific *conquest* of this disease but rather as a result of its medical and scientific *colonization.* It was, in other words, the vast expansion of breast cancer screening, treatment, and patient support practices, more than any significant progress in preventing, treating, or curing the disease, that reorganized the structure of stigma and hence created the preconditions for its resignification by breast cancer movements. In fact, what changed most dramatically in the last twenty years was not the *effectiveness* of breast cancer medicine, but its expansion.

Treatment regimens multiplied, support groups proliferated, and screening expanded into asymptomatic populations. This three-dimensional transformation in the management of breast cancer resulted in the formation of new social spaces, social networks, solidarities, and sensibilities among women with and without the disease. It resulted, in other words, in the production of new subjects and new socio-spatial relations of disease, and it was these subjects and socio-spatial relations that constituted the facilitating conditions of the social movements that ensued. In turn, the movements around breast cancer reshaped the social contexts in which breast cancer was experienced and encountered, and resignified the stigmas attached to it.

As this chapter demonstrates, the politicization and resignification of breast cancer in the Bay Area occurred in at least three different ways and according to three different logics. All three strands of the local field of activism challenged the stigma of breast cancer by building upon, strategically mobilizing, and reshaping these new subjectivities, solidarities, and sensibilities. And each strand of the breast cancer movement drew upon the material and discursive resources of pre-existing fields in order to do so. Race for the Cure drew upon the medical-industrial complex, corporate cultures, and the beauty, fitness, and fashion industries. The Women & Cancer Walk drew upon the women's health movement and AIDS activism. And the Toxic Tour drew upon feminist cancer activism and joined it with the environmental justice movement. What distinguished each strand of the local breast cancer movement was the way in which it mobilized these resources and shaped new discourses of disease and new forms of breast cancer activism.

The political logic of each strand of Bay Area activism—biomedical research and early detection; patient support and health care activism; and cancer prevention—was mirrored at the global level, although imperfectly, in the three main themes of the World Conference on Breast Cancer—diagnostics and treatment, caring for the whole woman, and breast cancer and the environment. But this apparent mirroring of activist agendas and organizing trajectories occluded what was actually quite extraordinary about both sites of activism. What distinguished both Bay Area activism and the Kingston conference was the incorporation of environmental justice issues into the center of breast cancer activism. Indeed, both the Bay Area field of activism and the Kingston gathering were exceptional, rather than representative, for having created a potent synthesis between the feminist health and environmental justice movements.

But this synthesis was neither automatic nor easy. Indeed, a quick glance in another direction demonstrates that a different trajectory of global organizing was simultaneously gathering momentum. This trajectory was spearheaded by the National Breast Cancer Coalition (NBCC), a feminist, Washington, D.C.-based breast cancer activist and lobbying organization that was formed in 1991 in order to raise awareness of breast cancer, increase the federal budget for breast cancer research, and expand the influence of breast cancer advocates in research and public policy arenas. In

March of 1997, the NBCC sought to expand the breast cancer movement and extend its assistance to breast cancer activists in other parts of the world by organizing a global gathering quite similar to the Kingston affair. The NBCC-organized event, the "First World Conference on Breast Cancer Advocacy—Influencing Change," was held in Brussels, Belgium, in March of 1997 and attended by approximately two hundred fifty breast cancer activists, health professionals, health educators, and industry representatives from forty-three countries.[48]

Although the Brussels and Kingston conferences shared a number of qualities, they differed along one key dimension.[49] Whereas in Kingston breast cancer was linked to issues of environmental justice and the post–World War Two chemicalization of the planet, in Brussels breast cancer was conceptualized strictly within a biomedical paradigm. The presentations and workshops on cancer and the environment that were so numerous in Kingston were noticeably absent from the Brussels agenda and its roster of speakers.[50] In their place, the chemical-pharmaceutical industry was well-represented—materially, as the underwriters of the conference, and discursively, as potential allies of the movement.[51] Whereas the Kingston conference moved the environment to the center of the agenda, the Brussels conference pushed it off into the silence of the margins. In fact, because the Brussels conference embraced an individualizing, biomedical model of disease, when the discourse of prevention actually appeared, it did so in the guise of individual risk-reduction "lifestyle" practices and pharmaceutical risk-reduction "treatments." The most obvious difference, then, was that the third prong of activism—cancer prevention—did not penetrate this global geography of action.[52]

The distinctiveness of the world conferences on breast cancer in Kingston and Brussels indicates that the nascent globalization of breast cancer activism is moving in two different directions. One trajectory, represented by the National Breast Cancer Coalition's (NBCC's) globalizing vision of breast cancer advocacy, has aligned itself with Sontag's dream of salvationist science and curative medicine. Its "lifestyles" approach to public health is symbolized by individually oriented practices of risk-reduction and early detection, and by a growing alliance with the pharmaceutical industry. A second trajectory, spearheaded by the Women's Environment and Development Organization (WEDO) and a diverse array of predominantly grassroots, North American, feminist, cancer activist organizations, has developed a global vision of public health that is oriented toward forms of cancer prevention that are neither individual nor pharmaceutical in origin. Here, the precautionary principle and the reduction of environmental carcinogens has replaced individual-level models of risk assessment; and here, an alliance with the global environmental justice movement has replaced alliances with the global pharmaceutical industry.

Despite their distinct trajectories, however, the global assemblies share something quite significant in common. Both global gatherings, despite the participation of activists, experts, and allies from around the world, are clearly the projects of local, specifically North American, movements that emerged out of local, specifically North American, contexts and conditions. Both global assemblies, in other words, are the projects and projections of very specific and privileged sites of activism. For activists and organizations from the San Francisco Bay Area, for example, the transition from the Bay Area to Kingston, and the translation from local to global sites of activism, was relatively effortless because the global site of activism mirrored, albeit imperfectly, the discursive constellations with which they were already engaged and familiar. But, although in some ways the Bay Area field of activism can be seen as the prototype of the Kingston conference, it must be remembered that it is a prototype that excludes most of the world. For those coming from elsewhere, the transitions to Kingston were bumpier, and the translations from the global to the local, and vice versa, were more partial and incomplete. It remains an open question whether either trajectory of breast cancer activism will be able to achieve relevance and resonance within local sites and struggles around health in other parts of the world.

What, then, can the history of breast cancer activism in the Bay Area teach us about global formations? If it can teach us anything, it is that the development of breast cancer movements is nurtured not only by shared visions of salvationist science, miraculous medicine, and environmental justice, but requires the prior restructuring of silence, isolation, and invisibility, and the creation of new subjects, solidarities, and sensibilities. Without the challenges to stigma that are made possible by these restructurings and recreations, private dreams can never be transformed into publicly enacted global visions.

NOTES

I thank the individuals and organizations, both named and unnamed, who participated in the events and movements written about here. Their visions and commitment inspired my analysis, and I hope they will see themselves reflected in this text. Thanks also to Barrie Thorne, Jennifer Pierce, Leslie Salzinger, Charles Kurzman, Ruth Horowitz, Judith Stacey, and Barron H. Lerner for their helpful comments. I also thank the Doreen B. Townsend Center for the Humanities; the University of California, Berkeley, Department of Sociology; and Sociologists for Women in Society for their generous support of this research. A different version of this paper received the 1999 Sally Hacker Graduate Student Paper Award from the Sex and Gender Section of the American Sociological Association.

1. Susan Sontag, *Illness as Metaphor*, p. 8.
2. Erving Goffman, *Stigma: Notes on the Management of Spoiled Identity*, p. 1.
3. Michel Foucault, *Discipline and Punish*, p. 183.

4. Sandra Steingraber, "We All Live Downwind," p. 43.

5. Nancy Scheper-Hughes and Margaret M. Lock, "The Message in the Bottle," p. 414.

6. Ibid.

7. James Patterson, *The Dread Disease*, p. 231.

8. For analyses of the "War on Cancer," see Robert N. Proctor, *Cancer Wars;* National Cancer Advisory Board–Subcommittee to Evaluate the National Cancer Program, *Cancer at a Crossroads;* Patterson, *The Dread Disease;* Walter S. Ross, *Crusade;* Paul Starr, *The Social Transformation of American Medicine;* Richard A. Rettig, *Cancer Crusade.*

9. In fact, organized cancer research had existed on an international level since the turn of the century—in England, there was the Imperial Cancer Research Fund; in Germany, the Institute for Cancer Research; and in Denmark, Sweden, and Switzerland there were other centers of research. The American Association for Cancer Research was founded in 1907, and the American Society for the Control of Cancer (ASCC), which later became the American Cancer Society, was founded in 1913. See Daniel de Moulin, *A Short History of Breast Cancer.*

10. Michael P. Coleman, Jacques Estève, Philippe Damiecki, Annie Arslan, and Hélène Renard, *Trends in Cancer Incidence and Mortality.*

11. Ralph W. Moss, *Questioning Chemotherapy.*

12. The patterns of breast cancer incidence and mortality that I am presenting here represent the dominant discourse at the World Conference on Breast Cancer in Kingston, Canada. This discourse is not out of the mainstream, however, and is based on figures gathered by the International Agency for Research on Cancer (IARC) and reproduced in many textbooks and reference books on cancer epidemiology. See David Schottenfeld and Joseph Fraumeni, Jr., *Cancer Epidemiology and Prevention*, for a widely accepted presentation of epidemiological patterns and data. The authors of this text state that: "The incidence of breast cancer is increasing slowly in most countries, the rate of increase tending to be greatest where rates were the lowest, e.g., 3.2 percent per annum for Singapore Chinese who have experienced an increase most noticeable in the under 50 age-group. Mortality rates have also been increasing in, for example, Japan and Hong Kong, but have had a tendency to remain stationary in Western countries. In the United States mortality in white women less than 65 years of age has fallen, but among older white women and black women of all ages mortality has been increasing." Schottenfeld and Fraumeni, *Cancer Epidemiology*, p. 156.

13. This assessment and those that follow are based on *SEER Cancer Statistics Review, 1973–1994.*

14. In 1994, the Northern California Cancer Center published data from the SEER cancer statistics and the International Agency of Research on Cancer showing that "white women in the San Francisco/Oakland Area have the highest rate in the world" and that Bay Area black women have the fourth highest rate of breast cancer in the world. See Northern California Cancer Center, *Greater Bay Area Cancer Registry Report.*

15. The Women's Cancer Resource Center (WCRC), a feminist organization that provides free, direct services to women with cancer, was the first of its kind in the country and was founded in 1986 in Berkeley, California. Over the years, it has functioned as a key site for the development of social, cultural, and political projects

around cancer. Also in 1986, the Cancer Support Community was established across the bay, in San Francisco. Out of the Cancer Support Community, the first breast cancer treatment activist organization in the country—Breast Cancer Action (BCA)—was organized in 1990. BCA has been a key activist organization in the breast cancer movement, both locally and nationally. At about the same time that WCRC and CSC were founded, one of the first chapters of the Susan G. Komen Breast Cancer Foundation was established in San Francisco. In 1991, the San Francisco chapter of the Komen Foundation began organizing annual "Race for the Cure" events and funding local early detection campaigns for medically underserved women. In 1992, Charlotte Maxwell Complementary Clinic, the only clinic in the country that provides free complementary therapies to low-income women with cancer, was founded in Oakland. And in 1992, The Breast Cancer Fund, an increasingly influential activist foundation, was established in San Francisco. The Toxic Links Coalition was founded in 1994, and in 1995 Marin Breast Cancer Watch was established.

16. This argument is developed in greater theoretical and historical detail in my dissertation, "Reshaping the Contours of Breast Cancer: From Private Stigma to Public Actions." There I conceptualize the breast cancer apparatus in terms of two regimes of practices and show how the second regime, "the regime of biosociety," altered the social terrain of breast cancer, reconstituted the subjects produced within it, and created the facilitating conditions of breast cancer movements. I argue that social movements theory within sociology is stuck in a modernist moment that fails to comprehend the growing significance of biopower, biopractices, and bioinstitutions for the emergence of postmodern social movements.

17. Theresa Montini, "Resist and Redirect"; Theresa Montini, "Women's Activism for Breast Cancer Informed Consent Laws."

18. Although this legislation did not abolish or criminalize the one-step procedure, it did require surgeons to inform their patients of their treatment options and to inform them, prior to undergoing a surgical biopsy, that they had the right to have this diagnostic procedure separated from any ensuing surgical treatment. Failure to inform patients of their rights to a two-step procedure was categorized as "unprofessional conduct." Theresa Montini, "Gender and Emotion."

19. The term "docile bodies" is taken from Michel Foucault, *Discipline and Punish;* "gaz[ing] back" is a reference to the concept of the "clinical gaze" in Foucault, *The Birth of the Clinic.*

20. See Theresa Montini and Sheryl Ruzek, "Overturning Orthodoxy," for pioneering work on the belated demise of the Halsted radical mastectomy and the resistance of American surgeons to less radical surgeries. The expansion of surgical repertoires occurred not only as a result of the development of new techniques and the clinical trials that proved their effectiveness, but also, and importantly, as a result of patient demands that grew out of the patients' rights and women's health movements. Also see Barron H. Lerner, "Inventing a Curable Disease."

21. Breast-conserving surgeries—a term which many assume refers simply to lumpectomy—include partial or segmental mastectomy, quadrantectomy, tylectomy, wedge resection, nipple resection, lumpectomy, and excisional biopsy, with or without dissection of axillary lymph nodes. Cyllene R. Morris and William E. Wright, *Breast Cancer in California.*

22. Ralph W. Moss, *Questioning Chemotherapy.*

23. Michael W. DeGregorio and Valerie J. Wiebe, *Tamoxifen & Breast Cancer.*

24. In 1986, two cancer support communities were founded by women with breast cancer who were frustrated by the lack of support groups in the Bay Area. In Berkeley, a group of women led by Jackie Winnow founded the feminist and lesbian-friendly Women's Cancer Resource Center and, in San Francisco, Victoria Wells and Treya Killam Wilber founded the Cancer Support Community. During the nineties, as these grassroots, alternative organizations expanded their outreach to communities of color, support groups for women with breast cancer became institutionalized within the Bay Area health care system.

25. The incorporation of support groups into the health care delivery system was given a boost when David Spiegel, a highly respected scientist-physician at Stanford University Medical Center, published the results of a follow-up to a case-control study. His results showed that women with metastatic breast cancer who had participated in a short-term support group ten years earlier had lived an average of eighteen months longer than those who had not. Spiegel had conducted the follow-up study to disprove what he considered to be exaggerated claims about the survival benefits of support groups. Much to his surprise, however, his findings reinforced this set of claims and propelled forward the institutionalization of support groups in the medical care system. David Spiegel, J. R. Bloom, and H. C. Kraemer, "Effects of Psychosocial Treatment on Survival of Patients with Metastatic Breast Cancer."

26. The first program, Reach to Recovery, was developed by an ex-breast cancer patient in 1952 and became an ACS-administered program in 1969 (Ross, *Crusade*). The second program, Look Good/Feel Better, reflected changes in patient needs and medical practices and was oriented toward women undergoing radiation and/or chemotherapy. It was incorporated into the ACS rehabilitative arsenal in 1988 (Sharon Batt, *Patient No More*).

27. Batt, *Patient No More;* Ross, *Crusade;* Lester Breslow, *A History of Cancer Control in the United States, 1946–1971;* Audre Lorde, *The Cancer Journals;* Rose Kushner, *Breast Cancer.*

28. The first study to assess the viability and cost-effectiveness of using mammography as a screening technology was actually conducted between 1963 and 1968 by the Health Insurance Plan of Greater New York (HIP). But it was the Breast Cancer Detection Demonstration Project (BCDDP), a collaborative project of the ACS/NCI that introduced the concept and practice of screening to a wider audience. Ross, *Crusade*, 1987.

29. Ibid.

30. Ibid.; Susan Rennie, "Mammography: X-rated Film."

31. These controversies include debates over whether there is any benefit to screening, in terms of increased survival, for women under the age of fifty (the standardized marker of pre- and postmenopausal status) and whether there is any safe level of exposure to ionizing radiation (in the form of mammography), especially in premenopausal women. Probably the most infamous controversy—but one that more or less died with the demonstration project itself—involved the discovery that mastectomies had been unnecessarily performed on more than sixty women. For discussions of the controversies and politics surrounding screening mammography, see Rennie, "Mammography: X-Rated Film"; Batt, *Patient No More;* and Roberta Alt-

man, *Waking Up, Fighting Back.* Whereas the controversy over screening mammography during the seventies centered around the questions of safety (whether ionizing irradiation of the breast—mammography—was ever risk-free), effectiveness, and age recommendations, the mammography debates during the nineties have centered around issues of age recommendations and access for the category of women referred to as "medically underserved"—primarily women of color and women without insurance.

32. Barron H. Lerner, "Seeing What Is Not There."

33. Batt, *Patient No More;* Kate Dempsey, Nechama Katz, Traci Sawyers, Ellen Taggart, "Screening Mammography."

34. Batt, *Patient No More;* Monte Paulsen, "The Cancer Business."

35. For critiques of Breast Cancer Awareness Month, see Batt, *Patient No More;* Paulsen, "The Cancer Business"; and Proctor, *Cancer Wars.*

36. Morris and Wright, *Breast Cancer in California.*

37. By 1994, the percentage of women over fifty who had ever received a screening mammogram ranged from a low of 68 percent among "Asian/Other" women, to a high of 90 percent among "Black" women. Rates among "non-Hispanic white" women were measured at 87 percent, and 76 percent of "Hispanic" women had received a screening mammogram. Among women between the ages of forty and forty-nine, the rates were 70 percent for "Asian/Other," 71 percent for "Black," 69 percent for "Hispanic," and 83 percent for "White." Data are based on the California Behavioral Risk Factor Surveillance System (BRFSS); Morris and Wright, *Breast Cancer in California.*

38. Barron H. Lerner, "Fighting the War on Breast Cancer."

39. Ibid.; Morris and Wright, *Breast Cancer in California.*

40. In 1991 federal legislation mandating partial reimbursement for the cost of mammographically screening women over the age of fifty with Medicare coverage was approved by Congress (Altman, *Waking Up, Fighting Back*). That same year, federal legislation was enacted that established the Breast Cancer and Cervical Cancer Program (BCCCP), administered through the Centers for Disease Control and Prevention (CDC). California immediately applied for participation and became one of the first test sites for that program. Then, in 1993, California enacted legislation that established a statewide Breast Cancer Early Detection Program (BCEDP) comprised of fourteen regional partnerships (the other arm of the legislation established the California Breast Cancer Research Program). Both the BCCCP and the BCEDP, which eventually merged administratively, were designed to provide free clinical breast exams and screening mammograms to poor and uninsured women, and both were targeted, primarily, to communities of color and older women. For additional administrative history and background information on each program, see BCEDP, "Request for Applications," and BCCCP, "Request for Applications."

41. The San Francisco chapter of the Susan G. Komen Breast Cancer Research Foundation held its first Race for the Cure in 1991 and has continued to do so, on an annual basis, ever since. I was a participant-observer at San Francisco's Race for the Cure in 1994, 1995, 1996, and 1997. Race for the Cure is a registered trademark. For the sake of easier reading, I have eliminated the trademark symbol ("®") in the remainder of the chapter.

42. The Komen Foundation is part of the national steering committee of NBCAM.

43. The first Women & Cancer Walk was held in 1992 as part of a larger, collaborative, fundraising effort. In 1993 the Walk was held as its own affair in Golden Gate Park and it has been held there on an annual basis ever since. I was a participant-observer and helped organize the Women & Cancer Walk in 1995 and 1996.

44. Originally formed in New York City in 1987 in order to spur pharmaceutical companies and the federal government to pay greater attention to the AIDS crisis and the needs of people with AIDS and HIV, ACT UP chapters quickly mushroomed across the country—Boston, Chicago, Los Angeles, New Orleans, Portland, San Francisco, Seattle, and Houston. Known for in-your-face politics and flamboyant street theater, ACT UP was "a magnet for radical, young gay men and women" (Steven Epstein, *Impure Science*, pp. 219–20). For an excellent study of ACT UP, see Joshua Gamson, "Silence, Death, and the Invisible Enemy."

45. The Toxic Links Coalition (TLC) is a synthesis of feminist cancer activism and the environmental justice movement. Formed in the summer of 1994 by activists from the Women's Cancer Resource Center, Breast Cancer Action, Greenpeace, and the West County Toxics Coalition, the TLC expanded within a few months to include more than twenty organizations, most of which were drawn from the environmental movement sector. I began attending monthly meetings and conducting participant observation during the fall of 1994 and was involved in the Toxic Tours of the Cancer Industry in 1995, 1996, and 1997.

46. In 1995 Zeneca bought a 50 percent stake in Salick Health Care, and in 1997 Zeneca's growing vertical integration came full circle when it bought the remaining shares of Salick and took over the management of eleven cancer treatment centers in the United States—including a cancer center just down the road from the Women's Cancer Resource Center, the meeting place of the TLC (Elisabeth Rosenthal, "Maker of Cancer Drugs to Oversee Prescriptions at 11 Cancer Clinics"). NBCAM was listed as the country's second most important censored story in 1998 by Project Censored, a media watchdog project that, for almost twenty-five years, has published an annual list of the top twenty-five stories that were censored or downplayed by the mainstream media. Project Censored is conducted by more than 125 faculty, student researchers, interns, and community experts around the country and is based at Sonoma State University in California. See Jim Doyle, review of *Censored 1999*. See also Gabriel Roth, "Not Fit to Print?"

47. Sontag, *Illness as Metaphor*, p. 84.

48. In fact, although the NBCC's world conference was held *before* the Kingston conference, the NBCC did not begin planning their global gathering until well *after* plans for the Kingston conference were finalized and publicized. And, although Susan Love, one of the founders of the NBCC, delivered a luncheon speech at the Kingston conference, neither she nor the NBCC leadership attended the conference proceedings. The significance of NBCC's absence at this global gathering was noted by many. My analysis of NBCC's First World Conference on Breast Cancer Advocacy is based upon their publication, *A Report on The First World Conference on Breast Cancer Advocacy—Influencing Change*, a one hundred page document that includes coverage of official papers, presentations, and workshops from the conference as well as excerpts from participants' feedback. It is available on the World Wide Web at http://www.natlbcc.org.

49. For example, both conferences were feminist in tone and in tools of analysis; both emphasized the importance of building grassroots movements relevant to

their local contexts, countries, and conditions; and both conferences drew upon discourses of "the global" and constructed visions of global movements. NBCC's report on the Brussels conference indicates, for example, that phrases such as "global standards," "influencing global change," "work[ing] together globally," and "the dream that one day we would join hands globally" were sprinkled liberally throughout the first day's plenary sessions.

50. In fact, according to my conversations and correspondence with a participant at the NBCC-sponsored conference in Brussels, those who were interested in networking and organizing around the issues of breast cancer and the environment were forced to meet informally in the hallways because formal meeting space was not made available to them. And obviously, their concerns about the chemical-pharmaceutical were not incorporated into the official conference proceedings.

51. In a plenary presentation entitled "Influencing Industry, Government & Science," Jane Reese-Coulbourne, former Executive Vice President of the NBCC, advised that "Some industries want positive press with their customers. Women are their customers and helping NBCC work on eradicating breast cancer is viewed positively. If you are thoughtful and careful, there can be mutually beneficial relationships with industry without giving up your independence" (NBBC, *A Report*, p. 52). In contrast to this, the Kingston organizers rejected the offer of a major pharmaceutical corporation to sponsor their conference because they viewed the practices of the pharmaceutical-chemical industry as part of the problem and thus believed that allowing this industry to attach its name to the breast cancer movement would create a false impression of the industry's innocence and would be a signal to others that the movement had been co-opted by the pharmaceutical-chemical industry.

52. For example, according to the official conference report, in a plenary speech on cancer causes and cancer prevention delivered by Dr. Susan Love (one of the founding mothers of the NBCC, a breast cancer surgeon, and the author of *Dr. Susan Love's Breast Book*), pesticides were mentioned briefly and only in passing—as substances that are metabolized as estrogens. But any analysis of the broader implications of this link was quickly abandoned as Love redirected her focus to the individual-agent model of biomedicine. Love's overview of approaches to cancer prevention, for example, focused exclusively on individual and "lifestyle" factors such as exercise, diet, prophylactic surgeries, and pharmaceutical forms of risk reduction—namely, tamoxifen. Here, she simply ignored the efforts of environmental movements to prevent cancer by eliminating and better regulating the production and circulation of endocrine-disrupting chemicals and carcinogens. And, although another speaker offered a brief analysis of the rapidly globalizing pharmaceutical industry, he did not link the pharmaceutical industry to its other arm—chemical and pesticide manufacturers—or to the actual production of cancer.

Conclusion

ELEVEN

Grounding Globalization

Michael Burawoy

For his BBC Reith Lectures for 1999, Anthony Giddens, distinguished sociologist and Director of the London School of Economics, chose as his topic "The Runaway World," a discussion of globalization and its effects. To give his five lectures a global feel he broadcast them from London (first and last), Hong Kong, Delhi, and Washington, D. C.[1] They were accessible all over the world on the World Wide Web, where you could watch or listen to the lectures, read interviews with Giddens, and debate with him through electronic mail. Through their transmission he recapitulated the very theme of his lectures. As we listen to him across sound waves, or through cyberspace, or watch him on video, we cannot but wonder how much of globalization talk signifies the privileged lifestyle of high-flying academics. Giddens proclaims, "We are the first generation to live in this [cosmopolitan] society, whose contours we can as yet only dimly see. It is shaking up our existing lives, no matter where we happen to be."[2] But who is the "we" he is referring to? For whom has risk been extended, tradition disinterred, the family made more egalitarian, and democracy become more widespread? To what slice of Hong Kong's, Delhi's, London's, or Washington's population do his sociological observations pertain? Is he talking about everyone or just the new cosmopolitan elite to which he belongs? What does globalization look like from the underside—for example, from Castells's "black holes" of human marginality?[3] This is the question that motivates our conclusion.

SKEPTICS AND RADICALS

Giddens himself divides his protagonists into two camps—"skeptics" and "radicals." There are those who believe that all the hype about globalization is just that, hype. It is ideology rather than reality. The world is not that different today than in earlier periods. On the other side are the radicals, who believe that globalization is not just talk but refers to very real transformations that have had dramatic consequences not only for the world economy but for the basic institutions of society—from sexuality to politics to the environment. By dividing the field in two, Giddens all too easily appropriates the radical label for himself, even though his position is anything but radical, since it takes for granted the totalizing vision of a runaway world. His rhetorical division into skeptics and radicals deftly forecloses other options—the perspectival globalization of anthropologists and our own grounded globalization. His categories are not only not exhaustive but they are also implausible, as I shall now try to show.

Is the novelty of globalization myth or reality? The skeptics say myth. They create a phantom opponent who believes the world economy has perfectly permeable national boundaries and free-flowing capital, resulting in more equal relations among geographical areas. The phantom is subjected to intensive demolition. The argument has three steps.[4] First, when it comes to levels of trade, capital mobility, labor migration, and monetary regulation, the period 1870 to 1914 was as open as any since. Second, while there has been an internationalization of money and of capital markets, significant leaps in foreign direct investment, and increased trade within supranational economic blocs, these do not add up to a new form of globalization. "In the bigger national economies, more than 80 percent of production is for domestic consumption and more than 80 percent of investment by domestic investors. Companies are rooted in national home bases with national regulatory regimes."[5] The level of openness may be increasing but this by no means implies a global economy in which nation states are powerless to regulate economic activities, in which multinational corporations have been supplanted by transnational corporations, or in which inequalities between First and Third World countries are dissolving. The third move is from the descriptive to the prescriptive. Using Japan and the Asian "Newly Industrializing Countries" (NICs) as their models but also European countries, they argue that the world economy not only makes it possible for states to regulate national economies, but economic success requires such regulation.

If there has been no significant change, one must ask how the skeptics explain the hype around globalization? How can they explain its topicality at the end of the twentieth century—the fact that Giddens has not "been to a single country recently where globalization isn't being intensively discussed"?[6] Globalization studies are, after all, a growth industry in the humanities and social sciences as well as in the mass media. Is this just an intellectual fad? The skeptics respond that the world has been hijacked by "neoliberal" ideology, spreading its pernicious influence to the furthest corners of the earth, energized by the collapse of communism, aided and abetted by such organizations as the World Bank and the International Monetary Fund. In their very explanations they point to profound changes of a global dimension. They are no longer skeptics. To be a consistent skeptic is to enter a schizophrenic world. It means being a hard materialist when it comes to studying the global economy but metamorphosing into an ethereal idealist when it comes to explaining the ubiquity and power of neoliberalism as something created ex nihilo. Consistent skeptics think that by sheer force of intellectual argument they can dispel the ideological grip of neoliberals. In practice, as our book has shown, their economic indices simply do not capture what is experienced on the ground, the ways globalization attaches itself to everyday life, the way neoliberalism becomes "common sense."

The radicals are the mirror inversion! For them all the talk of globalization confirms the fact that the world must be undergoing major global transformation. Ideology has to be the expression of underlying reality: "The global spread of the term [globalization] is evidence of the very developments to which it refers."[7] Here we have a simple reductionism of reality to ideology. Giddens traces the origin, invention and meaning of concepts—risk, family, tradition, democracy—rather than engaging the concrete history of institutions. He does not compile evidence against the skeptics that nothing fundamental has changed. Giddens's strategy is strangely beside the point. Instead of considering any actual trajectory of change in real space and time, he traces globalization to the origins of modernity in the sixteenth century. Globalization is the culmination of the project of modernity. His history is sweeping and largely irrelevant to the question of what has changed in the last century. But his cavalier approach to history is typical of the radicals. Manuel Castells's encyclopedic three volumes on the information age is just that—an awe-inspiring analysis of the ways in which information technology is reshaping the contemporary world, but there is no historical depth. It is as if what is "now" is new.[8] Of the radicals, David Harvey gets the nearest to a serious engagement with transformation. But even he, after documenting the postmodern condition, substitutes for history a plausible but nonetheless speculative Marxist periodization of capitalism, based on the successive resolutions of the crises it generates.[9]

Fredric Jameson is the apotheosis of the radicals, bringing together cultural epiphenomenalism and historical unconsciousness.[10] Like Harvey he claims that the cultural is "symptomatic" of and "functional" for "late capitalism," but his reflections on the economic are so thin as to amount to no more than handwaving. But at least he is consistent, since he argues that the peculiarity of late capitalism lies in the invisibility of its global logic. Taking a leaf out of the philosophical arsenals of Louis Althusser and George

Lukács, he claims that the economic determines its own mystification, bring-ing in its train cultural reification as loss of history and memory. Since the connection to the economic is so tenuous, his position easily slips into the view that just as the cultural is an epiphenomenon of an invisible economy, so the past is an epiphenomenon of the present. Both history and material reality are lost in an impenetrable cloud of postmodern fragments.

One has to wonder to what extent the radicals are giving expression to their own conditions of existence. Is it an accident that high-flying acade-mics, hotel-circuiting consultants, conference-hopping professionals, and netscaping virtuosos should develop concepts of the network society, should imagine a manichean world of placeless power and powerless places, should expound on time-space compression or aesthetic cognitive maps? It is per-haps fitting that Giddens should traverse the world from capital to capital as he delivers his Reith lectures, ruminating on risk in Hong Kong, tradition in Delhi, family in Washington, and democracy in London. Their theories of globalization are theories of privileged men, who appear in a privileged air-space above the world they theorize. Their absence from their own accounts aspires to objectivity, but it cannot hide the unspoken, unreflected, stratos-pheric situatedness of their knowledges. How much of their theorizing is the projection of insulated journeys, unspoken genealogies, self-referential worlds?

This brings me to a third species of globalizer, "perspectivalists" who are quite at home with the idea that we create images of globalization in accor-dance with our own global location. These are what we might call the con-sistent radicals who accept and sometimes even celebrate the inaccessibility of history. I am referring here, in particular, to anthropologists who hold onto their radicalism by being skeptics at the same time. They are radicals insofar as, having been thrown out of their tents, they have awakened to a world in which outsider and insider, anthropologist and native, colonizer and colonist, center and periphery are no longer neat and water-tight cate-gories. They confront a new world in which the tables are turned: the natives have put up their own tents on the anthropologist's doorstep. But these anthropologists are also skeptics when they wonder whether the world *ever* conformed to the presumptions of classical anthropology, whether what is new is the lens through which the world is viewed rather than the world itself. As Clifford and Marcus's collection on *Writing Culture* made famous, the isolated village, the symmetrical lineage systems, the peace in the feud were as much constructs of anthropologists and the way they conducted their fieldwork as they were faithful portraits of the world being studied. The differences and separations, the voices and silences, were the products of the anthropologist's location in imperial or racial orders that were occluded from the classical monograph. From here it is but a short and slip-pery step to a radical perspectivalism in which anthropology turns away from the study of *locality* to reflections on "epistemological and political issues of *location*."[11] The perspectivalists among anthropologists become skeptical that ethnography can say anything about the world beyond the ethnographer. Ethnography moves toward comparative literature, an interpretive exercise, a political stance, which justifies the thinnest of accounts, the most fleeting of engagements, and the most unsystematic of observations. To embrace the global they have substituted travel for dwelling, vignettes for theory.

We, however, have not taken this road. We still believe in a realist ethnography that can tell us much about the world inhabited by others. As sociologists, our epistemologies have not been traumatized by upheavals in our working conditions and, so we like to believe, our theories are not without relevance to the world we study. As ethnographers within sociology, we have never been at the center of our discipline, at least since the eclipse of the Chicago School. Rather, we have taken up a critical stance at its margins. In the past ethnographers have tried to drum a little *reality* into the twin tendencies of grand theory and abstracted empiricism. And in this book we used ethnography to drum some reality into theories of globalization, investigating to what extent globalization is a flight of academic fancy. Thus, in stepping outside our place of worship to plumb the worlds inhabited by other agents and victims of globalization, we hoped to recognize *our* own positionality. But we also wanted to do more than that, to construct perspectives on globalization from below, what we call *grounded globalizations*. Thus, we set out from real experiences, spatial and temporal, of welfare clients, homeless recyclers, mobilized feminists, migrant nurses, union organizers, software engineers, poisoned villagers, redundant boilermakers, and breast cancer activists in order to explore *their* global contexts. The link, however, was not fabricated tabula rasa. It was no immaculate conception but required hard theoretical work. We searched for theories that would help us stretch from local to global. We circled back to where we came from, to our theoretical moorings, only now more conscious of who we were, and what tools we needed to make global sense of our sites. Our grounded globalizations are the antidote to skeptics without context, radicals without history, and perspectivalists without theory.

RESTORING IDEOLOGY AND HISTORY

What are the cumulative insights of our grounded globalizations? To what collective vision do they contribute? I approach this question once more through a critique of both the radicals and skeptics and from there tentatively knit together our studies.

Radicals and skeptics suffer from two common defects: a simplistic view of ideology and a thin conception of history. I consider first the relation between the material and the ideological. The skeptics see neoliberalism, global ideology par excellence, as a mystification of reality; they do not attend to its powerful roots in economic and political life. Our studies, on the other hand, show how ideologies have their power because they are rooted in everyday life, because they speak to lived experiences. Neoliberal discourses of need do not of themselves dismantle socialist welfare but connect to the real interests of specific groups. Postsocialist ruling classes have lost one ideology and need another. Neoliberalism with its focus on the market panacea suits their purposes well, silently reproducing their domination while denying responsibility for economic failures and injustice. For welfare agencies it means more surveillance jobs, for sociologists it means new sources of funding—even if at the bottom of the ladder it receives an angry reception. Ideology does not circulate of its own accord. It is carried hither and yon by interested parties who weld it to economic and political institutions. Brazilian feminists self-consciously import Northern discourses first around the body and then around gender in order to bolster defenses against the authoritarian order or exploit spaces in the democratic aftermath. In the *bairros* of Recife, foreign discourses are refashioned and mixed in with local discourses of citizenship to create a combustible concoction.

If the skeptics cannot explain the power of ideology, the radicals have the opposite problem. For them ideology is epiphenomenal, trailing one step behind reality. Globalization is reflected in its discourse. Once again our studies show something different. First, ideology may be mobilized to resist globalization. Metropolitan elites may wield neoliberal ideology, turning away from class compromise and public services to demand class concessions and privatization, but they also confront a rising tide of opposition mobilized around local ideologies of justice and care. Second, ideology may offer a psychological defense against the effects of globalization. Thus, homeless recyclers dream of past glories, nostalgia for an era gone by, to bolster their defenses against present degradation. Finally, ideologies are multiple. Globalization is not just a single ideology but a constellation of ideologies that becomes a terrain of struggle. Thus, Hungarian villagers attach themselves alternatively to Green environmentalism or international incineration as they battle with each other for economic advantage.

The very organization of our book into global forces, global connections, and global imaginations presumes that ideology is neither merely mystification nor merely reflection of reality. While global discourses are intricately interwoven with global forces and global connections, they also have an autonomy and coherence of their own, becoming powerful ideological constructions that can arouse collective wills. They have real effects, if not always the ones they announce. In my own research I have wrestled with the paradoxes of Russia's entry into a world economy and polity. As Russia's ruling class appropriated the discourses of liberal democracy and

market freedom, it invigorated the old order of cartels, mafias, and appa-
ratchiki, turning them loose in an asset-grabbing war that makes a mockery
of the rule of law, democratic accountability, or market efficiency. We have
to attend to the manifold and complex ways ideologies are produced, proliferated, transformed, combined, disseminated, appropriated, and mobilized to change the world but also to arrest such change. They are not simply tool kits adopted by different groups, but they become the terrain, the
coordinates of struggles. Neither mystification nor reflectionism will do.

If our first criticism of both skeptics and radicals is directed to the place
of ideology, our second criticism is directed to their thin conceptions of history. Whereas skeptics argue there is nothing fundamentally new, the radicals find novelty around every corner. Both commit the fallacy of globalism—namely, that one can characterize changes of the whole without
examining changes of the parts or, to put the fallacy the other way round,
that the secret of the part can be found in the whole. Where the radical
finds traces of space-time distanciation or space-time compression in every
locality and institution, the skeptic presumes there is nothing fundamentally new on earth because the macro indicators of trade, price convergence, and labor flows are unchanged. Radicals and skeptics alike write history by postulating changes or continuities at the global level that are
presumed to imprint themselves on the local level.

We have found no such isomorphism between local and global. At both
levels movement is manifold and multiple, combined and reversible,
uneven and unpredictable. We, therefore, work in the opposite way, ascend-
ing from the local to the global by stitching together our ethnographies. But
this has its problems too. It cannot be done tabula rasa. We needed an ori-
enting map that is attentive to both global and local simultaneously, that
would allow us to compose the global from below. It had to be a vision that
identified what was new about globalization against the skeptics, but without
surrendering to the totalizing mode of the radicals. It needed to be a vision
that acknowledged limits imposed by globalization but also identified spaces
from which those limits could be challenged or negotiated. It needed to be
a vision that recognized itself as a product of the world it sought to grasp
without getting mired in perspectivalism. We found such a vision, such a
theoretical compass in the work of the sociologist Stuart Hall.[12]

Hall sets out from his own biography—an intellectual transplanted from
Jamaica to England, from colony to metropolis. From this vantage point he
distinguishes between "Global Imperialism" and the "Global Postmodern."
Global Imperialism is the era of empire, of British (English) domination in
which other human races are deemed inherently inferior and denied their
own voices, while the Global Postmodern refers to a decentered world of
American mass culture. Ironically, it is a world in which the previously
silenced have found a voice with which to fight for new places. Global

Imperialism describes a world centered around nations organized in a hierarchy of domination, while the Global Postmodern has lost any such hint of totalizing logic. It describes a world in which homogeneity calls forth diversity, in which difference is pluralized, deployed, and valorized rather than enclaved in water-tight compartments of superiority and inferiority.

The Global Postmodern appears unevenly with the reconstitution of world markets (commodity and finance), migration and decolonization, supranational regional bodies and ecological interdependence. Hall offers the following loose characterizations. At the economic level, capitalism adopts a new model of flexible accumulation which exploits and recreates difference. At the political level, the world of interacting nation states is transformed by relations that move above and below the nation. On the one side, above the nation, the global mobilizes rather than silences difference, while on the underside the local reclaims its own historicity. At the cultural level, in place of essentialist categories of nation, race, class, and gender—that is, entities with teleologies that drive history forward—we find the proliferation of hybrid, recombinant, often fragile identities.

Even though Hall does not fall victim to the fallacy of globalism—that is, he does not infer the character of the local from the global or vice versa—nonetheless, he too is bereft of micro-foundations, or what we might call *ethnofoundations*. Without ethnographies such as our own, ethnographies of global forces, connections, and imaginations, he cannot understand how globalization in whatever form is upheld and reproduced, or is challenged and transformed. Moreover, without ethnohistories, he cannot connect his two templates, Global Imperialism and the Global Postmodern, since there is no way of analyzing displacement and emergence without careful attention to movements at the local level. So with our ethnohistories we begin to peg the two globalizations together in terms of different modalities of displacement.

BETWEEN GLOBAL IMPERIALISM AND THE GLOBAL POSTMODERN

So far in this book we have organized our studies in terms of the lived experience of globalization—the way global forces, global connections, and global imaginations uphold, accommodate, resist, or contest the existing order. I now want to move from the synchronic to the diachronic, from the reproduction/contestation of globalization to the movement of and between Global Imperialism and the Global Postmodern. With this end in mind, it helps to think of our nine case studies as archeological sites scattered around the world. In our excavations we hope to piece together a picture of the emergence of the Global Postmodern and of the displacement of Global Imperialism. To advance toward this goal I have reorganized the studies into accounts of institutional change along the lines of Hall's analysis.

First, there is the displacement of old *economic* forms—Fordist manufacturing is losing out to information technology, service work, and independent recycling. Second, there is the displacement of old *political* regimes—Hungarian socialism and Brazilian dictatorship were replaced by liberal democracies. Third, old *cultural* identities are shunted aside in favor of a proliferation of new ones—the fracturing of blue collar identity and the rupture of enclaved womanhood coincided with the multiplication of work identities and femininities. I will consider each institutional sphere in turn, with a view to understanding the different "modalities" of displacement—that is, how the dominant becomes residual and gives way to the emergent.

Flexible Accumulation. I begin with the economic and the most dramatic transformation, namely Pittsburgh's move from "steel city" to "global city." Pittsburgh was at the heart of the Fordist era of class compromise between steel unions and the great steel corporations, a compromise protected from international competition and with a guaranteed market. When the steel industry entered its tailspin, Pittsburgh's corporate elite showed rare agility in restructuring its economy. The steel plants became museums or carcasses and alongside them arose high-tech manufacturing and a flourishing service sector. Pittsburgh's government followed the lead of its corporations, granting tax cuts, promoting the privatization of public services, and demanding lay-offs and wage concessions from county employees. But this aggressive neoliberalism did not always have its own way. It met with determined opposition from local service-sector unions, organized around local interests and identities. Flexibility from above engendered flexibility from below but not without its own frictions. The new unionism, rooted in local communities, was hampered by rigidities inherited from the Fordist past. Union officials were accustomed to backroom dealing, while the membership expected their leaders to deliver improvements. They did not expect to have to fight for their demands. Displacement of bureaucratic unionism in one space was obstructed by its tenacity in another.

If the arrival of Pittsburgh's global city required a seismic disconnection from its past, the Irish software industry had a smoother passage. Until the 1980s American computer businesses exported only their most peripheral operations to Ireland. But in the process they created demand for localized products, and, with inducements from the state and with abundant skilled labor, spin-off firms took root and produced their own agglomerations. Some even took off into the global arena. As the Celtic Tiger began to flourish, American transnational corporations expanded their Irish investment in research and development, and with them came the flexible workplace of software development. But this global workplace, far from being disembedded from place and time, calls forth and requires for its operation local solidarities. Even as they spiral through transnational labor markets, Irish software engineers are rooted in Irish communities. The old and the new are rebonded.

We can find flexibility not just in the sky but also on the ground. If anyone exhibits flexibility it is the homeless recycler who lives from the refuse of consumer capitalism. As the securities of Fordism and its welfare state crumble in advanced capitalism, and as structural adjustment delivers its blessings elsewhere, flexibility becomes the survival strategy of the poor everywhere. The break with the past is greatest here but still it is by no means complete. Homeless recyclers sustain themselves with a nostalgia for their past, their lives as blue collar workers, as servicemen, as heads of household. No matter the trauma of real displacement, memory is not so easily conquered. The past is imaginatively reenacted along the avenues of our cities.

Global-Local Synergy. Transnational corporations and independent recyclers operate in the shadow of the state, but in many places the state is itself withdrawing, creating new global-local synergies. We turn, therefore, to the modalities of displacement in the sphere of politics. The demise of authoritarian states and their replacement by weak liberal democracy encourages global invasions of civil society. Feminist groups in Brazil are no longer defending themselves against the state but, under the impulse of imported and indigenized feminisms, they set new agendas and proliferate into the hidden recesses of community life.[13]

Here the erosion of the state-society nexus creates a vacuum that draws in global connections. Similarly, in postsocialist Hungary, "democratization" has created spaces for global and local interests to converge, lock, tangle, and diverge. No longer marginal to the political process, villagers forge alliances with different international incineration companies or latch onto the oppositional Greens. The most marginalized localities under state socialism exploit their hazardous wastes to tangle with global actors. Erosion of the old state-society nexus allows the local to circumvent the state, but at the same time the state itself becomes vulnerable to new supranational predators. State agencies are seduced and coerced by the neoliberal packages for welfare "reform," prepared by the World Bank and IMF. Thus, the weakness of the postsocialist state is measured not only by its retreat from national politics but also by its subservience to global forces. It acts as a transmission belt, turning universal child support, for example, into the stigmatizing, claims-processing of "welfare mothers." The state-society nexus dissolves from both sides: the state is caught up in the magnetic field of supranational bodies while society is hooked into transnational flows and connections.

New Identities. Global Imperialism generated relatively stable and enduring subjects of class, race, gender, and nation. Such entities had a certain insularity and essentialist character. Their self-realization was in step with history. We could talk of the industrial working class, Third World poor, autonomous nation states, the racialized ghetto, the women's movement, and so on. With the demand for flexibility and the rise of the global-local nexus, boundaries have broken down, and identities proliferated. The modality of cultural displacement is fragmentation. Thus, as long as they are trapped within successive shells of family, community, and nation, Kerala nurses cannot escape their subordination and stigmatization. Breaking into global labor markets threatens to disrupt these patterns. As first movers in migration, they challenge conventional gender identities, especially when their husbands, who follow, can find only lower-status employment in the United States. Gender and class relations are no longer "given" but have to be negotiated in the family, at work, and in the community. Although the transnational community attempts to reenclave women and their husbands—and so once again the past never disappears—nonetheless exigencies of migration, as well as rebellion from second-generation immigrants, challenge and break through conventional boundaries. These experiences become more common as migration cuts national identity adrift from states, building new diasporas within fluid boundaries.[14]

Even more remarkable is the deenclaving and proliferation of identities around breast cancer. Where women previously lived with their breast cancer as a private trauma, the last twenty years have seen them come out of the closet. The transformation of medical practices—the extension of screening, multiplication of treatments and diagnoses, and the rise of support groups—created the grounds for turning private stigma into public movement. Where difference was previously hidden, silenced, colonized, it is now openly uncovered, exposed, and expressed. In this case the emergent identities—survivor, resister, victim—feed into tenuous, overlapping, intermingling social movements.

But the dissolution of old identities does not always foreshadow movement. Far from it. The unraveling of working-class identity among shipyard workers leaves them tripping in many directions—taxi-driver, salesman, photographer, union official, sociologist. Unitary subjects splinter and then recombine in hybrid forms. They congeal into movements when cemented by an imagination of an alternative, better world.

TOWARD GROUNDED POLITICS

We have compiled our ethnographies and ethnohistories into the displacement of, first, an economic order based on detailed division of labor, organized relations between classes, and economies of scale; second, a political order centered on the nation state around which revolved civil society and which mediated unequal international relations; and, third, a cultural order that was connected to enduring and relatively homogeneous identities firmly entrenched in economy or state. In its place we have found an emergent order of flexible accumulation, global-local mutuality, and new hybrid identities.

Displacement of the old order took many forms: burial, erosion, retreat, dissolution, subordination, transmutation, recombination, fragmentation. Do these modalities of displacement of Global Imperialism add up to a transition to the Global Postmodern? A simple linear transition might serve our purposes well. It would challenge the skeptics by identifying transformations in the global order along lines that they cannot so easily measure. It would also bring the radicals down to earth, challenging their teleology of increasing globalization by insisting instead on the transition between two incommensurable, qualitatively different globalizations.

But this formulation is problematic. Many qualifications are in order, and none more important than the most obvious. The transition, if that is what we were to call it, is *uneven* across the globe, whether within or across national boundaries. Liberal democracy, for example, has been around as long as Global Imperialism, but some are only just entering or reentering its orbit. Change is also *combined* in that the Global Postmodern works with the preexisting capital, state, and identities. It works in part on the terrain of preexisting Global Imperialism. That is why we speak of *supranational* forces, *transnational* connections, and *postnational* imaginations to underline the repositioning rather than demise of the nation state. The transition cannot be unilinear because interests congeal around each of the orders. Every step in the direction of flexible accumulation, global-local mutuality, and new identities calls forth a reaction, the reassertion of Fordism, the state, and old essentialist subjects. The dinosaurs of Fordism are still around, not least the auto companies themselves. Welfare states have not disappeared, however trimmed down they may be. The economy still requires and receives ample regulation, ideology notwithstanding. Old identities have not dissolved in a welter of hybridity. Blue collar workers still organize themselves into unions and in some countries they even have parties. Xenophobic nationalism and even racism still greet foreign workers. Indian nurses are still stigmatized. It was the great achievement of Thatcherism and Reaganism that they could bring up the rearguard of Global Imperialism while presenting themselves as the vanguard of the Global Postmodern.

We do not, therefore, subscribe to the view that there is a *transition between globalizations,* between Global Imperialism and the Global Postmodern, even understood in this open-ended and indeterminate manner. Instead we prefer the more agnostic perspective of *globalization in transition.* Our studies point to the displacement of an old order while the contours of the new one are simply not clear. But more than that, we would also argue that the Global Postmodern is a world without a grand narrative. There is no path toward a homogeneous world capitalism or for that matter a single

world socialism. There are many capitalisms just as any renaissance of socialism would have to be multiple. A totalizing theory too easily stifles imagi-
naries from below, silences diversity of the local, and becomes a new ideology, presenting what *is* as natural and inevitable. As Inderpal Grewal and
Caren Kaplan intimate, in their evocative use of "scattered hegemonies,"
constructing any vision of the Global Postmodern is as much a political as a
theoretical project.[15]

Instead of reaching for a global theory of the Global Postmodern, we
should try to map out its distinctive and emergent political terrain. If Global
Imperialism governed through coercion, the forcible domination of center
over periphery, metropolis over colony, empire over satellite, the Global
Postmodern is a world governed by hegemony in which consent prevails
over coercion. It is dominated by a constellation of ideologies—market
freedom and liberal democracy, sovereignty and human rights—that recognizes and works through difference. To be sure, hegemony is always "protected by the armour of coercion,"[16] but the latter is deployed only episodi-
cally (if dramatically) and in the name of universal principles. Global
Imperialism called forth wars of movement, violent anticolonial struggles,
inter-national wars, but in the Global Postmodern wars of movement are
doomed to defeat. Just as national hegemony cannot be overthrown by revolution, so Western global hegemonies cannot be overthrown through violence. Instead, we turn to wars of position in which different groups with
multiple identities have to be woven together around universalistic interests
such as human rights or environmental justice. It is a war of position
because it builds up a mosaic from multiple locations. Its trenches lie in the
burgeoning transnational society of ethnic diasporas, deterritorialized
nations, nongovernmental organizations, professional associations, the
global civil society that becomes denser by the day. It is not so much a matter of creating movements outside the hegemonic order but rather on its
terrain, radicalizing the meaning of democracy, appropriating the market,
democratizing sovereignty, and expanding human rights.

Grounded globalizations call for a grounded politics. Where the "skeptics" (de)mythologize neoliberalism and uphold a social democratic politics
revolving around the nation state, where the "radicals" see no alternative
but to work with the forces of globalization, we have tried to show that a politics from below is also possible, a politics that can arrest or divert the tide
of globalization, play off its different tendencies, and invent its new meanings. To Giddens's cosmopolitanism from above we propose, following
Boaventura de Sousa Santos, a new cosmopolitanism from below.[17] Globalization cannot be reduced to an inexorable force; it is also a process in
which we participate; it is a process embedded in imaginations we construct.
It opens up opportunities as well as closes them down.

Even as I write, in this last month of the millennium, unprecedented
protest from labor, human rights, and environmental groups has laid siege

to the meeting of the World Trade Organization in Seattle. With its over-whelmingly American presence, it is premature to call this dramatic inter-vention from the streets a "counter-hegemonic globalization."[18] None-theless, this frontal challenge to a supranational organization on its own terrain—the regulation of trade—beckons the proliferation of transna-tional social movements, propelled by imaginations of a global dimension.

NOTES

Special thanks to Erik Wright for always demanding clarity and veracity.

1. Anthony Giddens, *Runaway World*.
2. Ibid., Lecture 1, p. 6.
3. Castells, *End of Millennium*, pp. 161–65.
4. See, for example, Paul Hirst and Grahame Thompson, *Globalization in Question*; Robert Wade, "Globalization and Its Limits: Reports of the Death of the National Economy are Greatly Exaggerated"; Peter Evans, "The Eclipse of the State? Reflections on Stateness in an Era of Globalization"; and Linda Weiss, "Globalization and the Myth of the Powerless State." They all contribute to the same argument, challenging the "radical" interpretations of globalization.
5. Wade, "Globalization and Its Limits," p. 61.
6. Giddens, *Runaway World*, Lecture 1, p. 1.
7. Ibid.
8. Castells, *The Information Age*, volumes 1, 2 and 3.
9. Harvey, *The Condition of Postmodernity*.
10. Jameson, "Cognitive Mapping"; *Postmodernism or, The Cultural Logic of Late Capitalism; The Cultural Turn*.
11. Gupta and Ferguson, "Discipline and Practice: 'The Field' as Site, Method, and Location in Anthropology," p. 39. Italics added.
12. Stuart Hall, "The Global and the Local: Globalization and Ethnicity"; "Old and New Identities, Old and New Ethnicities"; "When Was 'The Post-colonial'? Thinking at the Limit."
13. Boaventura de Sousa Santos describes similar moves from defensive politics under the Brazilian authoritarian order to a more aggressive politics, buttressed by the Catholic Church and international norms, around human rights (Santos, *Toward a New Common Sense*, chapter 5).
14. Basch, Schiller, and Blanc, *Nations Unbound*.
15. Grewal and Kaplan criticize much postmodern thinking for its "Western" bias and instead stress the transnational connections of postcolonialism—a post-colonialism which of course includes advanced capitalist countries as well as the so-called "Third World." They seek a transnational feminist politics that will knit dif-ferent groups together, across borders and from below. See "Introduction: Transnational Feminist Practices and Questions of Postmodernity."
16. Gramsci, *Selections from the Prison Notebooks*, p. 263.
17. Santos, *Toward a New Common Sense*, chapter 4.
18. See the prescient article by Peter Evans, "Counter-Hegemonic Globalization: Transnational Networks as Political Tools for Fighting Marginalization."

BIBLIOGRAPHY

Abbott, Andrew, and Emanuel Gaziano. "Transition and Tradition: Departmental Faculty in the Era of the Second Chicago School." In *A Second Chicago School?*, edited by Gary Alan Fine, pp. 221–72. Chicago: University of Chicago Press, 1995.

Ação Mulher/Brasil Mulher. Letter requesting funds for women's health projects. Unpublished document in SOS Corpo archives. Recife, Brazil: December 23, 1980.

Acuff, Stewart. "Expanded Roles for the Central Labor Council: The View from Atlanta." In *Which Direction for Organized Labor?* edited by Bruce Nissen, pp. 133–42. Detroit: Wayne State University Press, 1999.

Adam, Jan. "Social Contract." In *Economic Reforms and Welfare Systems in the USSR, Poland and Hungary,* edited by J. Adam, pp. 1–25. New York: St. Martin's Press, 1991.

Altman, Roberta. *Waking Up, Fighting Back: The Politics of Breast Cancer.* New York: Little, Brown, 1996.

Alvarez, Sonia E. *Engendering Democracy in Brazil: Women's Movements in Transition Politics.* Princeton, N. J.: Princeton University Press, 1990.

Alvarez, Sonia E., and Evelina Dagnino. "Para Além da 'Democracia Realmente Existente': Movimentos Sociais, a Nova Cidadania e a Configuração de Espaços Públicos Alternativos." Paper presented at the XIX Annual Encounter of the National Association of Graduate Study and Research (ANPOCS). Caxambú, October 17–21, 1995.

Alves, Maria Helena Moreira. *State and Opposition in Military Brazil.* Austin: University of Texas Press, 1985.

Anderson, Benedict. *Imagined Communities.* London: Verso, 1983.

Anderson, Nels. *The Hobo: The Sociology of the Homeless Man.* 1923. Chicago: University of Chicago Press, 1967.

Andorka, Rudolf. "A Társadalmi Egyenlötlenségek Novekedése a Rendszerváltás óta." *Szociológiai Szemle* 1 (1996): 70–92.

Andorka, Rudolf, and Zsolt Speder. "A Szegénység Magyarországon 1992–1995."
    Esély 4 (1996): 25–52.
Andorka, Rudolf, and Istvan Tóth. "A Jóléti Rendszer Jellemzöi és Reformjának
    Lehetöségei." *Közgazdasági Szemle* 1 (1995): 1–29.
Andrews, Kunnuparampil Punnoose. *Keralites in America: Community Reference Book.*
    New York: Literary Market Review, 1983.
Anonymous. "The Shipbuilding Industry in Korea," on the World Wide Web at
    www.iworld.net/Korea/industry/f206.html.
Appadurai, Arjun. *Modernity at Large.* Minneapolis: University of Minnesota Press,
    1996.
Aquino, Estela de, and Dina C. Costa. "Entrevista realizada com Betânia, integrante
    do grupo SOS-Corpo, Recife." Interview with SOS member conducted by Mas-
    ters' students in the Instituto de Medicina Social, Universidade Estadual de Rio
    de Janeiro. July 1983.
Arato, Andrew. "Revolution and Restoration: On the Origins of Right-Wing Radical
    Ideology in Hungary." In *The New Great Transformation,* edited by C. Bryant and E.
    Mokrzycki, pp. 99–119. New York: Routledge, 1994.
Ávila, Maria Betânia. "Modernidade e Cidadania Reprodutiva." *Revista Estudos Femi-
    nistas* (segundo semestre 1993): 382–93.
———. "PAISM: Um Programa de Saúde para o Bem Estar de Gênero." Pamphlet.
    Recife, Brazil: SOS Corpo, 1995.
Baden, Sally, and Anne Marie Goetz. "Who Needs [Sex] When You Can Have [Gen-
    der]? Conflicting Discourses on Gender at Beijing." In *Women, International Devel-
    opment and Politics: The Bureaucratic Mire,* edited by Kathleen Staudt, pp. 37–58.
    Philadelphia: Temple University Press, 1997.
Banks, Andy. "The Power and Promise of Community Unionism." *Labor Research
    Review* 10 (1992): 17–31.
Barnard, Elaine. "Creating Democratic Communities in the Workplace." In *A New
    Labor Movement for a New Century,* edited by Gregory Mantsios, pp. 4–15. New
    York: Monthly Review Press, 1998.
Barnes, Patricia G. "Safer Streets at What Cost?" *ABA Journal* 84 (1998): 24–25.
Baron, James, M. Diane Burton, and Michael Hannan. "The Road Taken: Origins
    and Early Evolution of Employment Systems in Emerging Companies." *Industrial
    and Corporate Change* 5 (1996): 239–75.
Barrett, Alan, Tim Callan, and Brian Nolan. "Rising Wage Inequality, Returns to
    Education and Labour Market Institutions: Evidence from Ireland." *British Jour-
    nal of Industrial Relations* 37 (1999): 77–100.
Basch, Linda, Nina Glick Schiller, and Cristina Szanton Blanc, eds. *Nations Unbound:
    Transnational Projects, Postcolonial Predicaments and Deterritorialized Nation-States.*
    Luxembourg: Gordon and Breach Publishers, 1994.
Batt, Sharon. *Patient No More: The Politics of Breast Cancer.* Charlottetown, Canada:
    Gynergy Books, 1994.
Baum, Alice S., and Donald W. Burnes. *A Nation in Denial: The Truth about Homeless-
    ness.* Boulder, Colo.: Westview Press, 1993.
Bauman, Zygmunt. "After the Patronage State: A Model in Search of Class Interests."
    In *The New Great Transformation,* edited by C. Bryant and E. Mokrzycki, pp. 14–35.
    New York: Routledge, 1994.

————. "Hol az osztályérdek mostanában?" [Where is class interest these days?] *2000* 5, no. 8 (1993): 9–16.

BCCCP. "Request for Applications—Breast and Cervical Cancer Control Program for Early Detection of Breast and Cervical Cancer." Sacramento: California Department of Health Service—Cancer Detection Section, 1997.

BCEDP. "Request for Applications—Breast Cancer Partnerships for Early Detection of Breast Cancer." Sacramento: California Department of Health Services—Cancer Detection Section, 1996.

Becker, Howard. *Outsiders: Studies in the Sociology of Deviance.* New York: Free Press, 1963.

Beckett, Katherine. *Making Crime Pay: Law and Order in Contemporary American Politics.* Oxford: Oxford University Press, 1997.

Belko, Mark. "Control of Kanes May Be Shifted." *Pittsburgh Post-Gazette,* September 4, 1996.

————. "Dunn Gives Ultimatum to Kane Unions." *Pittsburgh Post-Gazette,* January 11, 1997.

————. "Dunn Halts Proposed Transfer of Kanes." *Pittsburgh Post-Gazette,* March 25, 1997.

————. "Keep Kane Homes Public, Group Asks." *Pittsburgh Post-Gazette,* January 29, 1997.

————. "Lucchino: Privatization of Kanes Just a Quick Fix." *Pittsburgh Post-Gazette,* March 5, 1997.

————. "Privatization Hits Strong Opposition: Commissioners Booed, Questioned by Crowd." *Pittsburgh Post-Gazette,* October 3, 1996.

————. "Unions, County Expect Progress." *Pittsburgh Post-Gazette,* September 1, 1997.

Berman, Marshall. *All That Is Solid Melts into Air: The Experience of Modernity.* London: Penguin, 1982.

Blau, Joel. *The Visible Poor: Homelessness in the United States.* New York: Oxford University Press, 1992.

Bluestone, Barry, and Bennett Harrison. *The Deindustrialization of America.* New York: Basic Books, 1982.

Blum, Joseph A. "The African-American Struggle for Equality in the World War II West Coast Shipyards." Unpublished paper, 1993.

————. "San Francisco Iron: The Industry and Its Workers—From the Gold Rush to the Turn of the Century." Master's thesis, San Francisco State University, 1990.

Blum, Linda. *Between Feminism and Labor: The Significance of the Comparable Worth Movement.* Berkeley: University of California Press, 1991.

Blumer, Herbert. *An Appraisal of Thomas and Znaniecki's The Polish Peasant in Europe and America.* New York: Social Science Research Council, 1939.

Böröcz, József. "Dual Dependency and Property Vacuum: Social Change on the State Socialist Semiperiphery." *Theory and Society* 21 (1992): 77–104.

Boston Women's Health Course Collective. *Our Bodies, Our Selves.* Boston: New England Free Press, 1971.

Bourdieu, Pierre. *The Logic of Practice.* 1980. Stanford, Calif.: Stanford University Press, 1990.

————. *Outline of a Theory of Practice.* 1972. Cambridge: Cambridge University Press, 1977.

Bourgois, Philippe. *In Search of Respect.* New York: Cambridge University Press, 1995.

Braverman, Harry. *Labor and Monopoly Capital: The Degradation of Work in the Twentieth Century.* New York and London: Monthly Review Press, 1974.

Breslow, Lester. *A History of Cancer Control in the United States, 1946–1971.* DHEW Publication Numbers. (NIH) 79–1516 (volume 1) and 79–1518 (volume 2). Los Angeles: History of Cancer Control Project, University of California School of Public Health, for the Division of Cancer Control and Rehabilitation, National Cancer Institute, 1979.

Bronfenbrenner, Kate, and Tom Juravich. "It Takes More Than House Calls: Organizing to Win with a Comprehensive Union-Building Strategy." In *Organizing to Win: New Research on Union Strategies,* edited by Kate Bronfenbrenner, Sheldon Friedman, Richard Hurd, Rudolph Oswald, and Ronald Seeber, pp. 18–36. Ithaca, N. Y.: Cornell ILR Press, 1998.

———. "The Promise of Union Organizing in the Public and Private Sectors." Working paper. Silver Spring, Md.: Institute for the Study of Labor Organizations, George Meany Center for Labor Studies, 1994.

Brosch, Erich. "No Place Like Home." *Harper's,* April 1998, pp. 58–59.

Brown, Richard. "Passages in the Life of a White Anthropologist: Max Gluckman in Northern Rhodesia." *Journal of African History* 20 (1979): 525–41.

Brown, S., and K. Eisenhardt. "The Art of Continuous Change." *Administrative Science Quarterly* 42 (1997): 1–34.

Bryant, Christopher, and Edmund Mokrzycki. "Theorizing the Changes in East-Central Europe." In *The New Great Transformation,* edited by C. Bryant and E. Mokrzycki, pp.1–13. New York: Routledge, 1994.

Bull, John. "County May Offer Buyout Packages: Republican Takeover Could Frighten Many to Take Money, Leave." *Pittsburgh Post-Gazette,* November 22, 1995, p. B-2.

Bulmer, Martin. *The Chicago School of Sociology.* Chicago: University of Chicago Press, 1984.

Bunce, Valerie, and Mária Csanádi. "Uncertainty in the Transition: Post-Communism in Hungary."*East European Politics and Societies* 7 (1992): 240–74.

Burawoy, Michael. *The Colour of Class on the Copper Mines: From African Advancement to Zambianization.* Manchester, England: Manchester University Press for Institute for Social Research, University of Zambia, 1972.

———. "Consciousness and Contradiction: A Study of Student Protest in Zambia." *British Journal of Sociology* 27(1976): 78–98.

———. "The Extended Case Method." *Sociological Theory* 16 (1998): 4–33.

———. *Manufacturing Consent.* Chicago: University of Chicago Press, 1979.

———. *The Politics of Production: Factory Regimes under Capitalism and Socialism.* London: Verso Books, 1985.

Burawoy, Michael, and János Lukács. *The Radiant Past.* Chicago: University of Chicago Press, 1992.

Burawoy, Michael, et al. *Ethnography Unbound: Power and Resistance in the Modern Metropolis.* Berkeley: University of California Press, 1991.

Burgess, Ernest. "The Growth of the City: An Introduction to a Research Project." 1980. In *The City,* edited by Robert Park and Ernest Burgess, pp. 47–62. Chicago: University of Chicago Press, 1990.

Burt, Martha R. *Over the Edge: The Growth of Homelessness in the 1980's.* New York: Russell Sage Foundation, 1992.

Burton, Alice. "Dividing Up the Struggle: The Consequences of 'Split' Welfare Work for Union Activism." In Burawoy et al., *Ethnography Unbound,* pp. 85–107. Berkeley: University of California Press, 1991.

Camurça, Silvia, and Taciana Gouveia. *Cidade, Cidadania: Um Olhar a partir das Mulheres.* Recife, Brazil: SOS Corpo, 1995.

———. *O Que É Gênero? Um Novo Desafio para a Ação das Mulheres Trabalhadoras Rurais.* Brazil: MMTR/DED/SOS Corpo: Gênero e Cidadania, 1995.

Castells, Manuel. *End of Millennium.* Vol. 3. The Information Age. Cambridge, Mass., and Oxford, England: Blackwell, 1998.

———. *The Informational City.* Oxford, England: Basil Blackwell, 1989.

———. *The Power of Identity.* Vol. 2. The Information Age. Cambridge, Mass., and Oxford, England: Blackwell, 1997.

———. *The Rise of the Network Society.* Vol. 1. The Information Age. Cambridge, Mass., and Oxford, England: Blackwell, 1996.

Castells, Manuel, and Peter Hall. *Technopoles of the World.* New York: Routledge, 1994.

Castoriadis, Cornelius. "The Social Regime in Russia." *Telos* 38 (1978–79): 32–47.

Castro, Mary Garcia. "A Dinâmica entre Classe e Gênero na América Latina: Apontamentos para uma Teoria Regional sobre Gênero." In *Mulher e Políticas Públicas,* edited by Maria da Graça Neves and Delaine Martins, pp. 39–69. Rio de Janeiro: Editora Rosa dos Tempos/Fundação Carlos Chagas, 1992.

Castro, Mary Garcia, and Lena Lavinas. "Do Feminino ao Gênero: A Construção de um Objeto." In *Uma Questão de Gênero,* edited by Albertina de Oliveira Costa and Cristina Bruschini, pp. 216–51. Rio de Janeiro: Editora Rosa dos Tempos/ Fundação Carlos Chagas, 1992.

Center for Advanced Ship Repair and Maintenance, Norfolk, Virginia. March 10, 1997. "Background." On the World Wide Web at www.odu.edu.gnusers/miatc_v/casrm1.htm.

Chartrand, Sabra. "Unions Try to Secure a Place in the Changing Work World." *New York Times,* February 23, 1997.

Cirtautas, Arista Maria. "In Pursuit of the Democratic Interest: The Institutionalization of Parties and Interests in Eastern Europe." In *The New Great Transformation,* edited by C. Bryant and E. Mokrzycki, pp. 36–57. New York: Routledge, 1994.

City of Pittsburgh. "Mayor's Annual Report." Pittsburgh, Pa.: City of Pittsburgh, 1997.

Clifford, James. "Notes on Travel and Theory." *Inscriptions: Traveling Theories, Traveling Theorists* 5 (1989): 177–88.

———. "Spatial Practices: Fieldwork, Travel, and the Disciplining of Anthropology." In *Anthropological Locations,* edited by Akhil Gupta and James Ferguson, pp. 185–222. Berkeley and Los Angeles: University of California Press, 1997.

———. "Traveling Cultures." In *Cultural Studies,* edited by Lawrence Grossberg, Cary Nelson, and Paula A. Treichler, pp. 96–112. New York: Routledge, 1992.

Clifford, James, and George Marcus, eds. *Writing Culture: The Poetics and Politics of Ethnography.* Berkeley: University of California Press, 1986.

Cohen, Larry, and Steve Early. "Defending Workers' Rights in the Global Economy: The CWA Experience." In *Which Direction for Organized Labor? Essays on Organizing, Outreach, and Internal Transformations,* edited by Bruce Nissen, pp. 143–64. Detroit: Wayne State University Press, 1999.

Cohen, Lizabeth. *Making a New Deal: Industrial Workers in Chicago, 1919–1939.* Cambridge: Cambridge University Press, 1990.

Coleman, Elizabeth. "From Population Control to Reproductive Health." *Ford Foundation Report,* Summer 1994, p. 32.

Coleman, Michael P., Jacques Estève, Philippe Damiecki, Annie Arslan, and Hélène Renard. *Trends in Cancer Incidence and Mortality.* Publication no. 121. Lyon, France: International Agency for Research on Cancer (IARC), 1993.

Comaroff, Jean, and John Comaroff. *Of Revelation and Revolution: Christianity, Colonialism, and Consciousness in South Africa.* Chicago: University of Chicago Press, 1991.

Comaroff, John, and Jean Comaroff. *Ethnography and the Historical Imagination.* Boulder, Colo.: Westview Press, 1992.

Connell, R. W. *Gender and Power: Society, the Person and Sexual Politics.* Stanford, Calif.: Stanford University Press, 1987.

———. "Why Is Classical Theory Classical?" *American Journal of Sociology* 102 (1997): 1511–57.

Corrêa, Sonia. "Direitos Reprodutivos como Direitos Humanos." In *Os Direitos Reprodutivos e a Condição Feminina,* edited by Ana Paula Portella, pp. 4–8. Recife: SOS Corpo/Liber Gráfica e Editora Ltda., 1984/1989.

———. "PAISM: Uma História sem Fim." Pamphlet. Recife: SOS Corpo, 1993.

———. "Uma Recusa da Maternidade? Causas e Condições da Esterilização Feminina Voluntária na Rede Metropolitana do Recife." In *Os Direitos Reprodutivos e a Condição Feminina,* edited by Ana Paula Portella, pp. 26–38. Recife: SOS Corpo/Liber Gráfica e Editora Ltda., 1984/1989.

Costa, Ana Alice A., and Cecilia M. B. Sardenberg. "Teoria e Praxis Feministas na Academia: Os Núcleos de Estudos sobre a Mulher nas Universidades Brasileiras." *Revista Estudos Feministas,* special issue (segundo semestre, 1994): 387–400.

Costa, Claudia Lima. "Being There and Writing Here: Gender and the Politics of Translation in a Brazilian Landscape." Paper presented at the XX International Congress of the Latin American Studies Association, April 17–19, 1997, in Guadalajara, Mexico.

Costner, Pat, and Thornton, Joe. *Playing with Fire: Hazardous Waste Incineration.* Washington, D. C.: Greenpeace USA, 1993.

Craft, James. "The Community as a Source of Power." *Journal of Labor Research* 11, no. 2 (1990): 145–60.

———. "Unions, Bureaucracy, and Change: Old Dogs Learn New Tricks Very Slowly." *Journal of Labor Research* 12, no. 4 (1990): 393–405.

Cressey, Paul. *The Taxi-Dance Hall.* Chicago: University of Chicago Press, 1932.

Crumb, Joseph. "Religious Leaders Put Out Call for No Privatization." *Pittsburgh Tribune-Review,* March 25, 1997.

Culhane, Dennis P., June M. Avery, and Trevor R. Hadley. "Prevalence of Treated Behavioral Disorders among Adult Shelter Users: A Longitudinal Study." *American Journal of Orthopsychiatry* 68, no. 1 (1998): 63–72.

Davis, Mike. *City of Quartz: Excavating the Future in Los Angeles.* London and New York: Verso, 1990.

———. "Who Killed L.A.?" *New Left Review* 197 (1993): 3–28.

Deacon, Robert. "Social Policy, Social Justice and Citizenship in Eastern Europe." In *Social Policy, Social Justice and Citizenship in Eastern Europe,* edited by R. Deacon, pp. 3–18. Aldershot, England: Avebury, 1992.

DeGregorio, Michael D., and Valerie J. Wiebe. *Tamoxifen & Breast Cancer: What Every-*

one Should Know about the Treatment of Breast Cancer. New Haven: Yale University Press, 1994.

Dempsey, Kate, Nechama Katz, Traci Sawyers, and Ellen Taggart. "Screening Mammography: What the Cancer Establishment Never Told You." Unpublished report prepared for the Women's Community Cancer Project, Cambridge, Mass., 1992.

Devault, Marjorie. *Feeding the Family: The Social Organization of Caring as Gendered Work.* Chicago: University of Chicago Press, 1991.

Doyle, Jim. Review of *Censored 1999: The News That Didn't Make the News—The Year's Top 25 Censored Stories,* by Peter Phillips and Project Censored. *San Francisco Chronicle,* June 6, 1999, Book Review Section, p. 5.

Duneier, Mitchell. *Slim's Table: Race, Respectability, and Masculinity.* Chicago: University of Chicago Press, 1992.

Dunn, Larry, and Bob Cranmer. "Our Campaign Is Different." *Pittsburgh Post-Gazette,* November 5, 1995.

Durkheim, Emile. *The Division of Labor in Society.* 1893. Translated by W. D. Halls. New York: Free Press, 1984.

Duster, Troy. "Pattern, Purpose, and Race in the Drug War: The Crisis of Credibility in Criminal Justice." In *Crack in America: Demon Drugs and Social Justice,* edited by Craig Reinarman and Harry G. Levine, pp. 260–85. Berkeley: University of California Press, 1997.

Early, Steve. "Membership-Based Organizing." In *A New Labor Movement for a New Century,* edited by Gregory Mantsios, pp. 82–103. New York: Monthly Review Press, 1998.

Eisenscher, Michael. "Critical Juncture: Unions at the Crossroads." In *Which Direction for Organized Labor? Essays on Organizing, Outreach, and Internal Transformations,* edited by Bruce Nissen, pp. 217–45. Detroit: Wayne State University Press, 1999.

Epstein, A. L. *The Politics of an Urban African Community.* Manchester, England: Manchester University Press, 1958.

Epstein, Steven. *Impure Science: AIDS, Activism, and the Politics of Knowledge.* Berkeley: University of California Press, 1996.

Espiritu, Yen Le. *Asian American Women and Men: Labor, Laws and Love.* Thousand Oaks, Calif.: Sage Publications, 1997.

Evans, Peter. "Counter-Hegemonic Globalization: Transnational Networks as Political Tools for Fighting Marginalization." *Contemporary Sociology* 29 (2000): 230–241.

———. "The Eclipse of the State? Reflections on Stateness in an Era of Globalization." *World Politics* 50 (1997): 62–87.

Fact Betéti-társaság. *A Garé térségében épitendö hulladékégetö társadalmi hatástanulmánya* (The Social Impact Study of the Incinerator to Be Built in the Vicinity of Garé). Pécs, Hungary: Fact Betéti-társaság, 1995.

Fantasia, Rick. *Cultures of Solidarity.* Berkeley: University of California Press, 1988.

Feinberg, Madaline. "The Boston Women's Health Book Collective Celebrates Its 25th Anniversary!!" *The Network News* 21, no. 3 (May/June 1996): 1.

Ferge, Zsuzsa. "A Célzott Szociálpolitika Lehetösegei." Paper presented at the conference "A Jóléti Rendszer Reformja," ELTE Szociálpolitika Tanszek, Budapest, Hungary, March 24, 1995.

———. *Javaslat a Szociálpolitikai Rendszer Módosítására.* Budapest: MTA, 1982.

———. "A Magyar Segélyezési Rendszer Reformja II." *Esély* 1 (1996): 25–42.

———. "Recent Trends in Social Policy in Hungary." In *Economic Reforms and Welfare Systems in the USSR, Poland and Hungary,* edited by J. Adam, pp. 132–55. New York: St. Martin's, 1991.

———. *"A Society in the Making: Hungarian Social and Societal Policy, 1945–1975.* New York: M. E. Sharpe, 1979.

———. *Szociálpolitika Ma és Holnap.* Budapest, MTA, 1987.

Ferge, Zsuzsa, and Júlia Szalai. *Fordulat és Reform.* Budapest: MTA, 1985.

Ferguson, James. *Expectations of Modernity: Myths and Meanings of Urban Life on the Zambian Copperbelt.* Berkeley and Los Angeles: University of California Press, 1999.

Fernandez, Cida, and Silvia Camurça. *Relações de Cooperação ao Desenvolvimento e a Política de Gênero: Experiências e Perspectivas no Brasil.* Proceedings of seminar held in Recife, October 25–27, 1995. Recife, Brazil: SOS Corpo: Gênero e Cidadania, 1995.

Figueroa, Héctor. "International Labor Solidarity in an Era of Global Competition." In *A New Labor Movement for a New Century,* edited by Gregory Mantsios, pp. 304–19. New York: Monthly Review Press, 1998.

Filtzer, Donald. *Soviet Workers and De-Stalinization: The Consolidation of the Modern System of Soviet Production Relations 1953–1964.* Cambridge: Cambridge University Press, 1992.

———. *Soviet Workers and Stalinist Industrialization: The Formation of Modern Soviet Production Relations.* London: Pluto Press, 1986.

Fine, Gary Alan. *A Second Chicago School?* Chicago: University of Chicago Press, 1995.

Fine, Janice. "Moving Innovation from the Margins to the Center." In *A New Labor Movement for a New Century,* edited by Gregory Mantsios, pp. 119–46. New York: Monthly Review Press, 1998.

Fitch, Robert. "Explaining New York City's Aberrant Economy." *New Left Review* 207 (1994): 17–48.

Fletcher, Bill, Jr., and Richard Hurd. "Beyond the Organizing Model: The Transformation Process in Local Unions." In *Organizing to Win: New Research on Union Strategies,* edited by Kate Bronfenbrenner, Sheldon Friedman, Richard Hurd, Rudolph Oswald, and Ronald Seeber, pp. 37–53. Ithaca, N. Y.: Cornell ILR Press, 1998.

———. "Political Will, Local Union Transformation, and the Organizing Imperative." In *Which Direction for Organized Labor? Essays on Organizing, Outreach, and Internal Transformations,* edited by Bruce Nissen, pp. 191–216. Detroit: Wayne State University Press, 1999.

Foucault, Michel. *The Birth of the Clinic: An Archaeology of Medical Perception.* 1973. Translated by A. M. Sheridan Smith. New York: Vintage Books, 1994.

———. *Discipline and Punish: The Birth of the Prison.* 1975. Translated by Alan Sheridan. New York: Vintage Books, 1977.

Fraser, Nancy. "Rethinking the Public Sphere: A Contribution to the Critique of Actually Existing Democracy." In *Justice Interruptus: Critical Reflections on the "Post-Socialist" Condition,* pp. 69–98. New York: Routledge, 1997.

———. *Unruly Practices: Power, Discourse and Gender in Contemporary Social Theory.* Minneapolis: University of Minnesota Press, 1989.

Fynes, Brian, Thomas Morrissey, William K. Roche, Brendan J. Whelan, and James

Williams. *Flexible Working Lives: The Changing Nature of Working Time Arrangements in Ireland.* Dublin: Oak Tree Press, 1996.

Gamson, Joshua. "Silence, Death, and the Invisible Enemy: AIDS Activism and Social Movement 'Newness.'" In Michael Burawoy et al., *Ethnography Unbound,* pp. 35–57. Berkeley: University of California Press, 1991.

Gandy, Matthew. *Recycling and the Politics of Urban Waste.* London: Earthscan Publications, 1994.

Gapasin, Fernando, and Howard Wial. "The Role of Central Labor Councils in Union Organizing in the 1990s." In *Organizing to Win: New Research on Union Strategies,* edited by Kate Bronfenbrenner, Sheldon Friedman, Richard Hurd, Rudolph Oswald, and Ronald Seeber, pp. 54–68. Ithaca, N. Y.: Cornell ILR Press, 1998.

Gapasin, Fernando, and Michael Yates. "Organizing the Unorganized: Will Promises Become Practices?" In *Rising from the Ashes? Labor in the Age of "Global" Capitalism,* edited by Ellen M. Wood, Peter Meiksins, and Michael Yates, pp. 73–86. New York: Monthly Review Press, 1998.

Gedeon, Péter. "Hungary: Social Policy in Transition." *East European Politics and Societies* 9 (1995): 433–58.

George, Sheba. "Caroling with the Keralites: The Negotiation of Gendered Space in an Indian Immigration Congregation." In *Gatherings in Diaspora: Religious Communities and the New Immigration,* edited by R. Stephen Warner and Judith G. Wittner, pp. 265–94. Philadelphia: Temple University Press, 1998.

———. "Gendered Ideologies and Strategies: The Negotiation of the Household Division of Labor among Middle-Class South Asian American Families." Working Paper No. 8 for the Alfred P. Sloan Center for Working Families, University of California, Berkeley, 1999.

———. "Gendered Spheres in a Transnational Context: The Interaction of Work, Home and Community among Indian Christian Immigrants." Ph.D. dissertation, University of California, Berkeley, 2000.

Gerson, Deborah A. "Speculums and Small Groups: New Visions of Female Bodies." In "Practice from Pain: Building a Women's Movement through Consciousness Raising," pp. 97–125. Ph.D. dissertation, University of California, Berkeley, 1996.

Giamo, Benedict, and Jeffrey Grunberg. *Beyond Homelessness: Frames of Reference.* Iowa City: University of Iowa Press, 1992.

Giddens, Anthony. *The Consequences of Modernity.* Stanford, Calif.: Stanford University Press, 1990.

———. *Modernity and Self-Identity.* Cambridge, Mass., and Oxford, England: Polity Press, 1991.

———. *Runaway World.* Reith Lectures. London: British Broadcasting Corporation, 1999. On the World Wide Web at htttp://news.bbc.co.uk/hi/english/static/events/reith_99/.

Gindin, Sam. "Notes on Labor at the End of the Century: Starting Over?" In *Rising from the Ashes? Labor in the Age of "Global" Capitalism,* edited by Ellen M. Wood, Peter Meiksins, and Michael Yates, pp. 190–202. New York: Monthly Review Press, 1998.

Gingrich, Newt. *To Renew America.* New York: Harper Collins, 1995.

Glaser, Barney, and Anselm Strauss. *The Discovery of Grounded Theory.* Chicago: Aldine, 1967.

Gluckman, Max. *Analysis of a Social Situation in Modern Zululand.* The Rhodes-Livingstone Papers, Number 28. 1940 and 1942. Manchester, England: Manchester University Press for The Rhodes-Livingstone Institute, 1958.

———. "Anthropological Problems Arising from the African Industrial Revolution." In *Social Change in Modern Africa,* edited by Aidan Southall, pp. 67–82. London: Oxford University Press, 1961.

———. *Custom and Conflict in Africa.* Oxford: Blackwell, 1955.

———. "Ethnographic Data in British Social Anthropology." *Sociological Review* 9 (1961): 5–17.

———. *Order and Rebellion in Tribal Africa.* London: Cohen & West, 1963.

———. *Rituals of Rebellion in South-East Africa.* Manchester, England: Manchester University Press, 1954.

Gluszynski, Pawel, and Iza Kruszewska. *Western Pyromania Moves East: A Case Study in Hazardous Technology Transfer.* Warsaw: Greenpeace, 1996. On the World Wide Web at http://www.rec.hu/poland/wpa/pyro-toc.htm.

Goffman, Erving. *Asylums.* Chicago: Aldine, 1961.

———. *Stigma: Notes on the Management of Spoiled Identity.* New York: Simon & Schuster, 1963.

Goldman, Marshall I. *The Spoils of Progress: Environmental Pollution in the Soviet Union.* Cambridge: The Massachusetts Institute of Technology, 1972.

Gordon, David M. *Fat and Mean: The Corporate Squeeze of Working Americans and the Myth of Managerial "Downsizing."* New York: The Free Press, 1996.

Gosztonyi, Géza. "Hatóság + Szolgálat." *Esély* 4 (1993): 14–35.

Gouldner, Alvin. *The Coming Crisis of Western Sociology.* New York: Avon, 1970.

———. "Sociologist as Partisan: Sociology and the Welfare State." 1967. In *For Sociology,* pp. 27–68. New York: Basic Books, 1973.

Gramsci, Antonio. *Selections from the Prison Notebooks.* New York: International Publishers, 1971.

Grewal, Inderpal, and Caren Kaplan. "Introduction: Transnational Feminist Practices and Questions of Postmodernity." In *Scattered Hegemonies,* edited by Grewal and Kaplan, pp. 1–33. Minneapolis: University of Minnesota Press, 1994.

Gupta, Akhil, and James Ferguson. "Discipline and Practice: 'The Field' as Site, Method, and Location in Anthropology." In *Anthropological Locations,* edited by Gupta and Ferguson, pp. 1–46. Berkeley and Los Angeles: University of California Press, 1997.

Hall, Stuart. "The Local and the Global: Globalization and Ethnicity." In *Culture, Globalization and the World-System,* edited by Anthony King, pp. 19–40. Binghamton: Department of Art History, State University of New York at Binghamton, 1991.

———. "Old and New Identities, Old and New Ethnicities." In *Culture, Globalization and the World-System,* edited by Anthony King, pp. 41–68. Binghamton: Department of Art History, State University of New York at Binghamton, 1991.

———. "When Was 'The Post-colonial'? Thinking at the Limit." In *The Post-Colonial Question,* edited by Iain Chambers and Lidia Curti, pp. 242–60. London and New York: Routledge, 1996.

Haney, Lynne. "But We Are Still Mothers: Gender and the Construction of Need in Postsocialist Hungary." *Social Politics* 4 (1997): 208–44.

———. "Homeboys, Babies, Men in Suits: The State and the Reproduction of Male Domination." *American Sociological Review* 61 (1996): 759–78.

Hannerz, Ulf. *Exploring the City.* New York: Columbia University Press, 1980.

Haraszti, Miklos. *A Worker in a Worker's State.* Harmondsworth, England: Penguin Books, 1977.

Harden, Richard E. "Official Notification by Pacific Coast Metal Trades District Council." Oakland, Calif.: Pacific Coast Metal Trades District Council, July 31, 1996.

Hartmann, Betsy. *Reproductive Rights and Wrongs: The Global Politics of Population Control.* Boston: South End Press, 1995.

Harvey, David. *The Condition of Postmodernity: An Enquiry into the Origins of Cultural Change.* Oxford, England: Blackwell, 1989.

Hauk, Jake. "The Case For Privatizing the Kane Regional Centers." Pittsburgh, Pa.: Allegheny Institute for Public Policy, 1997.

Hegyesi, Gábor. "A Szociális Munka." In *Szociális Segítő,* edited by Zsuzsa Ferge, pp. 14–59. Budapest: MTA, 1991.

Heldman, Kevin. "On the Town with the U. S. Military." *Z Magazine,* February 1997, pp. 24–30.

Herberg, Will. *Protestant-Catholic-Jew: An Essay in American Religious Sociology.* New York: Doubleday, 1960.

Hiller, Ernest. *The Strike: A Study in Collective Action.* Chicago: University of Chicago Press, 1928.

Hirst, Paul, and Grahame Thompson. *Globalization in Question.* Cambridge, England: Polity Press, 1996.

Hirst, Paul, and Jonathan Zeitlin. "Flexible Specialization versus post-Fordism: Theory, Evidence and Policy Implications." *Economy and Society* 20 (1991): 1–56.

Hobsbawm, Eric. *Nations and Nationalism since 1780.* Cambridge: Cambridge University Press, 1990.

Hochschild, Arlie. *The Managed Heart: The Commercialization of Human Feeling.* Berkeley: University of California Press, 1983.

Hochstetler, Andrew L., and N. Shover. "Street Crime, Labor Surplus, and Criminal Punishment 1980–1990." *Social Problems* 44 (1997): 358–68.

Hondagneu-Sotelo, Pierrette. *Gendered Transitions: Mexican Experiences of Immigration.* Berkeley: University of California Press, 1994.

Horváth, Àgota. "Egy Segély Anatómiája." In *Oktatásról és Társadalompolitikárol,* edited by Zsuzsa Ferge, pp. 237–309. Budapest: Szociológiai Kutató Intezete, 1982.

Hulladék Munkaszövetség. No title. *Kukabúvár* 2, no.1 (1996): 19.

Hungaropec. *Tájékoztató a Garéban tervezett ipari hulladékégetöröl* [Information on the incinerator planned in Garé]. Budapest: Burson-Marsteller, 1993.

Hurh, Won Moo, and Kwang Chung Kim. "Religious Participation of Korean Immigrants in the United States." *Journal for the Scientific Study of Religion* 29 (1990): 19–34.

International Monetary Fund. *Social Security in Hungary.* Washington, D.C.: International Monetary Fund Fiscal Affairs Department, 1990.

Irwin, John, and James Austin. *It's about Time: America's Imprisonment Binge.* Belmont, Calif.: Wadsworth, 1994.

Ishi, Tomoji. "Class Conflict, the State and Linkage: The International Migration of Nurses from the Philippines." *Berkeley Journal of Sociology* 32 (1987): 281–312.

Jameson, Fredric. "Cognitive Mapping." In *Marxism and the Interpretation of Culture,* edited by Cary Nelson and Lawrence Grossberg, pp. 347–60. Urbana: University of Illinois Press, 1988.

———. *The Cultural Turn*. London and New York: Verso, 1998.

———. *Postmodernism or, The Cultural Logic of Late Capitalism*. Durham, N. C.: Duke University Press, 1991.

Janowitz, Morris. "Introduction." In *W. I. Thomas on Social Organization and Social Personality*, edited by Janowitz, pp. vii–lviii. Chicago: University of Chicago Press, 1966.

Jenks, Christopher. *Homeless*. Cambridge: Harvard University Press, 1994.

Joas, Hans. *The Creativity of Action*. Chicago: University of Chicago Press, 1996.

———. *G. H. Mead: A Contemporary Reexamination of His Thought*. 1980. Cambridge, Mass.: MIT Press, 1985.

———. *Pragmatism and Social Theory*. Chicago: University of Chicago Press, 1993.

John, Mary E. *Discrepant Dislocations: Feminism, Theory, and Postcolonial Histories*. Berkeley: University of California Press, 1996.

Johnston, Paul. *Success While Others Fail: Social Movement Unionism in the Public Workplace*. Ithaca, N. Y.: ILR Press, 1994.

Jowitt, Ken. *New World Disorder: The Leninist Extinction*. Berkeley: University of California Press, 1992.

Judt, Tony. "The Past Is Another Country: Myth and Memory in Postwar Europe." *Daedalus* 21, no. 4 (1992): 83–118.

Kanter, Rosabeth Moss. *World Class: Thriving Locally in the Global Economy*. New York: Simon & Schuster, 1995.

Katz, Michael B. *The Undeserving Poor: From the War on Poverty to the War on Welfare*. New York: Pantheon Books, 1989.

Kearney, Michael. "The Local and the Global: The Anthropology of Globalization and Transnationalism." *Annual Review of Anthropology* 24 (1995): 547–65.

Keck, Margaret E., and Kathryn Sikkink. *Activists beyond Borders: Advocacy Networks in International Politics*. Ithaca, N.Y.: Cornell University Press, 1998.

Kidder, Tracey. *The Soul of a New Machine*. New York: Avon Books, 1981.

Klawiter, Maren. "Reshaping the Contours of Breast Cancer: From Private Stigma to Public Actions." Ph.D. dissertation, University of California, Berkeley, 1999.

Kligman, Gail. "Reclaiming the Public: Reflections on Creating Civil Society in Romania." *East European Politics and Societies* 3 (1990): 393–438.

Kollar, István. *The Development of Social Insurance in Hungary over Three Decades*. Budapest: Tancsis Publishing, 1976.

Kornai, János. *Economics of Shortage*. Amsterdam: North-Holland, 1980.

———. "Lasting Growth as the Top Priority." Collegium Budapest, Discussion Paper No. 7, 1992.

———. "Paying the Bill for Goulash Communism: Hungarian Development and Macro Stabilization in a Political-Economy Perspective." *Social Research* 63 (1996): 943–1040.

Kornblum, William. *Blue Collar Community*. Chicago: University of Chicago Press, 1974.

Központi Statisztikai Hivatal (KSH). *A Gyermekgondozási Díj Igénybevétele és Hatásai*. Budapest: Társadalmi Statisztikai Föosztály, 1988.

———. *A Gyermekgondozási Segély Igénybevétele és Hatásai*. Budapest: Társadalmi Statisztikai Föosztály, 1981.

Kunda, Gideon. *Engineering Culture*. Philadelphia: Temple University Press, 1993.

Kushner, Rose. *Breast Cancer: A Personal History and an Investigative Report*. New York: Harcourt Brace Jovanovich, 1975.

Lamphere, Louise, et al. *Sunbelt Working Mothers: Reconciling Family and Factory*. Ithaca, N. Y.: Cornell University Press, 1993.

Lash, S., and J. Urry. *The End of Organized Capitalism*. Cambridge, England: Polity Press, 1987.

Lave, Jean, and Etienne Wenger. *Situated Learning: Legitimate Peripheral Participation*. Cambridge: Cambridge University Press, 1993.

LeBeau, Josephine, and Kevin Lynch. "Successful Organizing at the Local Level: The Experience of AFSCME District Council 1707." In *A New Labor Movement for a New Century*, edited by Gregory Mantsios, pp. 104–18. New York: Monthly Review Press, 1998.

Lee, Ching Kwan. *Gender and the South China Miracle*. Berkeley and Los Angeles: University of California Press, 1998.

Lee, D. J. "Skill, Craft and Class: A Theoretical Critique and a Critical Case," *Sociology* 15 (1981): 56–78.

Lerner, Barron H. "Fighting the War on Breast Cancer: Debates over Early Detection, 1945 to the Present." *Annals of Internal Medicine* 129 (July 1998): 74–78.

———. "Inventing a Curable Disease: Historical Perspectives on Breast Cancer." In *Breast Cancer: The Social Construction of Illness*, edited by Anne S. Kasper and Susan J. Ferguson. New York: St. Martin's Press, forthcoming.

———. "Seeing What Is Not There: Mammography and Images of Breast Cancer." Paper presented at "Intimate Portraits: Body Imaging Technologies in Medicine & Culture." Conference sponsored by Department of History of Health Sciences, University of California, San Francisco, April 4, 1998.

Lerner, Stephen. "Taking the Offensive, Turning the Tide." In *A New Labor Movement for a New Century*, edited by Gregory Mantsios, pp. 69–81. New York: Monthly Review Press, 1998.

Lewis, Flora. "The Red Grime Line." *New York Times*, April 10, 1990: A(21).

Liebow, Elliot. *Tally's Corner: A Study of Negro Streetcorner Men*. Boston: Little Brown, 1967.

Limtiaco, Leonard (Director, Enforcement & Investigations, Occupational Safety and Health Administration, U. S. Department of Labor). Letter to Carl Hanson (General Manager, San Francisco Drydock Inc.). Case number 72601040. Washington, D. C., December 26, 1996.

Lipschutz, Ronnie D., and Judith Mayer. *Global Civil Society and Global Environmental Governance: The Politics of Nature from Place to Planet*. Albany, N. Y.: State University of New York Press, 1996.

Lobo, Elizabeth. "Mulheres, Feminismo e Novas Práticas Sociais." *Revista de Ciências Sociais* 1 (1987): 221–29.

Lorde, Audre. *The Cancer Journals*. San Francisco: Aunt Lute Books, 1980.

Lupton, Tom. *On the Shop Floor: Two Studies of Workshop Organization and Output*. London: Pergamon Press, 1963.

MacLeod, Jay. *Ain't No Makin' It: Leveled Aspirations in a Low-Income Neighborhood*. Boulder, Colo.: Westview Press, 1987.

Magubane, Bernard. "Crisis in African Sociology." *East Africa Journal* 5 (1968): 21–40.

————. "A Critical Look at Indices Used in the Study of Social Change in Colonial Africa." *Current Anthropology* 12 (1971): 419–31.

Mahler, Sarah. "Theoretical and Empirical Contributions toward a Research Agenda for Transnationalism." In *Transnationalism from Below, Comparative Urban and Community Research*, vol. 6, edited by Michael P. Smith and Luis Eduardo Guarnizo, pp. 64–100. New Brunswick, N. J.: Transaction Publishers, 1998.

Main, Thomas J. "The Homeless of New York." *The Public Interest* 72 (1983): 3–28.

Malia, Martin. "Leninist Endgame." *Daedalus* 121, no. 2 (1992): 57–75.

Mani, Lata. "Multiple Mediations: Feminist Scholarship in the Age of Multinational Reception." *Inscriptions: Traveling Theories, Traveling Theorists* 5 (1989): 1–23.

Manser, Roger. *The Squandered Dividend: The Free Market and the Environment in Eastern Europe*. London: Earthscan Publications, 1993.

Mantsios, Gregory. "What Does Labor Stand For?" In *A New Labor Movement for a New Century*, edited by Gregory Mantsios, pp. 44–64. New York: Monthly Review Press, 1998.

Marcus, George. *Ethnography through Thick and Thin*. Princeton, N. J.: Princeton University Press, 1998.

Markowitz, Linda. "Union Presentation of Self and Worker Participation in Organizing Campaigns." *Sociological Perspectives* 38 (1995): 437–53.

Matthews, Fred. *Quest for an American Sociology*. London and Montreal: McGill-Queen's University Press, 1977.

Mauer, Marc. *Intended and Unintended Consequences: State Racial Disparities in Imprisonment*. 1997. On the World Wide Web at http//:www.law.emory.edu~ llevy/tsp/index.html.

McClelland, Keith, and Alastair Reid. "Wood, Iron and Steel: Technology, Labour and Trade Union Organisation in the Shipbuilding Industry, 1840–1914." In *Divisions of Labour: Skilled Workers and Technological Change in Nineteenth Century Britain*, edited by Royden Harrison and Jonathan Zeitlin, pp. 151–84. Urbana: University of Illinois Press, 1985.

McDonough, James. "John J. Kane Regional Centers: Privatization Options." Pittsburgh, Pa.: Allegheny Institute for Public Policy, 1996.

McLewin, Philip. "The Concerted Voice of Labor and the Suburbanization of Capital: Fragmentation of the Community Labor Council." In *Which Direction for Organized Labor?* edited by Bruce Nissen, pp. 113–32. Detroit: Wayne State University Press, 1999.

Mead, Lawrence. *Beyond Entitlement: The Social Obligations of Citizenship*. New York: Free Press, 1986.

Mejia, Alonso, et al. *Physician and Nurse Migration: Analysis and Policy Implications*. Geneva, Switzerland: World Health Organization, 1979.

Meyer, John, John Boli, George Thomas, and Francisco O. Ramirez. "World Society and the Nation-State." *American Journal of Sociology* 103 (1997): 144–81.

Meyer, John, and Brian Rowan. "Institutionalized Organizations: Formal Structure as Myth and Ceremony." *American Journal of Sociology* 83 (1977): 340–63.

Michelmore, David. "Democrats Match GOP Vow of 20% Cut in County Millage." *Pittsburgh Post-Gazette*, September 16, 1995.

Mitchell, Clyde. *The Kalela Dance*. The Rhodes-Livingstone Papers, Number 27. Manchester, England: Manchester University Press for The Rhodes-Livingstone Institute, 1956.

Molyneux, Maxine. "Mobilization without Emancipation? Women's Interests, State and Revolution in Nicaragua." In *Transition and Development: Problems of Third World Socialism,* edited by Richard Fagen, Carmen Diana Deere, and José Luis Coraggio, pp. 280–302. New York: Monthly Review Press, 1986.

Montgomery, David. *Workers' Control in America: Studies in the History of Work, Technology and Labor Struggles.* Cambridge: Cambridge University Press, 1979.

Montini, Theresa. "Gender and Emotion in the Advocacy of Breast Cancer Informed Consent Legislation." *Gender and Society* 10 (1996): 9–23.

———. "Resist and Redirect: Physicians Respond to Breast Cancer Informed Consent Legislation." *Women & Health* 26 (1997): 85–105.

———. "Women's Activism for Breast Cancer Informed Consent Laws." Ph.D. dissertation, University of California, San Francisco, 1991.

Montini, Theresa, and Sheryl Ruzek. "Overturning Orthodoxy: The Emergence of Breast Cancer Treatment Policy." *Research in the Sociology of Health Care* 8 (1989): 3–32.

Moody, Kim. "American Labor: A Movement Again?" In *A New Labor Movement for a New Century,* edited by Gregory Mantsios, pp. 57–72. New York: Monthly Review Press, 1998.

———. *An Injury to All: The Decline of American Unionism.* New York: Routledge, 1997.

———. *Workers in a Lean World: Unions in the International Economy.* London: Verso, 1997.

Morris, Cyllene R., and William E. Wright. *Breast Cancer in California.* Sacramento: California Department of Health Services, Cancer Surveillance Section, March 1996.

Morton, Margaret. *The Tunnel: Underground Homeless of New York City.* New Haven, Conn.: Yale University Press, 1996.

Morvai, Krisztina. *Terror a Családban.* Budapest: Kossuth Kiadó, 1998.

Moser, Caroline O. N. *Gender Planning and Development: Theory, Practice and Training.* New York: Routledge, 1993.

Moss, Ralph W. *Questioning Chemotherapy.* New York: Equinox Press, 1995.

Moulin, Daniel de. *A Short History of Breast Cancer.* Boston: Martinus Nijhoff Publishers, 1983.

MTESZ-MÁFI, *Waste Dump Survey.* Pécs, Hungary: MÁFI, 1986.

Murray, Charles. *Losing Ground: American Social Policy, 1950–1980.* New York: Basic Books, 1984.

National Breast Cancer Coalition. *A Report on the First World Conference on Breast Cancer Advocacy—Influencing Change.* Brussels, Belgium, March 13–16, 1997.

National Cancer Advisory Board—Subcommittee to Evaluate the National Cancer Program. *Cancer at a Crossroads: A Report to Congress and the Nation.* Bethesda, Md.: National Cancer Institute, 1994.

National Cancer Institute. *National Cancer Institute Fact Book, 1996.* NIH Publication No. 97–2789. Bethesda, Md.: National Cancer Institute, 1996.

Needleman, Ruth. "Building Relationships for the Long Haul: Unions and Community Organizing Groups Working Together to Organize Low-Wage Workers." In *Organizing to Win: New Research on Union Strategies,* edited by Kate Bronfen-

brenner, Sheldon Friedman, Richard Hurd, Rudolph Oswald, and Ronald Seeber, pp. 71–86. Ithaca, N. Y.: Cornell ILR Press, 1998.

Northern California Cancer Center. "Breast Cancer in the Greater Bay Area." *Greater
Bay Area Cancer Registry Report* 5 (1994): 1.

Nove, Alec. *The Soviet Economic System.* London: George Allen & Unwin, 1980.

Offe, Claus. "The Politics of Social Policy in East European Transitions: Antecedents,
Agents, and Agenda of Reform." *Social Research* 60 (1993): 647–84.

Office of Technology Policy. *America's New Deficit: The Shortage of Information Technology Workers.* Washington, D. C.: U. S. Department of Commerce, Technology
Administration, 1997. On the World Wide Web at www.ta.doc.gov/reports/itsw/
itsw.pdf.

Oliver, Melvin L., and Thomas M. Shapiro. *Black Wealth, White Wealth: A New Perspective on Racial Inequality.* London: Routledge, 1995.

O'Malley, Eoin. *Industry and Economic Development.* Dublin: Gill and Macmillan, 1989.

Ong, Paul, and Tania Azores. "The Migration and Incorporation of Filipino Nurses."
In *The New Asian Immigration in Los Angeles and Global Restructuring,* edited by Paul
Ong, Edna Bonacich, and Lucie Cheng, pp. 164–95. Philadelphia: Temple Uni-
versity Press, 1994.

Ó Riain, Seán. "The Birth of a Celtic Tiger?" *Communications of the ACM* 40 (1997):
11–16.

———. "An Offshore Silicon Valley?" *Competition and Change* 2 (1997): 175–212.

———. "Remaking the Developmental State: The Irish Software Industry in the
Global Economy." Ph.D. dissertation, University of California, Berkeley, 1999.

Pacific Coast Shipbuilding and Ship Repair Firms and the Metal Trades Department
of the A.F.L.-C.I.O., the Pacific Coast Metal Trades District Council, the Local
Metal Trades Council, and the International Unions Signatory Thereto. "1983–
1984–1985 Pacific Coast MASTER AGREEMENT." Monterey, Calif.: October 13,
1983.

Park, Robert, and Ernest Burgess. *The City.* 1925. Chicago: University of Chicago
Press, 1967.

———. *Introduction to the Science of Sociology.* 1921. Chicago: University of Chicago
Press, 1969.

Passaro, Joanne. *The Unequal Homeless: Men on the Streets, Women in Their Place.* New
York: Routledge, 1996.

Patterson, James. *The Dread Disease: Cancer and Modern American Culture.* Cambridge:
Harvard University Press, 1987.

Paulsen, Monte. "The Cancer Business." *Mother Jones* (May/June 1994), p. 41.

Pécsi Zöld Kör Environmental Affairs Team. *A király meztelen* [The Emperor Has No
Clothes]. Pécs, Hungary: Pécsi Zöld Kör, n. d.

Perlow, Leslie. "Boundary Control: The Social Ordering of Work and Family Time
in a High-Tech Corporation." *Administrative Science Quarterly* 43 (1998): 328–57.

———. *Finding Time.* Ithaca, N. Y.: ILR Press, 1997.

Pessar, Patricia R. "The Linkage between the Household and the Workplace in the
Experience of Dominican Women in the U. S." *International Immigration Review* 18
(1984): 1188–1212.

Peters, Ronald, and Theresa Merrill. "Clergy and Religious Persons' Roles in Organizing at O'Hare Airport and St. Joseph Medical Center." In *Organizing to Win:*

New Research on Union Strategies, edited by Kate Bronfenbrenner, Sheldon Friedman, Richard Hurd, Rudolph Oswald, and Ronald Seeber, pp. 164–77. Ithaca, N. Y.: Cornell ILR Press, 1998.

Piore, Michael J., and Charles F. Sabel. *The Second Industrial Divide: Possibilities for Prosperity.* New York: Basic Books, 1984.

Pittsburgh Post-Gazette. "County's Former Third Wheel Comes Full Circle." August 17, 1997.

Plate and Tank Division, California Metal Trades Association, and International Brotherhood of Boilermakers, Iron Shipbuilders, Blacksmiths, Forgers and Helpers of America, AFL-CIO. "Master Agreement." July 1, 1974–June 30, 1977. San Francisco: 1974.

Portella, Ana Paula, Cecilia de Mello Souza, and Simone Diniz. "'Not Like Our Mothers': Reproductive Choice and the Emergence of Citizenship amongst Brazilian Rural Workers, Domestic Workers, and Housewives." Translated by Jones de Freitas and Cecilia de Mello e Souza. Pamphlet. Recife/Rio de Janeiro/São Paulo: International Reproductive Rights Research Action Group: Brazilian Team, 1996.

Portes, Alejandro, Manuel Castells, and Lauren Benton, eds. *The Informal Economy: Studies in Advanced and Less Developed Countries.* Baltimore: Johns Hopkins University Press, 1995.

Powers, Brian. *Making Marginality: How High Schools Reproduce Inequality in the Inner City.* New Haven, Conn.: Yale University Press, forthcoming.

Pred, Allan, and Michael Watts, *Reworking Modernity: Capitalisms and Symbolic Discontent.* New Brunswick, N. J.: Rutgers University Press, 1992.

Proctor, Robert N. *Cancer Wars: How Politics Shapes What We Know and Don't Know about Cancer.* New York: Basic Books, 1995.

Rabinow, Paul. *Reflections on Fieldwork in Morocco.* Berkeley and Los Angeles: University of California Press, 1977.

Rachleff, Peter. *Hard Times in the Heartland.* Boston: South End Press, 1993.

———. "Organizing Wall to Wall: The Independent Union of All Workers, 1933–37." In *"We Are All Leaders": The Alternative Unionism of the Early 1930s,* edited by Staughton Lynd, pp. 51–71. Urbana: University of Illinois Press, 1996.

Ragavachari, Ranjana. *Conflicts and Adjustments: Indian Nurses in an Urban Milieu.* Delhi: Academic Foundation, 1990.

Rathgeber, Eva M. "WID, WAD, GAD: Trends in Research and Practice." *The Journal of Developing Areas* 24 (July 1990): 489–502.

Ray, Raka. *Fields of Protest: A Comparison of Women's Movements in Two Indian Cities.* Minneapolis: University of Minnesota Press, 1999.

Razavi, Shahrashoub, and Carol Miller. "From WID to GAD: Conceptual Shifts in the Women and Development Discourse." Occasional paper. Geneva, Switzerland: UNRISD, 1995.

Redburn, Stephens F., and Terry F. Buss. *Responding to America's Homeless: Public Policy Alternatives.* New York: Praeger, 1986.

Reed, Adolph, Jr. "A Slave to Finance." *Village Voice,* January 21, 1997, p.27.

Reich, Robert B. *The Work of Nations.* New York: Vintage, 1991.

Reiniger, Róbert. "Veszélyes hulladékok" [Hazardous Wastes]. *Anyaggazdálkodás Raktárgazdálkodás* 19, no. 6 (1991.): 1–7, and no. 7 (1991): 14–19.

Rennie, Susan. "Mammography: X-rated Film." *Chrysalis* 5 (1977): 21–33.

Rettig, Richard A. *Cancer Crusade: The Story of the National Cancer Act of 1971.* Princeton, N. J.: Princeton University Press, 1977.

Roediger, David R. *The Wages of Whiteness: Race and the Making of the American Working Class.* London: Verso, 1991.

Rosaldo, Renato. *Culture and Truth: The Remaking of Social Analysis.* Boston: Beacon, 1993.

Rosenthal, Elisabeth. "Maker of Cancer Drugs to Oversee Prescriptions at 11 Cancer Clinics." *New York Times,* April 15,1997, p. A1.

Ross, Walter S. *Crusade: The Official History of the American Cancer Society.* New York: Arbor House, 1987.

Roth, Gabriel. "Not Fit to Print? Project Censored Uncovers the Stories That Didn't Make the News in 1998." *The Guardian,* March 24, 1999, p. 20.

Roy, Donald. "Efficiency and the Fix: Informal Intergroup Relations in a Piecework Machine Shop." *American Journal of Sociology* 60 (1954): 255–66.

———. "Quota Restriction and Goldbricking in a Machine Shop." *American Journal of Sociology* 57 (1952): 427–42.

———. "Restriction of Output in a Piecework Machine Shop." Ph.D. dissertation, University of Chicago, 1952.

———. "Work Satisfaction and Social Reward in Quota Achievement." *American Sociological Review* 18 (1953): 507–14.

Rubin, Gayle. "The Traffic in Women: Notes on the Political Economy of Sex." In *Towards an Anthropology of Women,* edited by Rayna Reiter, pp. 157–210. New York: Monthly Review Press, 1975.

Rubin, Lillian B. *Families on the Fault Line.* New York: HarperCollins, 1994.

Saffioti, Heleieth I. B. "Rearticulando Gênero e Classe Social." In *Uma Questão de Gênero,* edited by Albertina de Oliveira Costa and Cristina Bruschini, pp. 183–251. Rio de Janeiro: Editora Rosa dos Tempos/Fundação Carlos Chagas, 1992.

Said, Edward. *Orientalism.* New York: Vintage Books, 1979.

———. "Traveling Theory." In *The World, the Text and the Critic,* pp. 226–47. Cambridge: Harvard University Press, 1983.

San Francisco Drydock. *EP.* San Francisco: San Francisco Drydock, 1996.

San Francisco Drydock, Inc., and The Metal Trades Department of the AFL-CIO, The Pacific Coast Metal Trades District Council, The Bay Cities Metal Trades Council, and The International Unions Signatory Thereto. "General Presidents' Pacific Coast Master Shipyard Industry Recovery Labor Agreement." July 30, 1996, through June 30, 2000. San Francisco, 1996.

Santos, Boaventura de Sousa. *Toward a New Common Sense.* London and New York: Routledge, 1995.

Santos, Maria Cecilia MacDowell. "The Battle for a Feminist State within a Context of Globalization: The Case of Women's Police Stations in São Paulo, Brazil." Paper presented at the XXI International Congress of the Latin American Studies Association. Chicago: September 24–26, 1998.

Sassen, Saskia. *The Global City.* Princeton, N. J.: Princeton University Press, 1991.

Sassen-Koob, Saskia. "Notes on the Incorporation of Third World Women into Wage-Labor through Immigration and Off-Shore Production." *International Migration Review* 18 (1984): 1144–1167.

Saxenian, AnnaLee. *Regional Advantage.* Cambridge: Harvard University Press, 1994.

Scheper-Hughes, Nancy, and Margaret M. Lock. "The Message in the Bottle: Illness and the Micropolitics of Resistance." *The Journal of Psychohistory* 18: 409–32.

Schiller, Nina Glick, Linda Basch, and Cristina Szanton Blanc. *Towards a Transnational Perspective on Migration: Race, Class, Ethnicity and Nationalism Reconsidered.* Annals of the New York Academy of Sciences, vol. 654. New York: New York Academy of Sciences, 1992.

Schöpflin, George. "Post-communism: A Profile." *The Public* 2 (1995): 63–72.

Schottenfeld, David, and Joseph Fraumeni, Jr. *Cancer Epidemiology and Prevention.* 2d ed. New York: Oxford University Press, 1996.

Schram, Sanford F. *Words of Welfare: The Poverty of Social Science and the Social Science of Poverty.* Minneapolis: University of Minnesota Press, 1995.

Schwartz, John, Carla Koehl, and Karen Breslau. "Cleaning Up by Cleaning Up." *Newsweek,* June 11, 1990, pp. 40–41.

Schwartzman, Kathleen. *The Social Origins of Democratic Collapse: The First Portuguese Republic in the Global Economy.* Lawrence: University of Kansas Press, 1989.

Sciacchitano, Katherine. "Finding the Community in the Union and the Union in the Community: The First-Contract Campaign at Steeltech." In *Organizing to Win: New Research on Union Strategies,* edited by Kate Bronfenbrenner, Sheldon Friedman, Richard Hurd, Rudolph Oswald, and Ronald Seeber, pp. 150–163. Ithaca, N. Y.: Cornell ILR Press, 1998.

Scott, Joan Wallach. "Gender: A Useful Category of Historical Analysis." In *Gender and the Politics of History,* pp. 28–50. New York: Columbia University Press, 1988.

SEER Cancer Statistics Review, 1973–1994. Prepared and edited by The Cancer Control Research Program, Division of Cancer Prevention and Control, National Cancer Institute. Bethesda, Md.: NIH Publication No. 97–2789.

Shaiken, Harley. *Mexico in the Global Economy.* San Diego: Center for United States–Mexican Studies, 1990.

Shailor, Barbara, and George Kourpias. "Developing and Enforcing International Labor Standards." In *A New Labor Movement for a New Century,* edited by Gregory Mantsios, pp. 277–85. New York: Monthly Review Press, 1998.

Sherman, Rachel. "From State Extroversion to State Extension in Mexico: Modes of Emigrant Incorporation, 1900–1997." *Theory and Society* 28 (1999): 835–878.

Shin, Eui Hang, and Hyung Park. "An Analysis of Causes of Schisms in Ethnic Churches: The Case of Korean-American Churches." In *Koreans in North America,* edited by S. H. Lee and T. Kwak, 231–52. Seoul: Kyungnam University Press, 1988.

Simai, Mihály. "Környezetbarát fejlödésünk" [Our Environment-Friendly Development]. *Valóság* 33, no. 9 (1990): 1–10.

Skidmore, Thomas E. "Brazil's Slow Road to Democratization: 1974–1985." In *Democratizing Brazil: Problems of Transition and Consolidation,* edited by Alfred Stepan, pp. 5–42. New York: Oxford University Press, 1989.

Skoll, Geoffrey R. *Walk the Walk, Talk the Talk: An Ethnography of a Drug Treatment Facility.* Philadelphia: Temple University Press, 1992.

Smith, Dorothy. *The Everyday World as Problematic: A Feminist Sociology.* Boston: Northeastern University Press, 1987.

Smith, Michael P., and Luis Eduardo Guarnizo, eds. *Transnationalism from Below, Com-*

parative Urban and Community Research, Vol. 6. New Brunswick, N. J.: Transaction Publishers, 1998.

Smith, Vicki. *Managing in the Corporate Interest.* Berkeley: University of California Press, 1990.

Snow, David A., Leon Anderson, and Paul Koegel. "Distorting Tendencies in Research on the Homeless." *American Behavioral Scientist* 37 (1994): 461–75.

Snow, David, Leon Anderson, Thoron Quist, and Daniel Cress. "The Homeless as Bricoleurs: Material Survival Strategies on the Streets." In *Homelessness in America: A Reference Book,* edited by Jim Baumohl. Phoenix, Arizona: Oryx Press, forthcoming.

Sontag, Susan. *Illness as Metaphor.* New York: Vintage Books, 1977.

SOS Corpo. *SOS: Corpo de Mulher.* Recife, Brazil: SOS Corpo, 1982.

———, ed. *O Que as Mulheres de Pernambuco Querem como Políticas Públicas Municipais de 1997 ao Ano 2000.* Recife, Brazil: Fórum de Mulheres de Pernambuco, 1997.

Spiegel, David, J. R. Bloom, and H. C. Kraemer. "Effects of Psychosocial Treatment on Survival of Patients with Metastatic Breast Cancer." *Lancet* 2 (1989): 888–91.

Stacey, Judith. *Brave New Families.* New York: Basic Books, 1990.

Staniszkis, Jadwiga. *The Dynamics of the Breakthrough in Eastern Europe: The Polish Experience.* Berkeley: University of California Press, 1991.

———. *The Ontology of Socialism.* Oxford, England: Clarendon Press, 1992.

Stanners, David, and Philippe Bourdeau. *Europe's Environment: The Dobris Assessment.* Copenhagen: European Environment Agency, 1995.

Starr, Paul. *The Social Transformation of American Medicine: The Rise of a Sovereign Profession and the Making of a Vast Industry.* New York: Basic Books, 1982.

Steingraber, Sandra. "We All Live Downwind." In *1 in 3: Women with Cancer Confront an Epidemic,* edited by Judy Brady, pp. 36–48. San Francisco: Cleis Press.

Stewart, Kathleen. "Nostalgia as Polemic." In *Rereading Cultural Anthropology,* edited by George E. Marcus, pp. 252–66. Durham, N. C.: Duke University Press, 1992.

Storper, Michael. *The Regional World: Territorial Development in a Global Economy.* London: Guilford Press, 1997.

Susser, Ida. *Norman Street: Poverty and Politics in an Urban Neighborhood.* New York: Oxford University Press, 1982.

Suttles, Gerald. *The Social Order of the Slum.* Chicago: University of Chicago Press, 1968.

Szalai, Júlia. "Poverty in Hungary during the Period of Economic Crisis." IBRD (International Bank for Reconstruction and Development) World Development Report, Washington, D. C., 1989.

———. "Social Participation in Hungary in the Context of Restructuring and Liberalization." In *Social Policy, Social Justice and Citizenship in Eastern Europe,* edited by R. Deacon, pp. 37–55. Aldershot, England: Avebury, 1992.

———. "Some Aspects of the Changing Situation of Women in Hungary." *Signs* 17 (1991): 152–70.

———. "Urban Poverty and Social Policy in the Context of Adjustment: The Case of Hungary." World Bank Working Paper, Washington, D. C., 1992.

Szalai, Júlia, and Mária Neményi. *Hungary in the 1980s: A Historic Review of Social Policy and Urban Level Interventions.* Washington, D. C: The World Bank, 1993.

Szelényi, Iván, and Robert Manchin. "Social Policy under State Socialism: Market

Redistribution and Social Inequalities in East European Socialist Societies." In *Stagnation and Renewal in Social Policy*, edited by G. Esping-Andersen, pp. 102–39. New York: M. E. Sharpe, 1987.

Szlávik, János. "Piacosítható-e a környezetvédelem?" [Is Environmental Protection Marketizable?] *Valóság* 34, no. 4(1991): 20–27.

TARKI (Tarsadalomkutatasi Informatikai Egyesulest). "A Szociális Csomagnál a Meg-takaŕitó Celzottság Finomhangolásáról." Working paper. Budapest: TARKI, 1995.

Thomas, Robert. *Citizenship, Gender and Work.* Berkeley: University of California Press, 1985.

Thomas, T. J. "The Shepherding Perspective of Seward Hiltner on Pastoral Care and Its Application in the Organizing of a Congregation in Dallas of East Indian Immigrants from the Mar Thoma Syrian Church of India." Doctor of Ministry thesis, Perkins School of Theology, Southern Methodist University, Dallas, Texas,1978.

Thomas, William I., and Florian Znaniecki. *The Polish Peasant in Europe and America.* 2 vols. New York: Alfred A. Knopf, 1927.

Thompson, Edward P. *The Making of the English Working Class.* New York: Vintage, 1963.

Thorne, Barrie, and Marilyn Yalom, eds. *Rethinking the Family: Some Feminist Questions.* New York: Longman, 1982.

Ticktin, Hillel. "The Contradictions of Soviet Society and Professor Bettelheim." *Critique* 6 (Spring 1976): 17–44.

———. *Origins of the Crisis in the USSR: Essays on the Political Economy of a Disintegrating System.* Armonk, N.Y.: M. E. Sharpe, 1992.

Tierney, Margaret. "Negotiating a Software Career: Informal Work Practices and 'The Lads' in a Software Installation." In *The Gender-Technology Relation: Contemporary Theory and Research*, edited by K. Grint and R. Gill, pp. 192–209. London: Taylor and Francis, 1995.

Timar, János. "Economic Reform and New Employment Problems in Hungary." In *Economic Reforms and Welfare Systems in the USSR, Poland and Hungary*, edited by J. Adam, pp. 156–76. New York: St. Martin's Press, 1991.

Tóth, István. "A Jóléti Rendszer az Átmeneti Időszakban." *Közgazdasági Szemle* (1994): 313–40.

Turner, Ralph, ed. *Robert E. Park on Social Control and Collective Behavior.* Chicago: University of Chicago Press, 1967.

Turner, Victor. *Dramas, Fields, and Methods.* Ithaca, N.Y.: Cornell University Press, 1974.

———. *The Ritual Process.* London: Routledge and Kegan Paul, 1969.

———. *Schism and Continuity in an African Society.* Manchester, England: Manchester University Press for The Rhodes-Livingstone Institute, 1957.

United States Bureau of Labor Statistics. "Relative Cost of U. S. Shipbuilding Labor." As supplied on the World Wide Web by Colton and Company at http://www.coltoncompany.com./index/shipbldg/wages.htm.

United States Department of Labor. *County Business Patterns.* Various years.

van Velsen, Jaap. "The Extended Case Method and Situational Analysis." In *The Craft of Urban Anthropology*, edited by A. L. Epstein, pp. 29–53. London: Tavistock, 1967.

————. "Labor Migration as a Positive Factor in the Continuity of Tonga Tribal Society." *Economic Development and Cultural Change* 8 (1960): 265–78.

————. *The Politics of Kinship*. Manchester, England: Manchester University Press for the Rhodes Livingstone Institute, 1964.

Verdery, Katherine. *What Was Socialism, and What Comes Next?* Princeton, N. J.: Princeton University Press, 1996.

Vergara, Camilo Jose. *The New American Ghetto*. New Brunswick, N. J.: Rutgers University Press, 1995.

Vincent, Joan. *Anthropology and Politics*. Tucson and London: University of Arizona Press, 1990.

Visvanathan, Susan. "Marriage, Birth and Death: Property Rights and Domestic Relationships of the Orthodox/Jacobite Syrian Christians of Kerala." *Economic and Political Weekly*, June 17, 1989, pp. 1341–46.

Voss, Kim, and Rachel Sherman. "Breaking the Iron Law of Oligarchy: Tactical Innovation and the Revitalization of the American Labor Movement." *American Journal of Sociology*, forthcoming.

Wade, Robert. "Globalization and Its Limits: Reports of the Death of the National Economy Are Greatly Exaggerated." In *National Diversity and Global Capitalism*, edited by Suzanne Berger and Ronald Dore, pp. 60–88. Ithaca, N. Y.: Cornell University Press, 1996.

Waldinger, Roger, Chris Erickson, Ruth Milkman, Daniel Mitchell, Abel Valenzuela, Kent Wong, and Maurice Zeitlin. "Helots No More: A Case Study of the Justice for Janitors Campaign in Los Angeles." In *Organizing To Win: New Research on Union Strategies*, edited by Kate Bronfenbrenner, Sheldon Friedman, Richard Hurd, Rudolph Oswald, and Ronald Seeber, pp. 102–20. Ithaca, N. Y.: Cornell ILR Press, 1998.

Walker, Dick. "California Rages against the Dying of the Light." *New Left Review* 209 (1995): 42–74.

Warner, Stephen. "Work in Progress toward a New Paradigm for the Sociological Study of Religion in the United States." *American Journal of Sociology* 98 (1993): 1044–93.

Waterson, Alisse. *Street Addicts in the Political Economy*. Philadelphia: Temple University Press, 1993.

Watson, William. *Tribal Cohesion in a Money Economy*. Manchester, England: Manchester University Press, 1958.

Weiss, Linda. "Globalization and the Myth of the Powerless State." *New Left Review* 225 (1997): 3–27.

Wellman, Barry, Janet Salaff, Dimitrina Dimitrova, Laura Garton, Milena Gulia, and Caroline Haythornthwaite. "Computer Networks as Social Networks." *Annual Review of Sociology* 22 (1996): 213–38.

Whyte, William Foot. *Street Corner Society*. Chicago: University of Chicago Press, 1943.

Williams, Alex (Safety Coordinator, San Francisco Drydock, Inc.). Letter to Pauline M. Caraher (Occupational Safety and Health Administration, Phoenix, Arizona). San Francisco, January 2, 1997.

Williams, Patricia. *The Alchemy of Race and Rights: Diary of a Law Professor*. Cambridge: Harvard University Press, 1991.

Williams, Raymond Brady. *Christian Pluralism in the U. S: The Indian Immigrant Experience*. Cambridge: Cambridge University, 1996.

———. *Religions of Immigrants from India and Pakistan: New Threads in the American Tapestry*. Cambridge: Cambridge University Press, 1988.

Willis, Paul. *Learning to Labor: How Working Class Kids Get Working Class Jobs*. New York: Columbia University Press, 1977.

Wilson, Godfrey. *The Economics of Detribalization in Northern Rhodesia*. The Rhodes-Livingstone Papers, Numbers 5 & 6. Livingstone, Northern Rhodesia: Rhodes-Livingstone Institute, 1941 and 1942.

Wilson, James Q. *Thinking about Crime*. New York: Basic Books, 1975.

Wilson, William Julius. *The Truly Disadvantaged: The Inner City, the Underclass, and Public Policy*. Chicago: University of Chicago Press, 1987.

Wirth, Louis. *The Ghetto*. 1928. Chicago: University of Chicago Press, 1956.

Wolf, Eric. *Europe and the People without History*. Berkeley and Los Angeles: University of California Press, 1982.

Wood, Ellen M. "Labor, Class, and State in Global Capitalism." In *Rising from the Ashes? Labor in the Age of "Global" Capitalism*, edited by Ellen M. Wood, Peter Meiksins, and Michael Yates, pp. 3–16. New York: Monthly Review Press, 1998.

World Bank. *Housing Policy Reform in Hungary*. Report no. 9031-HU. Washington, D. C.: The World Bank, 1990.

———. *Hungarian Health Services: Issues and Options for Reform*. Report no. 8772-HU. Washington, D. C.: The World Bank, 1990.

———. *Hungary: Reform of Social Policy and Expenditures*. Washington D. C: The World Bank, 1992.

———. *Hungary, The Transition to a Market Economy: Critical Human Resources Issues*. Report no. 8665-HU. Washington, D. C.: The World Bank, 1990.

Wright, Talmadge. *Out of Place: Homeless Mobilizations, Subcities and Contested Landscapes*. Albany: State University of New York Press, 1997.

Yamanaka, Keiko, and Kent McClelland. "Earning the Model-Minority Image: Diverse Strategies of Economic Adaptation by Asian American Women." *Ethnic and Racial Studies* 17 (1994): 79–115.

Zaretsky, Eli. "Editor's Introduction." In *The Polish Peasant in Europe and America*, by William I. Thomas and Florian Znaniecki, edited and abridged by Eli Zaretsky, pp. 1–53. Urbana and Chicago: University of Illinois Press, 1984.

Zorbaugh, Harvey. *The Gold Coast and the Slum*. 1929. Chicago: University of Chicago Press, 1976.

Zuboff, Shoshana. *In the Age of the Smart Machine: The Future of Work and Power*. New York: Basic Books, 1984.

INDEX

Global ethnographers at home. From left to right, Seán Ó Riain, Sheba George, Lynne Haney, Michael Burawoy, Millie Thayer, Maren Klawiter, Teresa Gowan, Steven H. Lopez, Zsuzsa Gille, and Joseph A. Blum. Photo by Joseph A. Blum.

Text:	10/12 Baskerville
Display:	Baskerville
Composition:	BookMatters
Printing and binding:	Friesens